Research Perspectives on English for Academic
Purposes

THE CAMBRIDGE APPLIED LINGUISTICS SERIES

Series editors: Michael H. Long and Jack C. Richards

This series presents the findings of recent work in applied linguistics which are of direct relevance to language teaching and learning and of particular interest to applied linguists, researchers, language teachers, and teacher trainers:

In this series:

Research Perspectives on English for Academic Purposes

EDITED BY

John Flowerdew

City University of Hong Kong

and

Matthew Peacock

City University of Hong Kong

CAMBRIDGE UNIVERSITY PRESS

PUBLISHED BY THE PRESS SYNDICATE OF THE UNIVERSITY OF CAMBRIDGE
The Pitt Building, Trumpington Street, Cambridge, United Kingdom

CAMBRIDGE UNIVERSITY PRESS
The Edinburgh Building, Cambridge CB2 2RU, United Kingdom
40 West 20th Street, New York, NY 10011–4211, USA
10 Stamford Road, Oakleigh, Melbourne 3166, Australia
Ruiz de Alarcón 13, 28014 Madrid, Spain
Dock House, The Waterfront, Cape Town 8001, South Africa

http://www.cambridge.org

First published 2001

Printed in the United Kingdom at the University Press, Cambridge

Typeset in Sabon 10.5/12pt   System 3b2   [CE]

A catalogue record for this book is available from the British Library

ISBN 0 521 80130 3 hardback
ISBN 0 521 80518 X paperback

Contents

Contributors

George Braine, Chinese University of Hong Kong
Geoff Brindley, Macquarie University, Sydney, Australia
Donna M. Brinton, University of California at Los Angeles (UCLA), USA
Suresh Canagarajah, City University of New York, USA
Yeonsuk Cho, University of Illinois at Urbana-Champaign, USA
Caroline Clapham, Lancaster University, UK
Tom Cobb, University of Quebec at Montreal, Canada
Averil Coxhead, Victoria University of Wellington, New Zealand
Fred Davidson, University of Illinois at Urbana-Champaign, USA
Tony Dudley-Evans, University of Birmingham, UK
Dana R. Ferris, California State University, Sacramento, USA
John Flowerdew, City University of Hong Kong
Liz Hamp-Lyons, Hong Kong Polytechnic University
Alan Hirvela, Ohio State University, USA
Christine A. Holten, University of California at Los Angeles (UCLA), USA
Marlise Horst, Concordia University, Montreal, Canada
Chris Kennedy, University of Birmingham, UK
Tony Lynch, University of Edinburgh, UK
Paul Nation, Victoria University of Wellington, New Zealand
Shuichi Nobe, Aoyama Gakuin University, Japan
Brian Paltridge, University of Melbourne, Australia
Matthew Peacock, City University of Hong Kong
Peter Robinson, Aoyama Gakuin University, Japan
Steven Ross, Kwansei Gakuin University, Japan
Sue Starfield, Formerly University of the Witwatersrand, South Africa; now University of New South Wales
Fredricka Stoller, Northern Arizona University, USA
Gregory Strong, Aoyama Gakuin University, Japan
John M. Swales, University of Michigan, USA
Steve Tauroza, City University of Hong Kong

Alan Waters, Lancaster University, UK
Mary Waters, Lancaster University, UK
Jennifer Whittle, Aoyama Gakuin University, Japan
Alistair Wood, University of Brunei Darussalam, Brunei
Bonnie Wenxia Zhang, Tsinghua University, China

Series editors' preface

In the English-speaking world, and also in many parts of the non-English speaking world, English is the major language of higher education. Both in these contexts, as well as in countries where English has a different role, it also serves as the major world language for the dissemination of research in science, industry and technology. These facts have an enormous impact on the educational experiences of vast numbers of students around the world, for whom fluency in the norms of English-language academic discourse is essential for the successful negotiation of both the processes and products of learning. The educational response to this phenomenon in tertiary institutions around the world has been the development of the discipline of English for Academic Purposes (EAP), that branch of English for Specific Purposes that provides teaching and other forms of language support for ESOL students completing academic studies in English-medium institutions of learning.

EAP is a field of activity that draws on 30 years or more of practical experience. It encompasses all aspects of language teaching including language analysis, curriculum development, teaching methodology, materials development and assessment. However, as the field has developed it has moved from being a largely practical activity to one that has much broader dimensions. A substantial theoretical basis has developed around key issues in EAP, as well as an active research agenda, and both theory and research are now seen as essential to the practice of EAP.

This book differs from many others books on EAP in that it adopts a research perspective on issues in EAP. It seeks to provide a comprehensive survey of research issues, methods and findings, as well as pedagogical applications of such research within this important field of applied linguistics. Contributors describe the history of EAP research, the development of theoretical paradigms, current issues in EAP research, testing in EAP, cultural and ideological factors, and approaches to the teaching of EAP in curriculum development, materials design, and pedagogy. A variety of research methodologies are illustrated, including discourse analysis, ethnography, experimental research, survey research, and action research. The advantages and limitations of different research approaches are also examined. At the same time the papers in this important collection provide a basis for a critical re-examination of assumptions about the scope and nature of EAP as well as its recent and current practices.

The accessibility and comprehensiveness of this timely survey will make it an essential reference source for EAP practitioners, applied linguists, curriculum developers, teachers and researchers as well as others interested in the role of language in the transmission of academic and other forms of knowledge.

Michael H. Long
Jack C. Richards

Preface

English for Academic Purposes (EAP) is a truly international phenomenon, linked in with the overall trend towards the globalisation of information exchange, communication and education. English is now well established as the world language of research and publication and an ever-greater number of universities and institutes of learning are using English as the language of instruction. With this tremendous expansion, there has been a parallel growth in the preparation of non-native English speakers (NNSs) for study in English. This has taken place, and is continuing, in English-speaking countries such as the United States, Canada, Great Britain and Australia, post-colonial territories such as South Africa, Zambia, Malawi, Hong Kong, Singapore and the Arabian Gulf States, and other countries where English has no official status, such as China, Japan, continental Europe and South America.

In recognition of this important development, it is time that serious attention was given to EAP in a scholarly work. The purpose of this book is to highlight the various key issues of the field and to demonstrate, through specially commissioned articles from leading scholars in the field, the scope, theoretical issues and pedagogical concerns of EAP. Individual contributions are original research articles, taking a broad definition of research to include philosophical enquiry and critical review. The majority of the chapters, however, contain empirical studies. Contributors have been chosen by reason of their track record in the EAP field, based on a literature review of the leading books and journals that deal with EAP. Given that one of the goals of the collection is highlighting the international nature of the EAP enterprise, scholars have been selected across a broad geographical spectrum, including North America, the United Kingdom, Australia, China (PRC), Hong Kong, Japan, Singapore, the Indian sub-continent, Canada, New Zealand, Brunei, and South Africa.

The two parts of the book are *Issues in EAP* and *The EAP*

Curriculum. Part I, *Issues in EAP*, is devoted to the more global, theoretical and practical problems with which researchers and practitioners are currently concerned. Part II, *The EAP Curriculum*, is more narrowly focused on the planning, implementation and evaluation of what goes on inside (as well as outside) the EAP classroom. These two areas overlap to some extent because the key issues, by virtue of the fact that they are issues, will be relevant to pedagogy and its planning, implementation and evaluation; at the same time, because of the fundamental relationship between EAP and pedagogy, some of the key issues derive directly from curriculum concerns. For example, needs analysis and methodology are intrinsic to any approach to the curriculum, but also figure greatly in the discussion of more global EAP issues. Where there has been doubt about where to locate an individual chapter we have applied the simple criterion of whether or not the issue is a key component of the curriculum – in which case we have placed it in the curriculum part – or can stand on its own as a research issue. In the case of assessment – which is, of course, a key curriculum component – we have two chapters: one is a case study of the historical development of an EAP placement test at one university; the other focuses on the more global issues relating to the major international tests, TOEFL and IELTS. The former paper is placed in the curriculum part, because it speaks most directly to curriculum planners and testers. The latter is in the issues part, because its ramifications are more wide-ranging and of international political significance.

It is envisaged that this book will be used as a set text for students on MA programmes in Applied Linguistics/TESL/ESP/EAP. As well as being used as a course book, this work is likely to appeal to the very large number of EAP practitioners working in institutions of higher education throughout the world. Finally, the book will appeal to university teacher educators and researchers in EAP.

PART I

ISSUES IN ENGLISH FOR ACADEMIC PURPOSES

Introduction

This first part of the two-part collection, *Research Perspectives on English for Academic Purposes*, presents a state-of-the-art collection of research and critical review studies of key issues in the field. Issues included in the collection are as follows: EAP and language planning, linguistic research related to EAP, the application of linguistic research to EAP, the concept of International Scientific English, the role of background knowledge in EAP competence, EAP testing and World Englishes, appropriate pedagogy in peripheral ESL contexts, the notions of power, culture and discourse community, and issues surrounding the international EAP placement tests TOEFL and IELTS.

The first, introductory chapter, by the editors, provides an overview of some of the key issues in EAP – the global need for English, the development of EAP as a discipline, the various types of EAP, EAP's defining characteristics, language description in EAP research, narrow versus wide angle perspectives on course design, collaboration with subject specialists, ethnography and culture, and critical perspectives.

The first chapter of the main body of Part I, on EAP and language planning by Chris Kennedy, begins by considering the growth of English worldwide, which Kennedy sees as a largely unplanned change. He then moves on to look at attempts by various bodies to control or expand the spread of English as an international language. This control is attempted through language planning, of which there are various types. Following on from there, Kennedy considers the need for English in academic situations and the language planning which has occurred in order to fulfil this need. Issues that arise here are links or the lack of them between higher level and lower level planning, cultural aspects in EAP and pedagogic models of language. Finally, Kennedy addresses the question of evaluation of the response of EAP to the demands created by English as an international language and by specific language policies.

Following the chapter by Kennedy, two contributions are devoted to the topic of linguistic research and EAP. Language description has been fundamental to EAP research, designed as it is to gain insight into the target discourses that confront students who are not native speakers of English. In the first of these two chapters John Swales, regarded by many as the doyen of the discipline, describes the historical development of language description, the beginning of which he traces back to the 1960s. Swales identifies each decade since then as making its own distinctive contribution. In the sixties the emphasis was on syntax and lexis. The seventies were characterised by innovative textbook projects, major EAP projects and methodological ferment. In the eighties there was a great deal of work in various types of discourse analysis, a revival of contrastive rhetoric, an appreciation of the socially constructed nature of academic language and an emphasis on disciplinary differences. Moving into and through the 1990s, we find the discipline marked by the use of technology (corpus linguistics and CALL), genre analysis and ethnographic studies. Most research has focused on the research article, but there has also been interest in lectures, oral presentations, and theses and dissertations. In his final section, Swales discusses two contemporary issues: the questioning of the notion of EAP as the acquisition of increasingly more complex generic forms on the grounds that induction into the disciplinary culture is not as 'neat' as this scenario portrays it to be, and the influence of critical pedagogy as discussed in Flowerdew and Peacock's introductory chapter.

While Swales's chapter focuses on linguistic research per se and its developing approaches and methodologies, albeit directed with a pedagogic goal in mind, Brian Paltridge in his chapter is concerned with the application of linguistic research in EAP. The first part of Paltridge's chapter reviews the different ways of teaching the various academic genres which have been informed by linguistic research. This review is followed by a case study of how Paltridge has applied genre analysis research in his teaching of academic writing. The case is illustrated by examples of work produced by a student from the People's Republic of China, writing a Master's thesis at an Australian university. Paltridge's chapter concludes with suggestions for teaching other academic genres, other skills and teaching at lower proficiency levels.

Caroline Clapham, in her chapter, investigates the important question of the relation between subject knowledge and EAP reading ability. In particular, she investigates the hypothesis that there might be a threshold level below which it is not possible to activate subject-specific background knowledge in text comprehension. Based on a large-scale empirical study, Clapham finds partial support for the threshold level hypothesis, especially where texts are highly subject specific. Apart from this, however, her findings also suggest that background knowledge becomes less important at higher ability levels, as learners become able to make use of all the linguistic cues in any given text. Clapham's results have important implications for both text selection in EAP reading comprehension and for the on-going debate concerning the relative merits of wide-angle and narrow-angle EAP syllabus design.

The next three papers in the collection all relate in one way or another to the question of World Englishes. In the first of these, Alistair Wood makes the case for a separate and distinct International Scientific English, particularly as it relates to the research article, a genre which, Wood argues, is determined and defined by the discourse community that creates it. Noting that non-native speakers may be at a disadvantage compared with native speakers when it comes to publishing the results of their research in international refereed journals, Wood argues that as non-natives are increasingly likely to become the majority, they will be the group who decide what constitutes appropriate scientific English. His case is supported by an empirical study of a corpus of scientific research articles designed to estimate the proportion of authors who are non-native speakers. Wood's research has important implications for EAP pedagogy. The pedagogic model should not be the prescription of the native speaker non-scientist, Wood claims, but the practice of scientists, of whom many are non-natives. It is important to note that Wood is only concerned with the natural sciences. The humanities and social sciences, Wood notes, have different, less international, rhetorical traditions.

Like Wood, Liz Hamp-Lyons and Bonnie Wenxia Zhang are also interested in what should be the appropriate model of English in EAP. Their perspective is rather different, however. They are concerned with what should be valued as a model in test development and use. Their research is prompted by calls from some language testers that high-stakes examinations should be rethought to take account of the multiplicity of World Englishes. In the empirical part of their chapter, Hamp-Lyons and Zhang report on the behaviour of raters focusing on the rhetorical patterns of candidates in a university-level essay test paper. Issues raised include the raters' level of tolerance of rhetorical diversity, the appropriacy of 'non-native-like' rhetorical patterns, the selection and training of raters and the implications of the study for English language writing assessment in localised and international contexts.

Like Hamp-Lyons and Zhang, and Wood, Suresh Canagarajah again considers the question of appropriate models of English for EAP. Taking a critical stance, Canagarajah reviews the dominant approaches to the teaching of academic writing in English as a Second Language (ESL). He finds the various approaches all deficient in not taking on board the important issues of culture differences and power as they influence ESL students in peripheral countries. He therefore argues for a focus on social contexts of writing where all the relevant cultural and political conditions influencing the students are taken into account. The approach is exemplified by means of a case study of a Sri Lankan student, which highlights the sorts of issues the approaches to writing reviewed in the first part of the chapter fail to address. The case study shows how the student, in confronting these issues, is able to produce a hybrid text that can be academically effective while reconciling the ideological struggles faced in academic writing in English. In addition, the case study questions a range of assumptions which the dominant approaches make about ESL students, e.g. that they are not total strangers to academic discourses, and that writing is a process of moving in a linear manner from the native to the non-native discourse.

Sue Starfield's chapter, like Canagarajah's, is grounded in the contextual parameters of culture and power. Her starting point is the notion of discourse community and the traditional conception of the role of EAP as inducting students into such communities by making their norms and conventions explicit. Echoing a concern raised by Swales in his chapter, Starfield argues that such a notion of discourse community – while bringing a welcome social dimension to teaching and learning – is monolithic and undifferentiated, tending to assume a homogeneous, unconflictual situation, free from the wider power relations which shape the social context. Basing her argument on a study of a social sciences department at a South African university, Starfield demonstrates that the black students, in particular, through their writing, struggled to negotiate entry into this complex community while academic staff were far from unanimous as to what constituted the criteria for successful access. Meaning was not fixed but subject to constant negotiation and renegotiation among the members of the departmental discourse community, with power relations and the status of the different members, as shaped by the wider social forces, affecting the outcomes. Starfield concludes that attempts to teach academic writing within a disciplinary context need to be based on careful ethnographic study of the target contexts, collaboration with content specialists and encouragement of students to themselves become ethnographers in the academic culture (Johns, 1988: 57).

In the final chapter in Part I, with the contribution of Geoff Brindley and Steven Ross, we turn to assessment issues. As in the majority of the chapters, Brindley and Ross begin with a critical review of the issues involved in their chosen area, the construction and use of large scale international tests of tertiary entry such as TOEFL and IELTS. These two tests are perhaps the most powerful gate-keepers in EAP, deciding which students will be allowed to study in English-speaking institutions, not only in the English-speaking countries of the United States, Great Britain, Canada, Australia and New Zealand, but also, increasingly, in other countries where English is not the national language but is used as a language of tertiary-level instruction. Brindley and Ross review a number of key issues with regard to these two tests, including the following: the way in which academic language proficiency is conceptualised by such tests; the question of content relevance, test score interpretation, test impact and use, and their relation to decisions on university admission; ways of assessing progress and achievement in EAP programmes; collaborative assessment involving subject specialists; and the related question of the overlap between assessment of language and the assessment of subject knowledge.

In the second, empirical part of their chapter, Brindley and Ross address the interface between TOEFL and the development of EAP listening, using longitudinal data from EAP listening course achievement outcomes and their relationship to TOEFL listening gain scores. The research focuses on the interface between syllabus content coverage, academic lecture simulation and classroom assessment of achievement. The chapter concludes with implications for programme evaluation in the light of comparisons of courses that do or do not affect TOEFL listening gain scores.

1 Issues in EAP: A preliminary perspective

John Flowerdew and Matthew Peacock

The need for English

English for Academic Purposes (EAP) – the teaching of English with the specific aim of helping learners to study, conduct research or teach in that language – is an international activity of tremendous scope. It is carried out in four main geographical domains, each of which exhibits particular characteristics and purposes. It is carried out, first, in the major English-speaking countries (the US, UK, Australia, Canada and New Zealand), where large numbers of overseas students whose first language is not English come to study. It is conducted, second, in the former colonial territories of Britain (and less importantly the United States) where English is a second language and is used as the medium of instruction at university level. It is conducted, third, in countries which have no historic links with English, but which need to access the research literature in that language (the countries of Western Europe, Japan, China, Latin America, Francophone Africa and others).[1] And finally, EAP is now increasingly being offered in the countries of the former Soviet-bloc, as they seek to distance themselves from the influence of Russia and its language and position themselves as participants in the increasingly global economy and academic community.

To give some indication of the demand for EAP, if we take the first of the four areas mentioned – the countries where English is a first language – in 1996–7, 457,984 foreign students were studying in the US (Davis, 1997) and 198,064 in the UK (Higher Education Statistics Agency, 1997). While these numbers are already very considerable, they are likely to comprise only a minority of the likely target EAP population. To start with, the figures for the US

---

[1] Some of these countries (e.g. Germany) are now indeed offering academic programmes of their own through the medium of English.

8

Table 1. *Native speakers of the world's major languages*

Mandarin	863
Hindi	357
Spanish	352
English	335

(*Source*: '*The World Almanac and Book of Facts*' [1998])

do not include the large number of ESL students – usually the children of immigrants – who have American citizenship. But more importantly, far more students are likely to require EAP in many of the post-colonial countries (e.g. Nigeria, India or Hong Kong), where there are many English-medium universities, and the countries in which English has no official status (e.g. many Latin American countries), where many students are required to take English, often EAP. Unfortunately, figures are not available for these countries.

One might imagine that the dominance of English as an international language is due to the fact that it is the language which has the greatest number of native speakers (NSs). However, this is not the case. According to *The World Almanac and Book of Facts* (1998), English is only the fourth language in the world in terms of the numbers who speak it as their first language; it is surpassed by Mandarin, Hindi and Spanish respectively (Table 1). However, English is by far the most popular language to learn as a second or foreign language.

Why is it, then, that so many non-native speakers (NNSs) want to learn English in preference to the world's other major languages? One important reason is undoubtedly to do with economic strength. As Graddol (1997) points out, in order to conduct trade one is likely to be more successful if one speaks the language of the customer. In terms of economic strength, the countries where English is the first language are by far the richest (Table 2). The economic power of these countries (most notably the United States) and the accompanying trend in using English for international business are strong reasons for NNSs to want to learn English. If one compares Table 1 with Table 2, it is notable that while the English language is only fourth in terms of the number of NSs (Table 1), English-speaking countries come out well above all other countries in terms of economic strength (Table 2). Chinese drops from first to seventh, Hindi drops down from second to twelfth, and Spanish declines from third to fifth.

Table 2. *The world's major languages and the economic strength of the countries where it is the first language*

	$billion
English	4,271
Japanese	1,277
German	1,090
Russian	801
Spanish	738
French	669
Chinese	448
Arabic	359
(Hindi/Urdu – 12th)	

(*Source:* Graddol [1997])

NNSs, of course, are not only attracted to learn the language of the English-speaking countries[2] because they want to sell their products there. They also want to gain access to their technology and expertise. This is another reason for the large numbers of overseas students studying in the English-speaking countries and the even greater numbers studying through the medium of English in their home countries, where it is a second language. The international language of research and academic publication is English and anyone who wishes to have ready access to this material needs to know the language.

The development of EAP as a discipline

If the economic and demographic factors just referred to provide a reason for the large numbers of NNSs learning and studying through the medium of English, they do not explain the development of EAP as a discipline. For this we need to turn to developments in linguistics, or more specifically applied linguistics, developments which took place primarily in Great Britain.

At the same time as English was beginning to establish itself as a World language in the newly independent countries of Africa and Asia, following pioneering work by Firth, British linguists (most notably Halliday) began to view language and language teaching in a new way. In contrast to theoretical linguists who traditionally saw

[2] This basically means the United States, which is far wealthier than any of the other English-speaking countries.

language as an abstract system, these applied linguists started to consider it as a resource for communication, a resource which varied in its application according to the context or situation in which it was produced. The ramification for language teaching of this perspective was that learners who mastered a language as an abstract system, as was the case with those who learned using the audio-lingual approach, which was prevalent in language teaching (especially in North America) during the 1960s, would not be prepared to communicate in the specific situations they were likely to find themselves when they wanted to use the language. What was needed was an approach to language teaching which was based on descriptions of the language as it was used in the specific target situations. The rationale for such an approach was set out in a seminal publication by Halliday, McIntosh and Strevens (1964), *The Linguistic Sciences and Language Teaching*. In this book Halliday *et al.* presented the concept of register analysis, the description of language varieties used in particular disciplines or occupations, based on statistical differences in lexis and syntax. As we shall see below, this book was very influential in encouraging theoretical work in language description and in its application to the production of EAP teaching materials.

Classifying EAP and its branches

EAP is normally considered to be one of two branches of English for Specific Purposes (ESP), the other being EOP (English for Occupational Purposes). Each of these major branches is then sub-divided according to the disciplines or occupations with which it is concerned. Thus, EAP may be separated into English for Biology, English for Mathematics, English for Economics, etc. and EOP branches out into English for Pilots, English for Doctors, English for Bank employees, etc. (Figure 1).

The distinction between the two major branches of ESP is not clear-cut, however. A lot of work conducted in the academy is in fact preparation for the professional occupations students are likely to go into when they graduate and might therefore be classified as EOP. If we take the example of English for Business in the university, aspects of the course designed to assist learners in their studies would clearly be EAP, but university business courses, like other vocationally-oriented courses, usually seek to prepare their students for business careers. English support for the more vocationally-oriented aspects of the Business course could perhaps be described as EOP as much as EAP. An English course designed to help students read economics

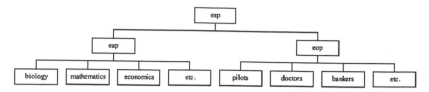

Figure 1 The two major branches of ESP

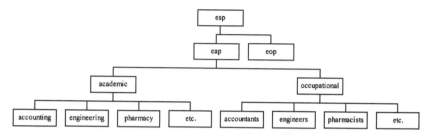

Figure 2 Sub-divisions of EAP

textbooks would clearly be EAP, but a course designed to teach learners how to participate in business meetings or take phone calls definitely has an EOP dimension to it. Perhaps we should sub-divide EAP into EAP designed to help students with their studies and EAP directed towards professional preparation. Both would be EAP by virtue of the fact that they take place in the academy, but they would be distinct in terms of the goal they were directed towards. This classification is represented in Figure 2, where the examples of 'pure' EAP areas are designated as subjects (accountancy, engineering, pharmacy, etc.) and the vocationally oriented dimensions by the target occupations (accountants, engineers, pharmacists).

However one may want to divide up the ESP/EAP cake, as A. Johns and Dudley-Evans (1991: 306) have noted, 'For most of its history, ESP has been dominated by English for Academic Purposes . . . [and it] continues to dominate internationally.' Elsewhere, Dudley-Evans (1998), co-editor of *English for Specific Purposes*, has described that journal as being 'dominated by EAP' (as opposed to EOP). This domination, at least in terms of research, is understandable, if only because EAP practitioners work in academic institutions, where research and intellectual enquiry are encouraged, while workers in EOP are more often located in the workplace, where professional endeavour is directed more towards the bottom line.

Characteristics and claims of ESP/EAP

In a frequently quoted article, Strevens (1988a) proposed four absolute characteristics of ESP/EAP. According to Strevens, ESP/EAP consists of English language teaching which is:

- designed to meet specified needs of the learner
- related in content (i.e. in its themes and topics) to particular disciplines, occupations and activities
- centred on the language appropriate to those activities in syntax, lexis, discourse, semantics etc., and analysis of this discourse
- in contrast with 'General English'

Strevens also listed two variable characteristics of ESP:

ESP may be, but is not necessarily:

- restricted as to the language skills to be learned (e.g. reading only)
- not taught according to any pre-ordained methodology

Furthermore he suggested that the rationale for ESP is based upon four claims:

- being focused on the learner's need, it wastes no time
- it is relevant to the learner
- it is successful in imparting learning
- it is more cost effective than 'General English'

A further set of factors not mentioned by Strevens, but which we would add are:

- authentic texts
- communicative task-based approach
- custom-made materials
- adult learners
- purposeful courses

Key issues in EAP

In the remainder of this chapter we will outline and discuss in more detail some of the features of EAP already mentioned, along with some others which we consider to be the key issues in EAP over the last 35 years or so. We will not discuss needs analysis or teaching methodology here, as, although key issues, these topics are better dealt with in Part II, *The EAP Curriculum*.

Language description

One of Strevens's premises about ESP/EAP was that pedagogy is focused upon the specific language appropriate to the target disciplines, occupations and activities. Pride of place in EAP research must go to descriptions of such target language. Such language description, many would claim, is the primary intellectual focus of the discipline. Indeed, while we have defined EAP as a pedagogic enterprise, there is also another definition in which it is conceived of as a type of language, or collection of types of language. Following this definition, the study of EAP thus becomes the descriptions of these special types of language.

A number of phases in language description work in EAP can be identified. The first of these, register analysis, has already been referred to above. An early example of register analysis is a paper by Barber (1962), 'Some measurable characteristics of modern scientific prose'. Swales (1988a: 1) begins his source book and commentary on the development of English for Specific Purposes, *Episodes in ESP*,[3] with this paper, describing it as 'a clear demonstration that the descriptive techniques of Modern Linguistics, as most influentially represented in *The Linguistic Sciences and Language Teaching* by Halliday, McIntosh and Strevens (Longman, 1964), could be successfully applied to the language of science and technology'. Overtly pedagogic in its intention, the paper clearly shows the distinctive use of lexis and syntax in scientific textbooks. As Swales points out (p. 1), at a time when language syllabuses typically covered all of the English tenses as parts of a system, the paper was particularly influential in its demonstration that the progressive verb forms are very rarely used in scientific writing. The implication of this for EST courses was clear; if progressive verb forms are rarely used, then there is no need to devote much, if any, time to them on courses on scientific writing.

A criticism of register analysis is that it is purely descriptive and not explanatory, i.e., it tells us the relative frequency of linguistic forms, but not the special functions these forms have in the specific register and what purpose their marked presence or absence may serve (Bhatia, 1993: 6). Starting in the 1980s, however, such considerations did begin to be addressed. Labelled 'contextual analysis', by Celce-Murcia (1980) and 'narrow and deep study' by Swales (1990: 3), perhaps the best known example of this approach is

---

[3] As a demonstration of the dominance of EAP in ESP, all of the 15 papers Swales presents deal with the former; none relate to EOP.

Tarone *et al.*'s (1981) examination of the use of the passive in astrophysics articles. In this study, which focuses on just two articles, frequency data is presented, but it is used to support the more important generalisations (for Tarone *et al.*) concerning the rhetorical, or communicative, purposes of the use of the passive in the selected genre, not just as an end in itself, as was the case for Barber (1962). Furthermore, where Barber's data made no distinctions between the different genres of scientific writing,[4] nor the different disciplines, Tarone *et al.*'s frequency data apply to a very specific context. Their data concerns one journal, one discipline, and one subject matter within that discipline (the two articles are on the same topic); not only that, but levels of frequency are distinguished across the various sections of the articles.

Prior to contextual analysis, another meaning-focused approach – termed 'pragmatic analysis' by Tarone *et al.* (1981) had developed. Instead of starting with a given linguistic form and seeking out its specific uses, pragmatic analysis starts with a particular rhetorical function – defining, describing, classifying, etc. – and investigates the linguistic forms through which the particular function is realised. The work of Selinker and his colleagues at the University of Washington (synthesised in Trimble, 1985) is typical of this approach. A limitation here, however, is that this work failed to differentiate the specific situations in which a given function was used. Thus, there was no distinction in Selinker's work between, say, defining or classifying in textbooks, popularisations, and training manuals. All such material is lumped together as 'scientific' English. As subsequent work was to demonstrate, language may vary across these different types of text.

In recent years, both rhetorical and pragmatic analysis have become much more sophisticated, facilitated by the use of computers. Large corpora of text can now be used to search for specific forms or functions, making reliable quantitative analysis much more feasible and allowing a concentration on specific text types (see, e.g., Swales *et al.* [1998] on the use of the imperative in research articles as an example of the former, and Hyland [1997] on *hedging*, of the latter).

In the early 1990s, researchers such as Swales (1990) and Bhatia (1993) developed a more focused methodology, which they referred to as *genre analysis*, as an alternative approach to satisfy the need for text-specificity. A genre is a particular type of communicative event which has a particular communicative purpose recognised by its users, or *discourse community*. By targeting specific genres as the

---

[4] The data was from both journal articles and textbooks.

object of linguistic analysis, one ensures that the description is valid for the specific situation and participants (especially where members of the discourse community are consulted as part of the analysis). Genre analysis has become a veritable industry in EAP research since the pioneering work of Swales and Bhatia. Studies have focused primarily on the research article and the various sections thereof (most notably introductions, but also abstracts and discussion sections [Nwogu, 1997]; introductory textbooks [Love, 1991]; graduate seminars [Weissberg, 1993]; conference presentations [Shalom, 1993]; lectures [Young, 1994; Thompson, 1994] and school genres [e.g. Martin, 1993]).

Genre analysis has more recently been further broadened. Some researchers are now no longer content to use representatives of the discourse community as specialist informants to confirm the linguistic interpretation, which is the primary focus of the study. Members of the discourse community (along with their physical situation) now become a primary focus of the analysis, equal to, if not more important than the actual text. Analysis thus becomes more ethnographic (Berkenkotter and Huckin, 1995) and genre is conceived of as a dynamic phenomenon, subject to change and adaptation by the participants, in contrast to the somewhat static original text-bound conceptualisation.

The relevance of all this activity in discourse analysis is that the descriptions produced may be applied to pedagogy. In the best examples of this work, discourse analysts not only provide linguistic descriptions, but also show how their findings could be applied to pedagogy.

Narrow vs. wide-angle perspectives

A question that often arises in the design of EAP courses concerns the level of specificity that should be adopted. Some argue that at the lower levels of general English competence, learners are not ready for discipline-specific language and learning tasks, while others argue that the most cost-effective teaching is that which focuses on the immediate specific needs confronting learners in their disciplines.

The issue is related to what Bloor and Bloor (1986) refer to as the *common core hypothesis* in applied linguistics. According to proponents of this hypothesis, there is a common core of grammatical and lexical items that predominates in any linguistic register. Thus, whatever type of text one analyses, a common set of linguistic structures and vocabulary items will run through it. When applied to language teaching, it follows, according to this position, that before embarking on any specific purpose course, learners may master the basic set of linguistic items which make up the common core.

There are a number of problems with the common core hypothesis, however. It is possible to specify a set of items to make up a common core because grammatical forms make up a finite set. This is to ignore the question of meaning, however. Any form has many possible meanings, according to the context in which it appears. The common core is a formal system, divorced from meaning and use. Because meaning is determined by context, if meaning is to be incorporated into the common core hypothesis, it is not possible to escape from the notion of specific varieties. Mastery of any language system, whether or not it is claimed to be a part of the common core, must take place within the context of a specific variety or varieties (Bloor and Bloor, 1986).

Turning this argument on its head, proponents of narrow angle EAP can argue that, because the common core is to be found in any variety, then it is possible to learn the common core at the same time as learning the specific variety. Such an approach is more cost effective, it can be argued, as mastery of the specific language of the target discipline can begin at any level of overall competence.

In its application to pedagogy, another problem with the common core hypothesis is that it assumes an incremental model of language acquisition. It assumes that learners can first master the common core and then go on to the variety-specific features. If there is one important finding of research in second language acquisition, it is that learning is not incremental. Learners tend to acquire features of the language system when they are ready, not necessarily in the order they are presented to them by their teachers and course books. If, after eight years of secondary school English, a university student has still not mastered third person subject verb agreement or the article system – both common errors in language users who are in other ways highly proficient in the language – then EAP curriculum planners are justified in moving on to more discipline-specific features, it can be argued.

Finally, with its focus on language items, a common core approach neglects language skills. An EAP discipline is defined as much by the activities performed within it as by its typical language forms and meanings. EAP needs to prepare learners to read text-books, listen to lectures, write essays, and do library research, among a range of other skills. Curriculum planners cannot wait until mastery of the common core is complete before focusing on these discipline-specific activities. It is far better to do remedial work on common core items – which will regularly be encountered in any variety – at the same time as developing the discipline-specific skills.

Some EAP practitioners have argued for wide-angle EAP/ESP on general pedagogic grounds. Widdowson (1983) has claimed that narrow-angle ESP is a type of 'training', as opposed to 'education'. If ESP is to play a role as part of the broader educational process, then broader competencies will be developed in courses with broader aims, courses which focus on 'purposeful activity' rather than specific language. Hutchinson and Waters (1987) argue for a broad-angle approach on similar grounds, claiming that competence in the skills required in the target situation is more important than the specific language of those situations. Ultimately, however, these positions fall back on the common core hypothesis in assuming that a basic set of language items exists, which learners already know and which they can use in the development of the target skills. Those who reject the common core hypothesis, however, argue that the specific language associated with the specific skills might just as well be the target of learning than a register which must be artificially created to employ only those items of language which purportedly belong to the common core.

Collaboration with subject specialists

A distinctive feature of EAP work is the increasing collaboration which takes place with subject specialists. The earliest account of systematic subject/language teacher collaboration in EAP is described by T. Johns and Dudley-Evans (1980), who claim that problems encountered by overseas students in the UK are rarely concerned with 'knowledge of the language', or 'knowledge of the subject' alone, but that these two factors are 'inextricably intertwined' (p. 8). Johns and Dudley-Evans believe that the language teacher

needs to be able to grasp the conceptual structure of the subject his students are studying if he is to understand fully how language is used to represent that structure; to know how the range of different subjects are taught during the course; and to observe where and how difficulties arise in order that he can attempt to help both student and subject teacher to overcome them.

(Johns and Dudley-Evans, 1980: 8)

Johns and Dudley-Evans's team-teaching experiment was conducted with small classes of postgraduate students. A larger scale application of a similar approach for beginning university students is described by Flowerdew (1993a) at Sultan Qaboos University,

Oman. In the course described by Flowerdew, the foundation year science course and the science support English course were team-taught by paired science and language teachers. The focus was primarily on the lectures, but also on the assigned reading that accompanied the lectures. The English teachers observed the science lectures and video recordings were made for exploitation in the English class. English and science staff also collaborated in the writing and editing of materials to be used in both the science and English classes.

Barron lists two other methods for working with subject specialists besides collaborative or team-teaching. The first of these is the subjects-specialist informant method, where the subject specialist provides insights into the content and organisation of texts and the processes of the subject. The second is the consultative method, where the subject specialist is brought in to participate at specific stages in a course. He/she may suggest topics for projects, give lectures, assist in the assessment of students' work, and run discussions, among a whole range of activities.

Taking content and language teacher collaboration a stage further is A. Johns (1997a), who calls for EAP literacy specialists to act as 'mediators' among students, faculty and administrators. Johns sees the role of the EAP literacy teacher as one who encourages students and subject specialists to collaboratively examine the interactions of 'texts, roles and contexts'. The literacy teacher needs to educate not only students but also content teachers as to the nature of academic literacy, so that they are able to appreciate the assumptions within their own disciplines regarding literacy, on the one hand, and the goals and intricacies of language programmes designed to initiate learners into these disciplines, on the other.

Ethnography and culture

Although both research and curriculum work in ESP have been much concerned with language and discourse, at the same time there has been a continuing, though less systematically documented, preoccupation on the part of some with more ethnographic approaches to both research and pedagogy. Indeed, the development of EAP linguistic research, as described above, already demonstrates a move away from a focus on language in isolation towards a consideration of discourse in context.

The rationale for more ethnographic approaches as far as pedagogy is concerned, lies in the potential mismatch between the academic culture of the EAP provider and the background culture of the learner. Such mismatches may occur both where curricula with an 'Anglo' bias are employed in non-Anglo settings and where overseas NNSs study in Anglo countries. The approach is predicated on the idea of getting away from what Coleman (1996) calls an *autonomous* approach to the classroom, which assumes that classroom phenomena everywhere are and should be much the same, in favour of an *ideological* position, which is culturally embedded and recognises social processes as influencing classroom activity.

In line with the ideological view, grounded in an ethnographic investigation of a large scale, internationally-funded EAP project in Egypt, Holliday (1994) argues strongly against the imposition of alien pedagogic models in such non-Anglo EAP settings, in favour of greater sensitivity to the social context. Barron (1992) also argues for local input to EAP curricula, in his case the traditional local culture and technology in Papua New Guinea.

As an outcome of an ethnographic study of an English-medium university in Hong Kong, Flowerdew and Miller (1995) offered a grounded model of culture in lectures where expatriate NSs of English lecture to Cantonese L1 students. Flowerdew and Miller posited four dimensions of culture where cross-cultural communication breakdown is likely to occur: ethnic culture, local culture, academic culture and disciplinary culture. Ethnic culture is concerned with the socio-psychological make-up of students and overseas lecturers, which may differ due to their contrasting ethnic background; local culture is concerned with aspects of the local setting with which students are familiar, but with which lecturers may not be. Academic culture refers to values, roles, assumptions, attitudes, patterns of behaviour, etc., which may differ across cultures; disciplinary culture refers to the theories, concepts, norms and terms of a particular discipline with which lecturers are familiar and students, as apprentices, by definition, are not.

Turning now to English L1 contexts, ethnographic research has again revealed cross-cultural difficulties. An early study was that of Dudley-Evans and Swales (1980) who highlighted problems likely to be encountered by Arab students in British universities. Cortazzi and Jin (1994) have described the contrasting expectations of Chinese research students and their British supervisors. Benson's (1988) ethnographic study of an Arab student in the United States, while not written from a cross-cultural perspective, provided a number of insights as far as preparation for lecture listening is concerned. Benson discovered, for example, that whereas in his EAP listening classes his Arab student had been listening to 'comprehend', to get some facts, in his content lectures he was listening to 'learn', to get the facts, but also to understand the attitudes that underlay their selection and presentation (p. 441). Benson also discovered that in lectures, listening is only one of a range of skills employed. The other macro-skills of reading, writing and speaking are also required, along with note-taking.

A common cultural problem in both L1 and L2 contexts is attitudes towards plagiarism. A number of articles have considered contrasting cultural views on this issue (Cortazzi, 1990; Scollon, 1996; Pennycook, 1996a). These articles highlight how different academic cultures can view the 'borrowing' of others' words in different lights.

Critical perspectives

In a 1997 article John Swales, the doyen of EAP, confessed to a certain self-deception in his 30-year involvement with the enterprise. He admitted to having accepted the view during the 1970s that, in his words, 'what Third World countries needed was a rapid accelera- tion in their resources of human capital, which could be achieved by hurried transmission of Western technical and scientific know-how delivered through the medium of English and supported by appro- priate EAP programmes' (p. 377). Swales had viewed his experience working overseas in scientific English as, in his words again, 'a culturally and politically neutral enterprise'. Having read the work of authors such as Phillipson (1992) and Pennycook (1994a), however, which highlights certain 'neo-colonialist' aspects of English – for example, how it is 'marketed' as a global 'commodity', its association with the maintenance of socio-political structures that rely on a linguistic 'overclass' proficient in English, and the link between the teaching of technical language and the manufacture and export of technical equipment – Swales is now sensitive to some of the more contentious ideological implications of English as a world language and EAP as an important part of that phenomenon.

In his reassessment, Swales has coincided with a more critical turn in EAP on a number of fronts (e.g. Santos, 1992; Benesch, 1993; Pennycook, 1994b, 1997a). Various practitioners have criticised EAP for avoiding important ideological issues and being too ready to accommodate to the status quo at the expense of their second language students (e.g. Santos, 1992; Benesch, 1993). Santos (1992), for example, critiqued Horowitz for arguing against process writing in favour of a needs-based approach which emphasised realistic simulations and writing essay exams under time pressure. Similarly Benesch (1993) was critical of Reid (1989) and her emphasis on students '[understanding] what the professor wants' and 'feel[ing] secure about being able to fulfil those expectations.' (p. 233). 'Reality and authenticity [for EAP practitioners such as Reid],' Benesch (1993) argues, 'are located in current academic institutions, departments, lectures, discourse, genres, texts, and tasks. These academic structures are given in the EAP literature, not areas of debate or resistance.' Instead of this accommodationist stance, EAP should be ready to argue that the academy bears a responsibility to adapt itself to the cultures, world views and languages of second and foreign language students, Benesch argues. In being too ready to accommodate traditional academic practices, EAP limits the participation of NNS students in the academic culture. 'The politics of pragmatism leads to a neglect of more inclusive and democratic practices, such as negotiating the curriculum and collaborative learning because these are rarely practiced in non-ESL classes' (Benesch, 1993). An example of the more *critical* approach argued for by Benesch is the needs analysis she conducted at her university (Benesch, 1996), which resulted in the EAP teacher running classes which aimed at modifying the target situation. In another study, Benesch (in press) has developed a framework for EAP learners' rights.

Taking the critique of the pragmatic approach to EAP a stage further, Pennycook (1997a) argues that EAP has a responsibility to develop students' linguistic and critical awareness in the broadest possible context, well beyond the needs of the specific target disciplines. 'A curricular focus on providing students only with academic-linguistic skills for dealing with academic work in other disciplines', Pennycook claims, 'misses a crucial opportunity to help students to develop forms of linguistic, social and cultural criticism that would be of much greater benefit to them for understanding and questioning how language works both within and outside educational institutions' (p. 263).

Given the radical, potentially confrontational, nature of these critical positions, they have, unsurprisingly, been subject to dispute. Allison (1996), for example, has argued that it is misleading to represent *pragmatism* – which he glosses as 'reinforcing conformity in thought and expression under the guise of pragmatic concerns' – as a uniform ideology underlying all EAP. He cites a range of examples of collaborations between EAP practitioners and mainstream faculty that highlight, in his words, 'EAP decisions and practices [which] take account of and change wider realities of power'.

There are a number of other important critical issues which have a bearing on EAP. One of these is what have come to be called *World*

Englishes (McArthur, 1998). In many post-colonial countries indigenous varieties of English have developed which have phonological, grammatical, lexical, and discoursal features which diverge from British and American standards. The question arises as to what is the appropriate model for EAP in these countries, the local variety or the international standards (Kachru, 1988)? The indigenous variety will perhaps have greater currency locally, but the international standard will be more useful in accessing the international literature, study overseas, interacting with other academics internationally and publishing their research results in international journals.

Variation in World Englishes has given rise to calls in some quarters for greater tolerance of different rhetorical styles in international publication. Tickoo (1994: 34) has written on this issue as follows: 'Academics share disciplinary cultures. But before they gain entrance into such cultures, they are, in every case, members of ethnic cultures which influence the way they use language for a purpose.' Mauranen (1993a, 1993b) has argued that international journals should show greater tolerance of different rhetorical styles. Similarly, Yakhontova (1995), writing from a Ukrainian perspective, has argued that Ukrainian scholars want to publish their research internationally in English, but that they want to retain their own distinctive Ukrainian voice. Perhaps such tolerance should also be extended at the instructional level. University faculty should be taught to accept different rhetorical styles in the writing of their NNS students.

Another critical issue in EAP is the dominance of NSs in setting the agenda in the discipline (Tickoo, 1994). Many early EAP projects in NNS settings were set up by expatriates and although most EAP teaching is now done by NNSs and more NNSs are now publishing research in specialist journals (itself, perhaps, evidence of the success of EAP), Anglo practitioners and researchers still predominate in the EAP literature. The situation is one in which most of the EAP literature is written by NSs, but most of the EAP teaching is done by NNSs.

Finally, the EAP issue with perhaps the most significance outside the field itself, concerns the important part played by EAP in the increasing global hegemony of English (Crystal, 1997). English as an international language brings with it great benefits, but it is not without its costs (Phillipson, 1992; Pennycook, 1994a). On the academic front one important effect of the tendency towards international scholarly publication in English is that academic genres are dying out in some languages. Mauranen (1993b) has noted, for example, that the research article in Finnish has just about disappeared. As well as impoverishing national cultures, such a loss may have international ramifications: 'Insofar as rhetorical practices embody cultural thought patterns, we should encourage the maintenance of variety and diversity in academic rhetorical practices – excessive standardisation may counteract innovation and creative thought by forcing them into standard forms' (Mauranen, 1993b: 172).

Conclusion

This chapter has reviewed some of the key issues in EAP. It has been fairly selective in its choice of issues and fairly cursory in its treatment of these issues. Space has precluded a more detailed treatment. Nevertheless, we hope the chapter will have prepared the ground for a reading of the more in-depth and specific treatments of some of these and related issues in the chapters which make up the main body of this collection.

2 Language use, language planning and EAP

Chris Kennedy

Introduction

In this article I will be looking at the current situation regarding the spread of English as an international language, the relationship of English with other languages, the attempt at intervention through language policy or language planning, and some of the implications of both the situation of language spread and of policy/planning for the practice of English for Academic Purposes or EAP.

I shall restrict the meaning of EAP to cover those educational activities in higher education, the purpose of which is the teaching and learning of the English language required by undergraduates, post-graduates and/or staff. Their subject of study is not the English language, which is a 'carrier' subject. They need English language and communication skills for access to subject knowledge or 'content', either, in the case of undergraduates and post-graduates, prior to their studies ('pre-sessional') or during them ('in-sessional'). Such 'content' skills will cover the whole range of higher education curricula, in the sciences, humanities and social sciences.

I shall not be dealing with issues arising in EAP contexts at school level, interesting and important though this area is. I do not deal with language across the curriculum in bilingual education, for example, an area which is arguably a form of EAP. This activity is expanding as command of at least two languages, typically a first language and English as a working second language, is beginning to be perceived important and, by some, an expected part of social competence, particularly for those who can afford private education or who are dissatisfied with state provision (Brewster, 1999; Clegg, 1999).

Although the specific focus of this volume is EAP, we must remember that EAP is an area of speciality within the field of ESP (English for Specific Purposes) (Dudley-Evans and St John, 1998), itself a part of ELT, and that much of what I say will be applicable to other ESP and ELT contexts. We should also be careful not to assume that EAP is independent of more general educational concerns. EAP, just as any other educational endeavour, responds to economic and socio-political pressures and it is to these influences that I shall turn first.

The social context of English as an international language

Over the last two centuries, the spread of the West's economic and political power, represented initially by the UK and subsequently the USA, has been not surprisingly linked with the majority language used within those countries, English. Crystal (1997) gives a detailed guide to the spread of English in the 20th century. Kachru's (1985) now familiar set of concentric circles of English-using countries reflects these past political and economic movements and the language users associated with them. To remind readers, Kachru describes 'inner circle' countries in which the major use of English is as a first language (e.g. Australia, UK, USA); the 'outer circle' consisting in the main of territories who had inherited English as a colonial legacy and who still use English within the country as a lingua franca (e.g. India, Malaysia, Nigeria); and the 'expanding circle' of countries where English is used for mainly for communication with those from other countries (e.g. Brazil, Germany, Japan).

The major use of English within a country as a lingua franca, primarily in outer circle countries, I shall refer to as English as an Additional Language (EAL); English used for external relations with other countries I shall term English as an International Language (EIL) (Kennedy, 1987a; Nayar, 1997). The speakers in the nations of the three circles (inner, outer and expanding) use English (in fact different Englishes) in various ways within their respective borders, and categorising English use within a country or outside it as EAL or EIL respectively, as I have done, is admittedly a crude generalisation (Tripathi, 1998; Crystal, 1999). There will be much individual and group variation in different social circumstances and code-mixing and code-switching will occur (McArthur, 1998). However, all countries (but not all discourse communities with them), irrespective of the 'circle' in which they are situated, use English for international communication, and this fact has considerable effect on the introduction and maintenance of EAP programmes.

Domains and discourse communities

Both Graddol (1997: 8) and Crystal (1997: 78ff) list a number of domains in which English is now being used internationally. These include professional domains such as international organisations; conferences; academic publishing, particularly though not exclusively in science and technology; banking, economic affairs and trade; tourism; and transport, particularly air and sea transport. Considerable exposure to English takes place through advertising, the media and popular culture, and a major medium of communication, the Internet, is attracting use in English. However, it is almost impossible to obtain valid figures of those exposed to English, and almost as difficult to estimate the numbers of users of English internationally. The discourse communities operating in the professional domains mentioned above may in fact be relatively small as a proportion of national populations, but given the expertise required to enter such domains, they are likely to be those communities with the greatest power and influence in any society.

There will be a strong link between the use of English in the specialised domains listed above (and hence EAP students who need to gain access to those domains) and the high socio-economic status of the users. Figure 1 (from Walters, 1998) illustrates the range of English use in Tunisia (one of the expanding circle countries). The majority of the population will use either Arabic or French in their daily lives. Those using English in the specialised domains we have referred to are a relatively small proportion of the population (those shaded in the diagram) and their language proficiencies will vary from limited to excellent, depending on their social and educational experiences. Although relatively small in number, such an EIL-using group are likely to have considerable influence in their societies, particularly perhaps in countries like Tunisia where the society is socially stratified and the power base small. It is not the facility in English per se which creates these influential groupings (clearly elite groups do not owe their existence to their use of a particular foreign language), but English is closely associated with the hopes, aspirations and lifestyles of such groups. It is an important resource. For this reason the academic activity giving access to such English (EAP) has been accused of being an instrument of elitist language policies (Tollefson, 1991).

The predominance of English is not a stable state of affairs. Other languages are still powerful; some are already or will become powerful regionally and Internet communication is expanding into other-than-English use. Translation and interpretation (as an alternative to communication between two or more parties conducted in English as an international language) is still a major activity, and likely to develop further as machine translation techniques develop (see below). At present, however, English remains attractive for many

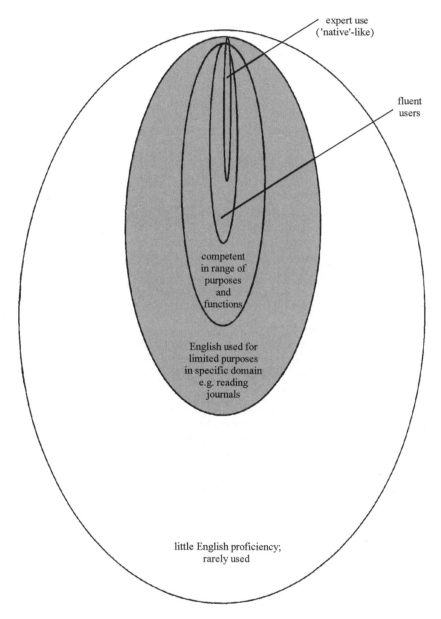

Figure 1 (Walters, 1998) English language users in Tunisia

users as the international language. This is not meant to be triumphalist but reflects an opinion held by many, including those who question whether the monopoly of English is beneficial (e.g. Phillipson and Skutnabb-Kangas, 1996).

Power and influence of English-users

The users of EIL from inner circle countries are obviously advantaged since English is generally their first language. Kachru was originally concerned with what he regarded as undue influence from inner to outer/expanding circles, deriving from the power of first language speakers. This imbalance in direction of influence still remains and Goh (1998) shows how ESP practices in the outer/expanding circle (termed 'domestic' ESP) can be harmed by applying the approaches of inappropriate and irrelevant inner circle ESP. The situation is very slowly changing. The speed of change is slow since a concentration of economic and political power, together with use of English as a first language, still remains predominantly in inner circle countries, most evidently in the USA. There is, however, more interaction in the reverse direction both from outer/expanding circles to inner, and probably even greater interaction within outer/expanding circles. One must be careful, however, not to assume that activity within an outer/expanding circle country is necessarily evidence of an actual rather than cosmetic shift – it may be a form of globalisation emanating from inner circle countries. Thus, inner circle publishers may publish under a local name in outer/expanding circle countries, or there may be a high concentration of inner circle English L1 speakers in a country who control ELT activity. Hong Kong and Brunei have arguably been examples of this, with a high proportion of inner circle representatives in outer/expanding circle higher education ELT positions. Where there is awareness of imbalance, and attempts made to restore it, there is the danger that power may be given as a gesture of political correctness rather than as a belief. Students may choose to study in outer/expanding universities rather than those in inner circle countries for financial reasons or convenience rather than conviction.

However, the signs of shift, though slight, are there. In 1980, the first Editorial Board of *English for Specific Purposes Journal*, which is arguably the journal that represents the international ESP academic community, had 12 inner circle representatives, 9 from North America and 3 from the UK; and no members from the outer/expanding circle. Recent comparative figures (Volume 18/2, 1999) are an Advisory Board of four, all from the inner circle and an

Editorial Board of 23, 17 of whom are inner circle representatives and 6 of whom are from the outer/expanding circle. The editors and publishers are still from inner circle countries. Imbalance is still apparent (and there may be pragmatic rather than ideological reasons for this), but a minor shift has been initiated. There are more regional conferences in ESP with local organisation, and a few local ESP journals exist (e.g. *ESP Malaysia Journal* with Malaysian editors and Malaysians constituting 3 out of the journal's 5 advisors).

The ESPecialist [sic] is of interest. This is a Brazilian bilingual journal with six out of the seven articles in Volume, 19/2, 1998 written by Brazilian teachers, and three out of these six written in Portuguese, the remaining three in English. The reasons for the bilingual language policy have clearly been that while the editors hope for an international readership, they also see the journal as fulfilling a local role in Brazil acting as a means of communication between ESP teachers in Brazil and encouraging local teachers who prefer to use their first language to contribute.

The reasons for such shifts, and their slowness, are complex, and relate to political and socio-economic developments, which in turn influence the development of local EAP professionalism and expertise. English language interaction between outer/expanding circle users and within them has certainly caused a shift in the ownership of English. All users of the language, from whichever of the circles, own English in the sense that they use it regularly and are using varieties which are part of their international and local identities (Svalberg, 1998). This raises questions of a language policy addressing what forms of English should be taught and is particularly an issue within business English (Van der Walt, 1999; Connor, 1999). Whether users from outside the inner circle countries own English in the sense of managing, controlling or planning its use, to the extent that that is anyway possible, is the subject of current debate. The argument, developed mainly by representatives of the inner circle (e.g. Phillipson, 1992; Pennycook, 1994a) has now been taken up by those who use English in outer/expanding contexts (e.g. Bisong, 1995 from Nigeria; Fonzari, 1999 from Estonia), so in this area, too, we are beginning to see a balance of contributions from all three-circle representatives, though there is still an imbalance in areas of ELT and ESP in general (Holliday, 1999).

English for academic purposes and EIL

Widdowson has said (1997) that EIL is the result of ESP. Engagement in certain international activities, what I have called domains above, is now necessary for economic and political survival, and English is commonly used within the domains internationally. Widdowson was not referring to the teaching and learning of ESP but to the use of English for specific purposes in such domains. However, it is clear that the teaching and learning of ESP derives from the need to use English in those domains. If individuals wish to enter the professional communities represented by the domains, they will need access to both the knowledge and skills of the profession (content training) and the language and discourse through which those skills and knowledge are communicated, in this case English (carrier training). The educational activity of ESP and the subdivision of EAP within it, is of course concerned essentially with ways of reconciling the familiar tension between content and carrier.

Let us look at this relationship further with an example from the genre of academic discourse. Because so much academic discourse is conducted through the medium of English, whether in journals, at conferences or through the Internet, academics will need a competence in English, if they are to keep up with developments in their field, ensure that their own work is available to their colleagues internationally and interact with each other. If the academics wish to publish for an international academic community, they will be forced to write in English, however much we may dislike this element of covert coercion (Medgyes and Kaplan, 1992). Such societal pressure gives an added motivation to EAP to provide the means by which academics can produce texts in English which in turn will be read by post-graduates who themselves will require language training (see below).

The alternative to intervention through EAP programmes is translation. It is difficult at the moment to see how translation could keep pace with scientific development and associated publication, though the provision of texts in the L1 is clearly going to develop over the next few years as machine translation becomes more sophisticated. Whether machine translation will move further from dealing with restricted, highly specific (and hence more easily translatable) genres is at present an open question and the subject of debate (see Attwell, 1999). If, indeed, automatic translation becomes a reality in the future, this may affect EAP, since as we have seen, EAP is an attempt to provide the means (the language skills) required to access subject-specific information which at present is not available in the relevant L1.

However, a further interesting question is whether, even with accurate, speedy and cheap translations available, those professionals wishing to publish internationally will be forced, as at present, to publish in English if they wish their work to be read. It is highly likely that this will be the case if their own language has a relatively low usage in the hierarchy of major international languages (see Graddol, 1997, for discussion of future language hierarchies). Much will depend on both the attitudes and language policies of English-users (not only English L1 speakers but more significantly English L2 speakers) towards language of publication. Even with satisfactory translation facilities available, will journals published in languages other than English have sufficient status (when compared to English-language journals) for English-users to access them; and will those journals at present publishing in English (since it is the international language) change their policy to include papers in other languages? If not, then the necessity to publish in English will continue, and this will either mean an increasing demand for translation from L1 to English from those who are not confident of their composing skills in academic English, or increased demand for EAP provision both from actual and potential contributors and from those requiring access to the subject matter at undergraduate and post-graduate levels.

For undergraduates and post-graduates, the need for English is as apparent, though of a different nature. They are being trained in the specialisation of their choice, and even if the language of instruction in their institutions is not English but their own language, they will find because of the power and status of EIL we have described above, the books and articles they will need to refer to will be in English. Some may be undertaking vocationally oriented courses, such as the Masters in Business Administration (MBA), and will find that they may be expected at the end of their course to be familiar with professional as well as academic genres in English, such as report writing. Such EAP situations are common in those countries within the expanding circle.

The situation becomes more complex where the medium of higher education is English, since the needs for English will be much wider in scope. Not only do students require access to English for reference purposes, but they will need English in order to understand lectures and seminars and other study genres. English-medium situations are typically found in outer circle countries where English is an additional language (EAL). In the past, such situations have been the result of a colonial history, but there is likely to be increasing demand for such English-medium universities. Some parts of the outer circle will wish to attract students from other countries of the region who will use what Goh, 1998, refers to as 'new' EAP.

The other rapidly expanding area of EAP is occurring in the inner circle where English is a medium of education in English L1 communities. Such inner circle countries are finding students from outer circle or expanding circle countries an attractive source of income in the face of government cuts in funding. The students themselves register in inner circle countries for many reasons, because the courses they attend cannot be provided in their own country, because they cannot gain admission to their own universities either for logistical or political reasons, or because the real or perceived status of an inner circle degree is higher than a degree in their own country. Such 'classic' EAP programmes (Goh, *op.cit.*) have to respond to the same study needs found in EAL situations but additionally have a social element since the students have to operate in an English-medium environment both inside and outside the university. These are generalisations of course. There will be occasions when a bilingual policy will be adopted with certain subjects in English and others in the students' first language, and there are instances of English-medium universities (often within the private sector) in expanding circle countries (EIL), where education would normally be provided through the first language. Examples exist in Germany, the Netherlands and Turkey. Such bilingual institutions may require a large investment in EAP programmes if they are to succeed (O'Dwyer *et al.*, 1995).

So far I have described EAP as a teaching and learning process responding to the spread of English as an international language, itself a consequence of a constellation of economic and political factors, as if EAP were part of a process of unplanned change. There is, of course, always an element of chance and 'drift' attached to change, but underlying the development of EAP as a teaching and research discipline is perhaps more policy and planning, and intervention in the process of change, than we might think. Choices have consciously been made between the use of English and other languages in various domains. The result of these choices is language policy, sometimes written, at other times less explicit, but policy nonetheless. International corporations have to decide in which language or languages they will conduct their business (Nickerson, 1998). Journal publishers will decide which languages their authors can use. These are examples of language policy decisions. Where the policy is to use English, the effect on EAP is immediate. Other language-in-education policy decisions we have inferred above, including whether institutions will be English-medium or not. I have now explicitly introduced the concept of language policy to which I now turn.

Language policy and planning (LPP)

In this article I will conflate the terms policy and planning and use the single term language policy and planning (LPP). Where I need to distinguish policy (as a statement of aims and objectives) from planning (the attempt to turn a policy statement into action and implementation), I shall use the respective individual terms.

We have already seen that the present socio-economic context is encouraging the spread of EIL. Essentially, this is a reflection of language behaviour. More people are using English, are needing, or wanting to use it, in the various domains I have listed above. This is an example of relatively unplanned change influenced by market forces. Some will object that market forces imply a situation of supply and demand and that demand is often created and supply provided by interested parties. The argument is that linguistic choices are being made not 'naturally' but in response to a perceived need for English, which is the result of particular political and ideological systems controlling people's choice (Tollefson, 1995 ed.) and to which Pennycook, for example, believes certain discourses 'adhere' (Pennycook, 1998: 7–8, 207–214).

I sympathise with the argument but wish to try to distinguish language behaviour (largely unplanned and unconscious), from explicit attempts (planned and conscious) by individuals, groups, institutions or governments to influence that behaviour and control it, either by encouraging it (maintaining or spreading use), or limiting it (decreasing use), though I recognise the difficulty separating the two as they are part of a circle of development. Attempts at explicit control constitute language policy and planning (LPP), and my description of it comes close to Cooper's (1989) definition of LPP.

LPP and pedagogy

There is debate about the point at which language policy/planning ceases and other forms of policy/planning begin. All models of LPP agree that there are connections between various levels of action (whether at national, institutional, or classroom levels), but some maintain a definition of LPP that places it at higher levels of policy/planning, particularly governmental levels. Others (Kennedy, 1986; Cooper, 1989; Wiley, 1996; Hornberger and Ricento, 1996) argue that LPP occurs at all levels, from state policy to language decisions made by individual teachers and students in classrooms. It is this latter view I will be taking in this article. A more appropriate term for this broader view of LPP may well be 'language management', a term suggested by Neustupny (1985), and Jernudd (1990), and taken up by Cameron (1995) who is similarly in need of a term to describe various forms of language intervention not normally classified as LPP.

This approach, by broadening the scope of LPP may well weaken its focus, but it presents us with a powerful way of looking at situations which would not be normally classified as LPP, and more importantly creates a new, more active role for those who would not normally regard themselves as 'language planners' such as teachers and teacher trainers. I have referred to these groups as 'change agents' (Kennedy, 1996 and 1997) and Wiley (1996) refers to them as 'language strategists'. Extending the definition of LPP to include groups of language planners such as EAP materials writers and teachers, not normally associated with LPP as traditionally defined, enables such groups to look at broader issues of LPP outside the classroom. This may help in diagnosis of particular problems that EAP students face.

Rather than assuming a particular learning problem (for example, motivation, [Kennedy, 1988]) lies with the students, teachers or materials, it is worth considering that its source may lie at many levels beyond the classroom. There might be a mismatch between, at level 1, the use of English within the country concerned (minimal use of most functions being taken here), at level 2, an LPP decision at government level on medium of instruction (politically motivated but inappropriate in the context of language use above) and, at level 3, a further LPP institutional decision on the introduction of an EAP course (an attempt to remedy student failure in an English-medium learning environment). Problems at level 3 can be traced back to policy decisions at level 2 based on a misunderstanding of level 1. If teachers or instructors are able to locate the sources of their problems by adopting an LPP diagnostic perspective, they are more likely to be able to attempt appropriate and relevant solutions, even though they will have little power to reverse the higher level decisions themselves. This notion of mismatches (see Kennedy, 1999, from innovation, and Pascale, 1990, from management perspectives) between levels of LPP and their influence on EAP is an area I shall return to below.

A model of LPP

A model of LPP integrating a number of different approaches (Kennedy, 1985; Kaplan, 1989; Barkhuizen and Gough, 1996; Hornberger, 1994) is shown in Figure 2. This shows various levels of planning and can help diagnose problems by assigning their source at specific points in the planning process. It is the omission of these levels for which Munby (1978) was criticised in one of the early attempts to systematise ESP needs analysis. More recent writers on ESP and EAP (e.g. Holliday, 1994; Markee, 1997) have realised the

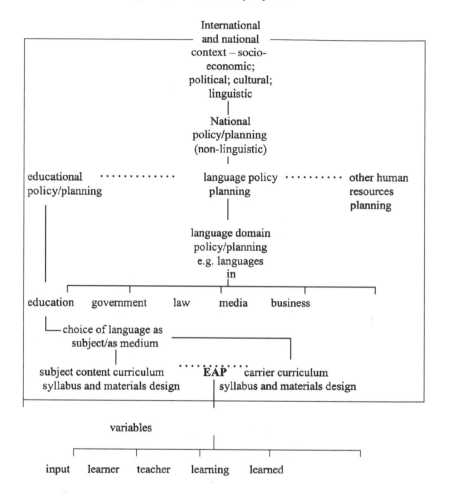

wider context is important. Such writers broaden the unit of analysis to include other levels as depicted in the model apart from the linguistic.

The model describes a process of LPP from national policy/planning at government level, to institutional planning, through to teaching in EAP classrooms. Unbroken lines indicate the links between levels, and dotted lines across levels. I have deliberately avoided indicating the direction of the links since although most influential LPP is top-down, bottom-up planning between various levels does occur. Language behaviour at a lower level may be later ratified in the form of policy at a higher level. Although the model suggests policy at one level is implemented by the next level below it (a typical top-down approach), such a neat sequence does not always occur. The reality of LPP processes are generally much messier and fuzzier. Levels may be missed; implementation may not occur; LPP may remain at one point in the system. Surrounding the whole LPP process is the international and national context, referred to in a previous section. Rather than putting the social context as the driving force at the top of the process, I have tried to show all levels of the process influenced by the wider context as a frame surrounding the LPP process.

In addition, each level within the system will itself be influenced by its own social context. This is represented diagrammatically in Figure 3. Each circle represents a 'planning community' whether at government, institution or classroom level. Policy set by one community is implemented by another. The amount of overlap between the circles represents the amount of matching between policy and implementation. The greater the overlap, the greater likelihood of successful implementation, at least in terms of the policy. Each planning community is influenced by its own local social context.

As I have suggested, all policy/planning at the various levels is influenced by the wider social context (the frame drawn around the model). Within that frame, non-linguistic national planning will take place which will then feed into different types of planning. Sometimes, the links between the social 'frame', LPP, and EAP are very clear. The political changes in Central Europe after the collapse of the Soviet Union had an immediate impact. Many students, given a choice of foreign languages to study, dropped Russian in favour of English. Easier access to the West and an explicit political agenda towards Western forms of democratisation expanded the demand for English. A large number of British government-funded ELT projects were consequently set up in Central Europe (Enyedi and Medgyes, 1998), many concerned with EAP, for example, the PROSPER Project to upgrade EAP in Romanian higher education. In China, the economic liberalisation process led to increasing ELT support from DFID (the British government aid agency) (Henry and Pritchard, 1999). Several EAP projects were set up, though these have now come to an end as DFID's social priorities have changed to poverty alleviation, a further example of the influence of a change in the external context on language policy. Other aid agencies, including those from Australia, Canada, Sweden and the USA have also been involved as partners in such language planning, raising once again the question of the ideological motivation behind aid-funded EAP projects which I alluded to above.

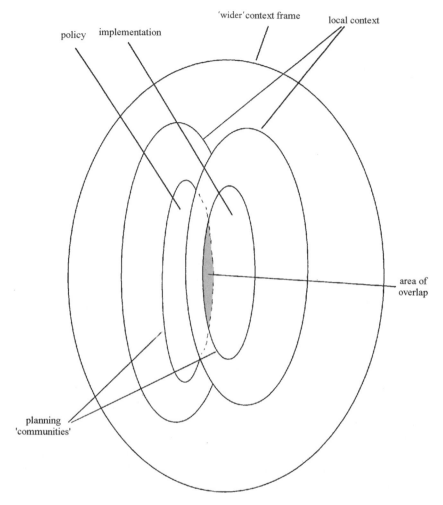

policy   implementation   'wider' context frame   local context

area of overlap

planning 'communities'

Figure 3 Planning communities

At lower levels, LPP occurs in different domains (see Figure 2). I have isolated as examples – government, law, education, media and business. This planning reflects the expansion of English into the domains discussed in a previous section. We are concerned here, of course, with the educational domain where educational and language planning come together. This is most apparent in the major planning decision on choice of medium of instruction. Clearly, the EAP enterprise will be different in approach and design where it is in support of learning content through the medium of English, rather than where English is used for reference purposes in institutions where the medium is in the students' first language.

The variables that influence the design of EAP curricula are listed at the bottom of Figure 2 (drawn from Tollefson, 1989). 'Input' refers to the amount of exposure that students have to English (whether inside or outside the classroom). 'Learner' refers to who the learners are, their age, class, gender, purposes for learning, motivation, personality and intelligence; 'Teacher' to the characteristics of teachers – their work conditions, their language and pedagogical skills, their training, their attitudes, beliefs and motivation. 'Learning' refers to styles of learning, and 'learned' to the content of the curriculum.

Decisions about the variables can be made at any level in the LPP process. The 'higher' the decision-point, the more centralised the LPP process is likely to be. Isolating the variables means we can evaluate failures and successes, and try to pinpoint sources of pedagogic or management problems. The higher the source of the problem, the less likely the EAP unit will be able to effect change, and it will have to adopt a strategy of optimising its own local conditions but working within the constraints of the wider situation.

Fortunately, in many EAP situations, the unit responsible for course delivery is relatively free from centralised control outside the educational institution in which it is based, though the institution itself may be highly centralised. Thus, a university director or dean may decide on a course of action to which the EAP unit has to respond. This may be positive in that the support of superiors is always important; on the other hand, such decision-takers may have unwarranted expectations about what can be expected from EAP courses, or may initiate policy without adequate resources.

The model is not intended to present a rational, non-political view of LPP and we follow the approach taken by Tollefson (1991) who is concerned with the ideologies and socio-economic forces behind LPP and the results on individuals, and Moore (1996) who uses a 'critical' rather than descriptive approach to explain LPP processes.

Mismatches between LPP and EAP practice

In presenting models of LPP we should remember that the process of policy formulation and implementation is not smooth. Many of the problems that arise in EAP contexts are the result of mismatches between language policies, the realities of the social situation outside the classroom, and pedagogical practice.

Universities in EIL contexts, Sultan Qaboos in Oman and the

University of Kuwait are examples, have to grapple with these realities. Markee (1986) and Zughoul and Hussain (1985) both emphasise the need for EAP practitioners to be aware of such mismatches. They describe higher education EAP situations in the Sudan and Jordan respectively, where the official institutional language policy at that time was English-medium teaching and learning. However, both staff and students adopted their own unofficial policies so that communication and transfer of information could take place. The higher level policy was at odds with educational realities, the level of students' English being too low for English-medium study. In these cases there was pressure to relieve the mismatch between policy and practice and create an educational equilibrium by relaxing the 'official' policy and using Arabic, a form of pedagogic contingency management (Smith, 1999). The choice of language (Arabic, English, or a mixture of the two) was influenced by a combination of factors including staff and student attitudes, the status of the languages in the wider community, and pedagogic mode (e.g. question/answer, lecture, discussion, note-taking). Mackay (1993) has termed these pedagogical strategies (a form of micro-LPP), used when there is a conflict between two sources of language policy, 'hygiene strategies', which teachers use to 'clean' problematic situations.

More recently, Pennington (1998) (at secondary level education) has shown how similar hygiene strategies are used in Hong Kong classrooms, and Flowerdew *et al.* (1998) investigated the use of Chinese (Cantonese) and English in content classes at their university, also in Hong Kong. They found that generally lecturers agreed with the current language policy, that English should normally be used as medium of instruction. Staff believed that English was important for Hong Kong's economy and status as an international city, and that proficiency in English provided access to greater knowledge/professional advancement. Accordingly, staff supported English as medium of instruction. However, in the lecturing situation, Flowerdew *et al.* found that lecturers modified the policy. In order to communicate with the students, some of whom did not have adequate levels of English, and to maintain solidarity with them (some were hesitant about using English rather than their mother tongue), the lecturers switched to Cantonese. This behaviour, seemingly at odds with the lecturers' expressed beliefs, is not surprising and conforms with current social-psychological theories of behaviour (Kennedy and Kennedy, 1996). One particular theory (Ajzen, 1991) suggests beliefs will not necessarily predict behaviour and that behavioural constraints (the low level of students' English) and peer influence (student attitudes to Cantonese and English) will also influence pedagogic behaviour (the hygiene strategies referred to earlier).

Conclusion

In terms of the 'local' management and administration of an EAP unit, and the teaching within it, much of what I have described in this article may seem remote. What I hope to have shown is that although certain LPP decisions have indeed been made outside the normal operating context of EAP units, their effect is considerable. EAP practitioners should at least be aware of these forces at work 'outside' but impinging on them. This article confirms recent appeals for greater socio-political awareness of the EAP teacher, but also shows to those wishing to adopt wider roles that the socio-political framework influencing EAP contexts is complex, and solutions to 'local' EAP problems are not easily resolved.

3 EAP-related linguistic research: An intellectual history

John M. Swales

Foundations

Investigations into EAP target discourses (content textbooks, research papers, lectures and the like in relevant areas) have now been going on for almost fifty years. While the definitive history of this important aspect of the EAP movement probably does not need to be written, some insight into how we have got to where we are today is useful, especially for those who have only recently moved into the field or who are on the verge of doing so. Indeed, the umbrella field of ESL/ELT is always in danger of losing its history, and thus 'reinventing the wheel' or 'repeating the mistakes of the past'. There has not been a book-length attempt at a history of ELT since Howatt's 1984 volume, and Howatt in today's terms seems overly focused on European developments to the neglect of other parts of the world. One partial exception is Spolsky's *Measured Words* (1995), which tells the inside story of ESL testing over the last decades. Two others are Phillipson's *Linguistic Imperialism* (1992) and Pennycook's *The Cultural Politics of English as an International Language* (1994a), which provide revisionist accounts of mostly British contributions to ELT. Alas, there seems little room on all those MA courses in Applied Language Studies (or their terminological variants) for a component offering a historical overview of developments over the last forty years of general ESL/ELT, let alone for one targeted on EAP (regarded as a subset of ESP in this paper). And, as far as I am aware, few, if any, applied linguistics master's or PhD theses are primarily interested in the *history* of their field (or some sub-section of it), or in tracing the evolution of ideas, delineating the impact of particular 'movements,' or in assessing the significance of particularly prominent individuals. The only exception known to me is Matsuda's forthcoming dissertation on the history of ESL writing instruction in the United States (Matsuda, in preparation).

With this past somewhat disregarded, one starting point is to place the beginnings of EAP linguistic inquiry in the 1960s within its broader cultural and academic milieu. This milieu, which dominated the middle decades of the century, was predominantly characterised by beliefs in objectivity and the experimental method in both natural and social sciences. Indeed, as a psychology student at Cambridge in the late 1950s, I remember being taught that we could learn most of what we needed to know about human behaviour by seeing how animals performed in experiments. Another reason for the dominance of the scientific method at that time was its ratification by armchair philosophers who continued to view science as 'a ship of reason powering its own way through a silent sea of social contingencies' (Barnes, 1982: 117). The sociology of knowledge and social-constructionism had yet to make their mark. As a result, the view prevailed that scientific and academic languages were rhetorically simple and transparent linguistic mechanisms for the display and transmission of knowledge, hypotheses, methods and experimental results. Scientific and academic discourses were thus sharply distinguished from literary ones; for example, the former might well be open to successful machine translation, the latter not. The following extract, published in 1938 by Leonard Bloomfield, the leading American structural linguist of that time, effectively captures these perceptions:

Thus, half-a-dozen differently worded treatises, say on elementary mechanics, will produce the same result, so far as science is concerned. In this uniformity the differences between languages (as English, French, German), far-reaching and deep-seated as they are, constitute merely a part of the communicative dross. We say that scientific discourse is *translatable*, and mean by this that not only the difference between languages but, within each language, the difference between operationally equivalent wordings has no scientific effect.   (original emphasis: 264)

Of course, such beliefs about the transparency, the neutrality and the universality of scientific language continue to be widely held both within academic and research communities as well as outside them, at least partly because they offer a value system of international understanding and collaboration otherwise hard to find in a world preoccupied with national, racial and political conflicts (Montgomery, 1996).

This then was the belief system sustaining the universes of discourse that EAP began to study in the 1960s. Although a pioneering paper on scientific language had been published in Sweden by Barber in 1962 and Mellinkoff's massive *The Language of the Law* had appeared in 1963, the major impetus for a new approach was the 1964 trigraph put together by three leading British (applied) linguists under the highly significant title of *The Linguistic Sciences and Language*

Teaching (Halliday, McIntosh and Strevens, 1964). The key passage for the development of ESP (and also EAP) is the following:

> Only the merest fraction of investigation has yet been carried out into just what parts of a conventional course in English are needed by, let us say, power station engineers in India, or police inspectors in Nigeria; even less is known about precisely what extra specialized material is required.
>
> This is one of the tasks for which linguistics must be called in. Every one of these specialized needs requires, before it can be met by appropriate teaching materials, detailed studies of restricted languages and special registers carried out on the basis of large samples of the language used by the particular persons concerned. It is perfectly possible to find out just what English is used in the operation of power stations in India; once this has been observed, recorded and analysed, a teaching course to impart such language behaviour can at least be devised with confidence and certainty.
>
> (Halliday, McIntosh and Strevens, 1964: 189–190)

The linguistic and textual studies inspired by this volume would have a number of characteristics that made them very attractive to the small numbers of EAP practitioners working in the field at that time. First, they would be properly descriptive (i.e., there would be no attempt to criticise any stylistic or other features in the target discourses). Second, they would be as broad and representative in their coverage of 'normal' science and social science as resources permitted (i.e., there would be no attempt to privilege discourses by particularly famous individuals, such as Nobel Prize winners). Third, the studies would be synchronic (i.e., they would be taken to be representative of the contemporary world with no looking back to the historical forces that might have shaped them). Fourth, the studies would be textual, with no contamination or complication arising from asking authors why they wrote (or more rarely spoke) as they did. Fifth, the studies would use the analytic apparatus of functional grammar, as largely developed by Halliday, rather than the terms and categories of traditional grammar. Finally, the investigations into 'restricted languages and special registers' would adopt, as a heuristic framing device, some version of the 'neo-Firthian' model of situational parameters such as field, mode and tenor.

In all respects, then, this was to be an agenda premissed on modern linguistics, setting itself firmly apart from literary approaches to the study of scholarly texts. Although all of these founding tenets have since been questioned at various times and places, the clarity and simplicity of this agenda has had a long-standing and profound effect on EAP practitioners and materials developers, precisely because it looked so eminently *doable*. No demands were being advanced that we had to have deep content

knowledge, understand the rhetorical history of the chosen discipline, or be trained as some 'fly on the wall' ethnographic observer.
Further, the grammatical model as well as the analysis of register
and registral characteristics were typically taught on Diploma and
MA courses (except in the United States). In effect, we were given
methods and means of studying texts in ways that made sense in
environments where we also had to teach, develop pedagogy,
produce course materials, evaluate students and the like.

I have stressed these foundations of the discipline not so much out
of a sense of 'filial piety', but rather because of their long-standing
influence on the forward trajectory of EAP linguistic studies over the
latter part of the century. Bloomfield's depiction – typical of its time
– of scholarly and textbook text as exposition rather than persuasion
would long prevail, and would therefore enhance the sense that
what remained of interest in such texts would be their surface
syntactic and lexical features – features that could then be appropriately examined as decontextualised textual artifacts. The ensuing
history of EAP-driven linguistic and discoursal analysis has either
been more or less faithful to this evolving systemic-functional
tradition or has attempted to move in some way beyond it (see
Hyon, 1996, and Bloor, 1998, for somewhat different interpretations
of this evolution).

Fast-forwarding thirty years

Five years after the appearance of *The Linguistic Sciences and
Language Teaching*, Crystal and Davy published *Investigating
English Style* (1969). This offered an alternate and somewhat more
sophisticated categorisation of registral varieties and provided original linguistic analyses of a range of language varieties, including
conversation, unscripted commentary, religion, newspaper reporting
and legal documents. Indeed, a number of these areas would only
become incorporated into mainstream ESP/EAP work very much
later, especially through the work of Vijay Bhatia (e.g. Bhatia, 1993).
A second major contribution from about that time was Huddleston's
*The Sentence in Written English: A Syntactic Study Based on an
Analysis of Scientific Texts* (1971). Essentially, this was Huddleston's
contribution, although now theoretically recast into the mode of
transformational grammar, to *Sentence and Clause in Scientific
English*, the final, but never published, report of a major research
project carried out at University College, London. Huddleston uses
that project's corpus of 135,000 words of written scientific English to
exemplify how certain syntactic structures are expressed in this

variety, such as voice, relativisation, comparison and modality. Even today, there remains much of interest here, perhaps especially in the final chapter on theme. Unfortunately, however, this pioneering study amalgamated three different types of text (from specialist journals, undergraduate textbooks and popularisations) into a combined corpus, so that the quantitative propensities of each text-type are not recoverable. This 'combinatory' tradition in corpus-based work, for all its merits in constructing a picture of the syntax and lexis of the language as a whole such as might be useful for general grammars and dictionaries, has not served the needs of EAP practitioners and their student constituencies so well.

The remainder of the 1970s was most remarkable for four developments. One was the initiation of major studies of oral discourses, such as lectures. A classic paper in this area remains Candlin, Bruton and Leather's 1976 study of the discourse occurring in casualty or emergency rooms in hospitals (where non-native speaker residents often find themselves working). A second strand, already evident in the investigation of oral discourses, was a growing sense that there was much to be learned about detectable patterns and regularities occurring above the level of the sentence or the utterance. Halliday and Hasan's landmark *Cohesion in English* was published in 1976. And beyond their discussion of basically intersentential links, there were new perceptions that whole texts were chunked into beginnings, middles and ends. These perceptions were strengthened by the publications of the so-called 'Washington School' in the north-west of the United States led by Lackstrom, Selinker and Trimble. Trimble (e.g. Trimble, 1985) in particular brought to EST (as a subset of ESP) insights into the rhetorical structures and arrangements of technical texts, and, at the same time, reminded people that academic and professional texts, despite surface appearances often to the contrary, were in the end constructed to persuade their audiences of the correctness of their arguments. The fourth and final voice that spoke during that decade for change and development in EST was that of Widdowson, whose work from that time is most accessible in the 1979 collection *Explorations in Applied Linguistics*. Indeed, as early as 1971 he could write:

I think it is possible that in language teaching we have not given language as an instrument of communication sufficient systematic attention. We have perhaps been too concerned with language system, taking our cue from the linguists, and in consequence there has often been something trivial in *our* proceedings. Now that we are turning our attention to the teaching of English for special purposes, and in particular to English for science and technology, we must take some principled approach to the teaching of rules of use, and restore rhetoric, in a new and more precise form, to its rightful place in the teaching of language.

(original emphasis, 1979: 17)

These four elements, oral discourses, discourse analysis, rhetorical modelling and rules of use, were to prove to be emancipatory for EAP as it moved into the final two decades of the century. They provided some freedom of manoeuvre outside of the rise of formal generative linguistics and variationist sociolinguistics, and opened the door for more multidisciplinary approaches and influences.

One of the first and most long-lasting of these emancipations was the emergence of the concept of genre. As far as I am aware, the term 'genre' first occurred in EAP literature in 1981. It was used that year (independently) in the important paper by Tarone *et al.* in the second issue of the journal *English for Specific Purposes* (or the *ESP Journal* as it was originally called) and by myself in the local Birmingham monograph, *Aspects of Article Introductions*. The concept has given rise to very considerable theoretical, pedagogical and ideological debate, the details of which cannot be reviewed here, but are discussed in such volumes as Swales (1990), Freedman and Medway (1994), Berkenkotter and Huckin (1995) and Johns (1997a). In effect, a focus on genre redrew the map of academic discourse by replacing rhetorical modes such as exposition or registral labels such as scientific language with text-types such as research article, term paper, final examination, MA thesis and conference abstract. The consequences were fairly dramatic. The genre categories had a self-evident validity (although within blurred definitional boundaries) for the academy in general and for the students in it. Dialogue became easier, and in hindsight it is probably no accident that the 1981 Tarone *et al.* study of two astrophysics papers included an astrophysicist co-author as a 'specialist informant'. The replacement of randomised sampling of texts by generic whole ones then led to separate analyses of 'parts' of a genre (such as the IMRD structure in many scientific papers) and the development of accounts of what seems to be happening within them, such as 'the move analysis' in Swales (1981).

As Flowerdew (in press) notes, approaches to genre can be essentially divided into those that are grounded in the textual and those that are grounded in the context or community situation. The former proponents by the end of the 1980s could number many of the contributors to *English for Specific Purposes* as well as a number of leading figures in the 'Sydney School' of systemic-functional linguistics, such as Hasan and Martin. (It has never been fully clear that Halliday ever accepted genre as a concept of equal status to that of register.) Genre could then also operate as some point of contact between the two groups.

Meanwhile, genre had become an important concept in the 'New Rhetoric' movement, especially following the publication in 1984 of Carolyn Miller's seminal article 'Genre as Social Action'. As its title suggests, this piece positions genre as a means of using communication in order to achieve certain ends and thus represents the contextual end of Flowerdew's polarity. Further, the new rhetoricians, who were mostly US English department faculty, were producing a fine body of EAP-relevant work of several innovative kinds. One, inspired by Charles Bazerman (e.g. Bazerman, 1988), focused on tracing the diachronic evolution of academic texts, such as his own study of physics research articles over much of the last hundred years. It became clear that today's textual characteristics of particular genres were complexly imbricated with their earlier formulations. Second, detailed studies of scientists and academics struggling on 'the agonistic field' to gain acceptance, such as those depicted in Myers (1990) provided further evidence of the rhetorical and social exigencies that affect academic life and work. Third, the 1980s saw a revival of interest in Contrastive Rhetoric (e.g. Clyne, 1987 on German, and Hinds, 1987, on Japanese). The earlier tradition of using comparisons of cross-linguistic discourse patterns in order to understand NNS student difficulties with writing English, became replaced by an interest in cultural effects on academic text per se. The assumptions behind this growing sub-field are, of course, totally different to Bloomfield's views quoted at the beginning of this chapter, and further reflect pressure on the EAP discourse analysis tradition from post-modern types of inquiry.

Another important influence on both the new rhetoricians and the EAP practitioners came from the sociologists of science and knowledge, particularly from the classic laboratory studies of Latour and Woolgar (1979) and Knorr-Cetina (1981). The emergent claims that scientific facts are socially and rhetorically constructed naturally proved to be highly seductive music to the ears of all parties who have contributed, either directly or indirectly, to the growth and development of EAP-related linguistic research, since those claims give the language specialist his or her own enhanced place in the study of academic tribes and territories. On the other hand, the arguments of the 'strong' social constructionists tended to antagonise those whose academic work they were in fact investigating, as well as traditional historians and philosophers of science. The search for a balanced position has been problematic, but one who apparently early achieved it was Rudwick (1985) in his superb account of the Devonian Controversy in geology in the mid-nineteenth century. He writes:

neither 'discovery' nor 'construction' is *by itself* an adequate metaphor for the production of scientific knowledge. The outcome of research is neither the unproblematic disclosure of the natural world nor the mere artifact of social negotiation. The metaphor of *shaping* – or, in the original sense of the term, *forging* – has been used allusively throughout this book, as a less inadequate image. For the Devonian controversy shows how new knowledge is shaped from the materials of a real natural world, malleable yet often refractory; but it becomes knowledge only as those materials are forged into new shapes with new meanings, on the anvil of heated argumentative debate.

(Rudwick, 1985: 454–455; original emphases)

A final component that needs to be mentioned in this brief intellectual history of EAP is the increasing attention being paid to the notion of *intertextuality*, particularly as articulated in Bakhtin (1986). Once again, the idea that any instance of discourse is at least partly created out of other discourses and in turn has the potential to affect its successors, is one that is likely to appeal particularly to language specialists because it again privileges the role of the word in scholarly and professional affairs. It also of course undermines any lingering beliefs in a solipsistic set of universes populated by individual creative authors, and thus questions the US obsession with the student crime of plagiarism (Pennycook, 1996a). Even more importantly, the view that texts are networked in the ways outlined by Bakhtin has been a strong impetus for seeing that the idea of *independent* genres, such as the free-standing research article, is an over-simplification, perhaps a necessary one in the early stages of analysis, but difficult to sustain over the longer term. Rather, as argued by Bazerman (1994) and others, genres themselves form systems, sets, colonies or some other kind of reticulation. Thus, the standard research article is situated within and influenced by other contingent genres such as the research proposal, the conference paper, the letter from the editor and the reviewer's report.

A broader picture

The potted intellectual history of the last forty years presented in the previous sections has attempted to show how the field has steadily moved beyond a detached lexico-syntactic analysis to ones that are variously multi-modal. More specifically, perceptions about the relations between texts and contexts have become much richer and more complex: on the one hand, discourse is indeed seen as being shaped by context; on the other, discourse, in its generic reiterations, is also seen as shaping the context (Giddens, 1984). However, and this is an important caveat, the EAP tradition has remained faithful to its founding fathers in its continued beliefs about the need to provide *linguistic* evidence for the claims being made. Papers appearing in *English for Specific Purposes* or *Applied Linguistics* continue to make their discoursal claims via quantitative textual data and/or detailed and rigorous linguistic exemplification.

Any evaluative intellectual history will be seen as being partial, at least in some eyes. Indeed, it is important to recognise that the previous focus on *intellectual* allegiances and influences has had the consequence of under-representing the world of EAP-related linguistic research in two important ways. It has insufficiently accounted for both the global reach of EAP and for the great increase in our knowledge about academic discourse as a result of numerous studies along fairly traditional lines. In my *Episodes in ESP* (1985), I remarked (in some dismay) that none of the fifteen episodes illustrating developments from 1962 to 1981 had been written by a non-native speaker of English. Today, the situation would be very different because many important contributions to EAP have been made by non-native speakers, including the following (with a sample publication for each): Anna Duszak (1997, Poland); Lars Evensen (1996, Norway); Britt-Louise Gunnarsson (1997, Sweden); Maria Horzella (Horzella and Sindermann, 1992, Chile); Anna Mauranen (1993a, Finland); Desiree Motta-Roth (1997, Brazil); Kevin Nwogu (1997, Nigeria); Francoise Salager-Meyer (1994, Venezuela); Claude Sionis (1995, France); Angele Tadros (1985, Sudan); and Eija Ventola (1996, Germany). Several of these scholars, as might be expected, have been prominent in the Contrastive Rhetoric sub-field (see Connor, 1996, for a comprehensive review). Further, a number of them, such as Gunnarsson, Mauranen and Tadros, have provided important methodological innovations. A second aspect of this global reach has been a shift in centre of influence from British universities and the British Council to other parts of the world – to places like the City and Polytechnic universities in Hong Kong, to Malaysian universities such as the technical university in Johor Bahru, and to Australian universities (Canberra, Melbourne and Sydney) and American ones (Illinois, Michigan, Ohio State).

Although the research article has long continued to be the most investigated EAP genre, if only because it has become the master academic narrative of the last fifty years, significant work has been produced in recent years in other areas. Although full accounts of *any* genre (especially given the complexities arising from disciplinary variation) are still some way off, the pieces of an extremely complex puzzle are slowly falling into place. Flowerdew (1994a) is a fine contribution to our knowledge of the important genre of the lecture. The so-called 'foreign teaching assistant problem' in the United States has been highly productive of discourse-based research into office hours, discussion sections and tutorials (see Briggs *et al.*, 1997, for a comprehensive annotated bibliography). Other genres that have been investigated range from complex oral events such as departmental colloquia (Tracy, 1997) to small-scale written texts such as conference abstracts (Berkenkotter and Huckin, 1995) and submission letters (Swales, 1996).

One important and relatively new development has been the emergence of studies devoted to particular discourse features – rather than syntactic ones such as tense – of written academic discourse. Major topics in this area have been metadiscourse, or text about the evolving text, as perhaps best represented by Mauranen (1993a); citations and their functions (Block and Chi, 1995; Hyland, in press); and various kinds of qualifications or 'hedges' (e.g. Hyland, 1997). Less usual topics began with Tadros's 1985 pioneering study into 'predictive structures'; for example, when an author writes 'there are three reasons for this', he or she is thereby committed to producing three reasons in his or her subsequent text rather than two or four as part of his or her 'contract' with the reader. Equally revealing has been the long series of studies by Dubois of the discoursal features of presentations at biology conferences, such as her analysis of the 'rounding' or 'non-rounding' of numbers for rhetorical effects (Dubois, 1987). Gosden (1992) is one of several who have investigated the form, function and distribution of initial pre-subject elements in academic sentences. Other *particularistic* investigations include Dudley-Evans (1984b) on thesis titles; Johns (1998) on visual elements; Swales *et al.* (1998) on the (surprising) role of imperatives in research articles in several fields; Giannoni (1998) on acknowledgements; and Bloor on humour (1996). While the pace of publication in this and other kinds of EAP-related linguistic research continues to accelerate, the range of disciplines covered continues to be patchy. Some fields continue to be well-tilled, such as physics, biology, economics and various branches of engineering, while others (e.g. architecture, geology and sociology) have been largely untouched.

Two closing contemporary issues

The focus of this chapter has been on language and discourse rather than the learner or the student, the latter being covered elsewhere in this volume. As a result, I have tried to map out our knowledge of the textual geography of the academy with little attention to those who have to navigate its terrain and scale its heights. One hidden assumption in this account is that academic progress and advancement can be seen, at least from a rhetorical perspective, as the climbing of some generic ladder. Thus, those interested in disciplinary discourse have tended to view that discourse as being most obviously and easily accessed in terms of its final published products, such as textbooks, scholarly monographs and research papers. Having analysed these texts with whatever linguistic, discoursal or interview techniques that seem appropriate, we can then set up our findings as some kind of desiderata, and then study how (graduate) students with greater or lesser skill attune to and approximate to the newly-described academic genres. In sum (graduate) education looks like a trajectory that requires mastery of increasingly complex genres, finishing with publications and a thesis.

Seductive as this scenario may appear, a number of fine-grained investigations have begun to question its accuracy. Such studies include Belcher (1994), Casanave (1995) and particularly Prior (1998). Prior's *Writing/Disciplinarity* volume argues that the foregoing account is essentially a 'strong text' approach that is over-hierarchical, too static, too cerebral and too discoursal. Rather, he argues, disciplinary enculturation is not so much a matter of novices serving apprenticeships with experts, but more a case of continual negotiation wherein much of the outcome depends on contingent and personal factors. In consequence, what gets written, and not written, by graduate students is partly affected by the fleeting epiphenomena of the educative moment. Graduate writing is no longer a straightforward cumulative process, but more a matter of new starts and unexpected adjustments. In order to get at how 'persons are produced' in the unfolding dynamics of a graduate class, now reseen as a key site for uncovering the presumptions and expectations of a particular disciplinary area, Prior once again makes use of Bakhtin and his concepts of dialogic intertextuality, but adds to this apprenticeship theories and the work of sociologists and psychologists interested in 'situated cognition'. It is unclear at the moment whether the influential genre analysis movement of the last decade is put at serious risk by the investigations of Prior and others, or whether the local, unstable and highly contingent processes of genre acquisition that they have uncovered are themselves local and unusual and perhaps symptomatic of their interdisciplinary character. Persons may be produced differently in engineering or medicine research laboratories, and indeed, this apparently happened in the university herbarium studied in Swales (1998). Overall, it would seem that genre study and genre skills are typically a necessary but not a sufficient condition for interpreting and creating academic discourse. As Briggs and Bauman (1992) observe, 'some elements of contextualisation creep in, fashioning indexical connections to the on-going discourse, social interaction, broader social relations, and the particular historical juncture(s) at which the discourse is produced and received' (p. 149).

A second major contemporary issue is also connected with our perceptions of academic discourse and the means of its acquisition. The debate was launched in 1992 when Santos expressed surprise that ESL/EAP continued to view itself as a 'pragmatic' service industry, while L1 composition in the United States had tended to offer radical pedagogies designed to challenge the academic and institutional status quo. Several years later, a number of matters have become clearer (at least to me). Ideological disputes and 'identity politics' in composition have had a deleterious effect on research (Charney, 1996). On the other hand, the debate within the EAP field has been important and broadly beneficial, recent contributions including Benesch (1996), Allison (1996) and Pennycook (1997b). Certainly today, few reflective practitioners in EAP would accept that the spread of academic English, the expansion of tertiary education, the 'publish or perish' syndrome, or the increasing role of the US as the world's academic gatekeeper should be simplistically viewed as *neutral* developments with no account taken of their darker sides. Few too, as this chapter has tried to show, would view academic and scientific discourses as transparent and objective in the way that Bloomfield proposed sixty years ago. The differences between the protagonists have been narrowing. Pennycook (1997b), in his advocacy for a 'critical pragmatism', expresses what he believes to be the tension at the heart of ESP as follows:

on the one hand we need to help our students gain access to those forms of language and culture that matter while on the other we need to help challenge those norms. On the one hand we need to help our students develop critical awareness of academic norms and practices, while on the other we need to understand and promote culturally diverse ways of thinking, working and writing.

(Pennycook 1997b: 265)

I think it would be generally agreed that Pennycook's two 'on the one hand' propositions are laudably designed to ensure that any EAP programme pay attention to critical awareness and student empowerment, however constrained that programme might be in time and space. Rather more problematic are the second clauses that advocate, challenge and promote a greater diversity than the institutional base may typically accommodate. A possible compromise would be, in the first instance, to restrict the focus to revealing how those norms have been historically and socially constructed, and, in the second, to use our increasing knowledge base in cross-cultural communication and contrastive rhetoric to reveal and discuss those 'culturally diverse ways of thinking, working and writing'. In the end, it would be our students' responsibility to decide what use, if any, they might want to make of the insights reached. When the dust settles, our *primary* responsibility may become best seen as providing opportunities for engendering those kinds of rhetorical awareness.

4 Linguistic research and EAP pedagogy

Brian Paltridge

Introduction

Early classroom based EAP work focused more on teaching the language and discourse patterns typically found in academic texts, in general, rather than the language and discourse of particular academic genres. More recent work has concentrated on the language and discourse of particular academic genres, as well as the process of academic writing, and the context of production and interpretation of academic texts. This chapter will review each of these approaches. It should not be read from this discussion, however, that as each new approach has emerged, the preceding one has faded away and gone out of use (Silva, 1990). Indeed, many EAP courses today draw on each of the developments listed below rather than focus, necessarily, on the one single perspective (Johns, 2000a).

Approaches to EAP writing

Controlled composition

Earliest work in EAP teaching was based on the notion of controlled, or guided, composition. This was the predominant approach from the mid-1940s to the mid-1960s. It was based on the behaviourist view that language learning involves imitation, repetition and habit formation. The view of language that underlay this approach was that of language as a set of fixed patterns that a speaker or writer manipulates in order to produce new utterances. There was a prime focus on accuracy and correctness and the learner's first language was seen as a hindrance to language learning and the source of errors in their second language development.

Classroom tasks employed in this perspective included substitution tables, written expansions, transformation and completion-type tasks which learners used in the manipulation and imitation of model texts. The texts students wrote became a collection of sentence patterns and vocabulary items with little concern for audience or purpose (Silva, 1990). Spencer's (1967) *Guided Composition Exercises*, Moody's (1974) *Frames for Written English*, and Kunz's (1972) *26 Steps. A Course in Controlled Composition for Intermediate and Advanced ESL Students*, are examples of books which draw on this approach.

Rhetorical functions

In the mid-1960s, teachers began to feel that controlled writing was not enough and there was a need to do more than enable learners to write just grammatically correct sentences. This led to an emphasis on more extended writing activities. This new movement, often referred to as 'current-traditional rhetoric', took textual manipulation beyond the sentence level to the discourse level, and focused on the teaching of 'rhetorical functions' such as descriptions, narratives, definitions, exemplification, classification, comparison and contrast, cause and effect, and generalisations. Classroom tasks concentrated upon arranging sentences and paragraphs into particular rhetorical patterns. Learners' attention still remained focused on form, but in this case, at a broader level.

Books which pay particular attention to the teaching of rhetorical functions include Kaplan and Shaw's (1983) *Exploring Academic Discourse*, Arnaudet and Barrett's (1984) *Approaches to Academic Reading and Writing*, Reid and Lindstrom's (1985) *The Process of Paragraph Writing*, and Jordan's (1990) *Academic Writing Course*. Other books which take this approach include Cooper's (1979) *Think and Link*, Johnson's (1981) *Communicate in Writing*, Sellen's (1982) *Skills in Action*, Wong et al.'s (1987) *Becoming a Writer*, Arnaudet and Barrett's (1990) *Paragraph Development*, Oshima and Hogue's (1992) *Writing Academic English* and Oshima and Hogue's (1998) *Introduction to Academic Writing*. These books take a mostly 'product-based' approach to the teaching of academic writing. That is, they are concerned, in particular, with the finished product, or text, rather than the process students go through in order to write their texts.

The process approach

The process approach of the 1970s emerged in reaction to controlled composition and current traditional rhetoric. Many teachers began to feel that the prevailing approach to teaching writing ignored individual thought and expression and that students 'were restricted in what they could write and how they could write about it' (Jordan, 1997: 164). It became more important, then, to 'guide' rather than control learners and to let content, ideas and the need to communicate determine form, rather than commence with the form of a text (Silva, 1990). The teacher's role in the perspective, thus, became less central and classroom practices more 'learner centred'.

Classrooms activities in this approach focus on the stages writers typically go through in producing texts, such as brainstorming, planning, drafting, revising, editing and proofreading their texts. Typical activities might be titled 'getting started', 'generating ideas', 'finding a topic', 'writing multiple drafts', 'adding, deleting and rearranging ideas', and 'focusing on grammar, sentence structure and vocabulary' (in the editing phase). The approach, thus, starts with the writer and the writing process itself, rather than linguistic and rhetorical form. If a focus on form is included, it is delayed until the writer has come to terms with the content and organisation of his or her text.

Books which concentrate on this approach include Hamp-Lyons and Heasley's (1987) *Study Writing*, Schenck's (1988) *Read, Write, Revise. A Guide to Academic Writing*, Kwan-Terry's (1988) *Interactive Writing*, Leki's (1989) *Academic Writing: Techniques and Tasks*, Benesch and Rorschach's (1989) *Academic Writing Workshop*, Frank's (1990) *Writing as Thinking. A Guided Process Approach*, White and McGovern's (1994) *Writing*, and Leki's (1995a) *Academic Writing: Exploring Processes and Strategies*.

The process approach was not, however, universally accepted by teachers with writers such as Reid (1984a, 1984b) arguing that it did not address issues such as the requirements of particular writing tasks, the development of schemata for academic discourse, and variation in individual writing situations. Others, such as Horowitz (1986a), questioned whether the process approach realistically prepared students for the demands of writing in academic contexts. In his view, the process approach gave students a false impression of what is required of them in university settings, and, in particular, its very special sociocultural context and expectations. This led to a focus on examining what is expected of students in academic settings and the sort of genres they need to have control of.

The genre approach

The 'genre approach' in EAP has taken place in different ways in different parts of the world. It has also had different underlying goals as well as focusing on different teaching situations. In Britain and the United States, for example, EAP applications have been mostly concerned with teaching international students in English-medium universities. Here, the emphasis has been on 'demystifying' the use of English in academic settings as well as providing students with the language resources and skills which will help them gain access to English-medium academic discourse communities. EAP classrooms in Australia, on the other hand, have had a rather different ideological focus from the British and American work. This, in part, draws from a concern for empowering underprivileged members of the community and providing them with the necessary resources for academic success.

The genre approach in EAP settings concentrates, as the term suggests, on teaching particular academic genres, such as essays, research reports, and theses and dissertations. This might include a focus on language and discourse features of the texts, as well as the context in which the text is produced.

Examples of genre-specific EAP materials include Dudley-Evans's (1985) *Writing Laboratory Reports*, Reid's (1988) *The Process of Composition*, Weissberg and Buker's (1990) *Writing Up Research. Experimental Report Writing for Students of English*, Webb's (1991) *Writing an Essay in the Humanities and Social Sciences*, Murison and Webb's (1991) *Writing a Research Paper*, and Swales and Feak's (1994) *Academic Writing for Graduate Students*. Other examples of genre-based teaching in EAP are described by Swales (1984a, 1987, 1990); Davies (1988); Drury and Web (1991); Dudley-Evans (1993, 1994a, 1995); Johns (1994, 1995a, 1997a, 2000b); Jacoby *et al.* (1995); Paltridge (1995a, 1995b, 1997a, 2000); and Clerehan and Moodie (1997).

As Hyon (1996: 714) observes, 'little work has actually investigated the impact of genre-based pedagogy in the classroom'. A number of studies are, however, beginning to emerge which suggest that a genre-based approach in EAP classrooms might be useful in helping students improve their writing. Reppen (1995), for example, reports on a case study where twenty ESL learners undertook a five-week, genre-based social studies course. She found that student writing, content knowledge, and attitudes towards the subject all reflected a positive change. Mustafa (1995) reports similarly positive findings. She examined the effect of providing formal instruction in the conventions of written term papers for ESL students at the Jordan University of Science and Technology. She found that her students' writing improved as a result of the instruction. Henry and Roseberry (1998) also report positive results in their evaluation of a genre-based academic writing course at the University of Brunei Darussalam.

An educational approach to the teaching of academic genres

Drawing together genre and process approaches, Flowerdew (1993b) argues for a procedure which focuses on the process of learning about, and acquiring genres, rather than one which concentrates solely on the end product, or specific variety of genre. Thus, he argues for an 'educational' rather than 'training' approach to the teaching and learning of genres. Flowerdew argues that we cannot hope to predict the wide range of genres our students will, in time, need to be able to participate in. In his view, we need to help our learners find ways of discovering how genres differ from one another as well as how the same genre may vary. Flowerdew, further, questions the rigid way in which genres are sometimes presented in the second language classroom, hoping teachers will 'adapt a genre-based approach in courses more broadly based than those courses in which it has mainly been applied until now' (1993: 315). He makes the important point, as do Swales (1990) and McCarthy and Carter (1994), that models of genres presented in the classroom should not be treated as 'fixed, rule governed patterns', but rather as 'prototypes' which allow for individual variation. Swales and Feak (1994), also, avoid laying down 'rules' for what a student should and should not write in a particular situation. Rather, they encourage students to explore, for themselves, exactly what the 'particular expectations' of their discipline might actually be. A similar approach is presented by Johns (1997a) in her book *Text, Role and Context*, in which she describes ways of helping students learn to interpret, critique, and produce texts in specific academic contexts.

Dealing with genres in EAP classrooms

Johns (1994) lists a number of important points to remember when dealing with genres in EAP classrooms. The first of these is that teachers should start genre-based activities with 'known texts', moving only onto 'unknown texts' when students are familiar with the basic principles and techniques of analysing genres. She suggests teachers always use texts that experts view as being representative samples of the particular genre. She adds that teachers should consult expert readers and writers about the purpose of a text, as well as its form and style. Teachers should also remember to ask these experts how the genre might be changing. It is important, further, to 'contextualise' texts in EAP classrooms. That is, teachers should make it clear to their students 'that texts exist in and for communities of readers and writers' (1994: 25). Teachers should, equally, be sure to remind their students that there are reasons 'beyond the text' for the linguistic choices that writers make.

Audience and second language writing

The issue of audience has only recently been taken up in second language writing research. This is notwithstanding the fact that for second language students, in particular, the ability to address a particular audience is essential to their success (Johns, 1993). This is somewhat in contrast with research carried out in the area of composition studies where the place of audience has been discussed for some time.

Drawing on the work of Ede and Lunsford (1984), and others in the area of composition studies, Johns (1990) discusses the expert, 'all-powerful reader' of EAP students' texts who can either accept or reject students' writing as coherent and consistent with the conventions of the target discourse community, or not. In her view, and in the view of Ede and Lunsford, knowledge of this audience's attitudes, beliefs and expectations is not only possible but essential for students writing in a second language. This audience, further, exists outside the text. Writers thus need to analyse the needs and anticipate the biases of their anticipated audience, as well as adapt their discourse to meet the expectations of their intended readers (Ede and Lunsford, 1984).

General and particular expectations

Dudley-Evans (1995) makes a distinction between 'general' and 'particular' expectations which is extremely helpful for EAP classrooms. By 'general expectations' he means general transferable patterns of textual organisation that might be transferred from one area of study to another, such as the overall organisation of the traditional thesis or dissertation. By 'particular expectations' he means the ways in which these general patterns need to be adapted to meet the expectations and requirements of a particular field of study. Developing this kind of discipline-specific sensitivity should, in Dudley-Evans's view, form part of the teaching of academic writing. As Dudley-Evans argues, 'an approach to the teaching of academic writing that implies that there are common patterns of organisation that always apply in all disciplines [can be] dangerously misleading'

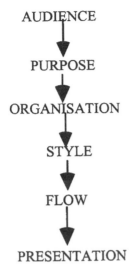

AUDIENCE

PURPOSE

ORGANISATION

STYLE

FLOW

PRESENTATION

Figure 1 Considerations in academic writing (Swales and Feak, 1994: 8)

(Dudley-Evans, 1993: 147). Thus, even though we can say how a thesis or dissertation might, in general terms, be written, we also need to be sure to consider the particular expectations of the academic audience our students are writing for. This is especially complicated by the fact that different types of theses and dissertations are increasingly being required in some areas of study (such as compilations of publishable articles in place of the traditional thesis or dissertation), and the particular local context of writing where, in some cases, the thesis or dissertation advisor might be one of the student's committee of examiners, and others where they are not (Dong, 1998).

Audience and EAP writing

Swales and Feak (1994), in their book *Academic Writing for Graduate Students*, also argue for the importance of audience in EAP classrooms. They provide a helpful overview of important characteristics of academic writing, showing how academic texts are a product of many considerations, such as audience, purpose, organisation, style, flow, and presentation (see Figure 1).

As Swales and Feak point out, even before students begin to write, they need to consider their audience. They need to have an understanding of their audience's expectations and prior knowledge, as these will impact upon the content of their writing. If the audience knows more than the writer, as is often the case with graduate writing, the writer's purpose is usually to display familiarity and expertise in the particular area, beyond simply reporting and reflecting on the research at hand (Swales and Feak, 1994).

Primary and secondary readerships

Brookes and Grundy (1990), in their book *Writing for Study Purposes*, discuss the notions of 'primary' and 'secondary' readership which is also helpful for EAP classrooms. Theses and dissertations, for example, are written for a primary readership of one or more examiners, but also a secondary readership of the student's supervisor and anyone else the student decides to show their work to for comment and feedback. It is the primary reader, however, who will be the final judge as to the quality of the piece of writing, rather than the secondary reader whose role is, rather, to guide the student through the research and writing process. As Kamler and Threadgold (1997: 53) point out, a dominant, or 'primary' reader, within the academy, 'quite simply counts more than other readers'.

Academic essays

Kusel (1992), in a discussion of the writing of academic essays, makes a number of points which are relevant to this discussion. As he argues, the essay, in normal practice 'has to be written in a way to appeal both to an imaginary reader as a communication and to the tutor as an exhibit' (1992: 459). In his view, this 'dual function' of essay writing is the cause of much difficulty in second language essay writing. Kusel suggests encouraging students to write for an imaginary audience, arguing that 'writers of many genres do this all the time' (1992: 467). Part of this involves anticipating what the imaginary audience already knows about the subject of the text, what knowledge the writer needs to 'display', as well as how well the imaginary audience would understand and react to what they read.

Thesis and dissertation writing

Shaw (1991), in a discussion of thesis and dissertation writing, argues that it is difficult for EAP students to write for their particular audience and to produce 'reader-based prose', 'caught as they are between knowledge-display and information transmission' (1991: 193). As he points out:

[The students'] relation to their audience is strange, in that they presume that the real readers (supervisor, external examiner) already know much of what they have to say. This unacknowledged knowledge-display function of theses must affect the writing process.

(Shaw, 1991: 193)

Some of the confusion, he suggests, is due to advice from supervisors, many of whom seem to recommend writing for an expert in a parallel area or merely for someone with background in the particular area. It is not, however, obvious, he argues, that following this advice would produce the traditional thesis or dissertation that supervisors are looking for in that students may assume they do not need to 'display the knowledge' their reader is expecting to see. To complicate matters, this 'display of knowledge', typical of much academic writing in English, varies cross-culturally. Chinese examiners of theses and dissertations, for example, have different expectations of what a thesis should contain than, for example, English examiners (Shaw, 1991).

Ramani, Chacko, Singh and Glendinning (1988) and Tickoo (1994) also remind us of the need to incorporate ethnographic or 'insiders' views' into genre-based descriptions of academic genres. Ramani and her colleagues found, in their teaching of the conventions of citation and referencing to PhD students, that they were forced to abandon developing a universal style guide for all PhDs as most research groups in their institution, they discovered, had their own conventions that they were reluctant to change. Instead, it became more worthwhile to encourage students to look at theses recently completed in their areas of specialisation to find out exactly how they were expected to refer to previous research.

The occluded nature of academic genres

Swales (1996) reminds us of the 'occluded', or hidden nature of the academic genres our students are learning to write. That is, it is often very difficult for students to obtain and identify highly regarded instances of texts without access to confidential information, such as the level of grade the piece of writing was awarded, and what amount of revision was required (in the case of a thesis or dissertation) by examiners before the final copy of the thesis was accepted by the university. Thus, even though a university department may have a collection of sample essays or theses for students to look at, it is often difficult for them to know which of these are 'best examples' of the particular genre and why.

Students as researchers

Johns (1988, 1997a) suggests training students to 'act as researchers' as a way of helping them write texts which meet the institutional and audience expectations of their particular field of study, as well as discovering the knowledge and skills that are necessary for membership of their particular academic community. This might include consideration of the role of students, tutors, supervisors and examiners. It might also involve identifying key topics and concepts in their particular area, as well as exploring the writing conventions of the particular field of study, and the kinds of knowledge claims which are permissible in the particular area (Johns, 1988). The particular focus, in this perspective, is on 'student discovery' of discipline-specific understandings, expectations and requirements. As Johns (1997a) argues, though we cannot hope to predict all of our students' possible literacy experiences, we can help them to ask questions of the texts they are required to produce, and the contexts in which these texts occur.

Context analysis

One further suggestion Johns (1995a) makes is to ask students to collect several examples of a text, then use the texts as catalysts to elicit sociocultural understandings about the context and community in which the text occurs, the roles and purposes of readers and writers, as well as typical textual patterns; that is, as the basis for an analysis of the context of production and interpretation of the particular genre.

The analysis of the sample texts might take an ethnographic approach to this examination (Grabe and Kaplan, 1996), considering aspects of the text and context in which they occur such as:

the social and cultural context of the texts, including:
the purpose of the texts
the content of the texts
the writer of the texts
the intended audience of the texts
the relationship between the writers and readers of the texts
the setting of the texts (e.g. in a university or other research setting)
the structure of the texts
the tone of the texts
the expectations of the target discourse community
shared understandings between the writers and readers of the texts

particular background knowledge that is assumed by the texts
the relationship the texts have with other similar such texts, as well
     as with other genres

This analysis might form the basis for a classroom-based discussion or for individual student/supervisor consultations in which students are led through each of these aspects, given advice on their characteristics, and (importantly) the interaction between them.

Audience analysis and expectations

Students can then proceed to consider, in more detail, who the 'primary reader' of their text is likely to be. In the case of theses and dissertations, this is a difficult task for students as at the point of writing, they may not know who that reader might be. They, therefore, have to consider an 'imagined reader' for their text, what that reader's purpose in reading the text will be, and what this reader is likely to expect in relation to the text as a whole, as well as each section of their text.

One way in which students can do this is by considering their text in relation to assessment guidelines given to examiners at the university where they are studying; that is, the criteria statement examiners are given for the award of each level of grade. Another helpful task is to ask students to consider their text in relation to advice given to examiners, such as the suggestions for reading theses and dissertations presented by Brown and Atkins (1988) in their book *Effective Teaching in Higher Education*. The student's tutor or supervisor can take them through each of these sets of guidelines, explaining and clarifying points for them as they go. This kind of task is especially helpful for keeping students' attention on the primary reader of their text, rather than the secondary reader they have contact with, and receive feedback from.

This, and a number of the other tasks suggested here, focus, in particular, on the *content* of the students' writing. A student, thus, needs to know not only how to structure their text, but also what it is important and appropriate to write *about* in such contexts (Berkenkotter and Huckin, 1995). Students also need to understand 'who they are expected to be' and how they are expected to position themselves textually (Cadman, 1997: 8–9). This is often difficult for second language students who come from a writing context where the demonstration of knowledge is quite different to the situation they now find themselves in (Cadman, 1997; Ballard and Clanchy, 1991). As Connor (1996) observes, students are very often given very little guidance on content in second language teaching and learning materials. This is especially the case with theses and dissertations where universities often present vast amounts of information to students on binding, presentation, width of margins, and punctuation, but very little real guidance on the actual content of the thesis (Kamler and Threadgold, 1997).

Students doing their own on-line genre analysis

Another useful task is for students to do their own 'on-line genre analysis' (Flowerdew, 1993b) to identify the typical 'generic structure' and linguistic characteristics of the genre they are currently studying. Students can, with the help of their tutor or supervisor, examine the way a sample text is divided up into identifiable stages, as well as consider the function each of these stages performs in achieving its overall goal (Veel and Coffin, 1996). Students can then use this analysis as a checklist for examining their own piece of writing to ask themselves if they have achieved these goals.

Students can also be asked to examine other similar texts for examples of 'metadiscourse' (Swales, 1990; Vande Kopple, 1985) and the 'discourse about discourse' (Hyland, 1998) which is particular to much academic writing. For example, they might identify ways in which academic writers signal where they are going, where they have got to, and 'what they have achieved so far' (Swales, 1990: 188). Students might also consider the rhetorical strategies thesis writers use to convince their readers of their claims (Mauranen, 1993b), and the strategies they use to direct their reader towards an 'intended interpretation' (Hyland, 1998).

Using the results of genre analysis

The results of previous genre studies are also useful for providing a framework for students to use, in combination with other aspects of genre knowledge (Berkenkotter and Huckin, 1995), as a 'scaffold' for writing their own texts. Hopkins and Dudley-Evans' (1988) analysis of the discussion section of MSc dissertations is useful for this sort of task, as is Swales and Feak's (1994) list of 'points' (rather than 'facts') that are typically found in the Discussion section of research articles. It is important to point out to students, however, that these points do not represent a fixed order. Hopkins and Dudley-Evans, and Swales and Feak also remind students that Discussion sections often move through particular move sequences more than once. They, further, point out that Discussion sections vary from discipline to discipline and urge students to examine what actually happens in their own field of study.

Comparing student texts

Another useful task is to ask students to compare and discuss sections of each other's texts (Swales, 1981, 1984a). This comparison can be based on some set of guidelines, such as a list of the main points students are expected to cover in a literature review. Students use this list of points to read and critique each other's texts. They then discuss their observations with the student who wrote the text. Each student then reworks his or her text on the basis of the fellow student's observations. The teacher can facilitate this activity by drawing students' attention to, and explaining, key aspects in the writing guidelines and keeping the focus on the particular 'part-genre' (Ayers, 1993) they are examining.

An example

Qi (not her real name) is a student from the People's Republic of China who came to Australia as a government-funded student to undertake a Master's degree in the area of applied linguistics. Her first language was Mandarin and, at the time of arrival, she had an overall IELTS score of 6.0 (out of 9.0), with a score of 5.0 in the writing component of the test. After a year of intensive English study in Australia, her IELTS score had increased to 7.5, with a score of 8.0 in the writing component of the test. Qi's first degree was in science. She also had an English teaching certificate from the University of Foreign Languages in Beijing. In China, she worked as a lecturer in English at a university of science and technology.

Qi was enrolled in the thesis component of her degree for a year. She wrote her thesis on opening sequences in Chinese telephone calls. Her decision to make this her thesis topic was influenced by a course she did in her Master's degree on discourse analysis as well as by the ease of obtaining the data: friends and family members in China collected the data and sent it to her in Australia. She saw her supervisor every two or three weeks throughout the year. Field notes were taken during the supervision sessions, during which each of Qi's written drafts were closely examined and discussed. She was also interviewed after the thesis had been completed.

The supervision process commenced with a review of Qi's thesis proposal. The proposal outlined the overall purpose of the study, relevant background literature, the research question, a proposed research methodology, the theoretical approach that would be employed for the analysis of the data (conversation analysis), a discussion of limitations and problems that might be encountered in the study, and a statement of the significance of the research.

The readership of her thesis had already been brought up in a research proposal workshop Qi had attended prior to enrolling in the thesis. Early supervision sessions returned to this topic and, in particular, discussed who her potential readers might (in general terms) be, and what they would expect in terms of content, presentation, analysis and discussion. She had also, prior to commencing her thesis, read our 'suggestions for reading a thesis or dissertation'. In her words, 'these were extremely useful, before, during, and at the end of the thesis'. This was especially the case, she said, for writing the review of the literature and discussion sections of her thesis.

Early on, Qi prepared a chapter outline for her thesis by doing her own 'on-line' genre analysis of other theses written in the department on similar topics. In the supervision sessions, this outline was discussed in relation to the purpose and expectations of each of the chapters she had proposed. As her research progressed, Qi revised and further refined this chapter outline. Her analysis of previous theses also helped her with the presentation and discussion of her data and the particular expectations and conventions that she would be expected to follow using her particular approach to the analysis of her data. Her on-line analysis also revealed metadiscourse strategies she was able to employ in her thesis such as outlining the structure of the thesis in her introductory chapter, and 'linking' sections at the beginning and end of each chapter.

Later in the writing, Qi worked with Hopkins and Dudley-Evans's (1988) and Swales and Feak's (1994) descriptions of Discussion sections of theses and dissertations to address the general expectations of a Master's level thesis. She found these analyses particularly useful, drawing on both of them equally. They were very helpful, she said, for planning the Discussion section of the thesis, as well as for reviewing what she was writing. This section took her the longest to write, and was, she found, the most difficult section of the thesis to write. The final piece of writing was, however, detailed and substantive, making constant links back to her analysis as well as to the results of the studies she had summarised in her literature review.

In summary, Qi found the kind of activities described in this chapter extremely helpful. This was especially so given that she had not written a text of this kind before. She discovered early on that the thesis required much more of her than had the coursework component of her degree. The focus on audience helped her considerably to adapt her writing to the particular level and task she was undertaking. As Ballard and Clanchy (1984) observe, Asian students often have difficultly, at this level, with the more analytical and critical kind of work expected of them. Qi was able, through the attention given to audience and expectations, to do this very capably.

Qi was awarded a very high grade for her thesis, with the examiners saying her work was clearly defined, well argued and convincing in the observations and claims that it made – much of which was the result of the attention she paid to genre and audience throughout the process of her research and the writing up of her text.

Conclusion

This chapter has reviewed approaches to the teaching of academic writing which has been informed by research into the language and discourse of particular academic texts. The activities described here are for a particular genre and a particular audience. However, they might equally be used for the teaching of other academic genres and for teaching other skills such as listening, reading and speaking in academic settings. For example, many of the suggestions made in this chapter for thesis and dissertation writing can be used for teaching the academic essay (see Paltridge, 2000) and for teaching listening in academic settings (see Paltridge, 1997b). They might also be drawn on in the teaching of reading in academic settings (see Paltridge, 1999, 2000) and for teaching spoken genres such as the seminar presentation.

Similar such tasks might be designed for students with a lower level of language proficiency than the example described in this chapter. It is important, however, that the tasks be 'designed for success'. That is, the activities should be ones which the learners are likely to succeed in doing, rather than being beyond their present capabilities (Ur, 1996).

The tasks described in this chapter might also be integrated with teaching applications currently being developed which draw on corpus-based studies of genre-specific academic language such as those described by Master (1987), Dudley-Evans (1994b), Flowerdew (1994b), and Thurston and Candlin (1997, 1998). This work is especially important as the patterns of language use that are revealed in corpus studies often run counter to our expectations based on intuition (Biber *et al.*, 1994). There is, further, often a mismatch between the language presented in published second language teaching materials and the observations that are made of language use in corpus-based studies (Ljung, 1991; Kennedy, 1992). Corpus studies, thus, clearly have much to offer descriptions of academic genres and their application in EAP settings.

Similar kinds of tasks might also be employed in critical analyses of academic genres and, in particular, classroom-based tasks which aim to 'make visible' the social construction and transmission of ideologies, power relationships, and social identities (Threadgold, 1989). A critical perspective on academic genres might explore issues such as gender, ethnicity, cultural difference, ideology and identity, and how these are reflected in particular texts (Pennycook, 1997a). It might also explore how these relations can be drawn to learners' attention so they are aware of how they are positioned by particular texts. These kinds of questions clearly need a reasonable level of language proficiency in order to deal with them in a second language classroom. They can, however, be used selectively to help learners better understand what a text might assume of them, as well as how they can present a particular position, should they wish to do so.

5 International scientific English: The language of research scientists around the world

Alistair Wood

English as the international language of science

A Yugoslav pharmacologist once told me that, in addition to his other linguistic accomplishments (he spoke Serbian, Slovene, Russian, German, Flemish and French) he was also fluent in the international language of science, 'bad English'. He was not serious, but behind the joke lie some serious points that will be the focus of this paper. Is there a 'language of science'? Is this 'bad English' or a particular variety of English, and who are its speakers?

My friend's description of his linguistic abilities, though, does reflect the perception that English is indeed the international language of science. Although precise figures are hard to establish, it is certainly true that English plays an increasingly prominent role in scientific publication round the world (Baldauf and Jernudd, 1983; Gibbs, 1995; Swales, 1990, 1996). There are a number of factors behind this dominance of English, ranging from the geopolitical to the local. The pre-eminence of Russian in the old Soviet bloc has been superseded by English with the end of the Cold War, while the pre-war dominance of German in chemistry has declined to the extent that *Angewandte Chemie* is now published in English. This trend towards the publication of national scientific journals in English rather than the national language is found not only in Germany but around the world from Scandinavia to Mexico (Gibbs, 1995; Swales, 1996).

The reasons for this are not hard to discern. For scientists to become recognised and successful their work must be read and cited by their peers as frequently as possible. To ensure such citation it is imperative that their work be accessible to as many as possible and thus that it be written in English, the global language spoken by more people around the world than any other, perhaps 1,200–1,500 million, of whom only around a quarter are native speakers (Crystal, 1997). Moreover, the requirement for citation means that inclusion in the Science Citation Index (SCI), which analyses the number of times a paper has been cited by researchers and is thus a measure of its importance, increases the pressure to publish in English (Gibbs, 1995). Another push in this direction is the practice, more common in research in the natural sciences, to rank publication in journals in terms of impact factor, with those in fast moving fields like molecular biology all published in English.

This dominance of English varies from field to field, and in certain fields other languages may have a disproportionate place (Swales, 1990). While this is certainly the case, and the dominance of English language journals in the 3,300 published by the SCI does not reflect the overall place of English among the 70,000 scientific journals published worldwide (Gibbs, 1995), it is evident that the most prestigious and cited journals in the majority of fields of science are published in English, and that scientists are more likely to cite their own work published in English rather than their L1 (Grabe, 1988a).

In the humanities and social sciences rather than the natural sciences there may still be a considerable amount of publication in languages other than English in national journals, or in English in national journals not widely available outside the country (Burgess, 1997). Cultural factors may also lead towards national publication in non-English-language journals. Thus, in China, it may be the case that political realities dictate that 'to publish in, say, *Science*, or *Nature*, is of less importance than to be covered by the *People's Daily*', as one eminent Chinese scientist observed (Tsou, 1998: 520).

Despite this, however, the pressure to conform to international or Western research criteria is growing and many countries in East Asia are introducing Western concepts of research assessment (Swinbanks and Nathan, 1997), with South-East Asian countries moving in a similar direction (Mervis and Normile, 1998). As a result there has been a rapid increase in papers published by the countries of the Pacific Rim in journals included in the SCI: double in China, three times more in Hong Kong and Singapore, four times more in Taiwan and five times in South Korea (Swinbanks, Nathan, and Triendl, 1997).

We may predict that the use of English as the language of international science is likely to continue. This choice of language has been described by de Swaan in an economic analogy in terms of language as 'hypercollective goods' (de Swaan, 1998). Applying this concept to scientific English we find that as more and more users decide to use scientific English, the value of knowing this variety correspondingly increases as more scientific papers are available in the language. In addition, there are network effects such as the benefit of knowing scientific English increasing for existing users as more new users join the international network of scientific English.

The increasing use of English, however, does not necessarily mean that scientific English as a specific variety exists. In the next section we shall examine how far we can identify a particular variety of English that can be described in this way.

Characteristics of scientific English

Within the framework of EAP, English for Science and Technology has long been one of the standard divisions (e.g. Hutchinson and Waters, 1987; Jordan, 1997; Robinson, 1991; Swales, 1985). However, there are a number of reasons why we might want to distinguish scientific English from academic English in the broader sense. Although there are certain broad genres of academic English that students will contact regardless of disciplinary background, such as the lecture, it may be somewhat dangerous to overgeneralise regarding EAP. However, it is not claimed that all disciplines, especially the humanities, have the same type of unitary international character as the natural sciences.

A considerable amount of research, back to the pioneering work of Kaplan on contrastive rhetoric (Connor and Kaplan, 1987; see also Connor, 1996) has demonstrated that there are considerable differences in the styles of writing of particular cultures (see Hinds, 1987 for Japanese, and Egginton, 1987 on Korean), including other European cultures. Clyne has demonstrated that academic German has a less linear structure than English, while both Finnish and Spanish are less likely to signal the direction of argument in the text as explicitly as does English (Clyne, 1987; Mauranen, 1993b; Valero-Garces, 1996). However, much of this work has been carried out on the social sciences – Clyne specifically states that his conclusions do not apply to chemistry texts, which follow the Anglo-American model, while Oldenburg (1992, cited in Clyne, 1994) found substantial similarities in English and German engineering texts.

Even in cultures which differ regarding the discourse structures in the humanities, such as Chinese, Taylor and Chen found that Chinese scientists ranging from geologists to metallurgists broadly follow the standard pattern of introductions to scientific articles (Taylor and Chen, 1991). If scientific texts are not influenced by the traditional rhetorical patterns of the humanistic or social science disciplines, what are the determining factors involved?

Researchers working within a number of different research traditions have demonstrated that scientific texts also have a definite rhetorical structure, and that scientists manipulate their texts to achieve a particular rhetorical purpose. These arguments have been put forward by proponents of various approaches to the analysis of scientific texts from a genre analysis point of view (Hyon, 1996; Yunick, 1997), e.g. the British, following Swales (1981, 1984a, 1990), the Australian systemic-functional approach of Halliday and Martin (Halliday and Martin, 1993; Martin and Veel, 1998) and the American New Rhetoric (Berkenkotter and Huckin, 1993; Miller, 1984).

Perhaps the work which has had most impact on EST has been that of Swales and those generally following his approach to genre analysis. In addition to Swales's well-known work on introductions to scientific research articles (RAs) (Swales, 1981, 1984a, 1990), other researchers have confirmed that further sections or types of RA also have particular move structures (e.g. Hopkins and Dudley-Evans, 1988; Thompson, 1993; Wood, 1982). Such work has demonstrated that the scientific RA has a particular rhetorical structure aimed at advancing the argument of the authors of the text and having their claims accepted by the scientific community. Common to all types of scientific RA is the fact that they have a particular type of rhetorical pattern, which in the experimental sciences at least is usually encapsulated in the traditional I-M-R-D, or Introduction-Methods-Results-Discussion format (Biber and Finegan, 1994; Swales, 1990). Although this traditional pattern may be modified, and there are clear differences between different disciplines (e.g. Salager-Meyer, 1994; Tarone *et al.*, 1981), these rhetorical conventions may be developed and manipulated because they are so accepted and so standard that they are often given in journal guidelines to contributors.

We may characterise scientific English, therefore, not in terms of the use of a particular type of vocabulary, but by the fact that scientific RAs have a particular type of rhetorical structure. Other types of scientific writing besides the RA can also be characterised in such terms (e.g. the MSc dissertation investigated by Dudley-Evans, 1994a), but we shall concentrate on the RA as the prototypical type of writing produced in international scientific English. That these texts have clear and characteristic structure grows out of the purpose for the scientist in writing the RA: to have the scientific claims taken up and accepted by the wider scientific community, a process described by a number of writers working in, or influenced by, the framework often called the sociology of scientific knowledge.

Gilbert and Mulkay (1984) demonstrate that there is a considerable difference between what they term the contingent repertoire of the informal discussion in the laboratory and the empiricist repertoire of the formal scientific paper. Scientists try in this way to bring about the 'construction of scientific facts', as Latour and Woolgar (1986) put it. Historically, in response to the shifting rhetorical demands of the scientist vis-à-vis the changing audience for science, a paper written by a member of the Royal Society bears little resemblance to the research article of today (Bazerman, 1988). This process of change over centuries is mirrored in microcosm by the detailed process of negotiation that goes on between author, referee and editor before a scientific paper is published, as shown by Myers (1990). In his work on the framing of claims, what the researcher has to try to do is demonstrate the strongest claim compatible with the evidence that is put forward, but which is acceptable to peers in the scientific community (Myers, 1989, 1990).

It is quite apparent, therefore, from the work of sociologists of science such as those cited above, as well as that of Bloor (1976), Collins (1992), Collins and Pinch (1993), Woolgar (1993) and Fuller (1997), that science is a social construction which is created by scientists in terms not just of the science they are carrying out but of what is accepted by the scientific and wider communities. If the science of research articles is not simply a matter of what takes place in the laboratory, but is related to what is accepted by the society as a proper scientific claim, it may be interesting to try to characterise who is involved in the negotiation of such claims of acceptance for new scientific work.

The role of the native speaker

It is important to examine what part the status of the scientists as speakers of English might play in the achievement of this aim. Does the fact that a scientist is a native speaker of English affect the likelihood of success in this endeavour?

This question brings forward the problem of what constitutes being a native speaker (NS) of a language. The former unchallenged primacy of the native speaker has been replaced by an increasing questioning of the unique and privileged nature of their status. Davies (1991) noted the many different aspects involved: are we concerned with the first language the speaker has learnt, the language habitually used, the dominant language or a mixture of these criteria? Rampton (1990) attempted to separate out the three strands of language expertise, language affiliation and language inheritance. That language expertise need not be the sole preserve of the NS has been emphasised, for example, by White and Genesee (1996), who show that the supposed differences in attainment levels between native and non-native speakers (NNSs) are exaggerated and that near-native levels are indistinguishable from native.

If the levels of expertise in a language do not automatically correlate with the NS/NNS boundary, is the NS user of scientific English in a more secure position than the NNS? As Rampton points out, expertise (as opposed to an innate concept of nativespeaker-hood) is learned, partial and relative. This means that not only the NNS but also the NS must learn how to do science. Science is a craft that can only be learned by doing and is not just a matter of knowledge, as stressed by current sociologists of science (e.g. Pickering, 1992; see also Fujimura, 1996; Collins, 1992). Part of this learning of a craft is the acculturation process of learning how to write in the way deemed appropriate by the mature practitioners of the craft (Bazerman and Paradis, 1991). This is true both for the NS and the NNS, so that Dudley-Evans discovered that errors made by an NS 'scientific apprentice' learning her trade by writing her PhD dissertation were no different in kind from those of NNSs. She too had difficulty with cohesion, lexical choice, sentence order and tense choice, and Dudley-Evans concluded that 'there is only quantitative rather than qualitative difference between production in L1 and L2' (Dudley-Evans, 1991: 50).

This similarity between NSs and NNSs in the problems they face in academic writing is supported by other researchers: it has been noted that higher level discourse problems are more significant than are the grammatical problems of practising scientist NNSs writing for international journals (e.g. Dudley-Evans, 1994a; Mauranen, 1993b; St John, 1987; Swales, 1990; Swales and Feak, 1994). Even NNSs may often be aware that language is not a significant problem, so that among the Hong Kong academics investigated by Flowerdew, 32% thought they were at no disadvantage vis-à-vis NSs, while among those who did think they were at a disadvantage, only 51% said they had technical problems with the language (Flowerdew, forthcoming).

NNSs must, of course, still overcome the obstacle of acceptance by the gate-keepers of journal editors and referees. Myers (1990) has shown that this is a significant hurdle and requires a lot of negotiation even among NSs, while a glance at the date of submission and acceptance of any scientific journal will show that papers are rarely accepted without revision. In some cases, as evidenced by Carter-Sigglow (1996), it may be that perception of possible language problems by NNSs will impede publication. However, Flowerdew notes that journal editors are not usually worried about grammatical errors, since these can be edited out easily (Flowerdew, forthcoming).

This is not to say that NNSs do not have additional problems compared to NSs in writing in English, in that they may require additional time to complete a manuscript, including more revisions, etc. NNSs may also use various strategies to counteract a perceived deficiency in English language skills, such as greater reliance on mathematics (Sionis, 1995), seeking the help of an NS and using translation services (St John, 1987). Despite these qualifications, however, it is not the case that the NNS is automatically at a disadvantage compared to the NS.

Even if we consider the discourse-level skills identified by those authors cited above as problematic, it is normally the case that these are a problem, as in the case studied by Dudley-Evans, for the beginning writer. Experienced NNS writers are familiar with the discourse requirements of their discipline. The reasons are not hard to determine. Before NNS scientists write their first papers in English they will have spent several years reading such papers in English and will be familiar with the conventions of the field. This follows from what has been said above about the dominance of English internationally as a medium of scientific publication, so that the NNS scientist who can attempt to write an RA in English will have been reading the journal literature in English for a long time.

A related factor derives from the nature of scientific rhetoric. The rhetoric of scientific RAs comes from the need of the authors to convince their audience of the validity of the new claim and to have that claim accepted: this pattern is discipline-specific rather than culture-specific, as may be the case with the humanities or social sciences. An RA on the molecular biology of cancer, for example, will not vary according to the cultural background of the main author, since the background is that of cancer research, not that the author is Japanese.

This analysis of the status of the NS versus the NNS implies that the NNS is not as disadvantaged as is often thought, at least in the scientific field. But (as we saw above) NNS authors have difficulties publishing their work in English. We shall now investigate this by examining a corpus of RAs in English and see how difficult it is for NNSs to publish in English.

The NNS as author of the scientific RA

Canagarajah (1996), St John (1987), Jernudd and Baldauf (1987), and Swales (1990, 1996) have tended to emphasise the difficulties that the NNS has in publishing in English. Other authors, principally Phillipson (1992) and Pennycook (1994a), have taken the argument further and tried to show that the use of English around the world continues and extends the hegemony of the English-speaking countries at the centre and the interests of international capitalism. Considering the position of scientific English as a variety, the world of science seems to be similarly dominated by the developed world and the English-speaking countries in particular. The G7 countries plus the other important developed countries of Australia, Denmark, the Netherlands, Sweden and Switzerland, account for 80% of world investment in scientific R and D (May, 1998), while the USA alone accounts for 34.6% of scientific papers (May, 1997). This hegemony in the world of science parallels that in the political and economic spheres. Looked at more carefully, however, there is no such clear-cut dominance of English-speaking countries in the field of science: of the twelve countries investigated by May (1998), relative to GDP the UK, the US and Canada were all among the bottom four in the table.

The world of scientific research does not demonstrate the clear hegemony of the native English-speaking world, whether we measure this in terms of authorship of papers or R&D expenditure and output. However, these overall statistics still do not indicate how difficult it is for the NNS to publish in English. In an attempt to obtain a clearer picture, a corpus of RAs was examined to ascertain the proportion written by NNSs and NSs. The corpus was taken from the two most prestigious international scientific journals, *Nature* and *Science*, on the basis that if it is very difficult for the NNS to publish in English it will be more difficult to publish in the highest-level scientific journals.

The corpus was made up of one year's issues of the two journals, minus the combined Christmas-New Year issues, a total of 50 issues for each journal. In each journal the standard type of RA only was examined, i.e., 'Reports' in the American and 'Letters to Nature' in the British journal. The issues ran from June 1997 through to the following May for *Nature*, and because two issues of *Science* from 1997 were missing, through to June 1998 for *Science*.

As is standard for scientific RAs, the large majority of papers were multi-authored. The main author was taken to be the first author listed, with the team leader usually being the last mentioned. In order to establish whether the first author was likely to be an NS of English two criteria were used, one strict and one broader and more realistic but still relatively conservative in terms of erring in favour of a low number of NNS authors. The strict criterion was to take as an NNS a first author with a name which was not an English name but one native to the country concerned. For example Tetsuo Irifune, the lead author of a paper with ten other authors, all with Japanese names

Table 1. *Numbers and percentages of RAs by NS and NNS in* Science *and* Nature

	Science	Nature	Combined
Total no. of articles	754	838	1592
NS strict crit. nos./%	609/80.77	633/75.54	1242/78.02
NNS strict crit. nos./%	145/19.23	205/24.46	350/21.98
NS realistic crit. nos./%	414/54.91	452/53.94	866/54.4
NNS realistic crit.nos./%	340/45.09	386/46.06	726/45.6

(Strict crit. = NNS in country of origin. Realistic crit. = NNS regardless of residence. See text for full explanation.)

and at Japanese institutions, was taken to be Japanese and an NNS of English (Irifune *et al.*, 1998). The less strict criterion was to recognise as an NNS a first author whose name indicated that they were not an NS of English, despite being at an institution probably not in that scientist's home country. Thus Zhu Gang Wang was taken to be an NNS of English, despite being affiliated to a US Graduate School of Medical Sciences (Wang *et al.*, 1998). As many Americans have non-English surnames, only those scientists whose whole names appeared to be non-English were taken as NNSs. Thus many scientists who were quite likely from their surnames to be NNSs were not counted as such because only initials and surname were given. It is not claimed that every scientist taken on these criteria to be an NNS is in fact an NNS, merely that the overall proportion of NS/NNS will be approximated by such an operational definition.

The findings from this analysis are shown in Table 1. As can be seen, even following the strict criterion of counting as NNS of English only those scientists who are clearly natives of the country they are resident in (labelled 'strict crit.' in the table), we see that almost a fifth (19.23%) of papers in *Science* and almost a quarter of papers in *Nature* (24.46%) are written by NNSs. If we take the more realistic, but still conservative, criterion and recognise that many scientists, especially graduate students, will not be resident in their country of origin (labelled 'realistic crit.' in the table), 45.09% of papers in *Science* and 46.06% of papers in *Nature*, or an average of 45.6% of RAs in these two journals, are written by NNSs. This figure approaches half the total number of papers in the journals and does not count those other scientists who were part of the same team who are clearly NNSs under even the stricter criteria. Taking these researchers into account would give well over half of the papers involving NNSs. If we allowed such criteria it would seem not at all difficult for an NNS to be published in prestigious journals. However, even if the NNS remained as first author, a figure of almost half NNS as first author in the two highest-ranking scientific journals in the world is far higher than would be anticipated from the kind of arguments given by Pennycook, Phillipson or Canagarajah.

Certainly many of the scientists concerned are at US or UK institutions, as can be seen from the difference between the NNS percentage under the strict or more realistic criteria. But this does not invalidate the finding that NNSs are able to publish in even the highest-level journal. Nevertheless this is in line with the argument put forward by Canagarajah on the difficulties that researchers in the developing world find in getting research published. Clearly it is difficult for them to publish, but this is because of the kind of physical and financial problems he outlines, not because of the language. From the data here the linguistic barriers for NNSs to be published in even the most prestigious journal do not seem high.

International scientific English

It seems clear that the NNS does write a considerable number of RAs even in the most prestigious journals in science. This is in agreement with the above arguments about the expertise of the NS and NNS, but it also receives support from other authorities who have discussed the question of the status of a community of NNSs vs. that of NSs. In a series of papers Kachru argued for the existence of three circles of English, the 'inner circle' of native speakers, the 'outer circle' of ESL speakers and the 'expanding circle' of EFL speakers (e.g. Kachru, 1985, 1991, 1995a). Though the three circles may differ in their English, Kachru suggests that outer circle users of English are as entitled as inner circle users to the status of owners of their English and that each variety has equal status with the others, with no need for an external standard taken over from another variety.

It might be argued that NNSs still cannot publish in their first language and to that extent the position of English is still a hegemonic one. The concept of ownership of English by all speakers of English regardless of whether they are NS or NNS implied by Kachru's arguments, however, means that although English is dominant, it is no longer the language of hegemony. 'English-knowing bilinguals' (Pakir, 1999) are increasingly the majority of English-speakers (see also Graddol, 1997). Knowledge of English, is, therefore, empowering rather than hegemonic as it becomes the language of globalisation (Pakir, 1999).

This argument, in terms of a community of English users who themselves define what constitutes their English and claim ownership of that form of English regardless of other groups has a parallel in the concept of discourse community (Swales, 1988b, 1990). The most interesting aspect of Swales's discussion, from the point of view of a community of users of international scientific English, is the idea that 'the discourse creates the community' (Swales, 1988b: 212). The community is constituted by the interaction between the members. In this respect the users of international scientific English make up a separate discourse community.

We seem on a number of grounds to be able to put the case for a variety which we may name International Scientific English, or ISE, the variety of scientific English used by scientists around the world of any linguistic background. This discourse community may be characterised by what they have in common, namely the use of English to write science. The two-sided nature of this definition, in terms of both English and science, enables us to avoid focusing on the NS as constitutive of the discourse community. The fact that some, or even most, of the members are native speakers of English is irrelevant. What constitutes grounds for membership in the community is an acceptance by members of that community of a scientist as a member. Although a minimum command of English is necessary before a scientist can publish a paper in English, level of expertise, as has been shown above, is not synonymous with the status of NS. What is much more important than level of expertise in English is the scientific quality of the research produced by the members of the community.

To become a member of the community, in other words to be accepted by the international community of scientists of a particular discipline or subdiscipline like molecular biology or cancer genetics, the scientist has to produce research claims which are accepted by the community. The more central the claim and the more widely accepted by the community, the more central a member of the community the researcher becomes. To achieve these goals the researcher must deploy a skilful use of language, which may be easier in some respects for the NS, but does not rule out the NNS. To the extent that the researcher persuades the rest of the research community of their claims, that researcher's status as NS or NNS is irrelevant.

In this respect the discourse community of those users of ISE is much less dependent on the concept of NS than that of the three circles of Kachru, for example, where the speakers of the outer circle are defined in terms of not being NSs (Wood, 1997). Since ISE is defined in terms of membership of a discourse community which has two equivalued definitive criteria, use of English and the carrying out of scientific research, it is as a result immune from the problems of relative status that have characterised the debates over inner circle and outer circle between Kachru and Quirk (Kachru, 1991; Quirk, 1991a, 1991b).

The difference arises from the fact that for ISE, English is a means to an end shared by all members of the discourse community, i.e., the advancement of scientific knowledge by the publication of research accepted as valid by the whole community. Both NSs and NNSs share in this aim and in doing so are members of the same discourse community, whereas for the members of the three circles, NSs and NNSs are members of different communities. For ISE, since the scientific research and not the language is the focus, the fact of being an NS or NNS is backgrounded and the science takes first place. As we shall see in the final section, this has interesting consequences for the teaching of EST.

Implications for teaching EST

If, as we have seen, there is a growing international community of scientists who use ISE as their common medium of expression, this facilitates the task of the teacher of EST. Certainly foreign learners of scientific English must still learn to express themselves via English. But if learners realise that this is part of becoming a scientist and is as much a part of the craft of doing science as being able to run a gas chromatograph or a statistical test on results, it is likely to be much more acceptable. If ISE is not the property of the native speaker but of scientists of any language background, it can become the property of student scientists as well, who will integrate the language into their developing practice and persona as scientists in a way which would be impossible if English is seen as the property of the English-speaking world in the sense of the countries of the inner circle.

In this respect the idea of International Scientific English parallels the arguments put forward by the proponents of World Englishes and that of Pennycook and Phillipson for the empowerment of the student who would take command of English. Where it differs is that it does not set up a barrier between NS and NNS since the discourse community concerned is united by sharing a disciplinary background as scientists. The language is free to be used for the purposes of the discipline. It has been argued by Swales (1996) that students should be free to make use of particular genres rather than follow them as recipes. Membership of an international community (apprentice scientist users of ISE) makes this much easier than being an apprentice speaker of a language which might seem to be fully mastered only by the NS.

What this implies in practice is that teachers of EST should not be content to use texts written only by NSs, but should also use texts written by NNSs. The ideal is to use texts written by the norm of international research, international teams from different countries made up of both NSs and NNSs. Although it is often impossible with undergraduate students to use actual RAs because of the difficulty of the science as well as the language, reports of research written in English by NNSs can be found in general news magazines or more specialist science journals like *New Scientist* or *Scientific American*. In addition, many countries have national science journals published in English that can be a source of materials.

More broadly though, if students recognise that learning the appropriate language of science is learning as scientists, rather than NNSs of English, then this can lead to better acceptance of the task. If the NS of English must also learn to write in English in this way, what the NNS student is doing is much easier to relate to. EST becomes not something extra, grafted onto training to be a scientist, which is how it is often traditionally seen by students of science, but an integral part of that training. If English is seen as ISE, it is part of science, not just part of English, and thus part of what it means for the student to become a scientist. If it is also seen as belonging to the international community of scientists, English is no longer a 'foreign' language, perhaps spoken by former colonists or contemporary neo-colonialists, but becomes owned by the community the science student is aspiring to join.

6 Discipline specificity and EAP

Caroline Clapham

Introduction

It is the custom in learner-centred EAP classes for teachers to give students a choice of topics to study. Some students ask for texts from subject areas outside their chosen field of study in the hope that such topics, being novel, might be more interesting (see Carrell, 1983 on salience, and Fransson, 1984 on interest). Others, however, prefer texts relating to their academic area so that they can gain practical experience of typical texts in their field of study. (By 'text' here, I am referring to both written and spoken texts.) It is these latter students that we are concerned with here, since their wishes tie in not only with theories about ESP teaching (see, for example, Dudley Evans, 1994; and Waters, 1997), but also with theoretical work in the area of cognition, notably schema theory and notions of how knowledge is stored in the brain.

Before I move on to discuss different theories of comprehension, I should explain what I mean by EAP. Since EAP is concerned with the English required for the specific purpose of studying at universities and colleges, it can be seen as being subordinate to ESP (see Jordan, 1989, and Robinson, 1991). EAP courses can be divided into those for English for General Academic Purposes (EGAP) and those for English for Specific Academic Purposes (ESAP) (see Blue, 1993; Jordan, 1997; Dudley-Evans and St John, 1998). ESAP courses range from ones for broad groupings of subjects, such as EST (English for Science and Technology), to highly specific ones, such as aeronautical engineering, that are suitable only for small groups in a narrowly defined discipline. The question I am addressing in this chapter is whether EAP courses should be based on ESAP or EGAP texts.

Theories of comprehension

I shall now return to theories of comprehension. Such theories abound, but I shall, in this next section, refer mostly to theories of reading. However, many of these theories also apply to listening. (For more about theories of listening comprehension, see Hansen and Jensen, 1994.)

It is now generally believed that reading is an interactive process in which readers use an interaction of bottom-up and top-down reading processes to make sense of a text (Grabe, 1988b). Bottom-up processing is a lower-level decoding of the language system, whereas top-down processing uses higher-level inferential processes as the starting point.

There have been several interactive models of reading comprehension (see LaBerge and Samuels, 1974; Samuels, 1977; and Rumelhart, 1977). Spiro (1980) emphasises that different people process text in different ways, depending on their purposes, attitudes, interests and background knowledge, and Stanovich (1980) suggests that if readers do not recognise a word or phrase because it is unfamiliar, they can compensate for this by using a top-down method of guessing. Similarly, if the topic is unfamiliar, bottom-up processes can sometimes be applied. This intuitively satisfying model may account for differences not only among first language readers, but also among proficient and less proficient readers in a foreign language.

In all top-down and interactive models of comprehension it is assumed that humans depend on memory or previous knowledge of some kind when they interpret textual cues. Without previous knowledge they would not be able to take an active part in comprehending a text, and would not be able to make inferences or hypotheses about what was coming next. Fundamental to all these models, therefore, is a system of storing and retrieving past knowledge. The group of theories which attempt to account for this come under the general umbrella term of 'schema theory'.

Schema theory

According to schema theory, knowledge is stored not in lists, but in hierarchies. Within these hierarchies are schemata which are embedded in other schemata, and which themselves contain other schemata. These schemata vary in their levels of abstraction, and represent all sorts of knowledge, such as objects, academic topics, rules, events, routines and social situations. They represent knowledge, rather than definitions, so they are not language based, but are symbolic representations of knowledge which may be used for understanding language. Schemata are not static, but fluid; they change according to the input. Schemata can be refined and new ones can be developed by the process of accommodation, that is, the modification of previous schemata in the light of new information. Two of the most celebrated schema-theoretic models are those of Minsky (1977) who introduced what he called 'frame system theory' and Schank and Abelson (1977). (For more about schema theory see Bransford, 1979; Anderson and Pearson, 1988; Goldinger, 1996; Alba and Hasher, 1983; and McClelland, Rumelhart and Hinton, 1986.)

A convincing advocate of the importance of the reader's own input is the psychologist John Bransford (1979). He and his colleagues reported on a series of experiments in which they asked L1 subjects to describe or remember pictures or texts. They found that passages that were hard to understand or remember when presented in a vacuum became clear once the text was accompanied by the appropriate title or picture. The effect of adding a simple context to such a text was dramatic. (By 'context' I mean the setting or topic of a text.) From this the researchers deduced that not only do readers need background knowledge to make sense of a passage, they also need to be able to activate this background knowledge. It is no use, for example, knowing about a given process, such as washing clothes, to cite a Bransford topic, if readers do not realise that they are reading a description of this process.

Many researchers have studied the effect of prior knowledge on comprehension, some comparing the performance of students from different cultural or educational backgrounds, and others comparing students with different amounts of knowledge of a topic. Many of these researchers have based their research on schema theory.

Research into ESP testing

Since 1981 there have been several studies into the effect of background knowledge on EAP test performance. These can be divided into two kinds, those concerned with world, that is, content and cultural knowledge, and those relating to knowledge of the formal or linguistic structure of texts. In this chapter I am concerned with both.

Alderson and Urquhart (1985) investigated the effect of background knowledge on students attending English classes in Britain in preparation for courses at British universities. They gave groups of students in three different disciplines – business and economics, science and engineering, and liberal arts – the Social Studies and Technology Modules of the English Language Testing Service (ELTS) test. The students' scores on the modules were somewhat contradictory in that, for example, science and engineering students did better than the business and economics students on the Technology module, but the business and economics students did no better than the science and engineering group on the Social Studies module. The researchers concluded, therefore, that although students in some disciplines achieved higher scores if they were given tests in their own subject areas, these findings were not consistent across disciplines.

Other studies (for example Koh, 1985; Shoham, Peretz and Vorhaus, 1987; Tan, 1990) have also proved inconclusive, but several points emerge from them. Firstly, language proficiency levels seem to play at least as important a role as background knowledge in the comprehension of reading texts. Secondly, background knowledge itself is not easily assessed: a student who is in business studies may well have previously worked in another discipline such as science, or may have scientific interests in his or her spare time. Thirdly, in these studies there seemed to be a tendency for science students to perform better than other students on science-based tests, but to perform as well as the humanities students on humanities-based ones. (I shall discuss a possible reason for this later.) Finally, the level of specificity of the subject-based texts probably varied widely in the different studies, but this was not fully taken into account in the research. (A 'specific' test is one which is based on content which is only appropriate for students in the relevant subject area.)

None of the above studies related their work to schema theory, but Jensen and Hansen (1995), investigating the effect of prior knowledge on the listening comprehension of academic students, discussed how the students' activation of the appropriate schemata allowed them to make use of their background knowledge.

Background reading

One of the reasons for the inconclusive findings of researchers such as Alderson and Urquhart (1985) and Tan (1990) may have been that for research of this sort it is difficult, if not impossible, to place students into appropriate subject areas. In all the above studies, students were allocated according to their academic field, but the fact that people study in one particular subject area does not, of course, mean that they are ignorant about other subjects and unfamiliar with other rhetorical styles, since they may well read books and articles in subjects outside their own academic field. In an investigation into students' background knowledge (Clapham, 1966), students were asked about their leisure reading. Their responses agreed with popular conceptions about the differences between scientists and non-scientists in that while 36% of the business studies and social science (BSS) students did not read outside their own broad subject area, most of the life and medical sciences (LMS) and physical science and technology (PST) students did; only 8% of the LMS students and 9% of the PST students read nothing but texts in their own subject area. Similarly 87% of both LMS and PST students said that they read at least some BSS materials, whereas only 64% of BSS students said they read science texts. Most people, whether they are scientists or not, are expected to read novels, and to comment on social and political events, but it is widely accepted that many non-scientists show little interest in scientific matters. It is also true that although it is possible to function adequately in society with little or no scientific knowledge, it may not be possible to do so without some knowledge of the main social and economic issues of the times. In addition, there is now a trend in many universities for students to follow multidisciplinary courses, where, for example, medical students may take courses in counselling, and biology students may study business management. (Once again, though, there is an imbalance between the science and the social science students in that whilst the science students may also study subjects in the social sciences, few social science students will take science courses, because of the content knowledge requirements of such courses.)

All this suggests that because of the breadth of their interests beyond their academic subject areas it is impossible accurately to assign students to particular subject areas, and therefore that dividing students up into different fields of study may be unnecessary if not impossible. In addition, the fact that 35% of the BSS students read nothing but BSS texts, whereas only 8% of the LMS and 9% of the PST students read only in their own subject area, suggests that there is a lack of symmetry in the world knowledge of BSS and science students.

The empirical study: research into the effect of background knowledge on EAP reading comprehension

Since designers of tests such as the International English Language Testing System (IELTS) assumed that students would achieve their highest scores on tests in their own subject areas, and since current research into the area was inconclusive, I carried out a large scale study into the effect of background knowledge on reading test performance (Clapham, 1996).

For this I initially divided the students up into the three IELTS academic fields (at that time IELTS gave academic candidates a reading module in one of the three broad subject areas reported above – BSS, LMS, and PST). The subjects were a heterogeneous sample of 842 non-native English speakers, most of whom were about to start undergraduate or post-graduate studies at English medium universities. The students were each given two versions of the IELTS reading test, one in their own subject area and one outside it, so the BSS students took the BSS module (M)BSS, together with either (M)LMS or the (M)PST. Similarly, LMS students took (M)LMS and another module, and the PST students took (M)PST and another module. Each student, therefore, took two reading tests.

The scores on the reading modules were compared to see whether the students had higher scores on the test in their own subject area. Three repeated measures analyses of variance were carried out, one for each pair of reading modules: (M)BSS and (M)LMS (M)BSS and (M)PST (M)LMS and (M)PST. There was a significant interaction effect in each of the three groups – in each case the students achieved higher scores on the module in their own subject area than on the other. These results are what we might expect, and would not be surprising were it not for the fact that in a pilot study, based on different reading modules and different students (see Clapham, 1996), there were no significant subject area effects. Why were the results so different? Was it because the number of cases in the previous study was much smaller, or was it because of differences in the specificity of the reading passages? No analysis had been made of the main study reading passages because the texts came out of journals and magazines in the appropriate subject areas, and were therefore assumed to be appropriate to the relevant reading modules. However, this was not necessarily so: academic papers, let alone magazine articles, vary in their level of subject specificity, ranging from those that are comprehensible to all educated readers to those highly technical ones which can only be read by experts in some limited sub-field. It might well be that the reading passages in this study varied in just this way. One of the PST passages, for example, on fuel resources, seemed to be the sort of general informative text that could be read by anyone in the BSS field, whereas two of the LMS texts seemed more subject specific as they depended on at least some basic medical or biological knowledge. Appearances can, of course, be deceptive, but it was worth seeing whether these texts were at the appropriate level of specificity for these modules.

Table 1. *The reading passages*

Title	Abbreviation	Subject Area
BSS Module		
Quality Circles	(Qual)	Business Studies
The Purposes of Continuing Education	(Educ)	Education
Access to Higher Education	(High)	Education
LMS Module		
The Mystery of Declining Tooth Decay	(Tooth)	Dental Health
Our Children's Teeth	(Child)	Dental Health
How to Make a Transgenic Beast	(Genes)	Genetics
Nitrogen Fixation	(Nitro)	Plant Biology
PST Module		
Life Without a Sunscreen	(Sun)	Physics
Energy from Fuels	(Fuel)	Physics
The Recovery of the Mary Rose	(Ship)	Engineering

Text specificity

Table 1 lists the reading passages, together with their abbreviated titles and the subject areas to which they belonged.

Each subtest contained one of these texts and a series of related questions. The subtests varied in length but since the reliability of each was acceptable, all subtests were included in the statistical analyses. (See Clapham, 1996, for more details about the performance of the individual subtests and the individual test items.)

In the same way as I had compared students' performance on the total modules, I now used repeated measures analysis of variance to compare students' performance on the individual subtests. In each case the analyses were carried out in pairs, so that, for example, the performance of BSS and LMS students on (BSS)Qual and (LMS)Tooth was compared, and similarly that of BSS and PST students on (BSS)Qual and (PST)Sun, and LMS and PST students on (LMS)Tooth and (PST)Sun. In this way all possible pairs of subtests were tested for subject area effect. Table 2 shows the difference in the effect of academic subject area for each pair of subtests. Table 2.1 shows the subject area effect when BSS and LMS students took the BSS and LMS subtests, and when BSS and PST students took the BSS and PST ones. Similarly, Tables 2.2 and 2.3 show the pairings with

Table 2. *Level of significance of subject area effect for pairs of subtests*
(Repeated Measures Analysis of Variance)

2.1		LMS Module				PST Module		
		Tooth	Child	Genes	Nitro	Sun	Fuel	Ship
	Qual	NS	NS	.01	.001	<.001	NS	NS
BSS	Educ	NS	NS	<.001	<.001	<.001	NS	NS
Module	High	NS	NS	<.001	<.001	<.001	NS	NS
		BSS and LMS students				BSS and PST students		

2.2		PST Module			BSS Module		
		Sun	Fuel	Ship	Qual	Educ	High
	Tooth	NS	.05	NS	NS	NS	NS
LMS	Child	NS	NS	NS	NS	NS	NS
Module	Genes	NS	.05	NS	.01	<.001	<.001
	Nitro	.01	<.001	.01	.001	<.001	<.001
		LMS and PST students			LMS and BSS students		

2.3		LMS Module				BSS Module		
		Tooth	Child	Genes	Nitro	Qual	Educ	High
	Sun	NS	NS	NS	.01	<.001	<.001	<.001
PST	Fuel	.05	NS	.05	<.001	NS	NS	NS
Module	Ship	NS	NS	NS	.01	NS	NS	NS
		PST and LMS students				PST and BSS students		

LMS students and PST students respectively. It will be seen from this chart how the subtests varied in their 'specificity', that is, in the extent to which they appeared to have significant subject area effects when paired with subtests from other modules. The LMS subtest Nitro, for example (Table 2.2), had significant subject effects when paired with all the subtests from the other modules (p = .01, <.001 and .01 with the PST subtests Sun, Fuel and Ship respectively, and .001, <.001, and <.001 with each of the three BSS subtests). On the other hand (LMS)Child (Table 2.2) had no significant subject area effects with any of the BSS or PST subtests, and when BSS and PST students' scores were compared on (BSS)Qual and (PST)Sun (Table 2.1) there was a highly significant subject area effect (<.001), but when those same students' performances were compared on (BSS)Qual and (PST)Fuel there was no significant difference.

When a subtest has highly significant subject area effects when paired with all or almost all the other subtests it can be assumed that the subtest is highly specific to students in that subject area. So (LMS)Nitro was a highly specific subtest. Subtests such as (BSS)Qual and (PST)Sun, which had highly significant effects with some but not all the other subtests, might be called 'specific', and subtests with few or no significant effects 'general'. (LMS)Tooth (LMS)Child (PST)Fuel and (PST)Ship were all 'general' according to this definition. One intriguing finding was that in all three subject area interactions between (PST)Fuel and the three BSS subtests, the students did slightly, but not significantly, better at the test that was *outside* their subject area.

This was not surprising as it later transpired that the Fuel reading passage was taken from a textbook explaining scientific facts to arts and social science students; although the passage contained material in a suitable subject area, it was not presented in a scientific manner or genre.

The other test with surprising results was PST(Ship): in only one case did it show a significant subject area effect (.01 with (LMS)Nitro, the highly specific text), and there were no significant subject area effects between it and the BSS passages. These results were particularly surprising as, on the whole, the chart showed strong background effects between BSS and LMS texts, and some-what lower ones between LMS and PST ones. However, this subject area effect was caused by the interaction of two texts, one of which might have been more specific than the other. To find out more about the individual texts, I investigated students' and academic lecturers' views on the appropriacy of the reading passages.

Familiarity of subject area

In the questionnaire, students were asked whether they were familiar with the subject area of each reading passage they encountered. For example one question was as follows:

Were you familiar with this general area of physics before you read the passage? (Question relating to (PST)Fuel)

Students were asked a similar question about each of the passages, whether the module was in their own discipline or not. The results are reported in Table 3. I assumed that if a text was specific, more students in the appropriate subject area would be familiar with it, than would students in the other areas. A typical example of a specific text is:

(BSS)Educ
BSS students: Familiar: 64%   Unfamiliar: 36%
LMS students: Familiar: 39%   Unfamiliar: 61%
PST students: Familiar: 47%   Unfamiliar: 53%

Table 3. *Subject Area Familiarity*

3.1 M(BSS)

	BSS	Students LMS	PST
	N = 282	N = 60	N = 85
	%	%	%
Qual Circles	1. 50	1. 27	1. 32
	2. 50	2. 73	2. 68
Education	1. 64	1. 39	1. 47
	2. 36	2. 61	2. 53
Higher Educ	1. 54	1. 33	1. 33
	2. 46	2. 67	2. 67

Key: 1 = Familiar   2 = Unfamiliar

3.2 M(LMS)

	BSS	Students LMS	PST
	N = 160	N = 112	N = 90
	%	%	%
Teeth	1. 29	1. 59	1. 31
	2. 71	2. 41	2. 69
Genes	1. 11	1. 66	1. 19
	2. 89	2. 34	2. 81
Nitro	1. 9	1. 64	1. 41
	2. 91	2. 36	2. 59

3.3 M(PST)

	BSS	Students LMS	PST
	N = 147	N = 60	N = 140
	%	%	%
Sun	1. 33	1. 77	1. 69
	2. 67	2. 23	2. 31
Fuel	1. 55	1. 68	1. 83
	2. 45	2. 32	2. 17
Ship	1. 4	1. 11	1. 10
	2. 96	2. 89	2. 90

The results indicate that 64% of the BSS students said they were familiar with the subject area of the passage, as compared to 39% of the LMS students and 47% of the PST group. Differences of this kind between the answers of the three groups of students were particularly marked for (LMS)Nitro, which the Level of Significance Chart (Table 2) had identified as being highly subject specific (see Table 3.2).

However, not all the results were as expected. (PST)Sun, for example, appeared to be slightly more familiar to LMS students than PST ones (see Table 3.3), and (PST)Ship appeared to be unfamiliar to almost everyone. In both cases these results can probably be explained. The Sun passage dealt with the effect of ultraviolet waves on living forms, and might therefore have been equally at home in an LMS textbook. On the other hand (PST)Ship might have been so subject specific that it was unfamiliar to students in all three subject areas. Or possibly its linguistic style posed a problem. It contained a description from an engineering journal on the raising of a Tudor warship from the sea bed and the text was unlike any of the others in the three modules. It was in a narrative style, giving a step by step account of the stages and dangers of the salvage process, and included some highly technical terms. It also included a surprisingly large number of passive verbs. It seems likely that its approach was familiar to only a small group of engineers and that it was unsuitable for most of the PST students who took this module.

Subject specialists' views

In order to investigate this further, university lecturers in different academic fields at Lancaster University were asked to read all ten passages and to say how appropriate the texts were for their students, and how familiar these students would be with the subject matter (see Clapham, 1996). On the whole, the lecturers' answers agreed with the other findings relating to the texts, and their responses explained one or two of the interesting findings. For example (LMS)Child, one of the 'general' passages, was considered highly appropriate for doctors but not for biologists. This lack of appropriacy is likely, at least in part, to account for the reduced subject specificity of that subtest. On the other hand (LMS)Genes and (LMS)Nitro, the two 'highly specific' subtests, were considered highly appropriate by the LMS lecturers, and not at all appropriate by those in BSS. They were also considered highly inappropriate by the physics lecturer and the two engineers, but one of the two chemists thought they were fairly appropriate, and the other thought they were highly appropriate. This emphasises the disparate nature of the lecturers in the PST subject area, and also the indeterminacy of the boundary between LMS and PST. One intriguing discovery, which was unlikely to have been anticipated by the item writers, was that the two engineering lecturers both thought that (BSS)Qual, which was a business studies report about producing high quality goods in factories, was highly appropriate for their students, and one of the

Table 4. *Specificity*

Text	Intuition	Significance	Familiarity	Specificity
Qual	S	S	S*	S
Educ	S	S	S	S
High	S	S	S	S
Tooth	G	G	S	G
Child	G	G	S	G
Genes	S	S	S	HS
Nitro	S	S	S	HS
Sun	S	S	S (for all sciences)	S (for all sciences)
Fuel	G	G	G	G
Ship	S	G	TS	TS

Key: S   = Specific
      HS = Highly Specific
      TS = Too Specific
      * Although unfamiliar to 50% BSS students

engineers said that it was more appropriate than the engineering text (PST)Ship.

Table 4 summarises the main specificity findings. My intuitive views before I started the empirical investigations are listed under 'Intuition', the results of the Table 2 Significance Chart come under 'Significance' and those of Table 3, under 'Familiarity'. The information from all the columns is combined to produce one overall classification under 'Specificity'.

Reasons for variation in specificity

It is clear that the reading subtests varied in their specificity, but it is still not clear why this was, and whether this could have been anticipated in advance. It might, of course, have been that the reading passages varied according to their sources. For example, a passage might tend to be more specific if it came from an academic journal than if it came from a popularisation such as the *New Scientist*, where scientific discoveries are rewritten for the educated layman.

Table 5 shows the source of each of the reading passages, and it can be seen from this that the passages came from varied sources. The BSS module contained the greatest variety of texts: one came from a study document, one from a British government paper and one from an adaptation of a paper on career education. The sources of the science texts were more uniform: with one exception, the passages came from either academic journals, *Nature*, *The British Medical Journal*, and *The Structural Engineer*, or popularisations of academic science reports, the *New Scientist* and the *Scientific American*. The one exception was the (PST)Fuel text which, as we have seen, came from a textbook written not for science students but for young *non-scientists*. The content of the passage was not sufficiently specialised for PST students, and it was therefore insufficiently academic. It seemed likely that the more academic a piece of writing was, the more highly specific would be its subject matter, as it would be aimed at a progressively more specialised audience. Articles in learned journals are considered to be more academic than ones in popularisations such as the *New Scientist* and the *Scientific American*, and these in turn are thought to be more academic than, for instance, articles in quality newspapers. However, there appears to be some uncertainty about what the word 'academic' means.

As another part of my study, I asked three EAP teachers to rate the reading texts according to Bachman's Test Methods Facets (Bachman *et al.*, 1995). One of the questions related to how academic the texts were. Although the raters were in total agreement that Nitro (a highly specific text from a popularisation) was academic, they were less certain of the general texts, and indeed for Tooth and Child (the two texts that came from medical journals) there was no agreement. One rater said they were academic one said they might be academic, and one said they were definitely not academic. (See Clapham, 1996, for more about this.)

Everyone would probably agree that a research article is academic. Writers such as Fahnestock (1986) and Myers (1991) have described the differences between research articles and popularisations, and imply that popularisations are less academic.

Presumably the more academic an article is, the more closely it is related to one discipline, so it might follow that texts from academic journals would be more subject specific than popularisations. Since all but one of the texts from the two IELTS science modules came from either academic journals or popularisations, we can see whether this is the case here.

Contrary to expectations, with the exception of (PST)Ship, which has been shown to be 'too specific', *none* of the passages from academic journals were specific, whereas all the three popularisations *were*. This may seem surprising. However, although genre analysts such as Swales (1990) may show that research articles are highly specific to their field of study (see also Bazerman, 1988), academic articles as a whole take so many forms that it is difficult to generalise

Table 5. *Source and rhetorical function of the reading passages*

Specificity	Passage	Source	Rhetorical Function
S	Qual	Study Document	Description of organisation
S	Educ	Adaptation of a university paper	Enumeration of list of aims
S	High	Government report	Record and prediction of facts
G	Tooth	Academic Article	Introduction: reporting research
G	Child	Academic Article	Introduction: listing findings
HS	Genes	Popularisation	Description of processes
HS	Nitro	Popularisation	Description of process
S	Sun	Popularisation	Introduction: explanation
G	Fuel	Textbook for non-scientists	Description of facts
TS	Ship	Academic Article	Description of plans and narration of outcomes

Key: HS = Highly Specific
     S   = Specific
     G   = General
     TS = Too Specific

about them. Even in one discipline they may vary from general survey articles which are comprehensible to the lay reader, to ones which are so technical that even experts in the esoteric sub-discipline have difficulty understanding them. In addition, different sections of an article may vary in their specificity. Within one publication there are likely to be many kinds of discourse. The introduction, for example, may contain an easily accessible review of the literature, but this may be followed by a highly specialist description of an experiment or process. Authors such as Dudley-Evans and Henderson (1990) have described the different styles used in different parts of a single article. Although the two 'general' LMS passages came from learned journals they were both so general in approach that they presented no problems to a BSS reader. The first passage, Tooth, introduced the concept of fluoridation in water supplies, and reported on some studies on the effect of fluoridation on tooth decay. Very few technical terms were used, and those that were, were explained in the text. The second passage, Child, discussed tooth decay in children, and showed how this was related to social class. This passage was perhaps slightly more technical than the first in that it included some statistics, but there were no concepts or terms which would be unfamiliar to a social scientist. The section of an academic article from which a passage is selected will, therefore, itself have an effect on the suitability and easiness of the passage.

Unlike the two LMS texts which came from academic articles, the two that came from popularisations were not introductions or surveys. They were either wholly or partially descriptions of processes, and this may have partly accounted for their difficulty for non-LMS students. (LMS)Genes described methods of transferring genes to mice, and (LMS)Nitro described the process of nitrogen fixation. Both passages had unexplained technical vocabulary, and both demanded an understanding of biological concepts. To a biologist such concepts are elementary, but to a non-scientist they are obscure. Myers (1991) has shown how the lexical cohesion which makes scientific research articles so difficult to read for non-scientists, is replaced by more helpful, explanatory cohesive devices in popularisations, but in (LMS)Genes and (LMS)Nitro any such devices seemed inadequate for the layman. The texts were not contextualised for non-life-science readers (see Bachman, 1990), and therefore BSS and PST students had difficulty with them.

In Table 5, the fourth column shows the rhetorical function of each passage and this does appear to have some relationship with the specificity or non-specificity of the passages. The passages from academic journals came from general introductions. The two 'highly specific' texts came from popular rather than academic journals, *but* they were descriptions of processes. I have already shown that the fact that a passage is extracted from an academic article will not itself guarantee that the text is subject specific, and although it is unwise to generalise from such a small number of texts, it seems as if the rhetorical function of an extract may be more important than the source.

It seems likely that in the early days of IELTS the role of genre and rhetorical function were not well understood and that the test writers, therefore, concentrated simply on the content of their reading passages.

Conclusion

The research described here mainly related to the *assessment* of reading comprehension, and not all the findings necessarily transfer across to *teaching*. However, it is possible to draw some conclusions which relate to the EAP classroom:

1 It is difficult, if not impossible, to classify students according to their academic background knowledge since they acquire this knowledge not only from their recent academic work but from other sources including their leisure reading and earlier scholastic studies.
2 It is difficult to find texts which have suitably specific content in an intended subject area, and the suitability of such texts cannot always be known in advance.
3 If specific texts are to be used, not only their topic but also their genre should be checked with specialists in the field. It may indeed be that genre is more important than the topic.
4 There seems to be no agreement about what an 'academic' text consists of. Until this is clearer, texts may have to be considered academic only if they come from academic sources.
5 The rhetorical function of a reading passage may have an effect on the specificity of a text. In my study, texts describing scientific processes were more specific than introductions to academic articles.

From the above findings it is clear that selecting comprehension passages for EAP students is very difficult: texts vary widely in their specificity, and students vary widely in their background knowledge. It may be impossible in EAP classes, therefore, to be certain of giving students appropriate texts which will enable them to bring their background knowledge to bear. Even if the teacher's aim is simply to give students practice in reading texts similar to those they will read in their studies, it cannot always be known in advance which texts will be appropriate for which students.

Since it is rare for all students in a language class to be in the same sub-discipline, and since even when they are they will have different backgrounds and aims, it seems sensible for EAP teachers to teach what Dudley-Evans and St John (1998) call 'common core' EAP. Since it also seems to be the case that genre and rhetorical function have as important an effect as topic on comprehensibility, students should read and listen to a range of EGAP academic texts, with teachers ensuring that these texts include the different rhetorical functions such as introductions, reports of research methods and discussions of results which are common across most disciplines. However, there may be certain rhetorical functions, such as descriptions of processes, which require knowledge of underlying concepts. If, during their language courses, students are to read texts containing such functions, they will have to tackle some ESAP texts. Dudley-Evans and St John (1998) suggest that in these cases students should, where possible, provide their own materials – such as tapes of recent lectures or examples of their own writings – since these have more immediacy than published texts. If teachers do use such ESAP texts, though, they must make sure that before their students read or listen to them, they (the students) are familiar with the underlying concepts – that is, that they have the appropriate background knowledge.

7 World Englishes: Issues in and from academic writing assessment

Liz Hamp-Lyons and Bonnie Wenxia Zhang

Introduction

The purpose of this paper is to study the implication of the World Englishes issue in academic writing assessment through a small scaled investigation of how raters' judgements of Chinese EFL student writers' examination essays interact with their perceptions of the culture-specific or nativised rhetorical patterns. The behaviour of examination essay judges in responding to the rhetorical patterns found in exam essays written by tertiary-level EFL students shows us how these essay judges' perceptions of rhetorical patterns and characteristics interact with their perceptions of the culture-specific or nativised discourse features; it also raises questions about whether some rhetorical patterns should be privileged over others in written English discourse. Given the small sample and qualitative nature of the study, the differences between the two rater groups would not be reliable for any attempt in making general assumptions. This study thus can be taken as one case for consideration in the area of language 'norms' and the status of 'World Englishes' especially in assessment contexts.

World Englishes: concepts and developments

The term 'World Englishes' is used to refer to a belief in the existence of, and respect for, multiple, varied models of English across cultures (Kachru, 1982, 1995b). Brown (1993: 59) summarises three major elements that characterise the World Englishes paradigm as follows:

a belief that there is a 'repertoire of models for English'
a belief that 'the localised innovations (in English) have pragmatic bases'
a belief that 'the English language now belongs to all those who use it'

According to Kachru (1982), English is spoken (used) mainly by three types or 'circles' of people: the inner circle, e.g. Britain, the United States, where English is the first language; the outer circle, e.g. Singapore, Hong Kong, where English, though not the first language of their people, is an official language of the country/region; and the expanding circle, e.g. Japan, China, where English is becoming more and more widely used. English is now used by more non-native speakers than native speakers (Kachru, 1995b; Brown, 1993; Norton, 1998; Scollon, 1997). The development of research on nativised models of English has not only addressed important issues concerning the spread of English, but also put forward very serious questions to language test developers, especially: what model(s) of English should be valued and what standard should be used in high stakes examinations? Lowenberg (1993: 95) challenges the assumption that he believes has long existed in language testing 'that the criteria for measuring proficiency in English around the world should be candidates' use of particular features of English which are used and accepted as norms by highly educated native speakers of English'. He suggests that:

In order to assess this proficiency accurately, examiners must be able to distinguish deficiencies in the acquisition of English by these speakers (errors) from varietal differences in the students' usage resulting from their having previously learned such nativised features.

*(ibid.:*101)

and his analysis shows that, at least in the case of the TOEIC (Test of English for International Communication, one of ETS's standardised tests, used commonly in Asia), assumptions about a privileged 'standard' form of English raise questions of validity for some items.

Davidson (1994) and Spolsky (1993) also argue that the sole use of the multiple-choice test format in TOEFL (Test of English as a Foreign Language, ETS's largest and best-known English test, used by universities in the United States to accept candidates from non-native, English speaking countries) has suppressed the richness of human language and suggest that test **users** should become a major force in test development. Davidson (*ibid.*: 382) cautions us that 'in the heyday of progressive education, as now, in the fervour of learner-centred language learning, we seem to have ignored the potential for individualising testing as well as teaching'.

Rater characteristics in writing assessment

The term 'rater characteristics' refers to the variables or patterns observable in the behaviour of raters, that is, people who mark or score performance tests. (For example, some raters may be harsher or more lenient than other raters when they are assessing the same essay. A consistent, relative severity or leniency can become one rater characteristic.)

The reason why variable characteristics of raters in making judgements is of concern with performance testing is that these characteristics are possible sources of measurement 'error' (Bachman *et al.*, 1995). When judges vary in critical judgements on high stakes performance tests such as IELTS (Internal English Language Testing System, a gate-keeper test used by universities in Britain and Australia to accept candidates from a non-native, English-speaking country), for example if one judge gives a '5' for IELTS writing, and another gives '6', and if '6' is the acceptable passing score for most English-medium universities, the consequence of this variation may be destructive to the real person, the test candidate.

An investigation of rater characteristics can reveal what is really going on in a rater's mind (Vaughan, 1991; Lumley, in progress), and can also provide tentative explanations of how these variations in characteristics might be linked to some very complicated social, political and ethical issues for World Englishes.

The study

Research question

The present study is part of a large-scale investigation of the relationship between the rhetorical patterns found in Chinese EFL student writers' examination essays in English and the influence of these patterns on rater response. The major research question was as follows:

• How do English native speaker raters perceive observable rhetorical patterns in Chinese students' examination essays in English?

In this study 'patterns' mean features that recur predictably and 'rhetorical patterns' refer to the choice or management of any textual features that have a communicative effect on a reader/rater.

Method

Data came from a comprehensive investigation of the rhetorical patterns found in Chinese EFL student writers' examination essays in English and the responses of raters to these patterns. The essays were collected under an examination setting. Students were given 45 minutes to write an essay on the topic 'Do you think it is fair to pay tuition fees for higher education?' and were instructed to support their arguments with their own ideas and experiences. Six native speaker, trained raters (university teachers of English in Hong Kong, hereafter NS raters) and six non-native speaker raters (Chinese university teachers of English from mainland China, hereafter CS raters) were asked to score the selected essays according to the scoring guide provided to them. Both groups of raters were also trained to talk aloud into a tape-recorder, giving their perceptions of the use of rhetorical patterns in these essays. Such 'think-aloud protocol' methodology has been widely used, and is considered a valid way to investigate cognitive processes (Smagorinsky, 1989; Cohen, 1996). These protocols were transcribed and analysed. All raters responded to thirty essay scripts, but in this chapter we report only their interactions with rhetorical features in two scripts, where their judgements and perceptions, as revealed in what they say, raise particularly interesting questions for issues of rhetorical 'standards' for English, and therefore, for World Englishes.

Results

Raters' perceptions of the use of paragraphs in script A (see Appendix A)

Table 1 shows the scores given by the two groups of raters to script A on its overall communicative quality, overall organisation and paragraphing on a four-point scale (where 4 is high). From the scores given by the two kinds of raters, there does not seem to be any sharp difference between the two groups, though the scores given by native speaker raters are slightly higher than those of the non-native speakers. However, an examination of the native-speaker raters' protocols for their reactions to the rhetorical patterns in student script A (see Appendix A) provides much more interesting insights, suggesting that what affected them most is 'paragraphing', i.e., 'the use or choice of paragraphs', which was one of the assessment categories raters were asked to make judgements and comment on.

The following are some extracts from native speaker raters' protocols on script A:

Extract 1 (NS Rater 1)

. . . there's a nice build up . . . a kind of intelligent sophistication of language and it's nice that he intersperses it with a little short statement like 'From this point, it's unfair.' . . . there are two sophisticated paragraphs and

Table 1. *Scores given by two rater groups to script A*

Raters	Overall Communicative Quality	Overall Organisation	Paragraphing
Native Speaker			
NS1	3	4	4
NS2	3	4	2
NS3	3	3	2
NS4	2	3	1
NS5	2	3	1
NS6	2	1	1
Non-Native Speaker			
CS1	3	3	1
CS2	3	3	3
CS3	3	3	3
CS4	2	2	1
CS5	2	2	2
CS6	2	1	1
1			

1 = Poor   2 = Adequate   3 = Fairly good   4 = Good

then the shorter ones around them are also sophisticated in style because it's pleasing to the reader to have that kind of variety if it is well used and it is well used. . . . I like the paragraphing and the opening paragraph works and the final one.

Extract 2 (NS Rater 2)

. . . I don't like the paragraphing. It's adequate. I don't mind the short one in the middle. Well, not really a paragraph, it is a sentence. I don't really like the way that he just put the sentences . . . and break them up like this. It hinders fluency . . . The beginning is good but of course too short.

Extract 3 (NS Rater 3)

The paragraphing is a little bit odd but in a sense you can see why the person has done the things they have. . . . I don't really see any particular reason for making 'From this point, it's unfair', 'This question should be set in two aspects' separate paragraphs. I think it is okay. . . . the beginning perhaps could be joining the second one in my opinion in order to make it more substantial.

Extract 4 (NS Rater 4)

When we come to paragraphing, I have to say, poor. The first paragraph has only two sentences. . . . if you put one line separately with the gaps on either side, it's a paragraph. So, she doesn't have a concept of paragraphing. And on line 19, 'From this point, it's unfair.' That's one paragraph on its own! . . . So she has no concept of paragraphing at all. . . . I have to say the beginning or opening paragraph is poor because it's too short.

Extract 5 (NS Rater 5)

Paragraphing, well, this kind of splitting up, a little bit unusual. I mean, he splits the first three sentences into paragraphs and then he has a large paragraph about one of his ideas that if the fees are too high, the students cannot afford them. And then, he seems to be making statements and trying to make them stand out more by organising his text into sort of statement sentences, for example 'From this point of view, it's unfair.' . . . So, I'd say, actually, his paragraphing is pretty poor.

Extract 6 (NS Rater 6)

My first impression is that it has been rather badly structured. It's split up into many attempted paragraphs. Full of divisions, mostly artificial divisions, not really appropriate for an essay format. It begins with a re-statement of the essay question, and then it just splits up a division and then 'This question should be considered in two aspects', a statement separated from any other context in another unacceptable fashion and followed up by another sentence. . . . And then, a kind of dangling summary or judgement, 'From this point of view, it's unfair.', . . . unclear and very confusing division. . . . extremely poor paragraphing.

A look at how the non-native speaker raters (CS raters) react to the paragraphing of this script, however, reveals a quite different picture. Two of them did not mention the paragraphing at all and judged the script as 'fairly good' on paragraphing. The other four found the ideas clear to them, but in their view the way the essay was structured did not conform to English rhetorical convention in terms of paragraph use. The following are some extracts from the Chinese raters' protocols:

Extract 7 (CS Rater 1)

Obviously, the student has problems in paragraphing. It is unnecessary to put one sentence into one paragraph. The information is well sequenced, but the paragraphing does not conform to what is required in English writing.

Extract 8 (CS Rater 4)

There are too many paragraphs, which may be influenced by his Chinese writing habits.

Extract 9 (CS Rater 6)

This student has a very good command of register, but the paragraphing is not appropriate.

Thus it can be seen that all the NS raters and most of the CS raters commented particularly on the paragraphing of this script, but NS raters paid more attention to it than did CS raters, that is, paragraph structuring as a rhetorical pattern was more salient to NS raters than to CS raters.

Raters' perceptions of 'rhetorically expressed ideology' in script B (See Appendix B)

Script B is interesting because it is the only script on which CS raters gave higher scores than NS raters. We examined the protocols to discover whether, and what kind of, rhetorical patterns caused CS raters to give higher scores than NS raters on this particular script.

In the protocols, the NS rater group all mentioned that this script was of a standard essay format: a beginning paragraph, some ideas or arguments in the middle and a concluding paragraph. They did not seem to detect any serious problems with the overall organisation and paragraphing, though NS raters 4 and 6 had given low scores to this script on these two categories. However, they did state in their protocols that they had problems, to different degrees, in comprehending the text, or that the ideas the student intended in the text were not clear, or rather, not acceptable to them.

When they were commenting on the use of rhetorical patterns in this script, NS raters 1 and 6 claimed that they could 'feel propaganda', which, according to them, might have caused their negative reaction to the text. NS rater 1 actually mentioned the word 'propaganda' five times during her on-line perception of the script. Additionally, NS rater 5 mentioned that she could feel the student's strong patriotic attitude in this script, which had affected adversely her judgement and perception of the objectivity and persuasiveness of the text because she did not agree with the argument the student writer made:

Extract 10 (NS Rater 5)

. . . she is less objective than the other two. She seems to have this 'We must think of it as rebuilding our country'. It's very patriotic, a kind of attitude. So I'd say 'poor'.

Throughout their protocols most NS raters experienced a kind of struggling with the use of the language in this script, or to be more exact, the student's choice of words and sentence structures in building her argument or expressing her ideas, which made raters either fail to understand/comprehend the argument, or unwilling to accept it if they otherwise understood it, because of the points or attitudes intended by the student in so expressing.

In contrast, all but one CS rater commented that this was a very well written script in terms of language use, overall organisation and paragraphing, focus and clarity of ideas, discourse markers, overall cohesion, register and objectivity. The only CS rater who down-graded this script is CS rater 4. He commented that this piece of writing was strongly influenced by the student's L1 (Chinese) and such students were the most difficult group to be trained to follow the English rhetorical conventions.

The study of the raters' protocols suggests that the major problem NS raters identified in understanding the intended meaning of the arguments in this script lay in whether they would accept the ideas in which the student's own ideology might be well embedded. While CS raters could understand and appreciate the student's clear presentation of her standpoint and arguments, NS raters reported themselves unable to comprehend fully the content of the text, which, as one of the CS raters suggested, was strongly influenced by the student's L1 (Chinese) transfer, or would not accept the way the student developed her arguments.

Discussion

These are only two of the thirty scripts that the raters judged and reported on; nor are these the only differences between the two rater groups. Interesting differences emerged in terms of such rhetorical patterns/expectations as appropriate content and amount of content in beginning paragraphs; the rhetorical purpose of concluding paragraphs; use of discourse markers; and others. But even this small amount of data, against the backdrop of the larger study, suffices to exemplify the issues to be considered about the role of assessment in furthering 'norms' or 'standards' of English; and in fronting some of the problems of a world Englishes perspective.

Attitudes towards rhetorical diversity: the level of structure

In Chinese rhetoric, short paragraphs can be used for emphasis or as a transitional paragraph which functions as the summary of the previous paragraph and the leading or sign post of the next one. This kind of paragraphing, i.e., one short paragraph followed by a relatively longer paragraph, is actually encouraged in Chinese rhetoric: for instance, Wang and Wu (1990) in their textbook entitled *Composition (Chinese)* instruct students to arrange paragraphs in this way. They state: 'When arranging and organising a text, ensure that its paragraphing is a kind of ups and downs just like wave upon wave' (*ibid*: 80). It is not surprising that in the raters' protocols, native-speaker raters react more negatively than Chinese raters towards this use of short or one sentence paragraphs in an academic, or rather, argumentative essay in English. This feature seems unusual and rhetorically deviant to the native speaker raters, probably because of their unfamiliarity with this nativised 'rhetorical' or 'culture-specific' textual feature. Their attitudes towards this rhetorical 'diversity' are well reflected in their protocols and the scores they have given.

Attitudes towards rhetorical diversity: the level of ideology

The sharp differences between NS and CS raters in judging and perceiving script B have raised very important issues for contrastive rhetoric and the teaching and assessing of EFL writing. As was observed earlier, a text analysis of this script showed a clear linear pattern which conformed to English expository rhetorical convention. The major cause for the difference lay in the textual manifestation of the student's ideology, which could be perfectly understood and appreciated by CS raters but made no sense to, or would not be accepted by, the NS raters. A close examination of the script indicates that the student showed her social-political stance, which seemed very strong, to support her attitude towards paying fees for higher education. As a first year student who has just stepped into a tertiary institution, this student writer might indeed feel patriotic, as one of the NS raters guessed. It is possible, therefore, that in writing this essay in response to the question of whether it is fair to pay tuition fees for higher education, she might try to apply the social-contextual, cultural norms of the values which she had most probably acquired during her years of formal schooling in China. This clear and strong manifestation of the student writer's ideology or socio-political stance in the essay could be seen in the protocols to have a great effect on raters, positively on CS raters and negatively on NS raters. The student's ideology or values conveyed by the essay seemed to have triggered some level of resistance in NS raters, which was not the case for CS raters. This strongly suggests that raters' cultural background and the values associated with it may play a very important role in their judgement of EFL writing quality. As one of the NS raters honestly explained after marking script B:

A Chinese teacher may have read that and felt that 'Yes', you know, 'That's right. We have to do this for this country. We should sacrifice some other things and try to pay our fees', because they are from their cultural background. They are understanding where the students are coming from, they are understanding their situation and their students because a Chinese teacher may have been in exactly the same situation, whereas from my cultural background, I have a lot of ideas about China, which may or may not be true, but they are still my ideas and my opinions and as an outsider, I'll say 'well you can't make these people pay, what about poor people in the provinces where they can't afford to?' I mean I would have my own opinions based on my own cultural background. So, of course, I'm looking at this argument and say 'well she has put an argument forward well but it's not persuasive and I don't agree with it.' So that would have an effect on how I rate the section and how I rate the persuasiveness. I felt it was 'adequate', but actually I thought someone from that background or a Chinese teacher might put 'good'.

Implications

Contrastive rhetoric

The contrastive rhetoric hypothesis in its original sense refers to the existence of different writing conventions across cultures (Kaplan, 1966, 1987; Connor, 1987, 1996). For example, according to this hypothesis, Chinese EFL students tend to use an 'indirect' rhetorical pattern in their English writing while English native speakers prefer a 'linear' and direct rhetorical pattern. This hypothesis has been challenged by Mohan and Lo (1985) and Scollon (1997) for its over-simplified generalisation of the rhetorical patterns, and it has been further challenged by the finding from the current study that NS raters could not understand the script – not because of its paragraph pattern but because of an ideology that they would not accept. A great deal of research has been conducted to test Kaplan's original hypothesis and the various later adaptations to it, most of which has focused on describing and comparing the writing conventions of different languages mainly through linguistic or textual analysis. This study has suggested that a focus on grammatical accuracy and conformity to English rhetorical conventions is simplistic: social/ contextual and cross-cultural variables can strongly and saliently influence responses to an EFL/ESL student writer's examination essay in English. An awareness of this will have implications for contrastive rhetoric, in that such perspectives or insights need to be included in order to understand better the dynamic role of contrastive rhetoric in cross-cultural written communication.

Writing assessment

This study also has implications for assessing EFL written texts in terms of designing prompts, giving instructions and training raters. For example, it is often found in the instructions given to test candidates that in addressing an essay question candidates are required to express their own opinions and to support their arguments with evidence from their own experiences. There might be a risk, however, if candidates do follow these instructions. If test candidates do express their ideas, which very often might be a reflection of their mind-sets or cultural ideology that are different from NS raters' expectations, their writing might be judged negatively because of the effect of the ideology they express. This issue may not arise as long as writing tests are scored by Chinese teachers of EFL writing, because they come from the same cultural background and may share the same ideology with their students. But when these same students take internationally-administered tests such as TOEFL (with the new computer-based writing component) or IELTS and their work is scored by NS raters, shared assumptions are not warranted.

At a time when more and more researchers are calling for fair evaluation of EFL/ESL student writing in terms of designing and assigning written tasks (Kroll and Reid, 1994; Reid and Kroll, 1995) and considering ethical issues in preparing EFL students for international high-stakes tests (Hamp-Lyons, 1998), we need to be very cautious when assessing EFL student writers' use of different rhetorical patterns, which may be a manifestation of their cultural background or ideology and not in any sense a cognitive or educational deficiency (Leki, 1991a; Connor, 1996; Silva, 1997, 1998). But since IELTS and TOEFL are used as gate-keepers for universities in Western countries and are tests for predicting whether the candidates will succeed in the English speaking countries, a mono-cultural setting, we must ask the complex question of whether readers would be justified in responding negatively to culturally-different ideology in essays. Further, if research confirms that this variable, whether legitimately or not, is affecting raters' scores, should the candidates be instructed to avoid showing their ideological stances? At this stage we are only able to problematise this issue and not resolve it. There is clearly much more to be done in investigating and understanding the role of social and ideological variables that have affected both EFL and ESL student writers in their use of rhetorical patterns, and raters in their responding to and assessing student writings.

World Englishes

Findings from the present study have suggested that when rhetorical patterns related to the writer's cultural and ideological background emerge in their examination essays in English, these patterns can impact raters' judgements differentially depending on the rater's own cultural and linguistic background. If the writing expresses a cultural norm or social ideology that is under-comprehended or resisted by a rater from a different cultural background with a different ideology, i.e., if there is a clash between a writer's ideology and that of a rater, as happened with script B, is there anything that rater training can do to ensure fair and consistent ratings of such scripts?

This question so far remains unanswered. Although the script reveals its ideological position more obviously than others in the data set, if the fact that this script, voicing as it did the student writer's ideology, was so homogeneously and negatively assessed by NS raters, it is likely that other such cases might elicit similar reactions. While some researchers have claimed that 'it should be clear that English is less likely to be a major cognitive, social, or cultural influence in the life of a person who has learned it as an adult than in the life of a person who has spoken the language since infancy' (Scollon, 1997: 355), this is questionable in the case of English in China. In reality, English proficiency is in some ways of greater consequence to Chinese EFL learners/users than proficiency in their L1 (Chinese). In China at present, English tests are everywhere. There are international testing systems such as TOEFL, IELTS and BEC (Business Certificate Tests), as well as English tests developed in China and used nationwide, such as CEE (College Entrance Examination, taken by 3.2 million secondary school graduates [Wu, 1998]) and CET (College English Tests, taken by about 2 million tertiary students each year). The results of English tests are used for different purposes such as college entrance and programme selection; screening students for more advanced studies; applying for funding for going abroad; getting promotion, etc. The more important the results of a test candidate's performance in English, the more careful test designers, administrators and raters, who are already in a much more advantageous position in this special power relationship, need to be in every stage of assessment so that what is valued in EFL/ESL writing assessment makes sense for EFL/ESL writers (Hamp-Lyons, 1991a, 1996). However, this study has raised worrying questions about how to deal with the issue of the difference between a writer's and a rater's ideology in writing assessment.

How, then, should the use of non-standard forms, whether grammatical, lexical, structural or ideological, be judged in writing assessment? People who take World Englishes' political positions may argue that in a society where variety and diversity are respected and emphasised, an open mind towards new things, especially when they come from a different culture, would certainly help in understanding people from that culture and thus enhance inter-cultural communication. But, to what extent is it possible to tolerate cultural 'variety' or 'diversity' in an international examination context? If nativised models of English such as Indian, Singaporean or Black English are to be respected and accepted as many of the 'language rights' proponents have insisted, can there still be a place for a standardised worldwide international test? If there is no shared, commonly accepted model and every culture is allowed to use its own nativised form of English, leading to increasingly diverse and varied forms of Englishes, will inter-cultural or inter-dialectal communication remain possible? Language testing researchers typically argue that any high stakes, internationally-used English test, such as TOEFL or IELTS, should possess validated test standards based on a well-defined model of language proficiency. Without these things, it becomes difficult to see how the use of any English test across cultures would be possible. This is a very important issue for researchers in World Englishes and also a very practical issue for policy-makers.

Conclusion

The findings concerning NS raters' attitudes towards the use of culture-specific (Chinese rhetorical) paragraphing in script A and the student writer's ideology reflected in script B have raised important issues for contrastive rhetoric, for writing assessment and for World Englishes.

First, what to assess? If there is a possibility that a candidate's written text that voices an ideology is adversely assessed because of factors beyond the textual features themselves, as shown in script B, the components of a writing test including task topics, task specifications, prompt instructions to students, categories of rating scales, etc. may need to be redefined.

Second, how to assess? The scoring procedure and the weighting of assessment categories need to make sense to EFL writers as well as be acceptable and operational in rater training. At a time when in the writing classroom, students are allowed, even encouraged, to choose the topic and theme to write on so that potential ethnic and other biases can be avoided (Silva, 1997, 1998), the question is whether to provide test candidates with a choice of topics to write on, as is done in some high stakes tests: For example in the FCE (First Certificate English) writing component, candidates are provided with a list of topics to choose from.

Third, who should carry out the assessment? If native speaker raters and raters from the writers' own culture use different sets of linguistic, cultural and ideological values to guide their judgements, whose judgements are 'right'? This controversial question is far from being resolved.

Fourth, what decisions should EFL/ESL writers and their teachers make on the use of specific rhetorical patterns in academic writing assessment contexts? At a time when individualism is gaining more attention, when an increasing number of researchers in language testing are expressing concerns about the impact of test results on the real life of test candidates and when proponents of World Englishes consistently claim that 'English belongs to people who speak it' (Norton, 1998), a practical issue that emerges from this study is: should EFL/ESL writers adopt different rhetorical patterns in different academic assessment contexts? If the scoring will have to be conducted by NS raters only, as is the case in some international high-stakes tests like TOEFL and IELTS, EFL/ESL writers will have to give up their nativised rhetorical patterns in order to avoid the potential of being disadvantaged in an international assessment context. If the scoring is conducted by raters from the same culture in an intra-national or local assessment context, EFL/ESL writers might choose those nativised or context-relevant rhetorical features that will be accepted or appreciated by the local raters or teachers. EFL/ESL teachers will also have to decide whether and/or how to inform their students of different rhetorical patterns in different contexts, which may be problematic, for teachers too come from a certain culture and may hold different perceptions of what are the appropriate rhetorical patterns in different contexts.

In this study we have discussed only two facets of one aspect of a writing assessment, and yet we have raised important issues for World Englishes and writing assessment. The many issues to be understood in this area are not of theoretical interest only; they may significantly affect the lives of many young people every year.

Appendix A: Script A

Is it fair to pay for study?

Nowadays, a lot of higher education students pay fees for their studies. Is it fair?

This question should be considered in two aspects.

First, to pay for studies, obviously, will limit the higher education to only those who are able to pay for it, not those who are intelligent and capable.

The fees for studies may be very high, including fees on books, lectures, talks, classes and money on other educational facilities and materials. If a student hasn't so much money, how could he pay for the fees? If a student can't pay for the fees, that means he will never receive the higher education no matter how he is anxious for and capable. So this system of fees will undoubtedly lower the educational qualities by keeping capable students without money out of the door – maybe they are more fit to work and devote than some of those who have the money but without capability. This abandon the object of education.

From this point, it's unfair.

On the other hand, we should also realise the real status of education system. Since our country hasn't developed very well, she is not able to give so much money to support all the students to study without paying anything. Many other fields such as industry, trades, science field and military field need financial backing too. So to call on all the people to support education career is necessary. In other words, every student pay some money for studies is not too much. Only how much should he pay should be considered. From this point, it is fair.

To solve this problem, we should lessen the fees properly. What do you think?

Appendix B: Script B

A lot of higher education students pay fees for their studies. Someone considers it unfair. But I think that's fair.

The problem we are to discuss is an important part of our country's education reform. First of all, our country is still a developing country. We cannot afford the whole fares of higher education for all the college students. At the present time, a lot of higher education students have to pay fees for their studies mainly because of the existing state of affairs in China. But we should point out paying fees for their studies means assuming part of the load of national education. With the developing of our country, we have enough reasons to be sure that we'll receive higher education freely in the future.

Secondly, making students pay fees for their studies may help to create a more reasonable and profitable system in Campus. That will include a more competitive atmosphere, a more suitable environment and so on. For example, these measures can make every student who has paid money for his study have a sense of urgency and duty. They will know they must assume the responsibility, or more directly speaking they will study and work hard. Thus we can get the competition in campus to be more intensive. This helps to cultivate and choose qualified personnel.

On another hand, these measures seem to be good for students, if we consider them from a long-term point of view. We can receive education in universities, but more important to us I think is character-training. Sense of duty, Going all out for our society, Unselfishness, these virtues are important to us all through our whole life. Having paid our own fees, we can think of these problems such as 'How to develop ourselves' now and then. We can create a definite destination of life and learn to fight to get it.

To sum up, the measure is fair in my opinion. Just try your best to develop yourself in universities, wish you great success!

8 Addressing issues of power and difference in ESL academic writing

Suresh Canagarajah

To become literate in a globally powerful language that is also prestigious in academic communication, language-minority students have to negotiate a place for their local discourse conventions, intellectual traditions, cultural practices and the vernacular. Second language composition teachers are not unaware of the conflicts of power inequalities and cultural difference involved in language acquisition. However, they do not have at their disposal the methods and approaches which would enable them to teach writing with a sensitivity to such concerns. Although recent philosophical and intellectual movements (such as critical theory and post-structuralism) have seeped into all academic or educational domains today, such awareness has not always translated itself pedagogically. There is therefore a gap in the present state of second language (L2) composition scholarship.

If the available approaches to L2 writing ignore issues of power and difference or, even, lead to the political and cultural domination of language-minority students, it may become imperative to construct new approaches consonant with our emerging recognitions. In order to venture into this challenging and exploratory enterprise, this paper will first analyse the philosophical and ideological foundations of the existing approaches from the perspective of L2 students. I will go on to narrate a case study of a student's research writing to illustrate the ways in which issues of power and difference may be negotiated in L2 writing.

Revisiting L2 writing pedagogy

It is convenient to use for our purposes the classification of composition teaching approaches offered by Raimes (1991) in her state of the art paper. She divides the schools into four: those that focus on form, on the writer, on content and on the reader. The *form-focused* approach is generally known as product oriented, conceiving writing as the mastery of correct grammatical and rhetorical structures on the text. Typically, sentence-combining exercises and imitation of model essays are prescribed in the classroom. Although this approach is considered old-fashioned in sentiment, many teachers still use this widely, motivated partly by strictly timed and controlled assessment procedures. The *writer-focused* approach, better known as cognitive process approach, attends to the skilled mental strategies that go into generating the finished text. Exercises for generating and organising thought, for revision and audience orientation are typical classroom practices. This pedagogical approach informs nearly all the composition textbooks today and has passed into professional common sense. *Content-focused* approach ties academic writing to the knowledge base which informs the texts of the respective disciplines. Teaching is linked to the specific courses followed by the students, providing access to the related cognitive skills, linguistic structures and information content characterising each discipline. This approach (and the next) constitute the cutting edge of academic writing programmes today, partly because administrators feel that tying writing to the specific content areas is more purpose oriented in terms of their institutional goals. *Reader-focused* approach, according to Raimes, perceives writing as influenced by the values, expectations and conventions of the discourse communities addressed by the students in each discipline, following pedagogical practices as in the preceding approach. (There is, however, more to the notion of 'discourse communities' than being simply reader-conscious, as we will see below.)

A critique

The simplest observation to begin with is that the four approaches outlined by Raimes do not originate in L2 writing research or instruction. They have been the dominant paradigms in L1 composition scholarship before being imported to the second language context. Although subsequent research in L2 typically endorses the relevance of these approaches to this context, such research activity smacks of influences from the bandwagon. The form-focused approach derives its roots from the 'current-traditional paradigm' (see Hairston, 1982) that was dominant in the mid sixties and attended to the textual structures in the finished product of writing. The paradigm is so named because it is a revitalisation (in L1 circles) of the classifications and structuration of rhetoric offered by classical Greco-Roman philosophers. The writer-focused approach stems from cognitive process theory in L1 which attended to the thought processes and cognitive strategies employed by writers, shifting attention from the written product. The origins of the latter two approaches, however, may appear less clear. Although Raimes attributes the development of the content-focused approach to Bernie Mohan and his associates in the L2 context, this too has prior development in L1 circles as a version of the process paradigm. The basis of the content approach on a 'common cognitive/academic component manifested in discourse across cultures' (Mohan and Lo, 1985: 516) and its pedagogy of helping students with 'the language of the thinking processes and the structure or shape of content' (Mohan, 1986: 18) make clear its cognitivist orientation (even though it also borrows somewhat from developments in English for Academic Purposes – EAP – and Writing across the Curriculum – WAC). The difference is that while process scholars like Raimes (1985, 1987) and Zamel (1982, 1983) focus on thinking strategies, Mohan and his associates focus on thought content in their characterisation of the processes accompanying writing. However, the notion of writing as a way of knowing had already developed an emphasis on content within the L1 process paradigm in the early seventies. On the other hand, while Raimes associates the reader-focused approach with the EAP movement and the process versus product debate in L2 from the mid eighties, this approach too has been anticipated by the WAC school in L1 context from the seventies (see Emig, 1977; Beach and Bridwell, 1984; Fulwiler, 1982). (Not much purpose is served, however, by considering the content-focused and reader-focused approaches separately, as Raimes does, since they have common influences from ESP, EAP and WAC, and are usually treated as related movements – see Shih, 1986: 635–640; Spack, 1988: 34–36.)

The moorings of L2 writing approaches in L1 scholarship should be emphasised for many significant reasons. Firstly, these approaches do not constitute the local knowledge (i.e., day-to-day classroom insights and first hand observations) on writing of teachers and students in the L2 context. Hence these pedagogies do not – and cannot – grapple with the complexities of writing for specifically L2 students. Perhaps the underlying assumption here is that the acquisition of L2 writing follows the same processes involved for L1 writing. This was in fact the dominant assumption (popularly known as the L1=L2 hypothesis) in language acquisition in the past. However, this has been challenged by the realisation that there are many social, cultural, cognitive, and affective variables that mediate L2 acquisition. Hence it is important to focus on L2 writing acquisition in its own right and develop approaches unique to L2 if we are to construct an effective pedagogy for such students.

We must also critique the ideologies that inform the current approaches. Since composition scholars have not performed this ideology critique, we have to borrow for our purposes constructs formulated by Henry Giroux (1983: 205–231) to analyse literacy models. The preceding discussion on the underlying assumptions and preferred practices of L2 writing approaches enable us to identify the ideologies clearly. The form-focused approach is informed by what Giroux labels *instrumental ideology* which is associated with the 'culture of positivism', technocratic social orientation, and behaviourist pedagogical practices. This approach treats writing as a mechanical 'skill' for expressing pre-defined, value-free knowledge through abstract structures of language by passive subjects. By considering issues of power and difference irrelevant to the writing activity, it could influence writers to serve predetermined political ends and economic institutions, and confirms the status quo. Writer-focused approach, in considering writing as a goal-oriented, cognitive activity of negotiating knowledge through language, preserves the agency of the writer. It thus displays *interaction ideology*, which envisions meaning to be produced out of an interaction of the subject with the structures around him/her. However, in considering cognitive processes and strategies to be universal and differing only according to each individual's personality development and cognitive maturity, it simplifies (by personalising) power inequality and cultural difference. Acting on the objective of developing universal cognitive strategies, the approach poses the possibility of inducting ESL students into the 'accepted' thought patterns and discourse of dominant social groups. Content-focused and reader-focused approaches are sensitive to the different ways in which knowledge is defined in different disciplinary communities and the different conventions used to talk about this knowledge. On the basis of inculcating communicative competence to talk to the chosen academic community, however, these approaches can influence ESL students according to the values behind these communities. This happens because the rules of use and forms of knowledge are not problematised adequately to realise their ideological nature. That is, though these approaches perceive difference, they do not relate it to power. Hence content- and reader-focused approaches display certain deterministic brands of *reproductive ideology* which, at best, consider an induction into the values, culture and knowledge forms of the respective disciplines as a necessary evil in order to communicate successfully with their members.

While there are differences between the approaches delineated above, there are also certain similarities in their basic assumptions.

These approaches assume that ESL students are total strangers to academic discourses;[1] that writing is a process of moving in a linear manner from one discourse or language to the other; and that texts are constituted wholly by one discourse or the other. The challenges students face are narrowly schematised into L1 vs. L2, native discourse vs. Anglo-American discourse, vernacular community vs. academic community or native culture vs. Western culture. But we have to remember that the discourses of post-colonial subjects are multiple, hybrid and overlapping. The global spread of English has already served to acquaint many communities with its discourse features. This means that second language students have to choose from among a range of discourses as they construct academic texts in English. The challenging question we need to explore is: how do students negotiate these conflicting and overlapping discourses to create coherence in their academic texts? We need to consider how ESL students may negotiate the discursive conflicts on their own terms, generating creative textual alternatives to write with integrity and relevance.

Strategies of negotiating discourses

I wish to narrate the strategies displayed by a graduate student – whom I call Viji – as she wrote a research paper for a professional degree in ELT in a university in Sri Lanka. This case study situates the writing process more firmly in the social context, unlike the approaches discussed above. In the tradition of thick description, I fully ground the writing activity in the backgrounds and motivations of the student. The experience of this student is interpreted in the light of the strategies displayed by six other students in the course.

Having followed course work on subjects ranging from descriptive linguistics to sociolinguistics and educational psychology, the students were to submit a research report on a subject of their own choosing relevant to ELT pedagogical concerns. Although they had a full year to research and write their project, in reality they focused on this component only in the final two months after they had completed the tests for their course work. Since they had already gained some experience producing a final year research essay in their undergraduate studies, they chose to consult the faculty according to their own need. The students following this course had served for some time as teachers of English, although their primary field of undergraduate study was not necessarily English or Applied Linguistics. Graduates

[1] See Swales, 1990.

who had followed courses in the English medium (in any disciplinary specialty) are recruited as English teachers in Sri Lanka in order to fill the shortage of ELT professionals in the country.

Viji's salient subject position was her association with a Pentecostal Christian church. She made no secret of her religious associations and often shared her faith with staff and students – to the extent of becoming comical sometimes. But she was the most closely integrated into the ELT academic community, having read English language and literature for her BA. She had been a teacher of English in tertiary level institutions throughout her career. She was less academically oriented than some of the other students, but more pedagogically grounded. She was a seasoned practitioner who was sensitive to the needs of her students. However, she was the most tenuously positioned socially and academically, compared to the others. As a Christian, coming from a traditionally Anglicised family, she was uneasily situated in the local political context of linguistic nationalism. Being a female and a religious fundamentalist, she was oddly positioned in the academic culture. But she never shied away from these uncomfortable identities. In fact, she was much more aware of the tensions in discourse one confronted in the academy, compared to the others. Since she was professionally secure, having a tenured instructorship in the university, her motivation was also less instrumental than others. She expressed the idealistic desire to take up the challenge of post-graduate research to obtain a sense of personal achievement.

The research process

An important concern in this narrative is to situate the writing process in the total context of knowledge construction. How do students' processes of research, reading and information gathering influence the written product? Viji wanted to choose a topic that she personally cared for. She initially began working on the broad title, 'English language teaching by missionaries in Jaffna'. She expressed the fact that she wanted to show how effective and successful the pedagogy of the missionaries was. Having studied in a missionary school herself, she had gained a lot of personal experience and useful information to develop her thesis. Viji's motivation for the choice of subject was therefore different from that of the others. Her personal interest differed from a choice based on mere convenience or an over-ambitious attempt to outsmart the faculty with esoteric subjects.

Unlike her colleagues who undertook research as primarily an individualistic activity, Viji was prepared to engage with her teachers and colleagues in dialogue about her project. Her collaborative approach provided opportunities to become aware of the controversial nature of her topic as the local nationalistic fervour generated a critical orientation to the missionary experience. This helped her realise that she had to adopt a more sober and detached attitude towards her topic. Furthermore, her discussion with others helped her narrow down her subject. Pointing to the fact that there were missionaries from many nationalities in Jaffna – i.e., Dutch, Portuguese, British, American, Italian, Belgian – she narrowed her focus down to American missionaries. Pointing later to the fact that American missionaries had an extensive history of work in Sri Lanka (continuing into the present), she further restricted her subject to the British colonial period when the activities of the American mission peaked. Her final title read, 'Approaches of the American Mission in teaching the English language during the British period in Jaffna.' This sharply worded, carefully qualified title shows the distance she has travelled in detaching herself from her religious sympathies to adopt a disciplined attitude towards her subject. This delimitation of her subject into very focused terms early in the research process helped her undertake the study in a constructive and productive manner.

Part of what influenced Viji gradually to adopt a sober attitude to her subject was the need to take painstaking effort to track down material relevant to her thesis. The missionary experience of teaching English was much discussed but rarely studied. In fact, very few scholars knew of documentation on this subject (compared to material on colonial politics or missionary theology, which were readily available). Therefore, Viji was forced to visit little known libraries in churches, rural missionary schools and private collections of priests to gather the handful of material that would at least indirectly answer her questions. Though it was frustrating at times not to get many documents on that subject, this experience only forced her to read the few she gathered more closely. Viji's focused research process influenced her to look for specific texts that answered the particular questions she had formulated.

Unlike some of her colleagues who conceived of research as a linear process of first gathering information and then writing it, Viji was forced to adopt a recursive process. She realised as she began working on her introduction and her initial chapters that there were gaps in her data that she had to fill with an additional search for sources. The new material then influenced her to revise her previous assumptions and rewrite her drafts. Though this was a risky and strenuous process, her research was more cogently argued and insightful for this reason (as we will see later).

It was also clear that the research work was endowing Viji with a sense of authority in her writing. This is the authority that comes from researching a little known area with little material. The faculty members, too, gradually found that her research was proving to be a learning experience for them, acquainting them with a provocative thesis supported by original material. Viji's choice of subject displayed a sound balance of personal interest, new information and interpretive challenge. Her insider status in the disciplinary community also provided her with the background to find her niche in the on-going academic conversation and to undertake focused and constructive research.

The writing process

Viji displayed a lot of care in undertaking the composing process. She had a rough outline of her work, which showed some attention to planning at the global level (delimiting the subject; identifying relevant material) and the local level (making tentative chapter divisions and sections). She also maintained good notes on the reading she was doing. Not only did she write two drafts by pen before she got the final draft typed, she also made it a point to get it read by her colleagues and supervisors. Apart from the process of negotiating her thoughts and revising her writing, she also displayed a careful eye for editing. She had in fact solicited the help of a colleague for help in the editing process. The entries in her Acknowledgments reveal her attitudes to writing: 'I am grateful to Dr— for his encouragement and *criticism*. I thank Mr— who untiringly went through the writing with a pair of eyes that hardly misses any *mistakes*' (emphasis mine). Thus her writing process displayed sound planning, collaboration, and care for textuality. It was also considerably recursive as she continued to narrow down her subject, reinterpret the limited primary sources she had, and reorganise the content of the chapters as she went on with her writing. It is possible that such writing practice was partly influenced by Viji's close association with the Anglicised literate community.

This is not to say that she, too, did not attempt to accommodate the oral tradition's predilection for spontaneous communication like some of her colleagues. Some typographical mistakes were corrected at the last minute by pen. Certain other spelling and grammatical errors were ignored. Despite advice from her reviewers, Viji still opted to display a certain amount of personal involvement, affect and passion in her writing. Advised to mention some of the criticism made by nationalist educators on the role of missionary education, she resisted this idea in the revision. She considered this simply an academic charade, i.e., writing something she did not subscribe to, simply because it was part of the convention. Such resistance during the revision process also showed influence from her religious discourse affiliations, which demanded whole hearted commitment to her beliefs. In a sense, she wrestled with competing traditions of communication as she composed her text.

The written product

Viji's is the briefest of the dissertations received, running to only 32 pages. Thanks to her timely work of narrowing down the scope of her research and undertaking it in a disciplined manner, her writing was very focused. She was also so confident about the thoroughness with which her subject had been explored that she did not have to pad the text unnecessarily.

The structure of her text is simple but logical. She adopts both a chronological and polemical organisation: after orientating readers to the colonial period, she introduces the main terms of the debate regarding the missionary educational enterprise in the introductory chapter. She uses this chapter masterfully to create a niche for her work in the scholarly conversation: she cites a variety of local educationists, linguists and social theorists of the post-colonial period who have criticised the missionary educational enterprise to show why a re-examination is necessary in order to arrive at a more balanced assessment. She also argues that since the missionaries did not leave adequate records of their teaching mission (as they were more focused on evangelisation), there is a need to reconstruct this dimension of their work. The political and academic significance of her thesis thus stands out as writing that is situated in the relevant discursive contexts.

At the end of the first chapter Viji outlines the content of the following three chapters, displaying her sound organisation of the material. She also provides reader-friendly signposts as she moves between the different sections of the work. In her second chapter titled 'A brief history of the foundations' Viji discusses the historical events that laid a foundation for the teaching of English in the local community. This provides the educational background for the times. In the third chapter she deals with the aims and objectives of the missionary teaching programme. The next chapter deals directly with the pedagogy of English language teaching, analysing the materials, testing, and teaching approaches employed. The final chapter on implications, appraises the effectiveness of the missionary approach while spelling out the exemplary features of their pedagogy for present day teachers. Thus, there is a clear, linear progression in the argument. While constructing a chronological narrative on the missionary experience, she is able to maintain an argumentative edge.

The discussion is sustained, and reader interest preserved, by the controversial thesis she develops in the text. In a social context where 45 years of decolonisation has led to the denigration of the missionary education, her intention is to give it more complexity. She makes several useful points to clarify the role of the missionaries – that they were not always collaborating with the colonial administration; that there was tension between the colonial bureaucracy and the missionary church; and that the church had a liberal streak that was attacked by the colonial administrators. She also points to the lasting impact of English language education on native culture and society to prove that what the missionaries did still bears fruit. In the light of recent teaching pedagogies and ELT research she is able to show that some of the modes of teaching adopted by the missionaries – i.e., non-formal, skills integrated, collaborative, whole-language oriented, and literature aided – in fact sound quite modern and effective. Thus, she undertakes a masterful reinterpretation of the missionary teaching experience.

The bibliography of Viji differs interestingly from that of the other students. She does not include any theoretical, scholarly or pedagogical publications. All her citations are those that are directly used in her work. Therefore, she lists local historical and educational writings – half of them articles or unpublished manuscripts – that discuss the colonial educational policies and practices. Since these texts are inadequate to answer all her questions, she has to read between the lines in order to make valid inferences. Her writing shows that she is careful not to exaggerate things to suit her perspectives. She struggles with the texts to make reasonable interpretations. Furthermore, since there have been remarkable developments in language teaching in the post-colonial period, the policies of the missionaries have to be contextualised in contemporary scholarship and their practices have to be interrogated in the light of current knowledge. Viji pays close attention to the writings to interpret them carefully and show the relevance for her argument. Though Viji does not cite pedagogical literature, it is clear that she is drawing from her insider status in the professional community and employing this knowledge actively to interpret the teaching practices of missionary teachers. Moreover, the tension between her faith and profession, personal religious ideology and nationalist political ideology, endows her with a critical interpretive attitude. Her discursive background thus accounts for this remarkably judicious reading strategy. The type of sources she uses and the modes of reading them thus differ from the other two writers discussed.

Her writing also displays the sharpest use of language among the dissertations received. This is not to deny that she too has some sections which are badly edited or contain a more personal use of language. She begins her first words in the thesis with the following words in her Acknowledgments: 'I thank my Lord and Master Jesus Christ for enabling me to complete this study with very limited sources at my disposal.' Though this language is permissible in this somewhat more personal section of the dissertation, it is eschewed in the body of the text. Thus, there is a recognition of the appropriate genres of discourse to be employed in the different sections of the dissertation. She also finds a permissible way of expressing her religious identity in the pages of the work. The next page, which presents her Abstract, suggests a scholarly prose with a more detached tone: 'This is an attempt at tracing the approaches of the American Mission in teaching the English language during the British period in Jaffna. From most of the findings the course has been a successful one. In fact it could be pointed out that at a certain period of time the cry for English and more English came from the natives themselves . . .' The impersonal syntactic structures, the hedging devices and the qualifications here suggest a switch to more research oriented discourse in the body of the dissertation. Viji's relative closeness to the literate, Anglicised discourse conventions helps her to be detached from her writing when she desires.

The creative fusion of these divergent discourses is also found in her use of citations in the first chapter:

'Ye shall be witnesses unto me unto the utmost part of the earth' (Holy Bible, Acts 1:8) – the final command of the Master to the disciples of Jesus Christ has been fulfilled through the centuries ultimately paving the way for a band of missionaries from the American Board to reach the shores of Jaffna in 1813. Though the supreme goal of the missionaries was to evangelise, they found themselves being compelled 'to seek the aids of learning' (Plan: 1823) in order to prepare the ground for sowing the seed of the Gospel. (p. 1)

It is interesting that the quotation from the Bible which was cited in earlier drafts as a proud announcement of the educational endeavours of the missionaries is cited here dispassionately to indicate the rationale for their educational activities. The quotation that follows is from the proposal by a school board for starting one of the first missionary educational institutions. This bureaucratic text is in tension with the previous Biblical quotation, suggesting the hybrid discourses embodied in the dissertation. The writer is also able to detach herself sufficiently from her biases to acknowledge how education is sometimes used for the utilitarian reason of evangelisation. This is a politically astute insight Viji is able to make in recognition of the dominant nationalistic sentiments in the local community. Making concessions of this nature is a good rhetorical strategy in order to win audience acceptance of her argument in favour of missionary pedagogy.

Though Viji's text displays some discursive tensions, they are quite constructive as they show the writer attempting to reconcile the religious and academic discourses to develop her unique perspective. While taking the academic conventions seriously, the writer also finds space for her own subjectivity to emerge through the text. She constructs a hybrid or multivocal text that is daring in realisation. Thus, she produces a text that not only contributes new knowledge to the field, but is also rhetorically creative and original. She cares sufficiently for her own values and convictions to engage closely with the dominant discourses of the academic context to present her message in a contextually appropriate manner. Her insider status in the ELT disciplinary community helps her in no small measure to use her familiarity with the relevant knowledge constructs to convey her message. Furthermore, the fact that her motivation for this writing is non-utilitarian may have enabled her to take more risks in her writing and seek ways of reconciling the discursive tensions she confronted. Her marginalised status may have created in her a keen sensitivity to the tensions she faces in order to wrestle with them for coherence.

An analysis of literate strategies

A perspective on the strategies adopted in Viji's writing emerges from the theorisation of 'voice' developed in post-structuralist and feminist circles. The usual temptation for subjects is to accommodate to preconstructed, legitimised, univocal discourses. These institutional discourses offer a ready-made and convenient way to solve communicative challenges. However, to use these institutionalised discourses uncritically is to let oneself be represented by the conventions and ideologies of each discourse. It is to be cast in the subject positions and roles preordained for speakers by the respective discourses. Therefore, the way to gain a voice is to negotiate the terms of speech comfortable to oneself in a critical and creative manner within the existing discursive constraints. In other words, one has to move strategically within the available discourse conventions and rules to find an advantageous position for one's voice. This may give birth to multivocal texts which infuse the dominant discourses with other conventions from the writer's background. Some of the writers in this study did give in to subtle forms of silencing as they solved their discursive problems by employing univocal discourses. They either immersed themselves in the academic discourse conventions or moved away from this to a vernacular discourse that they are more comfortable with. The uncritical and uncreative use of these univocal discourses denied them a distinct voice in their writing. But Viji attempts to find a space and voice for herself in the range of conflicting discourses to encode the messages she desires. Taking seriously the academic discourse, she yet brings into this her non-academic modes of communication to construct an independent text that takes a hybrid shape. This strategy of negotiating proves an effective way of reconciling the discursive tensions periphery students face in the academy.

Even oppositional writers who wish to be true to alternate (and presumably more 'native') discourses cannot simply turn their backs on the dominant communicative norms in a specific context for a particular audience. In addressing the academic audience, one has to take account of the existing conventions of that genre of communication and work through those structures in order to introduce the variant conventions, messages or ideologies of the writer. Ignoring the dominant conventions puts one in danger of losing the intended audience. Such a text may in fact be judged incoherent and irrelevant. Viji therefore negotiates with the conventions of the academic community for the strategic expression of her own thinking. Since she finds relevant ways of interjecting her personal religious ethos into the academic discourse, her text gains a creative and critical edge. While being unique and specific enough to show rhetorical effectiveness, the writing also makes an original contribution to knowledge construction in the field of applied linguistics. In other words, Viji appropriates the dominant conventions for her own purposes. Viji's strategy of discursive appropriation has the potential to interrogate academic discourses, reconstruct their conventions, and infuse them with vernacular discourses for critical expression – which suits Giroux's (1983) understanding of constructive, strategic forms of *resistance* to hegemonic discourses.

Viji confronts a range of conflicting discourses that offer the possibility of negotiating for original expression. The competing discourses are not paralysing for expression; they should be considered 'affordances' for effective expression. If students have the creativity, independence and boldness to take these conflicting discourses by the horns and negotiate for expression, they can channel them for constructive communicative purposes. We must therefore take into account the fact that all students (especially in multicultural periphery communities) generally confront conflicting, multiple discourses in practising literacy. A useful pedagogical strategy is to make students conscious of these discursive tensions, realise the positive potential of negotiating for expression and motivate them to engage with these discourses as they encode and decode texts. In other words, belonging to a different discourse community or being native to a marginalised discourse is not always a 'problem'. The conflicting discourses can also be a resource for critical expression and creative negotiation.

Conclusion

The narrative above shows that non-native students can go beyond the reproductive and deterministic influences of English language and discourse to display some agency as they creatively and critically compose English academic texts. This possibility of transcending discourse boundaries and constructing multivocal discourses (as displayed by Viji) should help us move beyond the pedagogies in ESOL that are motivated by cultural and linguistic determinism. Furthermore, periphery students already inhabit such a range of hybrid discourses that to categorise them as being native to only a single discourse may be a stereotype of well intentioned but uninformed teachers. In fact, so many of our students already come to classrooms with a range of centre-based academic and non-academic discourses (in addition to their indigenous variants) that what they need is not another introduction to these discourses but, more importantly, ways of employing them creatively and critically.

This focus on discourse strategies suggests significant pedagogical correctives. Hitherto, much of the teaching of academic or other Western discourses has taken place in a product oriented manner (see Kramsch, 1993). Instruction has been provided on features of the academic discourse – as if getting to know these discourse features will enable periphery students to adopt them. What we learn from the above narrative is that it is more important to teach students what to do with the competing discourses. After all, employing these discourses mechanically and uncritically is not desirable. It helps neither to construct rhetorically effective texts nor reconcile the ideological conflicts confronting periphery students.

The contribution of my narrative for the desired pedagogical corrective is to situate writing strategies in the ideological and social context as I consider how students negotiate conflicting discourses in their struggle for a critical voice. In fact, we can proceed along the above lines to understand a range of issues that will help us conduct learner strategy training for second language writers: which strategies are students comfortable with? Which strategies work well for negotiating their discursive conflicts? To what extent do students have a critical awareness of the discursive strategies they employ? What are the ideological and social implications of the strategies they use?

The narrative provides insight into the pedagogical approaches in composition surveyed at the beginning of this essay. We can see that situating the writing process of the students in the total context of the social and discursive background provides a more complex under-standing of both the challenges and the possibilities of academic writing for periphery students. While the product oriented approach, which treats literacy as the acquisition of decontextualised skills, misses much of the insight, even process oriented schools which conceive writing as cognitive strategies fail to understand writing as a social activity. When we understand the challenges confronting periphery students in the total social context, what we find is that for them to communicate is to resist – literacy for them is always *critical* literacy. While absorbing the dominant, institutionalised discourses passively may mean giving in to their hegemonic influence and being silenced, it is adopting a critical attitude towards univocal discourses and using them creatively for one's own purposes that ensures mean-ingful communication and ideological integrity.

9 'I'll go with the group': Rethinking 'discourse community' in EAP

Sue Starfield

Introduction

In the EAP literature, the notion of an academic discipline constituting an academic discourse community into which new students
will be 'inducted' or 'initiated' through EAP-type courses, particularly writing courses, while bringing a welcome social dimension to
the teaching and learning of writing, is of limited usefulness if it
presupposes a homogenous, unconflictual discourse community from
which the power relations shaping the wider social context are
absent. Theoretical frameworks and instructional models which over-
simplify reality (Zamel, 1993), may neither help prepare our students
to negotiate the complex social worlds they are entering nor necessarily assist EAP practitioners in their own negotiations with faculty in
the disciplines. My ethnographic research into the development of
the academic writing of black, ESL students, in their first year of
study in the sociology department at a South African university, has
led me to interrogate some current conceptions of discourse community which do not allow for sufficient understanding of the ways in
which social inequalities may be being reproduced within the discourse community.

Driving my research was a need to understand better the relative
lack of success of black, ESL students entering the university after the
exclusionary apartheid years.[1] The discourse community metaphor
appeared to provide a helpful conceptual framework: if I could come
to understand the norms and conventions, both implicit and explicit,
governing writing in the community, I would, as an EAP teacher be
better able to assist students in becoming successful in Sociology
One. As a staff developer, I would be better able to assist faculty
make their teaching and curricula more accessible to students from

---

[1] 1994, the year in which I carried out my research, was the year in which all South
Africans could vote for the first time and in which Nelson Mandela became President.

diverse backgrounds. As the research evolved, I began to question some of my own taken for granted assumptions about discourse communities. Whereas a number of studies of student enculturation into disciplinary communities (Berkenkotter, Huckin and Ackerman, 1991; Herrington, 1985; Herrington and Moran, 1992; McCarthy, 1987; Prior, 1991, 1995) have focused on the student (both native speakers of English and ESL) and have included data from student interviews and journals, interviews with professors teaching particular courses, classroom observation and examination of texts, in this chapter, I examine an event in which an academic discourse community communicates around its pedagogic duties. I propose a reconceptualisation of discourse community and consider some implications for EAP practitioners. I have taken seriously Harris's (1989) suggestion that rather than 'taking the kinds of rarefied talk and writing that go on at conferences and in journals as the norm' governing an academic discourse community, we study instead the 'everyday struggles and mishaps of the talk in our classrooms and departments' (p. 20).

Let me say at the outset that this chapter does not constitute a rejection of the discourse community metaphor – rather it seeks to argue that community is less a given than a goal to strive for.

Reviewing academic discourse communities

In the socioconstructionist account (Bruffee, 1993; Johns, 1992; Silva, 1992; Walvoord and McCarthy, 1990), learning is viewed as induction and socialisation into a discourse community which is governed by a range of norms and conventions: 'writers, like speakers, must use the communication means considered appropriate by members of particular speech or discourse communities' (McCarthy, 1987: 234). Typically, the discourse community is seen as an undifferentiated social grouping in which the members are fundamentally in agreement as to the group's activities. Johnson *et al.* (1994), for example, maintain that 'texts within the discourse community are produced and judged in relation to standards shared by its members' (p. 232).

Swales (1990) proposes a taxonomy for identifying discourse communities which, as Bizzell (1992) has pointed out, tends to overemphasise the degree of choice members have when 'joining' a community and also to promote a view of community as consensus. Discourse, she contends, is constitutive of the group's knowledge. In other words, a discourse community is constituted in and by its discursive practices. It is through discourse that new members are initiated into the group or as, I shall argue, are excluded from the group. When Bartholomae (1985) claims that 'every time a student sits down to write for us he has to invent the university . . . to try on the peculiar ways of knowing, selecting, evaluating, reporting, concluding and arguing that define the discourse of our community' (p. 134), he too depicts a university community in discursive agreement.

These views have had a powerful effect on teachers of writing in that they have helped make us aware of the normative weight of the conventions which govern the disciplines. Although there is some discussion over whether the university constitutes one discourse community or numerous disciplinary communities, the notion that these may be internally differentiated along complex sociopolitical faultlines is rarely encountered. The community metaphor, as Williams (1976) points out, is rarely negatively connotated, while for Anderson (1983), 'community' always promotes an 'imagined' solidarity which belies social inequality.

Some EAP practitioners have, however, begun to question such assumptions. Harris (1989) argues that discourse communities are structured by inequality and by power relations: 'there never really is a "we" for whom the language of the university . . . is fully invented and accessible . . . Like our students, we too must re-invent the university whenever we sit down to write' (p. 21). For Chase (1988), 'discourse communities are organised around the production and legitimation of particular forms of knowledge and social practices at the expense of others, and are not ideologically innocent' (p. 13). Clark (1992) adds that 'the academic discourse community . . . is not monolithic: power in the community is unequally distributed . . . It is the senior members of the community, the teaching staff, who establish the rules of behaviour for the community and it is easier for staff to flout those rules than students' (p. 118).

As a counter to the static, conventionalised view of discourse community, Prior (1991, 1995), Casanave (1995) and others have begun to carry out ethnographic studies grounded in specific disciplinary contexts, which attempt to capture the enormous variety of social contexts in which learning to read and write academic discourse takes place, even within a single department. In an attempt to avoid reductionist explanations of context, they tend, however, to foreground individual experience and remove the social from the explanation. In her study of a Latina student's struggles to succeed in a graduate programme in sociology, Casanave (1995) emphasises how difficult it is for students from outside of the US mainstream to challenge the established, frequently white and male, members of the community and how hard it seems to be for senior faculty to consider that culturally-diverse students might have a significant contribution to make to the discipline. Yet, when attempting to explain why it is that Richard, 'clean cut and confident . . . from a middle-class, white family' stays in the programme, while Virginia, 'of Puerto Rican ancestry' (p. 92) and Lu-Yun, from the People's Republic of China leave, Casanave resorts to an individualising explanation rather than a truly sociohistorical one which would explain why it is that the discourse community is not receptive. Richard's initially negative attitude shifts 'toward acceptance of the type of world he was being trained to enter'. He recognises the rewards which this will entail: 'there's the rules of the game. You have to get published . . .' (p. 101). On the other hand, Lu-Yun and Virginia 'perhaps coincidentally a foreign student and a minority student, each seemed to find it difficult to create contexts for writing from these local interactions' (p. 107). Casanave's explanation reduces interaction to inter-individual events, to coincidence, and fails to see how 'rewards' are shaped by the dense web of social, political and historical forces which shape every interaction. In this larger sense, the discursive practices of this community which made inclusion relatively easy for some and exclusion a likelihood for others, can be said to be constitutive of the community.

Left out of many accounts of the working of discourse communities are these dimensions of power and power relationships. While discourse communities are portrayed as having agreed upon norms and conventions, absent from many of these depictions is an account which looks at how power is exercised, resistance to that power and its effects on the functioning of the community. These notions of discourse community fail to take into account the larger, and frequently inequitable, social structures which are reproduced in daily interactions and neglect the potential implications for student success and failure. If academic communities are constituted by and through their discursive practices, then Bourdieu's (1982) concept of legitimate language becomes extremely useful in reconceptualising discourse community, precisely because it sees individual speakers and writer/hearers and readers as 'speaking subjects' who, in each and every social interaction, embody the sociohistorically determined relations of power which give them and the social groups they are members of 'speaking rights' endowed with greater or lesser authority. Bourdieu enjoins us to consider, in any social context, not only who has the right to speak but also who has 'the power to impose reception' and be heard. Through discourse, power is exercised symbolically. For Bourdieu (according to Wacquant):

linguistic relations are always relations of power and, consequently, cannot be elucidated within the compass of linguistic analysis alone. Even the simplest linguistic exchange brings into play a complex and ramifying web of historical power relations between the speaker, endowed with a specific social authority and an audience, which recognises this authority to varying degrees, as well as between the groups to which they respectively belong.

(Wacquant, cited by Jenkins, 1992: 154)

Bourdieu has also developed the economic metaphor of 'capital' to refer to accumulable social–symbolic resources: he is therefore able to refer to, for example, 'cultural' (knowledge, skills, education) and 'linguistic' capital (degrees of possession of the legitimate language in any educational or linguistic market). If the academic discourse community can be viewed as a 'field' or 'market' (Bourdieu's term for social context) then members can be seen to have accumulated varying amounts of 'academic capital' (PhD, tenure, published articles, etc.) within the field.

In the next section, I draw on Bourdieu's work to broaden and deepen the ways in which we think about academic discourse communities as I discuss data gathered in one of the few occasions in which members of the department met to discuss assessment, in an event which came to be known as the 'markers' meeting'. By examining data from several sources, I provide a 'thick description' (Geertz, 1975) of the complex microworld of the Department, in which meaning was not fixed but subject to constant negotiation and renegotiation.

The markers' meeting

The markers' meeting was instituted by the course co-ordinator of the first-year course in an attempt to attain greater intermarker reliability in the marking of first-year essays. The data which I will discuss are drawn from the markers' meeting following the students' submission of their first essay on the lectured topic, 'Introduction to sociological theory: Marx, Weber, Durkheim'. The required format was the traditional expository essay in which the student is expected to read a number of sources and synthesise these in response to the topic.

Essay marking was shared between a group of departmental staff which included the current lecturers, and four non-tenured, junior staff, known as tutors, who were responsible for running the weekly, small-group tutorials. The course co-ordinator, referred to above, was one of the four tutors. As the race, gender and status of the participants in the markers' meetings are significant for my analysis,

Table 1. *Grid of marks: markers' meeting, May 1994*

Essay	Steve	Anne	Michelle	Jeff	Craig
1	64	52	54	70	55
2	72	62	56	70	65
3	49	50	49	49	49
4	45	49	45	45	65

each participant will be identified in these terms in the next section. An analysis which did not take these factors into account, would, in my opinion, fail to grasp the complexity of the processes being examined.

Prior to the meeting, the markers had an initial meeting at which the course co-ordinator distributed four photocopied essays which she had selected at random, and a marking memorandum (memo) prepared by Lynne, one of the two lecturers, which set criteria for assessment.[2] It must be pointed out that this memo was not made available to students and had not been drawn up when the essay topics were set but just prior to the markers' meeting. Having each marked the four essays, the markers (except for Lynne) reassembled the following day. The meeting took place in the departmental tea-room, the markers sat in a circle and called out the marks which they had awarded to each of the essays. These were written up in the form of a grid (Table 1). Discussion then ensued, and markers were called upon to explain why a particular mark had been awarded, particularly in cases of discrepancies between the marks on a particular essay. Underlying the exercise was the belief that this discussion would help markers, particularly those who had tutored the course but not lectured it, to become familiar with the criteria that were to be used in assessing the essays.

Discursive struggles in the community

I will discuss the conversation over Essay 1 written by a student, Nazeema Mohamed (see Appendix for topic). The bulk of the discussion took place between Steve, the white, tenured lecturer who taught the course in conjunction with Lynne, and Jeff, a black, non-

---

[2] Informed consent was obtained from all participants and the names of all participants are pseudonyms.

tenured tutor. Also present were Michelle, a white, non-tenured tutor; Craig, a black, non-tenured tutor; and Anne, the course co-ordinator, a white, non-tenured tutor. Neither Craig nor Jeff were first-language speakers of English. Steve had been a member of the department for five years, but had never been a student in the department, while Michelle and Anne were former students who had become tutors while completing graduate degrees. Jeff and Craig had recently joined the department, having both studied at universities outside South Africa. All had been faculty for less than six years. Steve, who was the only member of the group with a PhD and to have published in academic journals, was also somewhat older than other members of the group. These histories are relevant to the discussion that ensued.

Once Anne has drawn[3] the grid of marks on the board, Steve opens the discussion by commenting on the markers' apparent agreement over Essays 3 and 4 which had all been failed, apart from Craig's mark for Essay 4.

Steve: We can tell what a borderline fail is. We're in agreement of what a fail is.

Jeff: Mohamed [Essay 1] is a very good essay – the only problem is no referencing but clear evidence that the student had read. Shows how Protestantism informed the work ethic.

Steve: This is not an abnormal distribution – compare this with the ASP/ASDEC workshop where the range of marks was much wider among people who had been teaching for 20 years.

Jeff then initiates the discussion of the essays, the marking criteria and the marks awarded, by taking up Essay 1 (Nazeema Moha-med's[4]) to which he has awarded 70% (an Upper Second), considered to be a very high mark. Steve 'responds' but not to Jeff's comments on Essay 1; he returns to his opening statement about 'agreement' referring to an earlier workshop on assessment run by the university's staff development units (ASP/ASDEC) where, during a marking exercise, more experienced lecturers produced a much wider distribution of marks. At this stage, Steve appears to be arguing that the difference between his and Jeff's marks and those of the other markers is not that significant. He also appears to be trying to build consensus, establish his authority, and play down differences in

---

[3] I use the 'ethnographic present' when presenting the discussion at the meeting as it seems to capture the flow of the interaction.

[4] The student whose essay was under discussion was a female student whose last name may have provoked some uncertainty as to her gender. Alternatively, markers may have been using the generic 'he'.

marking between those present at the meeting. He sets up an opposition between the markers present at the meeting and those who 'had been teaching for twenty years', drawing attention to the relatively junior status of those at the meeting. In these opening moments of the discussion, it is noteworthy that Steve and Jeff have both awarded high marks to the essay, whereas the other three markers gave what were regarded as 'borderline' passes.

Michelle then intervenes with a comment that is critical of Mohamed's approach to the essay and Anne supports her:

Michelle: Mohamed is very poor on method not very sophisticated.
Anne: It's not clear, he doesn't get it, doesn't fully answer the question.

Michelle (in particular) and Anne use a set of criteria to assess essays that differ from those of their colleagues. They articulate criteria which relate to generic form and which are taken up in the remainder of the interaction. These concerns re-emerge, often indirectly, in the course of the year.

Steve then re-enters the conversation, echoing Anne's criticism of the essay, and addressing himself directly to the essay, begins to question the '64%' he has awarded, putting forward a number of reasons for this change of heart. The intervention of the two women shifts the balance of power in the discussion as Steve moves away from his initial mark and from an initial solidarity with Jeff:

Steve: You don't answer the question. I don't know why I gave it a second the more I look at it the less I'm endeared to it. The introduction doesn't answer the question – inevitably the rest of the essay doesn't either, uses vague phrases, doesn't get the link between Calvinism and Protestant ethic, confused on rationality. On rereading it I wouldn't give it that much. It's clearly not even a good second, lower it.

At this point, Craig makes his only intervention in this exchange – in support of Steve and the two women tutors:

Craig: It's a fragmented answer, hides behind description, referencing not really adequate.

Steve then engages Jeff directly, while Jeff holds to and attempts to justify his position, despite Michelle's intervention:

Steve: What do you think?
Jeff: I still think it's a good essay. She mentions rationality, other students don't even do this.
Michelle: Don't you think she does this in a confusing way?

Jeff then begins to put forward arguments to support his position.

These are arguments which refer to the content of the essay and to how the writer has dealt with the topic's central themes:

Jeff: Well, she does relate it to the work ethic. The rationality of Calvinism compared to Catholicism which is concerned with the after life – the whole concept of rationality is very important here [he quotes approvingly from the essay]. Good concluding remark.

As the challenge to Jeff grows, the terrain starts to shift to question his authority as a marker. Is he able to 'detect' plagiarism?[5] Anne questions the origins of Jeff's quote and the spectre of plagiarism, described earlier by Steve in an address to the students as a 'capital crime', further shifts the balance of forces. Steve identifies Mohamed's words as being taken from Giddens, a leading sociologist whose book had been recommended to the students:

Anne: Are they her own words?
Jeff: Possibly not.
Steve: That comes right out of Giddens. We have to make a decision because she mentions rationality. Does she define it?

Steve asserts his authority as lecturer in charge of the course, attempting to conclude the discussion and to resolve the disagreement, using a 'we' which appears solidary and inclusive. At the same time, however, this move opens up a further exchange with Jeff over a fairly complex issue in Weber's theory by asking whether the student had defined the term 'rationality'. Jeff is forced to concede slightly but Steve persists, putting Jeff on the defensive. Anne intervenes in support of Steve and to further 'put down' Jeff. Jeff attempts to assert authority by displaying expertise in the finer details of Weber's theory but this challenge ultimately fails too:

Jeff: She doesn't take it and apply it.
Steve: Does she define it?
Jeff: Well, no.
Steve: Weber says the Protestant ethic is irrational, rationality means something else.
Anne: Saying it's a catalyst is only a beginning.
Steve: Other essays say it better.
Jeff: It's an upper second.
Anne: How many have you marked? You'll change your mind.
Jeff: I bet you don't find a better. I'll point out problems with the question. We're dealing with Calvinism – the student is confusing it

[5] The student handbook warned that students in whose work plagiarism was 'detected', would receive zero.

with Lutheranism. I could have failed it but I thought it wouldn't be failed. Calvinism deals with predestination, Lutheranism deals with a calling.

Anne: I haven't made that distinction Steve. Is it important?

Steve: If you say that, you're taking issue with Weber.

Anne: Isn't this a bit of a red herring?

Steve: A lot of students are slipping between Calvinism and Protestantism.

Jeff: Read the section on Lutheranism. [He reads from marking memo.]

Steve: Lynne did not mean this as a checklist. [Reads p. 64 of *Course Reader*, quoting Franklin.] I don't expect them to know the difference between Protestantism and Lutheranism. The memo is not a strict guideline.

Anne: Would you agree that you focus on content more than on structure of argument?

Jeff: No. I took that into account. You mentioned it yesterday. I like the flow of the debate. Should we take an average?

Steve: I'd be uncomfortable going more than a third.

Jeff: I'll go with the group.

In this exchange we have a rare instance of an academic discourse community discussing a central aspect of its pedagogic functioning: the assessment of written essay assignments. While the micro-purposes of the meeting may indeed have been to standardise assessment practices, what Clark and Ivanic (1996) refer to as macro-purposes seem less clear. Macro-purposes of a communicative event reflect social and ideological factors that are mostly unconscious. The consensus that many versions of the concept of discourse community would have us believe exists, seems absent, nor can the dynamics in the group be explained as mere coincidence. In other exchanges, similar patterns of interaction occurred. Jeff and Craig were relative newcomers to the department as well as the only two black faculty present and, unlike Michelle and Anne, were not graduates of the department. Steve's power was evident throughout the interaction. He could reframe the terms of the debate, open and close topics, appeal for consensus, refer to authorities (Weber, Giddens), question Jeff directly and respond to Jeff's challenges. While Steve, seeming to realise that he was 'out of synch' with the rest of the group and only 'in synch' with Jeff, rapidly conceded that he had marked too highly, Jeff, on the other hand, felt obliged to defend his mark. In the opening moments of the exchange, Anne and Michelle through a clear articulation of assessment criteria exercised the power to change Steve's mind and impose their and Craig's grade as what became the 'standard'. They then remained silent for much of the exchange, intervening only (particularly Anne) to support Steve as he and Jeff struggled discursively over who would have the power to set the norm.

Unproblematised notions of discourse community take for granted the conditions for the establishment of communication: that those who speak regard those who listen as worthy to listen and that those who listen regard those who speak as worthy to speak. 'Speakers without legitimate competence find themselves excluded from social universes where it is required, or condemned to silence' (Bourdieu, 1982: 42: my translation). Steve, because of his status as lecturer and tenured staff member, his gender and race, was endowed with the 'institutional' power and authority to impose reception. Ultimately, Jeff failed to impose reception and 'goes with the group'. By other members of the community, Jeff was positioned as an erratic and a lenient marker and in discussions and interviews was depicted as not responsible or reliable.

Anne's challenge to Jeff on the plagiarism issue positioned him as an outsider whose 'academic capital' might not enable him to recognise Giddens' words. Jeff attempted to mount a fundamental attack on Steve's 'academic capital' by challenging the topic he had set. He attempted to display academic capital of his own in fine distinctions between Lutheranism and Calvinism, and read from the marking memorandum in support of his position. Steve then exercised his power to flout the 'rules' by questioning the status of the memo itself: 'The memo is not a strict guideline'. In a rearguard attempt to maintain some vestige of power, Jeff proposed a compromise – 'an average' which Steve refused to accept. Jeff, his academic capital and legitimate competence under threat, 'goes with the group'. In fact, he went *from* the group, claiming another engagement. In the struggle over the power to set the norm, the group was constituted by the person excluded from it.

Jeff's insistence on staying with 70% can be seen as arising, at least in part, out of a sense of insecurity occasioned by his marginal status. Surrendering would be tantamount to admitting that he does not know how to 'do his job'. Steve, on the other hand, endowed with the symbolic power of his institutionally-given status and authority, and without endangering his academic capital, is easily able to align himself with the majority in the meeting. His 64% will not define him as an erratic marker. In ways analogous to the Mayor of Pau, described by Bourdieu (1982), who, adopting a *strategy of condescension*, maintains and demonstrates his symbolic power through speaking in the local dialect at an official gathering, Steve's admission of a momentary lapse in marking rigour, serves to reinforce his 'leadership'. Both the mayor and Steve draw profit from the tacit recognition by all parties that they are endowed with legitimate competence, the mayor as a fluent, educated speaker of French and Steve as course leader, tenured staff member, PhD graduate, etc. What has to be understood if we are fully to grasp the complexity of community is the extent to which the possibility of acquiring academic capital and legitimate language has been structured by previous inequality.

When I interviewed Jeff, he recounted a tale of perceived exclusion and marginalisation, which he expressed as not having known many 'rules' that seemed to govern behaviour and interactions between faculty. After repeated attempts to integrate into the department, he seemed to accept that his discoursal competence was not 'legitimate' in the eyes of his colleagues and retreated into silence. He was ultimately to resign from the department at the end of the year.

Although Anne and Michelle in interviews with me claimed to be marginalised in the department and that there was little support for their 'skills-based' view of teaching and learning, this episode from the markers' meeting shows them 'imposing reception', albeit indirectly. In an interview, Craig recounted feeling 'sandwiched' in the department – a black tutor understanding black students' experience and struggle at the university – while struggling himself to become a member of the still largely white world of the department where his status, his race and his 'unknownness' all placed him on the margins. Aware that his competence had not yet been deemed legitimate, he signalled his alignment with the dominant position in the meeting, and then stayed silent. Within a year, he too would have left the department, unable to secure the tenured position he was seeking.

What are the implications of these negotiations for student assessment? In the course of the discussion, the marking memorandum was effectively disavowed by Steve ('Lynne did not mean this as a checklist'), in what seemed to be part of a different struggle for control and power. While initially Steve seemed prepared to allow for a range of marks ('this is not an abnormal distribution'), by the end of the exchange he had shifted to needing to impose agreement. If the ostensible purpose of the meeting was to determine whether markers were adhering to the criteria for assessing students' essays, has this goal been met? Marked by Jeff and Steve, initially, Mohamed would have become a successful student. Marked by Michelle, Anne or Craig, she became a borderline student. Obviously not each student mark is negotiated in this way. But had the meeting not ensued, depending on which of the five had marked Mohamed's essay, her fate would have differed.

Student negotiations

The students I interviewed expressed constant anxiety over 'who is marking you'. They were acutely aware that there were multiple readings of their essays and frequently suggested to me that one person, who would get to know them, mark their assignments throughout the year. Rebecca's feelings were fairly typical of some of the black students:

In sociology you really won't know what is it . . . When coming to marking, I'm not saying it's bad and I'm not saying it's excellent but I'm saying the fact that you're being marked by different people, you can't just adjust to one person and know the style of marking; what that person expects. Today I'm marked by Jeff; tomorrow I'm being marked by Professor Wade and tomorrow it's Michelle; all of them have different ways of marking.

Rebecca, who was a fairly successful student, had realised that meaning was neither fixed nor shared within the department. Despite the considerable effort she put into consulting her lecturers and tutors, Rebecca never achieved the marks she felt her hard work deserved. The data from the markers' meeting give us some insight into why Rebecca might have experienced difficulty in 'figur[ing]' out and then adapt[ing] to the writing demands in academic contexts' (McCarthy, 1987: 262). Rebecca eventually developed a 'coping strategy' of her own. When dissatisfied with her assignment mark, she queried it with the marker or a tutor and successfully raised her grades on each assignment. Very few students have the self-confidence to enter into these kinds of negotiation.

Thandi, a fellow student, related a very different response when telling me about her friend Zodwa's experience:

like with Zodwa she has to go a long process last week, Jeff arguing with Professor Jenkins. They were arguing about her essay and at the end Jeff did win because Zodwa got 63 and it's not good really if every time they have to debate because of the marks of the student.

Thandi perceived that these discussions between lecturers over marks were battles with winners and losers and her way of dealing with the perceived unfairness of marking was to opt out, 'because sometimes this tutor will say this; you deserve this much and this one this much and then you find there is a conflict between the two, and I don't like people being in conflict because of me'. Thandi accepted that she had failed her essay by one mark and vowed to work harder.

Kress (1990) calls for discourse analyses that 'reveal the complex of processes involved in the production, communication, and reception/reproduction of texts' (p. 92). The markers' meetings provide a small window into the complex contexts in which student texts are being produced and received. A view of discourse community that is static, rule-governed and fixed in some a priori way cannot capture the dynamic, fluid negotiation and renegotiation that occurred in the markers' meeting and in other contexts. During the markers' meeting, the course leader himself redefined the criteria for the successful accomplishment of the essay. When marking the essay initially, Jeff and Steve both believed it met their expectations of a good essay. In the process of talk, meaning is shaped and reshaped, constantly shifting power relations affect the outcomes of student success and failure. Generic conventions are shaped by these shifting power relations rather than pre-existing them in neat sets of expectations. Socially-located individuals, who constitute the discourse community, with their varying amounts of academic capital, assess students' texts, not necessarily according to a pre-agreed upon formula. Assessment becomes the outcome of a 'complex of processes', some of which are revealed in the markers' meeting and are triangulated by data from other contexts.

Implications for the teaching of EAP

To conclude, I would like to reflect on what I see as some of the implications of these findings for the teaching of academic literacy in a tertiary context. Obviously, my research led me to question my initial assumptions about the nature of discourse communities. Induction into an academic discipline would seem to involve processes more complex than the acquisition of discipline-specific language. Attempts to teach academic writing within a disciplinary context need to be based on careful ethnographic study of the particular contexts in which students will be learning and teachers teaching.

Encouraging students to become ethnographers in the academic culture (Johns, 1988) has been proposed as a heuristic whereby students write about the rules of the lecture context, the writing conventions of the class and the kind of knowledge claims that are permissible. This intriguing idea could well be extended to prospective language educators who could then be exposed not only to the 'technical details of language acquisition, reading and writing, and so forth' (Pennycook, 1996b: 170), but to as wide a range as possible of texts and contexts that would enable them to see academic literacy acquisition as a profoundly social activity.

I would urge further exploration of EAP teachers' team-teaching with disciplinary specialists and the necessity for EAP practitioners to see themselves as faculty developers as well. Kusel (1992) advocates 'teachers of academic writing . . . engaging less with specialist texts and more with specialist subject teachers' (p. 468). Benesch (1996) not only spent time in the mainstream psychology class her EAP students were taking, she invited the professor to engage with her students in her adjunct class, enabling him to gain greater insight into who her students were and enabling the students to engage with a professor in ways they had probably never done before.

We need, as Rebecca's and Thandi's stories of success and failure tell us, to help our students develop their strategic competencies: the linguistic and critical abilities to negotiate the complex sociopolitical learning environments in which they find themselves. What, for example, are the tactful yet powerful ways in which a first-year, ESL student can tell a lecturer that 'this mark doesn't suit my essay'[6] and 'impose reception'? Current research into learning and coping strategies (Leki, 1995b) could fruitfully broaden its agenda to investigate strategies for students' discursive empowerment.

I believe that there is a role for 'language practitioners' within higher education but question whether they should be located in discrete 'language courses' or units. I feel that we need to 'redevelop' ourselves and those entering the EAP field to engage in the transformative, interactive and inter-disciplinary work which is needed in our institutions. Working in faculty development and teaching new students in a highly diverse society, in a period of rapid social change, I have to come to understand the significance of what I saw happening in the markers' meeting and in the discourse community and work towards ensuring that difference and diversity are recognised as the basic condition of our new society.

As faculty from historically-oppressed communities enter the university, they too will struggle to reinvent it, bringing with them new discourses, new voices, new genres and texts. EAP practitioners can mediate the challenge to the existing power relations and symbolic domination through critical ethnographic accounts that tell the stories of people like Jeff, Craig, Thandi, Rebecca and Isaac, struggling to contest the 'legitimate' forms of discourse.

What we find, as Prior recognised (1995), may complicate our professional lives rather than make them easier but if we choose to view academic environments as 'closed systems susceptible to taxonomic and rule-oriented description' instead of 'complex, constructed, unfolding events' (p. 77) then the game is perhaps not worth the candle.

---

[6] Isaac did not say these words to the marker of his second essay. However, he communicated his feelings about the essay mark to me in an interview.

Acknowledgements

I would like to thank Bonny Norton and Esther Ramani for their comments on an earlier draft of this chapter. Support from the Centre for Science Development enabled me to present an earlier version of this paper at the 1995 TESOL Convention in Long Beach.

Appendix

Essay topic

'Loss of time through sociability, idle talk, luxury, even more sleep than is necessary for health, six to at most eight hours, is worthy of absolute moral condemnation.' According to Weber, in what specific ways did these features of Calvinist doctrine compel believers to work in a manner that promoted the development of capitalism?

10 EAP Assessment: Issues, models, and outcomes

Geoff Brindley and Steven Ross

Introduction

The aim of this chapter is to provide an overview of issues in EAP assessment, with a particular focus on various ways in which information on student proficiency and achievement in EAP programmes is gathered for purposes of selection, curriculum monitoring and programme accountability. The first part of the chapter outlines the purposes for which assessment takes place in EAP contexts and examines issues surrounding the use of English language proficiency test scores as criteria for university admission. In this context, current debates concerning the validity and reliability of EAP tests are discussed. Methods of assessing course-related achievement in EAP programmes are then briefly canvassed, with particular reference to portfolio assessment. The second part of the chapter looks at the question of outcome measurement in EAP programmes. Following a survey of different approaches to measurement of language gains, we describe an empirical study of gains made over time by learners in an EAP listening programme in Japan. The results of the study suggest that if instruction is carefully targeted, achievement of specific course objectives will be reflected in gains in general academic listening proficiency.

Assessment in EAP programmes

Assessment in EAP programmes is carried out for a variety of purposes which can be roughly categorised under the general headings of achievement assessment and proficiency assessment. To provide a framework for the discussion that follows, these terms will be briefly defined and exemplified.

Achievement assessment

Achievement assessments are used to determine the extent to which learners have learned what has been taught during a course of instruction. They are designed to sample the specific skills or knowledge which form the basis of the course objectives and are thus intended to be optimally content valid. As Brown (1996: 14) points out, the results of achievement assessment can be used not only to inform teachers about individual learners' attainment of objectives, but also to provide feedback on the quality of the programme. In this way, achievement assessments may be used as the first line of evidence that a language programme is achieving its stated goals.

Proficiency assessment

Language proficiency assessment aims to establish the extent to which learners can use the language for their intended purposes. The main difference between proficiency and achievement assessment is that the former, by definition, cannot cover the syllabus content of any particular programme. Proficiency measures are often used as general indicators of attainment of programme goals for programme evaluation purposes, particularly in cases where no programme-internal measures are available. We will return to this point later.

EAP proficiency tests

In EAP contexts, probably the most widely recognised and influential forms of assessment are those high-volume English language proficiency tests which are used for purposes of admission to universities in English-speaking countries, particularly the Test of English as a Foreign Language (TOEFL) (Educational Testing Service, 1998a,b) and the International English Language Testing System (IELTS) (UCLES / British Council / IDP Education Australia, 1998). Because of the high stakes associated with tertiary entry and especially with the TOEFL, a large test preparation industry has emerged in many countries which has generated a huge commerce in textbooks, sample tests and specific purpose preparation courses (Hilke and Wadden, 1997).

Proficiency tests and university admission: issues and debates the use of test scores as admissions criteria

Testing agencies such as the Educational Testing Service (ETS) and the University of Cambridge Local Examinations Syndicate (UCLES), state explicitly that English language proficiency should not be the sole basis for admission decisions and that user institutions themselves should determine what score ranges or levels are acceptable in the light of their knowledge of course requirements. Test users are also advised that other factors such as the applicants' age, motivation, educational and cultural background, references, first language and language learning history, should also be taken into account (ETS, 1998a,b; UCLES / British Council / IDPEA, 1997).

There is evidence to suggest, however, that in some institutions, proficiency test scores are used in a somewhat cruder fashion as 'criterion-referenced pass-fail indicators' (Spolsky, 1995: 331). Some researchers have argued that such practices may result in the exclusion of otherwise qualified non-native speakers from tertiary study, since it has been shown that students admitted with scores below the university-determined cut-offs have been able to complete courses successfully (Allwright and Banerjee, 1997; Elder, 1993; Simner, 1997).

The on-going debate surrounding the application of cut-off scores for university entry raises the thorny question of what is an appropriate level of English language proficiency to undertake tertiary study. It is clearly desirable for institutions to be able to identify a threshold below which a candidate's chances of succeeding in university study would be seriously impaired. However, identifying such a threshold has proved to be very difficult. Research into the connection between English language proficiency test scores and academic success, as measured by such indices as grade point average or tutor evaluation, has frequently revealed a fairly weak relationship (Davies and Criper, 1988; Graham, 1987; Light *et al.*, 1987). This, of course, is not surprising since many factors other than language ability will clearly play a role in academic achievement. Moreover, the task of establishing a clear relationship is complicated considerably by the methodological problems involved in carrying out predictive validity studies, including reliance on truncated samples and the lack of adequate indicators of 'academic success' (Elder, 1993). In the light of the uncertain relationship between language proficiency and academic success, test development agencies continue to be appropriately cautious in their advice to test users on score interpretation and use.

Construct and content validity of EAP proficiency tests
The TOEFL

Language proficiency tests tend to reflect the views of the nature of language ability and language use which prevail at the time of their development. For this reason, proficiency tests which are used in EAP contexts differ in content and format. At the 'traditional' end of the continuum, tests such as the TOEFL, which were developed during the structuralist-behaviourist era, employ discrete point items and use the objectively scored multiple-choice format. Though it has consistently demonstrated very high reliability, there has been continuing debate concerning the extent to which the TOEFL reflects current understandings of the nature of communicative language ability (construct validity) (see, for example, Duran *et al.*, 1985; Bachman, 1986) and samples the types of activities which typically occur in EAP contexts (content validity) (Hansen and Jensen, 1994; Peirce, 1992). The appropriacy of the multiple-choice item format has also been questioned on the grounds, *inter alia*, that multiple choice questions do not test normal language processing and are subject to method effects (Buck, 1990; Weir, 1993, 1997).

In response to concerns such as these, ETS has initiated a major, long-term initiative, TOEFL 2000, the aim of which is to develop a new language proficiency test or battery to replace the current TOEFL. According to ETS, the new test will be one which is 'more reflective of the current understanding of communicative competence and performance-based language assessment and provides more information than current TOEFL scores about international students' ability to use English in an academic environment' (Taylor *et al.*, 1995: (1). In order to inform construct definition, ETS has commissioned the development of a model of communicative language use in academic contexts which is to serve as a framework for test design and validation (Chapelle, Grabe and Berns, 1997).

The challenge of performance testing

Although there appears to be an emerging consensus that EAP tests should be based on current views of communicative language ability and that they should sample a range of authentic academic tasks, the development of performance-based tests presents significant challenges which for reasons of space we can only sketch out briefly here. For more in-depth analysis of current issues in language performance testing, interested readers are referred to McNamara (1996), Norris *et al.* (1998) and Shohamy (1995).

Sampling and content validity

One of the major problems in testing any form of language performance is that of content representation. In order to make meaningful inferences about candidates' ability it is important to try to sample widely across a range of language use tasks. However, broad sampling is very difficult given the constraints of time and cost which prevail in most testing situations. Moreover, the type of performance which is elicited under examination conditions, may differ considerably from the academic work that students would normally produce in the classroom. The traditional timed essay test, for example, only samples the candidate's ability to write a draft in a single genre, whereas a final piece of student writing normally represents multiple drafts over a period of time with guidance from the teacher (Hamp-Lyons, 1991b; Purves, 1992).

This gap between formal tests and classroom practice has led to the adoption of methods of assessment such as portfolios, which are more closely aligned to EAP teaching programmes and which allow teachers to monitor and assess learners' work over a period of time. These will be described in greater detail below.

Tests of EAP proficiency: specific or general?

Another major question surrounding the content validity of EAP tests concerns the degree of subject specificity of the texts and tasks that are used. As Davidson (1998: 288) comments, common sense would seem to dictate that candidates in EAP reading tests should be given texts corresponding to their field of study. This view is supported by research evidence which suggests that EAP test-takers may be disadvantaged if they encounter a text drawn from a different discipline (Alderson and Urquhart, 1985).

However, recent research into the relationship between text specificity and test performance has revealed this question to be somewhat more complicated than hitherto assumed. In an exhaustive investigation of reading passages used in the IELTS test, Clapham (1996) found that not only was it very difficult to match texts to specific subject areas, but that enabling skills overlapped across different academic disciplines. She concluded (1996: 201) that students should be given a general purpose reading module instead of a subject-specific one. These findings, which were partially responsible for the replacement of the three separate, discipline-specific modules in the IELTS test by a single module (Charge and Taylor, 1997), highlight the need to review constantly the assumptions which underlie the construction of EAP tests.

Assessment in the EAP curriculum

In addition to the standardised proficiency tests described above, a wide range of methods, of varying degrees of formality, are used in EAP programmes for monitoring and assessing course-related achievement. These include teacher-made tests, journals, interviews, observations, projects, questionnaires and portfolios. For reasons of space and in view of their relevance to EAP contexts, we will deal only with the last of these methods here. Fuller description and discussion of the other methods can be found in Brindley (1989), Cohen (1994), Genesee and Upshur (1996), Hamayan (1995) and Shohamy (1998).

Portfolio assessment

Portfolios provide a range of samples of student work exemplifying different kinds of writing and thus offer a way of relating assessment closely to instruction (Fulcher, 1997; Genesee and Upshur, 1996; Kroll, 1998). Another claimed advantage of portfolio assessment is that the preparation of portfolios is often done collaboratively – students are encouraged to seek feedback and assistance from teachers and peers, thus encouraging learner autonomy.

However, the introduction of portfolio assessment has proven problematic in a number of ways. In the first place, there is by no means universal agreement on the type and amount of student work that should be included, the degree of student involvement in topic choice or the amount of outside assistance that should be allowed to learners (Fulcher, 1997). In addition, reliability studies have revealed low levels of agreement between assessors on the quality of a given sample of work, highlighting the need for regular standardising sessions and continuing discussion and renegotiation of assessment criteria (Hamp-Lyons and Condon, 1993: 188). Difficulties in scoring have been exacerbated by the lack of comparability between the samples submitted, leading to suggestions that there should be at least one common task which all students include in their portfolio. The logistics of collecting and marking large numbers of student texts on an on-going basis have also proved to be quite challenging in some academic settings (Belanoff, 1997).

Nevertheless, despite these difficulties, it has been argued that the positive impact that portfolios have on both teachers and learners is in itself sufficient reason to continue to use them, even if it cannot be demonstrated that portfolio assessment is technically more reliable than more traditional one-off tasks (Hamp-Lyons and Condon, 1993; Fulcher, 1997).

The role of technology

The advent of new technology is beginning to have a major effect on EAP language test design and delivery. The last few years have seen the widespread adoption of computer-adaptive assessment which enables tasks to be tailored to the test taker's level of ability and to receive immediate feedback on their performance (Brown, 1997; Gruba and Corbel, 1997). Candidates for both the TOEFL and IELTS are now able to take computer-based versions of these tests and in the near future the TOEFL will be available only on computer (ETS, 1998b). Researchers are now investigating a range of ways in which recent advances in electronically-mediated communication, computer technology and linguistic analysis can be incorporated into language tests. These include automated scoring of open-ended responses, handwriting and speech recognition, and Internet-based testing (Burstein *et al.*, 1996; Brown, 1997). Given the rapid progress which is being made in these areas, it may be envisaged that EAP tests of the future will incorporate many of these technological innovations.

Proficiency, achievement and programme evaluation

Up to this point, the discussion has centred on the use of assessment information for purposes of evaluating individual proficiency and attainment. However, this information has an equally important role in programme evaluation. In the second part of the chapter, we will therefore look at ways in which programme-specific assessments of achievement can be used in conjunction with external benchmarks of proficiency for the purpose of evaluating the impact of EAP programmes.

Assessing gain in EAP programmes

In EAP programmes, there is often considerable pressure on programme administrators to demonstrate that their programmes are producing the desired learning outcomes. The success of the programme is frequently gauged in terms of the extent to which gains are observed on achievement or proficiency measures. Crucial to the construct of 'gain', however, is a 'difference index' from a starting point to some other point occurring *later in time* after the impact of instruction has taken effect. Gain, in other words, requires either achievement assessments or proficiency measures to be conducted *before and after* the programme of instruction (Ross, 1998). Gain studies are, typically, logistically difficult to carry out – mainly because there are potentially numerous extraneous variables that can influence change over time (Cook and Campbell, 1979; Mohr, 1992).

EAP gain models

A variety of approaches to the assessment of gain in educational programmes are identified in the educational literature. These vary considerably in their complexity and sophistication (Lynch, 1996; Gottman, 1996). Six models typical of EAP programmes are outlined below, along with a discussion of the strengths and weaknesses of each.

The sequence of models begins with an outline of simple, and often problematic, pre-post assessments and progresses into integrated models, which demonstrate interrelations among achievement assessments and proficiency measures.

Model 1

A norm-referenced proficiency test (such as the institutional version of the TOEFL) is given before instruction and then administered again after instruction is completed (Figure 1). In order to determine the extent of the programme's impact, analysis of variance with repeated measures is carried out on the individual pre- and post-test scores. If there are significant within-subject mean differences, this is construed as evidence of positive programme impact.

Strengths: The observed gains may be accepted as evidence of programme success if the proficiency measure can be related to scores or levels on tests which are widely accepted as valid measures of English language proficiency such as TOEFL, IELTS, etc.

Weaknesses: The proficiency measures may be open to moderating influences (e.g. contact with native speakers outside the programme) and maturation effects (Cook and Campbell, 1979). It may not thus be clear to what extent the observed proficiency gains can be attributed directly to the effects of instruction (Beretta, 1986). In addition, if in-house proficiency measures are used, they may not be sufficiently generalisable unless considerable efforts are undertaken to validate the instruments. This may be difficult for institutions which do not have the necessary resources of time, expertise or funding to carry out validation studies.

Instructional Period

| Proficiency Test 1 | | Proficiency Test 2 |

Figure 1 Model 1

Model 2

This model (Figure 2) involves a criterion-referenced assessment of the specific objectives of the syllabus before instruction in order to establish learners' level of mastery. A parallel assessment is then administered at the end of the course and the results compared. Significant mean differences in performance on tasks, items and total scores (as shown by the results of repeated measures ANOVA) are interpreted as direct, simple evidence of instructional impact.

Strengths: Criterion-referenced tests are a useful way of measuring a candidate's standing in relation to the specific objectives of the course they are about to begin. By measuring the same objectives again at the end of the course, the course developers can determine how much of the course material learners have mastered. This, in turn, assists curriculum developers to determine the extent to which the programme content needs to be changed (Brown, 1993, 1996).

Weaknesses: Although learners may have mastered syllabus objectives, thus providing evidence of the impact of instruction, evidence of such gain may not generalise easily to programme-external criteria. In other words, achievement of specific objectives may not appear to translate directly into proficiency gains. In addition, parallel or equated forms of the tests are required so as to avoid pre-test bias on instruction or learner test-wiseness.

Model 3

A criterion-referenced pre-test of syllabus content knowledge is carried out as in Model 2. A post-test on syllabus content mastery is given after a suitable period of instruction. Additionally, a programme-external, construct-valid post-test is administered concurrently with the achievement post-test. The first criterion for detecting gain is a within-subjects significant difference between pre- and post-test mean scores as in Models 1 and 2. Model 3 (Figure 3) subsumes the earlier models in that it allows for within-subjects tests of gain. In addition, it introduces an important improvement, that is, it permits covariation over time to be assessed by comparing the

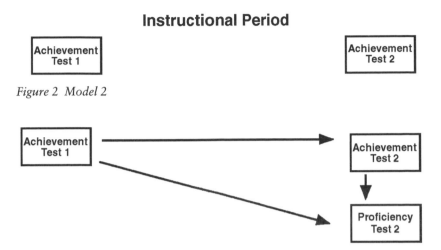

Instructional Period

Figure 2 Model 2

Figure 3 Model 3

relative magnitude of paths of influence. Covariation here indicates learners' relative standing on the pre-tests compared to their rank on the post-tests. If there are differential effects owing to learner variation in attendance, motivation, attention or learning, relative standings in proficiency (the post-test) can be expected to correlate with achievement status. The paths of influence are indices of influence on the post-tests attributable to individual differences in achievement.

Strengths: In this model, a syllabus-sensitive assessment is combined with an external proficiency-related criterion measure. This establishes an empirical basis for inferring that the achievement gains are construct valid by testing whether the achievement scores correlate with external criteria thought to measure the same skills as those developed through instruction (Gupta *et al.*, 1988, 1989). In addition to the mean difference comparisons, path models (standardised regression coefficients-*betas*) can be hypothesised and tested. The standardised regression coefficients indicate the relative influence scores that one assessment earlier in time have on a subsequent assessment or measurement. These influences (paths) can be tested for significance and size so as to allow inferences about their relative importance (Loehlin, 1987). In Model 3, for instance, the A2→P2 path would be predicted to be significant and positive, controlling for test effects from A1→A2 and A1→P2.

Weaknesses: Parallel or equated forms of the achievement tests are needed, as is a valid external criterion post-test. The logistics of test

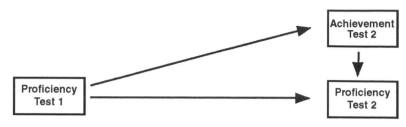

Figure 4 Model 4

construction and administration would make heavy resourcing demands on most EAP programmes.

Model 4

Here, valid pre- and post-proficiency tests are used in conjunction with a post-instruction achievement assessment (Figure 4). Valid gain is inferred if significant within-subjects mean differences are observed. The post-instruction achievement measure used here, however, must be derived from the actual instructional syllabus. The hypothesis of interest is that variation in achievement should covary with proficiency states at the end of instruction. This means that learners who are most successful in achieving the syllabus goals should also score relatively high on the proficiency measure after initial proficiency differences are controlled.

Strengths: External validity of gains can be established when a significant post-instruction path between achievement and post-test proficiency is observed. In Model 4, path A2→P2 can be assessed while holding paths P1→A2 and P1→P2 constant. No parallel forms of achievement measures are required, reducing the burden on programme staff to develop them. The only requirement is two proficiency measures that sample the same language skills as those taught and assessed in the EAP course.

Weaknesses: Parallel forms of a content-valid proficiency measure are required. Such measures (e.g. the institutional form of TOEFL) usually need to be interval-scaled (i.e., produce discrete numerical values based on a total score) if they are to detect small, medium and large gain scores after instructional periods typical of language training programmes. If there is a mismatch between achievement measure content and the proficiency measures, the validity may be depressed – that is, the path between achievement and proficiency may be no larger than what could occur by chance. Achievement measures lacking reliability may also depress validity. This may

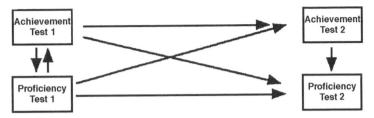

Figure 5 Model 5

happen when teachers opt to grade learners according to a 'freelance' scheme to the extent that composite achievement outcomes reflect teacher variation as much as learner achievement.

Model 5

The model considered here (Figure (5) includes repeated measures of both achievement and proficiency measures. Model 5 indicates that multiple paths can be examined for stability or change over time (Markus, 1979; Finkel, 1995). Two tests of gain can be formulated in Model 5. Tests of within-subjects mean difference can be conducted in parallel; an ANOVA for achievement differences and another one for proficiency. Different patterns of influence can be tested through cross-lagging achievement and proficiency measures over time (A1→P2, P1→P2 and A2→P2) so that the impact of achievement influences on proficiency change can be assessed.

Strengths: The major strengths of Model 5 emerge from the control over paths from pre-instruction individual differences (achievement and proficiency) on the main relationship of interest A2→P2. Assuming significant within-subject differences are observed between pre- and post-test achievement and proficiency means, the influence of syllabus-based achievement on proficiency gains can be tested with less ambiguity than in earlier models.

Weaknesses: The logistics of pre-testing and parallel achievement test form development make Model 5 quite rare in language programme evaluation.

Model 6

A variation on Model 5 includes achievement measures that are devised to assess syllabus content learning and mastery as a consequence of instruction. In contrast with earlier models, achievement in Model 6 (Figure 6) is assessed in a series of *waves* of measurements

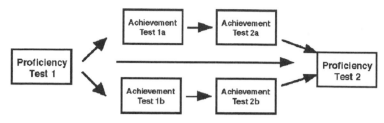

Figure 6 Model 6

and assessments that occur periodically over the length of the instructional programme. It is assumed that assessment waves may possibly influence each other across skill domains and time (cross-lags). Success in an EAP reading course, for example, may influence learner success in a writing course in the subsequent term. Language proficiency gain is assessed as in the other models with a pre-instruction proficiency test and a post-instruction parallel form. Achievement assessments are included in the model in order to represent learning outcomes within and across skill domains. These outcomes can then be tested for either influence on each other, as well as on eventual proficiency development.

In the Model 6 diagram below, Ach1a and Ach2a represent assessment of achievement in the skill of academic listening occurring over a longitudinal period of instruction. Ach1b and Ach2b may, for instance, be achievements in academic reading. Paths are devised to control for initial (pre-instruction) individual differences on achievement (P1→A1a), as well as 'carry-over' effects from one assessment wave to another (A1a→A2a). A path from within-skill achievement measures (A2a→P2) can be assessed for size and significance while controlling for prior proficiency (P1→P2) and skill-external achievement outcomes (A2b→P2).

Strengths: Model 6 has a major advantage over Model 5, in that no pre-testing of achievement is needed. The only pre-post measure is that of a valid external proficiency measure. Model 6 also permits within-subjects repeated measures gain assessment as well as tests of carry-over within skill domains. Contrastive (cross-lagged) paths between skills can also be modelled. Model 6 also controls for initial differences in proficiency (P1). This model allows administrators responsible for EAP programmes to build up a composite picture of the way their programme contributes to language proficiency gain.

Weaknesses: Achievement measures need to be contrastive (include more than one skill area) in order to create an optimal model of language gain outcomes. This typically requires reliable achievement assessment of different skill areas that can be compared with desired outcome measures. It also assumes that course assessments are devised to assess mastery of the course objectives, and that different teachers use a standard set of assessment procedures.

Assessing the outcomes of an EAP listening course

As an example application of Model 6, EAP listening development is analysed here. The method of analysis is a regression approach to impact analysis (Mohr, 1992) that tests whether achievement outcomes influence proficiency gain in listening as measured by TOEFL post-tests. The approach taken here is different from the usual impact analysis, which is predicated on the quasi-experimental *value-added* model of programme evaluation (Lynch, 1996). Rather, it involves one central hypothesis. It is that individual differences in achievement in EAP listening courses will lead to listening skill gain variance in proficiency. It is then that the EAP programme can be inferred to have the intended impact on learners' listening proficiency. In contrast, different skill achievements in EAP language courses are expected to lead to comparatively smaller influences in listening proficiency.

As an empirical study of EAP listening, an application of Model 6 to a three-cohort, ten-semester series of achievement assessments was examined for curricular impact validity. Achievement and proficiency test scores from 785 Japanese undergraduates enrolled in a two-year (288-hour) English for academic purposes programme at the School of Policy Studies, Kwansei Gakuin University, are analysed. In this analysis, the first year outcomes for three cohorts are examined.

As in Model 6, listening proficiency was measured before and after each instructional year with the use of the institutional TOEFL test given before and after approximately 144 hours of direct-method instruction in English for academic purposes. Of interest for this analysis are the paths from within-skill (listening) course achievements to post-instruction academic listening. Model 6 forces paths to 'compete' for influence on the post-instruction proficiency outcomes, which allows us to determine the size and significance of syllabus-based listening achievement assessments on listening proficiency gain relative to other achievements in reading or writing.

Two caveats will be introduced here in order to expedite the process of exposition: (1) only significant paths are shown from antecedent measures (earlier measures of proficiency or achievement) to consequent measures; (2) no synchronous influences are estimated

1995 First Instructional Year

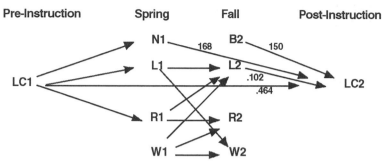

Figure 7

within a wave. These caveats thus create a left-to-right longitudinal path model of influences on TOEFL listening outcomes.

All course materials and assessments were standardised through a process of co-ordination and collaboration among the teachers assigned to each particular course. This provided the basis for a general uniformity in syllabus and assessment criteria across courses, teachers, and sections.

The 1995 cohort's first instructional year (n = 327; model[1] R^2 = .490) (Figure 7) shows several paths suggesting high impact on listening proficiency gain. First, the paths from TOEFL pre-test listening significantly covary with note-taking and listening achievement measures used in the first (spring) term. These paths suggest that the achievement assessments had some degree of domain content validity as assessments of listening. The second wave shows carry-over within skills (straight arrows), or cross-lags (angled arrows) between all four skill areas from spring to fall semesters. Such carry-over and cross-lagged patterns are not unexpected. Robust achievement in one language skill area in general influences other skills synergistically. Variance may be further increased by individual difference patterns of non-participation (poor attendance, motivation or attention), which tend to correlate across courses, sections and skills.

All three of the four courses with considerable academic listening focus (N1, B2 and L2) have unique paths to TOEFL post-test

---

[1] The model R-square indicates the amount of variance in the outcome (TOEFL post-test) that is accounted for by all of the antecedent variables together. A high R-square indicates that a large percentage of the individual differences in proficiency covary with the prior variables, which in all of the figures includes the TOEFL pre-test. A low R-square would suggest that post-test variance is unrelated to instruction or the pre-test.

listening. The relative size of the effect[2] indicates that achievement in the note-taking course (N1) is the most influential on TOEFL listening gains. Also, as Model 6 stipulates, within-skill achievements should influence gain, while across-skill achievements (below the centreline, here R1 and R2; W1 and W2), should, in principle, not. The data from the first instructional year impact study corroborate this expectation and thus support the hypothesis.

An examination of the 4–wave data for the first instructional year for the 1996 cohort (n = 258; model R^2 = .596) (Figure 8) reveals a slightly different pattern to that just observed. While there is considerable cross-skill influence between skills in the spring and fall achievement waves, some anomalies emerge when listening achievements are considered. N1 (first term lecture note-taking course) achievements carry over to B2 (support sections for sheltered content course), and influence L2 (listening) and S2 (reading and discussion seminar). It also yields, as in the previous diagram, an impact on TOEFL post-test scores. In contrast to the success of the lecture note-taking courses, are the ambiguous listening course achievements (L1 and L2). For these, there is covariance between pre-test TOEFL and L1 (end of spring listening achievement), but no carry-over to L2. Mysteriously, L1 influences B2 and the writing achievement in the third wave (W2). In contrast to the multiple influences on TOEFL post-test variance in the 1995 First Instructional Year, only N1 remains as an influence on gain in academic listening proficiency. This pattern suggests that the listening syllabus modifications may have had an unintended effect.

The apparent lack of influence of spring and fall wave achievements in listening-focused courses (L1, B2 and L2) on EAP listening gains might be explained by changes in syllabus content. An examination of syllabus documents for L1 and L2 courses, for instance, suggests that the focus of the listening materials was shifted away from academic and schema-building of content towards interpersonal communication in the form of pairwork and small group discussion. Achievement assessments (which included peer and self-assessments) for the L1 and L2 courses thus appear to cover a different skill domain than that of academic listening. B2 presents a similar shift in syllabus content, with a move to use 30% of class time for student presentations on ecology topics. The 1995 version of B2 was

---

[2] Effect here refers to change in the variable at end of an arrow. The magnitude of the change is in standard deviation units, such that one unit (1 sd) change in the variable from which the arrow comes leads to a percentage of 1 standard deviation change in the outcome variable. Thus a path of X - .30→Y implies that 1 sd change in X lead to 30% of 1 sd change in Y, holding all other influences constant.

1996 First Instructional Year

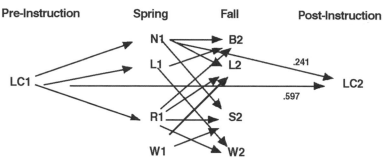

Figure 8

comparably more focused on sheltered-content course note-taking strategies and lecture processing, and thus had an impact on TOEFL gain. The 1996 version included more ecology theme-related reading of lecture handouts as well as the student presentations, which constitutes enough of a syllabus shift to account for the lack of a significant path to the TOEFL post-test.

Analysis of the achievement and proficiency test scores of the third cohort (1997 First Instructional Year – Figure 9) confirms the emergent patterning of influences. Here, as in the previous two diagrams, there is considerable cross-lagged influence from the second (spring) to the third (fall) waves. This cross-influence pattern (n = 200; model R^2 = .330) again suggests that achievements in one skill domain are likely to influence achievements in another. For example, success in N1 has a spreading effect to the reading/discussion seminar S2. N3 in Figure 9 likewise, influences achievement in S4. If cross-domain paths in all of the diagrams are tallied, there appears to be a rough parity between aural/oral achievements influencing subsequent reading/writing achievement – eight paths cross the centreline downward from aural/oral achievements, while ten paths cross it in an upward direction from reading/writing to aural/oral. In an EAP programme featuring direct-method language teaching (all instruction performed in the target language), synergistic or gestalt effects such as these imply a cumulative effect.

Discussion

If the programme evaluation question is 'How do syllabus-based achievements contribute to proficiency gain?', three answers appear to emerge from the foregoing analyses: (1) simulations of academic

1977 First Instructional Year

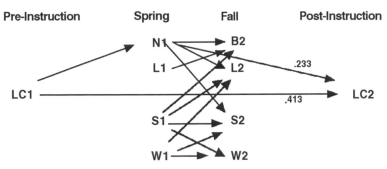

Figure 9

lectures in a note-taking course which provide ample examples of different lecture styles and content, as well as strategy training for successful note-taking, note-processing and review management, consistently influence EAP listening gains; (2) A general purpose 'listening' class may not lead to proficiency gains if the syllabus domain content drifts away from academic listening to conversational interaction; (3) There is domain-specific validity for EAP listening gain as measured by TOEFL. That is to say, no achievement scores in reading or writing appear to directly influence EAP listening gain, although there is considerable cross-influence of achievement in one skill domain to others, from antecedent achievement waves to consequent achievement waves.

The analysis of gains in the EAP programme reported here was based on cross-cohort longitudinal research on EAP listening gain over three years of instructional programmes, using scores in achievement and proficiency tests. Not all of the useful input to this analysis was, however, quantitative. Often useful programme evaluation needs to work backwards from profiles of outcomes – both desired and unexpected – to the original curriculum documents prepared by staff teachers and co-ordinators. Comparisons of 'what went right and what went wrong' are made possible only by conscientious archiving of such documents and data – which is one of the hallmarks of any successful EAP programme.

Conclusion

From the brief survey provided in this chapter, it can be seen that the EAP assessments used both at classroom and system level increasingly reflect a concern on the part of both test development agencies and teachers to ensure that the abilities tested are those actually required in tertiary study. Nevertheless, a good deal of further empirical work will be required in order to unravel the complexities of language use in academic contexts.

At the same time, we have shown how proficiency measurement and achievement assessment, which have tended to be viewed as separate processes in EAP contexts, can be brought closer together for purposes of programme evaluation (cf. also Hughes, 1988). The two forms of assessment provide complementary information: achievement assessment is context-sensitive, provides information on individual attainment of objectives at the individual level and informs the teaching process. The results of proficiency measures, on the other hand, can give teachers, learners and other interested audiences an indication of learners' overall level of ability in relation to their purposes for language use and provide information which is externally credible for purposes of programme accountability. Continuing efforts to develop assessments of both kinds that reflect research-based understandings of language use can do much to bring about a closer connection between assessment and learning in academic contexts and ultimately to improve the quality of EAP programmes.

PART II

THE ENGLISH FOR ACADEMIC
PURPOSES CURRICULUM

Introduction

This second part of the book provides readers with an overview of a representative selection of the numerous issues and research methodologies that are involved in curriculum design and the teaching of EAP as an international discipline. Broadly speaking, this part represents a model of the EAP curriculum and aims to describe and review the wide range of approaches to EAP syllabus design and to the teaching of EAP from the viewpoint of both practitioners and researchers. The aim is to highlight the various key issues in the field of EAP curriculum design and delivery and to provide case studies of the ways these issues can be researched.

This part falls naturally into two sections – the first covers curriculum design per se, and the second methodologies for the teaching of the different skills needed by the EAP student. The majority of the fourteen original chapters in Part II present empirical research from one EAP situation and describe the pedagogical and research implications of the findings. Topics covered include the following: needs analysis; course design and syllabus renewal; language and subject specialist team teaching; the place of grammar in content-based instruction; language learning strategies; student assessment; separate chapters on the teaching of reading, speaking, listening, writing, vocabulary, study skills; and finally, learner autonomy. The collection represents a variety of research methodologies including discourse analysis, ethnography, experimental research, survey research and action research. The geographical scope of the contributions is wide, reflecting the worldwide scope of EAP today.

The first chapter in this part, contributed by the editors, provides a broad overview of the EAP curriculum and discusses the following issues: needs analysis, the EAP syllabus, the roles of the EAP teacher and the EAP learner, classroom materials, teaching methodology for the four skills and for study skills, student assessment and programme evaluation. The aim of this chapter is to set the scene for the original studies which follow.

In the next chapter George Braine describes the many exercises in needs analysis he has conducted over the last twenty years in Asia and the US, and discusses how his approach has evolved over that time. He has been attentive to the necessity to vary his approach according to differences among the learning situations with which he has dealt. He also points out the necessity for course designers to enlist the co-operation of teachers from various disciplines, and discusses obstacles that inhibit this co-operation and ways to overcome them.

A somewhat under-reported aspect of the theory and practice of EAP is curriculum renewal. There is a great deal on how to design an EAP curriculum, but little on the necessary on-going renewal process of programmes once they are established. Fredricka Stoller points out that while some EAP programmes are content with the status quo, others see change as an integral part of programme life. She describes the three main stimuli for change as evolving faculty and student needs, programme changes and new findings in the professional literature. She also highlights the need to remain competitive as one important factor compelling continual curricular renewal, and asserts that reform is best advanced through collaborative efforts among stakeholders. After reviewing the literature on student needs and curriculum design, Stoller's chapter reports on the implementation and implications to wider settings of a ten-year cycle of EAP curriculum reform at Northern Arizona University. Reform involved the use of student and teacher feedback to fine-tune a programme combining content-based and discrete-skills instruction.

The team teaching approach developed by Dudley-Evans and Johns during the 1970s is now well known as an effective and useful option for the EAP curriculum in certain contexts. It entails a language teacher and a subject teacher teaching together in one classroom and was originally designed to help L2 students understand the content of lectures and of previous exam papers, and also to prepare for future exams. In this chapter Tony Dudley-Evans describes on-going work at the University of Birmingham on the approach, and particularly the changes to it since its inception. The focus of team teaching has shifted somewhat to oral presentational skills, writing research reports and the genres of professional writing, though students still work on examination skills. Another change since the 1970s has been that the courses are usually attended by L1 as well as L2 students, and partly as a result of this the courses have become credit-bearing. Dudley-Evans also discusses the reasons behind these changes, and compares the current model with other collaborative models, most importantly the American model for content-based instruction described by Brinton and Holten in this part of the book. Finally, he reflects on the reasons for the success of the courses, and implications of the relationship between the language teachers and the co-operating subject teachers.

Donna Brinton and Christine Holten begin their chapter on the teaching of grammar in content-based instruction by pointing out that while content-based instruction is one of the primary approaches used in the teaching of EAP, the approach does not readily lend itself to an explicit focus on form. They continue with a report on their research into the issue, carried out among the teachers and students on a number of university-level content-based courses. The data they use in their research includes end-of-term course reviews completed by teachers, student course evaluations and teacher questionnaires. Their general findings were that neither teachers nor students were satisfied with the quantity or quality of the grammar instruction on the courses. Based on their findings, the authors propose methods for adjusting the EAP content-based curriculum so that the authentic source materials (which they characterise as academic texts and lecture materials) typically used on these courses can also provide a suitable context for grammar instruction. Their aim with these proposals is to suggest a way to successfully integrate grammar input and practice with content-based instruction. They stress that to achieve this aim the target curriculum and materials will have to be modified and improved, and also that some pre- and in-service teacher training will be necessary.

Little research into the use of language learning strategies and their relationship to proficiency has focused on inter-disciplinary differences in EAP. Matthew Peacock in his chapter reports on an investigation into strategy use, associations with proficiency and EAP teacher and student opinions on useful strategies in seven EAP classes, and with 43 EAP teachers in Hong Kong. Students were studying physics, computing mathematics, or engineering. Data were collected from students and teachers using the 50-item Strategy Inventory for Language Learning (Oxford, 1990), interviews, essays and a proficiency test. Students reported frequently using 18 of the 50 strategies, primarily from two of Oxford's six categories – Cognitive (using all your mental processes) and Compensation (compensating for missing knowledge). Nine strategies were associated with proficiency (five positively, and four negatively). Two broad inter-disciplinary differences in strategy use were found: physics students used significantly fewer Cognitive strategies, and computing mathematics students used significantly fewer Metacognitive (organising and evaluating learning) strategies. Teachers rated 15 strategies as having high usefulness for EAP, primarily the Cognitive and Metacognitive categories; however, only 6 of the 15 strategies recommended by teachers were among those often used by students. Recommendations are that EAP teachers consider embedding strategy instruction in teaching tasks and materials. Additionally, as 5 out of 6 strategies ranked highest for usefulness by the 43 teachers in this study involve student work and study outside the classroom, it is suggested that teachers encourage and assist their students to increase their involvement in this area.

In the next chapter, Averil Coxhead and Paul Nation categorise vocabulary into four types – general purpose high frequency vocabulary (80% of academic text), academic vocabulary (around 10%), technical vocabulary (around 5%) and low frequency vocabulary. They stress that the second category, academic vocabulary, is very important for EAP learning and teaching because it is common to a wide range of academic disciplines, because it accounts for a high proportion of words in academic texts and because it is amenable to classroom instruction. Their proposed approach to instruction is to build up an academic vocabulary list, either through corpus studies of academic texts or frequency counts of the words learners need translations of in those texts. They point out the need for EAP instruction to focus directly on academic vocabulary; to consider its use for the four skills of reading, listening, speaking and writing; and to meet students' need for fluency development. Coxhead and Nation characterise EAP learners' familiarity with academic vocabulary as a vital part of their entry into their respective academic discourse communities.

In the next chapter, on student assessment, Fred Davidson and Yeonsuk Cho narrate the development of the *ESL Placement Test (EPT)* over the past twenty-five years at the University of Illinois at Urbana-Champaign, an institution with a strong commitment to international students. Their discussion focuses on three areas – the forces that made the test what it now is, the content and format of the current test, and the anticipated forces which may shape changes in the test over the next five or ten years. The authors of this chapter aim to demonstrate how these three areas is relevant to most EAP test settings and also how they affect the validity and reliability of most tests. The first issue they discuss is how an understanding of the history of a test and of the institution explains many of the features of any one EAP test and are relevant to an objective assessment of that test. The second is the role of empirical evidence (especially statistical evidence) in quality control, and how the application of new methods in norm-referenced statistical analysis has helped ensure that decisions about student placement based on EPT test results are reliable and valid. Davidson and Cho stress, however, that statistical quality alone is no longer sufficient but must be combined with consideration of richer models of test development and validation. Finally, Davidson and Cho assert that the different agendas of the three main stakeholders in test quality – the university, the students and their ESL teachers – must all be taken into account when developing and refining the EAP test.

Dana Ferris begins her paper on writing for academic purposes by surveying the current state of thinking on a number of major issues, including differences between L2 and L1 writing, the debate over discipline-specific versus general purpose EAP instruction, the role of reading in writing instruction, computer-assisted instruction, teacher and peer response and feedback, error correction, grammar instruction and student assessment. She then goes on to report on her own study of how teacher comments affect student revisions, and of which parts of those comments best helped students revise successfully. She examined 48 texts written by four strong and four weak student writers. It was found that the most useful teacher comments were those that were specific and called for micro-level changes; comments that addressed students' argumentation or called for global changes in the essays were less helpful. She also reports differences among teacher comments and in student revision across levels of ability and also across different types of assignment. In her conclusions Ferris argues that teacher comments and other feedback are of great importance to L2 writing students, and that they must be designed and handled carefully and cautiously by EAP teachers.

A central issue of Tom Cobb and Marlise Horst's chapter on EAP reading, is the discussion of finding appropriate instructional strategies to meet the challenge of what he calls the paradox of whether to teach depth or breadth – the fact that putting the main focus on the learning of vocabulary through time-consuming extensive reading may be at the expense of reading comprehension skills. He discusses the lexical problems of reading for EAP, proposes that one answer may be a concordance programme, and describes the adaptation of concordance software to learning vocabulary. Cobb says that the success of corpus analysis in describing the lexical problem of ESP reading led him to try a corpus-based teaching approach. He adapted concordance technology to an instructional system that takes the EAP learner through almost 3,000 words of general English in less than a year, and provides empirical data showing commerce students in Oman using the method to gain control of the required vocabulary within a few months.

The starting point of Alan Hirvela's chapter on incorporating reading in the writing class is his argument that while reading for academic purposes is usually classified and taught as a receptive skill, there have often been challenges to this viewpoint because (as has been pointed out before) reading is a productive as well as a receptive skill. He describes a qualitative study of 39 undergraduate students' reading during an integrated EAP reading and writing course in an American university. The aim of the study was to investigate the incorporation of reading into a writing course. The course aimed to ensure that the learners were taught as active rather than passive readers, and also that the texts they read came from their academic discourse communities. Data were collected through student self-assessment, an end-of-course survey, interviews and recall protocols on learner attitudes. The study found considerable variation in students' reactions and preferences for reading–writing tasks. Hirvela recommends flexibility in the selection of the types of text chosen for combined reading and writing on EAP courses, and also using a wide variety of text types and reading–writing assignments that are related to the particular academic discourse the students need to work within outside the EAP classroom.

Peter Robinson and his colleagues in their chapter on EAP speaking skills, focus on the issues of developing pragmatic competence, and conversational skills such as turntaking, topic nomination and control, and paralinguistic features of oral academic discussion such as appropriate eye contact and gesture. They discuss options in the design and implementation of courses for academic speaking ability, and conclude the first part of their chapter by describing two dominant approaches to EAP course design, skill-based and task-based. The second part reports on an empirical study of oral discussion skill development. The treatments and activities they describe are focus on certain skills, guided and structured focus on form and unguided focus on form. The measures of oral discussion skill development are described, including the analytic rating scale and the procedure for training raters, and then rating pre- and post-test videos of oral discussions. Finally individual difference measures are described, measures of language learning aptitude and strategy use, along with their research questions and results.

In his chapter on EAP listening, Steven Tauroza reports an investigation into whether encouraging students to predict, prior to academic presentations, leads to greater comprehension of what is heard. It has been suggested that prediction plays a major role in facilitating listening comprehension and, therefore, ESL learners should be encouraged to predict (see Brown, 1978). It seems likely that predictions activate schemata that help students to listen in a more focused manner. However, Rost (1990: 134–136) has examined ESL student predictions and found evidence that erroneous predictions might lead to misunderstandings. Tauroza's study of academic listening featured ninety Hong Kong-based undergraduates majoring in English who are in their first year at university. The study examined the relative efficacy of two methods that are designed to prompt ESL students to predict prior to listening to academic style speech. One method involved encouraging a group of listeners to make predictions about specific points of information they would hear. The other method involved encouraging listeners to make predictions about the issues and topics of an academic presentation. The comprehension of both groups of predictors was compared. In addition, the comprehension of the predictors was compared with that of students in matched groups who were not encouraged to predict prior to listening to the presentations.

In their chapter on skills for studying EAP, Alan and Mary Waters open with the remark that there is wide agreement that competence in study skills (e.g. note-taking and efficient reading skills for academic texts) is essential for EAP students. They argue that what they refer to as *study competence* – critical questioning, logical thinking and 'emotional intelligence' – is even more important than *study skills* for EAP students, and that EAP teaching tasks and materials therefore need to address the former as well as the latter. They continue by suggesting that problem-solving tasks are the most suitable type of classroom activity for developing study competence as well as study skills. They categorise these tasks as Direct Study Competence Tasks, Indirect Study Competence Tasks or Skills Transference Tasks. Direct Study Competence Tasks are activities that increase students' awareness of skills that make up study competence. Indirect Study Competence Tasks are those that allow students to see how the acquisition of study skills relies on them first developing study competence. Skills Transference Tasks are a set of related problems that together consist of a typical study cycle. Finally, Waters and Waters state that teaching materials for the development of EAP study competence need to be purpose-designed in terms of both content and the kinds of learning processes that they aim to activate.

Following a review of the relevant literature on autonomous learning covering the areas of strategic language learning, learner-centredness, learning styles, self-access learning, learner autonomy, syllabus negotiation, and self-directedness in evaluation and assessment, Tony Lynch suggests the main concern for EAP in this area should be to prepare learners to become members of their academic community. He claims that insufficient attention has been given to helping learners gain from exposure to English on their subject courses. In the empirical part of his chapter Lynch reports on research done at the University of Edinburgh since 1993 on the PROFILE (Principles, Resources and Options for the Independent Learner of English) project. The aims of the project are to design, test and revise materials that assist learners' exploitation of learning opportunities beyond the EAP classroom. Quantitative and qualitative data on materials evaluation are being collected through class observation, interviews and questionnaires and work is continuing on adapting, revising, piloting and evaluating the next generation of PROFILE materials and tasks. Particular attention is being paid to the incorporation of user comments and to keeping the focus of adaptation on helping learners become independent of teacher support.

11 The EAP curriculum: Issues, methods, and challenges

John Flowerdew and Matthew Peacock

English language teaching can be classified into two main branches, English for General Purposes (EGP) and English for Specific Purposes (ESP) (Strevens, 1988a; Hutchinson and Waters, 1987). Within English for Specific Purposes there are again two principal branches, English for Academic Purposes (EAP) and English for Occupational Purposes (EOP). However, within ESP, EAP tends to dominate, certainly in terms of research and research-based application.

The now widely accepted recognition of EAP as a separate and distinct discipline from EGP, on the one hand, and EOP, on the other (albeit with much overlapping), has made urgent the continuing search for the best approach to the design, implementation and evaluation of the EAP course. The teaching and learning of EAP presents its own unique challenges, problems, opportunities, failings and successes, and course and curriculum designers have to accept and meet those challenges and opportunities. One vital step in this process is producing a comprehensive description of the unique needs and wishes of the EAP student; another is shaping a detailed description of the nature of the EAP teaching and learning process; a third critical step in designing the EAP curriculum is accepting that the methodologies and approaches valid in any other area of ESL are not necessarily the most appropriate for EAP. The needs and wishes of EAP learners are distinct and clearly identifiable from those of EGP learners, as is the EAP learning context, and the EAP course designer must investigate and try to fulfil those needs and wishes within the context of the relevant EAP course.

This introductory chapter discusses key aspects of the EAP curriculum: needs analysis for EAP, planning the EAP course, syllabus design, methodology, teaching the different skills, assessment and programme evaluation. The key questions concerning each of these issues are introduced in this chapter, paving the way for the more in-depth research studies that will make up the main part of the rest of the book.

Needs analysis

There is a general consensus that needs analysis, the collection and application of information on learners' needs, is a defining feature of ESP and, within ESP, of EAP (e.g. T. Johns and Dudley-Evans, 1991; Robinson, 1991; Strevens, 1988a; Jordan, 1997). Needs analysis is the necessary point of departure for designing a syllabus, tasks and materials. With its concern to fine tune the curriculum to the specific needs of the learner, needs analysis was a precursor to subsequent interest in 'learner centredness' (Nunan, 1988a; Tudor, 1996). Early examples of needs analysis were simple affairs that sought to get a rough idea of the purposes for which learners would need English after their course. A more systematic and very influential model was that of Munby (1978), who provided a very detailed multi-dimensional model for specifying the uses of language that learners were likely to encounter in specific purpose situations.

Munby was criticised for only considering the target needs (referred to as *Target Situation Analysis*) of learners and neglecting other requirements. Needs analysis should be more than just a specification of learners' target uses of the language, subsequent curriculum specialists argued. It should also consider learners' *lacks* – that is, what they actually require, taking into account what they already know – and their *wants* – what they themselves wish to learn (Hutchison and Waters, 1987); target situation analysis may discover that learners need to be able to read academic textbooks, but learners, on the other hand, may feel that grammatical accuracy is what they need, or want to improve their social English.

An approach to EAP needs analysis can be to ask ourselves why the learners are doing an English course, in what situations they will need or already need English, and what they must do in those situations. Information can be gathered from people with responsibility for the course, learners, and others in the learners' academic department who are now using English. The information to be collected can also include the learners' primary motivation in learning English, their learning background, ESL proficiency (four skills) and an idea of how much they now use English outside the classroom – that is, their opportunities for reading, writing, listening and speaking English.

A further dimension of needs analysis is concerned with finding out about learners' language learning strategies (Oxford, 1990), defined by Oxford as conscious or unconscious methods of helping or accelerating learning. Strategy analysis is particularly important in EAP contexts where learners and teachers come from different cultural backgrounds, and where approaches to language learning may vary (Tudor, 1996).

Given the technical nature of the areas of language use with which EAP is concerned, in addition to the various dimensions to needs analysis just mentioned, there is an important role to be played by the specialist informant, a subject-matter expert who can interpret the conceptual content of the target situation on behalf of the needs analyst.

A range of methods is commonly used for conducting needs analysis. These include questionnaires, interviews, participant and non-participant observation, authentic language data (texts and recordings), case studies of learners, self-assessment, pre- and post-course testing, and learner diaries.

Given its increasing complexity, practitioners have come to realise that needs analysis cannot be just a one-off exercise, but that it needs to be on-going and continually refined, as teaching and learning develop (Tudor, 1996). Increasingly, detailed ethnographic studies are being used as on-going needs analysis. As with ethnography in general, the need for triangulation of perspectives is increasingly coming to be accepted.

Whatever approach to defining learner needs is taken by course planners, students need to be part of the planning process and teachers should ensure that they have an overview of the goals of the course, and of each lesson. This encourages student participation in the learning process and reduces potential frustration and disappointment. A link between individual activities and these wider goals is also needed, as is a variety of tasks and materials that will cater to the differences in learning styles, beliefs about language learning and modes of learning found particularly in pre-sessional courses. The EAP classroom is also very likely to contain learners of different levels of proficiency, and needs analysis needs to reflect this likely variation in target audience.

The EAP syllabus

Following the description of learner needs that is the outcome of conducting needs analyses, the syllabus designer must develop a detailed description of goals for the course as well as an evaluation of the potential difficulties learners will have in meeting those goals. An EAP syllabus, like any other syllabus, consists of a description of what will be included in the course, or course objectives.

Approaches to EAP syllabus design have been very much influenced by research in applied linguistics. Hall and Crabbe (1994) list a range of approaches to EAP syllabus design. The earliest they mention is the still influential Lexicogrammar-based approach, mostly focused on the teaching of structure and vocabulary and influenced by register analysis of the sixties and seventies. The second is the Function-notional-based approach developed in the 1970s, partly as a reaction against earlier form-focused approaches. Next came the Discourse-based approaches of the late 1970s, with an emphasis on cohesion and coherence at the level of the text. A further development was Hutchison and Waters's (1987) Learning-centred approach, which concentrated not on the language items and skills students needed, but rather on what they had to do in class to learn these processes; there is an emphasis on meaningful and appropriate content and on communication within the classroom. Finally, the Genre-based approach uses materials and tasks based on authentic linguistic data in order to promote student awareness of the conventions and procedures of the genre in question.

Another important approach, not mentioned by Hall and Crabbe (1994) is the skills-based approach, where the focus is on particular skills. This has been very important, given the rather precise needs of some EAP courses (for example, many learners in South America have traditionally only required a reading knowledge of English).

Another very influential approach to EAP syllabus design, especially in North America, but not mentioned by Hall and Crabbe (1994) is the *content-based* syllabus. Flowerdew (1993a: 123) cites Spanos (1987) in listing the precepts upon which content-based approaches are based:

- Language teaching should be related to the eventual uses to which the learner will put the language
- The use of informational content tends to increase the motivation of the language learner
- Effective teaching requires attention to prior knowledge, existing knowledge, the total academic environment and the linguistic proficiency of the learner
- Language teaching should focus on contextualised language use rather than on sentence level usage
- Language learning is promoted by a focus on significant and relevant content from which learners can derive the cognitive structures that facilitate the acquisition of vocabulary and syntax as well as written and oral production

There are a number of different types of content based instruction, including *theme-based*, *sheltered* and *adjunct* (Brinton *et al.*, 1989), and various hybrids of these basic types. Theme-based instruction is organised as a set of topics or a single topic selected by the teacher. Theme-based instruction focuses on developing overall academic skills and is not targeted at a particular discipline. Sheltered instruction consists of courses run by subject specialists for second language students in mainstream American colleges and universities. Second language learners can benefit from such instruction, it is claimed, because content teachers will naturally make adjustments and simplifications in order to communicate more effectively with their second language audiences. With adjunct language instruction, students are enrolled in both a content and a language course dealing with the same content. The second language students are integrated with mainstream students in the content class, but are segregated and receive extra help in the linked language support course.

The role of the teacher

Carver (1983) and Strevens (1988b) have both described the particular qualities that EAP teachers should possess if the EAP curriculum is to be successful. Teachers should be willing to adjust teaching activities and materials to the students' needs, to familiarise themselves with the language of the students' special subject and to take an interest in and to acquire a knowledge of the students' world. EAP teachers should understand that the students' knowledge of their specialist world is likely to be considerably greater than their own, have flexibility and skill in needs analysis, be able to design specialist courses, to design new materials or adapt existing ones, and to work with students of very different linguistic abilities within one classroom. In addition, in some EAP situations teachers must be able to co-operate with subject teachers.[1] The need for these skills is perhaps greater for EAP than in many other areas of ESL. Altered perspectives such as these should also affect how teachers view their classrooms (Woods, 1996).

The role of the learner

EAP learners need to be able to develop the skills they require to study alone and this makes it clear that an important part of EAP methodology is promoting learner independence. Learners have

---

[1] See, e.g., the chapters by Brinton and Holten and Dudley-Evans on collaboration with subject specialists.

many opportunities to promote their English and academic study skills outside the classroom, and teachers who neglect to foster their students' ability to use these opportunities are failing to help make their learners independent. By asking learners to research and investigate the resources available to them inside and outside the academy, as well as encouraging learners to take responsibility for their own learning, teachers will set their students on the path to full independence.

Teaching materials

Once a syllabus has been established, teaching materials need to be selected. A difficult choice for many EAP course designers and teachers is between published materials and materials made specifically for the target EAP course. Kuo (1993), however, recommends that we 'need not take an all-or-nothing approach . . . (EAP) textbooks may serve as a kind of data bank', allowing teachers to choose the materials that are most appropriate for any one class among those in a small collection.

Another choice is between authentic and non-authentic materials. Three common arguments in favour of authentic texts are that non-authentic texts cannot represent real-world language use, that simplified materials often lose some meaning with simplification and that the real-world situations learners will face or are already facing are best prepared for with authentic texts. Among the arguments against the use of authentic texts are that any one authentic text may not be authentic for a specific class, the fact that just because a text is authentic does not mean it is relevant (the distinction between authenticity of text and authenticity of purpose) and the obvious point that authentic texts are frequently too difficult linguistically, and for classes of students from various disciplines may require too high a level of specialised knowledge. Kuo (1993) concludes on the question of authenticity that it is almost impossible for authentic texts to be always appropriate, and that the important point with any text is appropriate selection and use. Certainly the choice of any language teaching materials must be made with the proper context in which the materials will be used kept firmly in mind. It must also be remembered that each EAP discipline has its own specialised style of language use (discourse), and that this style should – if possible – be incorporated into the teaching materials selected (see Widdowson, 1983; Hutchinson and Waters, 1987; Phillips and Shettlesworth, 1978, on the debate surrounding authenticity).

EAP methodology

EAP/ESP is generally claimed not to have a single specific methodology (Strevens, 1988b). On the other hand, methodology employed in specific ESP/EAP settings is quite often innovative or specialised (Bloor and Bloor, 1986; T. Johns and Dudley-Evans, 1991). Most consistently running through these innovative approaches to ESP/ EAP methodology is the notion of purposeful and authentic learning activity. EAP practitioners are concerned that the learning goals and activities that their learners engage in are meaningful in relation to the specific purpose of their target discipline. This has resulted in an emphasis on various types of task-based learning and the use of authentic materials. Space allows us to describe briefly only a few examples of such approaches.

A pioneering effort was developed by Herbolich (1979) at the University of Kuwait in the late seventies. In order to teach his students to read and write technical manuals, Herbolich set them the task of designing and building box-kites and writing the accompanying manual to go with them.

Working also in the Middle East (King Abdulaziz University, Saudi Arabia) at about the same time as Herbolich, and also concerned with the relationship between authentic task and language learning activity, Phillips (1981) developed an approach to ESP methodology based upon the following two precepts: (1) the structure of LSP tasks must be determined by the structure of the behavioural objectives of the learner's special purpose, and (2) this structure must be at the highest practicable level of focus. From this position Phillips developed four principles, as follows:

the principal of reality control: control of task difficulty should be determined by simplifying the task in terms of the specific purpose and not just by simplifying the language.
the principle of non-triviality: the learning tasks must be perceived by the learner as meaningfully generated by the special purpose.
the principle of authenticity: the language acquired must be authentic to the specific purpose
the principle of the tolerance of error: errors should be treated as unacceptable only if they compromise communicative adequacy.

Emphasising methodology over content, Hall and Kenny (1988) described a pre-sessional EAP course in a Thai university in which 'Our syllabus is specified in terms of its methodology rather than in terms of linguistic items or skills' (p. 20). Concerned that the course should prepare learners for the sort of activities that they will be confronted with in their real-life programme of study, the course begins with a deep-end strategy of confronting learners with actual tasks, which they will have to perform as fully fledged students in an English-medium university. In this way Hall and Kenny encourage a method of work that involves 'initiative, the sharing of ideas and a focus on the "how" and "why" of investigation rather than on the "what"' (p. 21). The emphasis is here again on purposefulness and authenticity.

With task-based approaches the role of the teacher becomes one of guide and advisor rather than omniscient source of knowledge. Such an approach fits in with recent work in North America based upon the work of the Soviet theorist Vygotsky. In pioneering literacy pedagogy at San Diego State University, A. Johns (forthcoming) describes how literacy teachers can provide *scaffolding* or *assisted performance* in the performance of such tasks. Citing Vygotsky's *Zone of Proximal Development*, Johns describes how the Soviet theorist argued for *whole* activities which could be partitioned into *units* that contain essential characteristics of the whole. Johns demonstrates how teachers can assist learners in various ways in the performance of these units, or tasks, through assisted performance: by *modelling* an activity, by providing *feedback* and by *cognitive structuring* (organisation of learners' cognitive activities). Fundamental to John's approach is close collaboration with content teachers, a methodology she has documented in an earlier publication (A. Johns, 1997a).

Teaching the different skills

Considerable research has been conducted in recent years into the teaching of the four macro-skills (reading, writing, listening and speaking) in EAP and a considerable literature has been built up on each. Here we can do no more than indicate some of the key issues.

Reading

Reading, as a skill for EAP students, is often linked to writing because the former often precedes the latter within the target disciplines. Students read textbooks and journal articles with the goal of extracting relevant information and ideas for writing up assignments, examinations and dissertations, etc. For this reason, reading teachers often focus on reading skills they believe will be useful when students write extensively (see Bloor and St John, 1988). Examples are distinguishing relevant from irrelevant information, note-taking skills, skimming and scanning skills, understanding connections between paragraphs and between sections, use of cohesive and other markers and interpreting the writer's point of view.

Reading is probably the skill needed by the greatest number of EAP students throughout the world. Many textbooks are available only in English and most of the specialist international journals are published only in English. Even if the medium of instruction is not English, therefore, students throughout the world need to be able to read in English. EAP reading involves a number of specific difficulties (Grellet, 1981). The registers/genres of different disciplines are different from those of 'general English'. Students may do well in 'reading lessons' in general English, but have difficulty in reading in their subject areas. Also the aims are different: reading narrative may be for enjoyment alone, but in subject areas students often read to perform some task – to learn about something, get information, learn how to do something or draw material for argument. This dichotomy was highlighted by Johns and Davies (1983) in the mnemonic for dealing with texts in the classroom, *Text as a Linguistic Object* (TALO) and *Text as a Vehicle for Information* (TAVI).

Reading is often neglected by subject teachers. Nuttall (1996) points out that although reading textbooks is vital for assignments, projects and exams, students are often not taught how to read textbooks and there is a tendency for subject teachers to use the following strategies: explain in spoken language, sometimes the L1, give notes because the textbook is 'too difficult' and even write the notes on the board, in which case students spend the lesson writing. These strategies may help students learn the content, but will not help them to improve their content reading skills or to be independent learners. The learning of the process of reading, particularly extracting and organising information into their own notes, is perhaps educationally more important than learning sets of information. When choosing texts for reading at lower levels, a strong argument can be made for using coursebooks. At higher levels, a problem emerges – if authentic texts are used, students may misunderstand or misinterpret the text; but if lower level texts are used, students may be bored or feel insulted by the low level of the content. One solution is to take topics the students have to study and look in technical journals for articles in the same subject area. Lower level EAP courses often use popular journals and these are a very good source.

There are a number of macro- and micro-reading skills that EAP students need to develop (Munby, 1978; De Escorcia, 1984; Nuttall, 1996). Among the former, students need to be able to make use of their existing knowledge to make sense of new material, and fit new knowledge into their schema. They need skimming and scanning skills in order to get an idea of the overall structure and organisation of a text, and the primary and secondary information in it, along with prediction skills. Students also need to learn how to select and organise information (to distinguish important from less important information in text) to read selectively for a particular purpose and know how to make notes from a text. Other important skills are the ability to evaluate and use information (particularly about the lesson focus, discussion purpose and exact tasks to be done), and to see the implications of the reading.

Important micro skills for EAP reading include recognising logical relationships (Sawyer, 1989), e.g. cause and effect, time, condition, comparison and contrast; recognising definitions, generalisations, examples, explanations and predictions; and distinguishing fact from opinion, which might be achieved by recognising markers (also see Huckin, 1988). Further necessary skills are coping with vocabulary (especially in lexically dense text), and identifying and learning technical, field-specific terms (as opposed to non-field specific terms) they may have problems with. Some useful strategies here are the use of context clues to work out meanings, the unpacking of classifier/ thing structures (compound nouns), the ability to recognise 'technicalised' everyday words and prioritising essential words from words that are important, but not essential for text comprehension.

Carrell and Carson (1997: 56) have suggested that EAP students need both intensive and extensive instruction and practice in reading skills – the former so that they can acquire the particular reading strategies such as (for example) reading for detail and distinguishing main ideas and evidence that they need, and the latter to gain the experience in extensive reading and ability to deal with large amounts of text required by all academic disciplines.

Writing

Writing as a skill for EAP has been described in idealised terms by Johnson, Shek, and Law (199: 86) as 'the most deliberative act of communication that we engage in . . . writers have an array of strategies to use at each stage of the writing process'. The reality, though, is different: first-year EAP students are normally set a number of writing assignments, often relatively simple, yet they often end up being accused – justifiably – of plagiarism. Students are often unaware of the range of genres among different disciplines and also unable to reprocess information, perhaps because they have not been taught the necessary steps and procedures in secondary school (Reid and Lindstrom, 1985). EAP students need to be able to plan for writing, select and organise content before writing, review and revise successive drafts and proof-read to ensure that the product is improved, based on their knowledge of the subject and their knowledge of the language.

As Leki (1995a) points out, it is difficult to design writing tasks for students that take account of the linguistic and conceptual stages they have reached, and to give the appropriate amount of guidance. Writing activities for the early stages might include gap-filling, sentence completion, dictation and information transfer; in the next or intermediate stage, instruction can focus on cross-disciplinary genres – the narrative, procedures, reports, explanations, exposition and discussion of their subject. Each academic discipline differs in its ways of arguing for a particular point of view, interpreting data, considering different sides of an argument and drawing conclusions. EAP writing, certainly at the more specific levels, places emphasis on the *socially constructed* nature of writing, how the norms and values of the target discipline shape the features of the target genres (Dudley-Evans, 1984a). Swales and Feak (1994) is a good example of an advanced writing course that focuses on disciplinary differences as well as general writing and research skills for postgraduate students.

Much discussion in EAP writing revolves around the question of whether to focus on product or process – to view writing as a single production or as a process (see Johns and Dudley-Evans, 1991). A typical product-oriented classroom writing cycle (Reid, 1988) is setting up a context (exploring the situations that require a particular register/genre audience, purpose, topic), modelling (by reading texts of the appropriate genre), noticing (setting tasks that draw students' attention to typical features of the texts, including staging, functions and grammatical features), explicit genre analysis (when students, prompted by the teacher, work out the major features of the text – the function, styles, schematic stages and linguistic features of the genre), information transfer (often pairwork), and text comparison. This can be followed by controlled production, e.g. text completion, text reconstruction and text reordering; and finally independent production of drafts, when students individually or in groups choose a topic within the target genre, do the necessary research and write the text. Feedback might include a degree of individual and group conferencing before publishing the final draft.

A typical process-oriented classroom writing cycle, has the following steps, generally with students working in pairs or groups: taking preliminary decisions, composing a rough draft, revising the rough draft, preparing a second draft, further revisions and re-working of drafts, further evaluation and writing the final draft (see also Leki, 1995a). Each stage needs input from the teacher and from classmates through the use of peer feedback (negotiation – the joint construction of a new text within the same genre, to prepare for the independent construction of a text), and also a balance between fluency, expression and accuracy.

Speaking

There is a general consensus among ESL educators that oral language is very important, yet speaking in EAP remains a relatively neglected skill. This is unfortunate because apart from the specific speaking needs learners may have, confidence and ability in speaking tends to carry over to the other skills. In addition, language proficiency of non-native speakers is often informally evaluated on the basis of spoken language. Subject teachers, for example, tend to judge NNS students by how they express themselves orally and this judgement can lead to teacher expectations that can strongly influence academic success.

Jordan (1997) describes typical EAP speaking skills as asking questions during lectures and tutorials, participating in seminars and discussions, giving presentations, interacting in laboratory and work-shop settings and describing data (see also Chirnside, 1986). Compared with the research article, which is the most researched academic genre, little work has been done to describe the spoken academic genres.

An important area of EAP speaking instruction is directed towards seminar participation. There is some literature on the discourse of seminars. The findings indicate a wide range of seminar types, ranging from a monologue by the seminar leader to a free for all discussion. Johns and Johns (1977) note that this variation tends to depend upon the different disciplines. More discussion is traditional in the humanities, with more teacher dominance in the natural sciences. However, there are also cultural differences; Asian cultures, for example, tend to encourage less student participation, with more deference accorded to the teacher (Flowerdew and Miller, 1995, 1996).

Lynch and Anderson (cited in Jordan, 1997: 197) list a range of problems in seminar speaking:

the publicness of the performance
the need to think on your feet

the requirement to call up relevant subject knowledge
the need to present logically ordered arguments
the fact that speakers may be being assessed on their contribution

In mixed classes of native and non-native speakers, native speakers tend to have the advantage over non-natives, who may have had little opportunity to practise speaking in English. In mixed seminars of NSs and NNSs Furneaux *et al.* (1991) noted very few examples of NNSs breaking into the discussion. In Hong Kong, where most of the universities are officially English-medium, while many Cantonese-speaking academic staff will lecture in English, very few conduct tutorials in the second language (Flowerdew, Li and Miller, 1998). As well as students' difficulties in expressing themselves in English in tutorials, lecturers claim that a greater sense of rapport is developed if the mother tongue is used. Although Cantonese is used in this *de jure* English-medium context, there is considerable code-mixing of technical terms.

Another important focus of EAP speaking instruction is the oral presentation. The discourse structure of the typical oral presentation has been described by Price (1977) as follows: general introduction; statement of intention; information in detail; conclusion; invitation to discuss. Lynch and Anderson (1991) recommend the following areas of focus for the teaching of oral/seminar presentations: sequencing; signposting; delivery; visual aids; body language; and concluding.

Cultural background is an important factor in EAP speaking. In many societies students are not expected to speak in lectures or seminars. The teacher is the authority and this authority is not expected to be challenged. Cultural background may thus explain the apparent reticence of NNS students to participate when they study overseas in English-speaking countries or when they are taught by Westerners in their own countries (Flowerdew and Miller, 1995, 1996).

Listening

Most of the work in academic listening research has focused on lectures (see, e.g., the papers in Flowerdew [1994a]), although seminar participation is another language event where listening skills are needed. Interactive, or conversational listening, however, is usually dealt with along with speaking.

The key issues in lecture listening research revolve around the question of authenticity and the goal of preparing learners to comprehend an extensive monologue presented in real time without the facilitative features of interactive listening, such as asking for repetition or clarification and speaker modification of delivery to make comprehension easier for non-native speakers. Should teachers adopt a 'deep-end' strategy of presenting learners with live or recorded authentic lectures and training them to extract key information, as they will have to do in their target disciplines, or should they use simplified texts, more easily understood by learners, but not a true reflection of what learners are likely to have to do in their target disciplines?

Comprehension theory assumes that linguistic messages are processed in two parallel processes – bottom up (decoding the sounds, words, phrases and sentences and then relating this to contextual knowledge) and top down (starting with inferential processes and contextual knowledge and then invoking the lower level processes where required) (Flowerdew, 1994a). Approaches to teaching reflect these two views. Bottom-up teaching methods emphasise decoding the individual components of the linguistic message as the starting point, while top-down methods emphasise the need for learners to apply their inferential processes to extract meaning, only focusing on the linguistic components where necessary. Given the limited time available for most EAP courses, the top-down approach is perhaps more cost effective, while the bottom-up approach is more applicable for more wide angle EAP where more time is available. Taxonomies of listening micro-skills have been produced by Munby (1978), Richards (1983) and Powers (1986), and these form the basis for designing many of the bottom-up, skills-focused, listening materials which predominate in the commercial marketplace.

A further reflection of the bottom-up/top-down dichotomy is the question of whether EAP listening pedagogy should be focused on simplified or authentic lecture discourse, as previously mentioned. Authentic lectures have a number of distinctive features which set this type of discourse apart from that of other genres. The phonological dimension, of course, differentiates it from written text and the fact that it is produced in 'real time' means that listeners do not have the opportunity to process lecture discourse more than once, unlike readers of written text who may backtrack and ponder over the language confronting them on the written page (Flowerdew, 1994c).

In many cases EAP listening materials are based on specially prepared recordings of written text. This means that they differ from authentic lecture discourse in that they have fewer false starts and redundancies, are structured into sentences marked by full stops rather than tone groups marked by pauses, filled pauses (ums and ahs) or discourse markers (now, so, OK, and, etc.) and have a more tightly structured grammar (Halliday, 1989). In many ways, listening to a recording of a written text is a more difficult challenge than listening to a spontaneous lecture. In a comparison of one authentic lecture with materials used in second language textbooks, Flowerdew and Miller (1997) highlighted a range of salient features in the authentic lecture which they believed to be important for learners to comprehend, but which were absent from the textbooks. In addition to the linguistic characteristics of authentic lectures mentioned above, Flowerdew and Miller (1997) noted the importance of the body language of the lecturer, a range of interpersonal strategies used by the lecturer to empathise with the audience and check on comprehension, the use of 'macro-markers' to refer backwards or forwards in the lecture or to other lectures in the course, the use of rhetorical questions, and the integration of the spoken monologue with visual aids, written handouts, pre- and post-lecturer reading and tutorial discussion. Arguing that such distinctive features are not conducive to treatment in a textbook, Flowerdew and Miller suggest that textbook materials should be supplemented by authentic lectures which would allow learners to develop top-down strategies and integrate listening with the other associated skills.

Flowerdew (1994c) suggests that a lot could be done to train lecturers who teach NNSs and that such training might indeed be more cost effective than investing yet more resources in improving the proficiency level of their students. Indeed, in North America, there is quite a literature on the training of international teaching assistants (TAs), but there are few accounts of such lecturer training outside North America (although see Lynch, 1994). Tauroza and Allison (1994) suggest ways in which lecturers could improve their delivery, including repetition, moderating speed, emphasising main points, summarising, and speaking loudly and clearly. One area of training which would be particularly beneficial, Flowerdew and Miller (1995, 1996) argue, is at the cultural level. In ethnographic research conducted in Hong Kong, these researchers identified a whole range of features where there were potential mismatches between the culture of the Hong Kong Chinese students and their Western lecturers. These cross-cultural mismatches relate to ethnic culture, local culture, academic culture and disciplinary culture.

Study skills

Because EAP is concerned with helping students use English to learn, EAP teaching has always been associated with the various study skills in which the language they teach their students is used. Study skills encompass a wide range of activities. They include listening and note-taking, reading skills such as skimming, scanning, guessing meanings from context and using the dictionary, seminar discussion, oral presentation, essay/thesis/laboratory report writing, using the library, using computers in their various applications (word-processing, the Internet, etc.), and even avoiding plagiarism (see Jordan [1997: 7–8] for a more extensive list). Given the very wide range of study skills needed in EAP, Waters and Waters argue that developing students study skill *competence* is more important than teaching the specific individual skills.

As technology comes to be used more in academic study, the student's repertoire of required study skills is rapidly expanding. One area worth special mention, because it is a language learning strategy skill rather than a study skill to be applied to the content subject, is the use of corpora and concordancing packages as a learning tool. There is a lot of interest currently in devising effective ways of helping students access the wealth of linguistic information available in specialist corpora by the use of concordancers and related computer software (Johns, 1988; Stevens, 1991a). Use of the internet has so far not figured in the EAP literature, but doubtless this important study aid will soon be researched.

Assessment

Student assessment for EAP is the measuring of students' language ability and can be undertaken at different stages in their study careers, by different means, and with different purposes. The main aim of a test is not to say how appropriate or successful a course is, but to measure the individual abilities of individual students so that a comparison – or ranking – between students and of any one student can be made. It is generally agreed that three different kinds of tests are relevant to EAP: placement tests, which measure abilities at the start of a course so that students can be placed in the right EAP class, achievement tests, which test to what extent students have learned the skills and items on a course, and proficiency tests, which do not refer to any one course, but are normally used to assess and describe students' linguistic abilities before enrolling on a course of study (examples are TOEFL and IELTS). Assessment is a key issue in EAP, given its important gate-keeping function within the institution or nationally or internationally. Minimum scores on the international proficiency tests are used by many universities as a guide to acceptance of students. Similarly, within the individual institution, proficiency scores or achievement scores on in-house English courses often affect decisions on student progress in their content subjects. In many universities, for example, students cannot graduate unless they have achieved the university English requirement.

Alderson (1988), writing about ESP, refers to three aspects of course design which are relevant to EAP assessment. The first aspect is test content, and particularly how close to the detailed content of a course the test content should be. In EAP, the closer the number and type of test items are to the content of the course, the stronger the effect of washback (the effect of a test on teaching and learning) is likely to be on that content. The second is test method, and here Alderson suggests that we should be less concerned with numerical or statistical validity than with making sure the items on the test match as closely as possible the items taught on the course. This is true in the EAP context for placement as well as achievement tests, and should as an added advantage make the task of the test designer easier. The third aspect is test validity, the examination of which calls for evidence that the test measures what it claims to measure. Here Alderson calls for the test to be a direct examination of student performance; this suggestion is very relevant for EAP test construction, due to the focus of the EAP course on study and academic skills and to the relative similarity of those skills across disciplines and across places of study.

Programme evaluation

Programme evaluation for EAP means evaluating or re-evaluating the course design – the syllabus, materials, tasks and methods as they were originally planned – to see if the course is meeting its stated objectives. Evaluation may be either formative – i.e., on-going, as the course progresses – or summative – i.e., at the end of the course. Course evaluation should involve as many participants as possible and this may mean students, teachers, subject teachers, the institution and administrators. The broad range of views that these interested parties can contribute will mean that a balanced and comprehensive view of the course and its achievements may be obtained. The aim of EAP course evaluation should be to measure the effectiveness of the EAP course, and perhaps to make suggestions for change. Mechanisms for course evaluation include learner and teacher questionnaires and interviews, learner diaries and teacher notes, materials evaluation, test and other assessment results, and classroom observation. This triangulated view may be comprehensive enough to act as an appropriate basis for recommendations for course improvement. The most comprehensive account of an EAP programme evaluation is Celani *et al.* (1988). A more general collection is Alderson and Beretta (1992).

Conclusion

As stated in the introduction, this chapter has provided an overview of the key aspects of the EAP curriculum, from the initial analysis of needs through to the final programme evaluation. It is important to bear in mind that the issues identified as components of the EAP curriculum should not be seen as a rigid series of procedures, but rather as a cycle with a central focus, or axis, which inter-relates each of the stages. Needs analysis cannot be undertaken without an initial consideration of what sort of syllabus might be appropriate in a given situation. Methodology cannot be formulated without consideration of the roles of teachers and learners. Programme evaluation, whilst considered the last stage in the curriculum process, should nevertheless be considered at the outset, as parts of the needs analysis. We hope that readers will bear this in mind as they read the individual chapters of the collection, each of which focuses on one particular dimension, but which cannot function in isolation from the others.

12 Twenty years of needs analyses: Reflections on a personal journey

George Braine

Hutchinson and Waters (1987) classify the development of ESP into a number of phases which include register analysis in the 1960s and early 1970s, rhetorical or discourse analysis in the 1970s and 1980s, and needs analysis from the 1980s onwards. They rightly identify the needs analysis phase as the coming of age in ESP because learner needs, defined by Johns and Dudley-Evans (1991) as the 'identifiable elements' of 'students' target English situations' would appear to be the obvious basis for designing ESP courses.

However, until the advent of ESP, course design in English language teaching may have been based mainly on teachers' intuitions of students' needs. The publication of Munby's *Communicative Syllabus Design* (1978), which consisted of parameters for categorising learners' needs and guidelines for applying them to course design, was therefore a watershed in the development of ESP in general and needs analysis in particular. Although the rigour and complexity of Munby's parameters have been criticised (see West, 1994), there is little doubt that needs analyses carried out since the late 1970s owe much to Munby's approach.

In his state-of-the-art paper on needs analyses, West (1994) claims that the term *needs* lacks an accepted definition. For instance, Hutchinson and Waters (1987) classify needs into *necessities* – 'what the learner has to know . . . to function effectively in the target situation' and *wants* – what the 'learners feel they need'. Further, they argue that course designers must be aware of the learners' *lacks*, defined as the gap between the existing proficiency and the target proficiency of learners. Although terms such as *necessities, wants* and *lacks* may appear ambiguous, few would deny the existence of *constraints* (Hutchinson and Waters, 1987), the external factors such as staff, time and prevailing cultural attitudes that must be taken into consideration when conducting needs analyses.

Another grey area is the methods or procedures by which needs analyses are conducted. Jordan (1997) lists fourteen methods of collecting data, which include advance documentation, language test at home, language test on entry, self-assessment (by students), observation and monitoring, class progress tests, surveys, structured interviews, learner diaries, case studies, final tests, evaluation/feedback, follow-up investigation and previous research. Although Robinson (1991) cites fewer methods of analyses, her list appears to be more comprehensive and reflective of current practices: questionnaires, interviews, observation, case studies, tests, authentic data collection and participatory needs analyses. Only Robinson mentions authentic data collection, now regarded as one of the most reliable methods of data collection in needs analysis. Nevertheless, the prominence given to questionnaires in both lists is surprising, given the doubts on the reliability of questionnaires for data collection in EAP by Horowitz (1986b) and Braine (1988a), among others.

ESP and EAP literature is replete with descriptions of the methodology and outcome of research into learner needs carried out in all parts of the world. ESP/EAP practitioners have surveyed students on their backgrounds and goals (Frodesen, 1995), consulted teachers on course requirements (Bridgeman and Carlson, 1983; Johns, 1981), collected and classified writing assignments (Braine, 1995; Horowitz, 1986b) and observed the language and behavioural demands of learning situations (Jacobson, 1987; McKenna, 1987). The design of English language curricula without some consideration of learner needs is almost unthinkable today.

Case studies

In the following account, I describe three case studies of needs analysis, recalling my personal journey in EAP beginning at the University of Kelaniya in Sri Lanka in the pre-Munby 1970s, continuing at the University of Texas at Austin in the United States in the late 1980s, and concluding at the Chinese University of Hong Kong in the late 1990s. To some extent, my journey reflects the growth and transformation of EAP itself, from its purely pedagogical roots in the less developed countries (the Periphery) to its current status as a research and pedagogical tool in Western countries (the Centre) as well. While describing the challenges of conducting EAP needs analyses in such widely different contexts, I examine how my approach has evolved over the past two decades, varying according to the target situation. Because the co-operation of teachers from other disciplines is vital to the success of needs analyses, I also discuss some obstacles that inhibit such co-operation and ways to overcome them.

University of Kelaniya, Sri Lanka

In Sri Lanka, all universities are under government control. Admission is based upon the students' performance in the General Certificate of Education – Advanced Level (GCE-AL) examination, which is also conducted by the government. Because university places are available for only about ten per cent of the examination takers, competition for admission is fierce. In the 1970s, only about a hundred students were admitted to the Faculty of Science at Kelaniya University each year.

The Faculty consisted of six departments of study: botany, chemistry, industrial management, mathematics, physics and zoology. Students taking botany, chemistry and zoology were generally known as Biological Science majors, and those taking a combination of chemistry, physics and mathematics or industrial management were known as Physical Science students. The medium of instruction was Sinhala. *Technical English* has been taught as a service course since the inception of the Faculty in 1967.

The teaching of science in the first language (either Sinhala or Tamil) in schools had been started only in the mid-sixties. Thus, the typical student gaining admission to the Faculty of Science in the late 1960s and early 1970s had a fairly high proficiency in English; their primary and middle school education was in the English medium and/or they were from bilingual (English-Sinhala speaking), middle-class homes.

In 1974, the Sri Lankan government introduced a District Quota system of university admission, under which students from rural areas were admitted to universities even with lower scores on the GCE-AL examination. This measure was taken because rural schools had fewer facilities than urban schools in the availability of qualified teachers, and scientific laboratories and students from these schools were thought to be unfairly disadvantaged on the GCE-AL examination. As a result of the District Quota system, a large number of rural students, often from less affluent families, gained admission to the medical, engineering, and science faculties of Sri Lankan universities. These students also had a much lower proficiency level in English than their urban classmates.

The language skill most emphasised in the required service course *Technical English* was reading. This was because of the lack of sufficient science textbooks written in Sinhala, which compelled the students to read books written in English for reference purposes. For instance, in 1979, the university library contained 875 titles in physics, listed under classifications such as mechanics, dynamics, hydraulics, electricity and nuclear physics. In contrast, only 20 titles were listed in Sinhala, some of which were prescribed texts for the GCE-AL examination (Braine, 1980). In the early years of the *Technical English* course, course material consisted mainly of reading passages gleaned from popular magazines such as *Readers' Digest*. These 'first generation' reading passages, prepared by the assistant lecturers who taught *Technical English* in the early years, were safe from the teachers' viewpoint: the passages were self-contained and would not embarrass teachers who were essentially literature majors with no background or interest in science.

In 1974, the admission of more rural students to the Faculty of Science coincided with the hiring of English instructors with a background in science. As a result, a set of reading passages, which could be considered 'second generation,' were introduced, along with grammar and vocabulary exercises. The reading passages were classified as Biological Science and Physical Science and bore seemingly relevant titles such as *Physiology 4 – Excretion* and *Physical Science 10 – Magnetic Fields*.

Most subject-area teachers in the Science Faculty were openly critical of *Technical English*. The criticism took on an urgency with the influx of rural students into the Faculty. Typically from middle-class homes where English was spoken as often as Sinhala or Tamil, these subject-area teachers, like others who have learned English as a second language, tended to have strong opinions about how best to teach English. These opinions were usually based on their own learning experiences in the days of grammar-translation or oral-aural methods, during which the teaching of language forms and structures occupied a prominent place, with exercises, drills and correction, or in which they memorised vocabulary. Thus, these teachers saw the more communicative approaches of the *Technical English* courses as being unproductive.

Another factor which contributed to the criticism of *Technical English* was low attendance, with only about 30% of the students attending regularly. Classes for second year physical science students were the least attended, with less than five students attending regularly. Obviously, an English course consisting of randomly selected, non-sequential reading passages did not appeal to science students. Did students need help with laboratory reports, which were written mainly in English? Could we assist them in the comprehension of English medium lectures? How important was speaking, especially for students of industrial management, who were required to visit factories and liaise with management? Although the questions were straightforward, no instructor had the qualifications or the expertise to design courses. None had a Master's degree in TESOL, which may have included coursework in curriculum design; most had undergone a two-year teacher training course conducted by the Sri Lankan Ministry of Education, which prepared English teachers for teaching in primary and secondary schools.

The breakthrough came when the Ministry of Higher Education, under the sponsorship of the British Council, invited an ESP Consultant to Sri Lanka. In 1980, at the invitation of the ESP Consultant, Tim Johns ran the first ESP workshop in Sri Lanka, providing university English teachers with the know-how and the tools to design curricula to meet their students' needs.

The urgent need for change propelled me to conduct a rudimentary needs analysis a few months after my return from the ESP workshop. With the help of handouts and my notes from the workshop, I designed two questionnaires, the first for students of the Faculty of Science and the second for the Faculty's teachers. The student questionnaire, which was in Sinhala, contained 30 items. I attempted to collect information on the students' proficiency in English, their attitudes towards and perceptions of the *Technical English* course and the amount and type of reading in English that they did. The teachers' questionnaire, designed after I had analysed the responses from the students, contained ten items which sought to match the teachers' responses with that of the students.

I had no difficulty in getting 100 captive students to return the questionnaire; however, despite repeated requests, only 10 of the 35 teachers did. In retrospect, I am unable to explain why I could not have visited the teachers, most of whom had offices down the hallway from mine. The Faculty of Science was located in a single, self-contained building, and I encountered many of these teachers almost everyday, often at the Senior Common Room. However, the ESP workshop had stressed the use of questionnaires, and, quite naively, I saw no alternative method of data collection. Were the teachers offended that I took the more formal approach of a questionnaire, instead of meeting them informally? Were they, for reasons best known to themselves, reluctant to state their opinions and suggestions in writing? While paying lip-service to the importance of English (which would align them with the Dean of the Faculty, who was a strong supporter of more English for students), did the majority of the teachers have no interest in improving the *Technical English* course? Or were they merely discouraged, having seen the gradual deterioration of English at the University and in the country as well? I will never know now, but a few face-to-face meetings would have provided me with a rich source of data.

The University of Texas at Austin, USA

When I began a Master's degree in Linguistics at the American University in Washington DC in 1984, I enrolled in a course titled 'Curriculum design in ESP' taught by Professor Grace Burkhart, a pioneer ESP practitioner and the founding editor of *The ESP Journal*. The course was an eye opener, providing a solid foundation in needs analyses and curriculum design as well as a thorough survey of the depth and range of ESP.

The beginning of my doctoral studies at The University of Texas at Austin coincided with the publication of Horowitz's (1986b) ground-breaking article 'What professors actually require: Academic tasks for the ESL classroom' in *TESOL Quarterly*. His premise was that analyses of writing assignments given to students would provide more reliable data on academic writing tasks than questionnaire surveys or interviews with teachers. Horowitz criticised the use of preconceived academic writing tasks in questionnaires because it compelled teachers to fit their responses to these tasks; the use of questionnaires in needs analysis might more plausibly reveal what teachers think they do, not necessarily what they do (1986). Horowitz later wrote to me that he was 'unaware of any other study which examined actual writing assignments'.[1] However, in my own research, I modified Horowitz's approach, arguing that the inclusion of data from widely different disciplines such as marketing and biology in his study could not justify a common classification of writing tasks (Braine, 1988a).

My teaching assistantship in the English Department at Texas had involuntarily transformed me from an ESL generalist to a writing teacher, and I had no doubt at all what my dissertation research would be. I would conduct a needs analysis of the writing tasks in undergraduate courses at Texas, and, building on my research in Sri Lanka, would focus on the Faculty of Science and the Faculty of Engineering. Texas was home to a clearly-defined, well-established Writing Across the Curriculum (WAC) programme, and this was a distinct advantage. Undergraduates were required to take two courses of the programme in order to graduate. In the semesterly course schedule, these courses were clearly labelled as 'substantial writing component courses' and listed under each academic department's offerings. Each semester, the course schedule listed 18 substantial writing courses in the College of Engineering and 21 courses in the College of Natural Sciences.

---

[1] Daniel Horowitz, personal communication, nd.

To be certified as a substantial writing course, each course had to include at least three writing assignments per semester, totalling approximately 16 double-spaced pages. Students were to be provided feedback on their writing and writing quality was a criterion in the final grade for the course. In fact, some academic departments had hired Master's or doctoral students of English as teaching assistants to help teachers handle the increased workload involved in substantial writing courses.

The move from a technologically barren, resource poor, Periphery context to an affluent, world-class university, which emphasised English skills across the curriculum was an EAP researcher's dream come true. Although the mid-1980s had not opened up the vast potential of e-mail, I did have access to telephones and fax machines that worked, computers, a first-rate library, generally helpful departmental secretaries and a printed course schedule that clearly listed the titles of courses and the names of teachers. However, there was one significant drawback: although the English Department did have renowned composition specialists, there were no ESP/EAP experts at Texas. My dissertation advisor distanced herself from the project early, claiming no knowledge of EAP and warning me that I would be on my own. But Horowitz had provided clear guidelines, and I was also armed with Munby's *Communicative Syllabus Design* (1978). In addition, I had begun a correspondence with John Swales, Ann Johns and Dan Horowitz, and their support, even from a distance, was a morale booster.

I knew that the academic status of the researcher was vital to the success of such research; in Texas, my status was even lower than in Sri Lanka. I was now a graduate student, a foreigner with an accent scrutinising writing assignments prepared by experienced, native speaker teachers in disciplines (engineering and the natural sciences) I had little knowledge of. I was, indeed, a stranger in a strange land, and I knew the challenge ahead could be daunting. With some trepidation, I telephoned the teachers of the other WAC courses in the two Colleges, explaining the purpose of my project and requesting copies of course syllabi and assignments.

The response was overwhelmingly supportive. Most teachers were not only willing to provide the data I needed, but also volunteered to give me laboratory manuals, laboratory notes and samples of student writing. A few invited me to attend their laboratory meetings so that I could observe what 'really went on' in their courses. Of the 39 WAC courses for the two Colleges in the course schedules for that year, some courses had to be eliminated due to cross listing, leaving a total of only 34 courses suitable for study. In the end, I collected syllabi from 17 courses and 80 writing assignments from these courses,[2] a much higher response rate than that of Horowitz (1986b): only 38 of the 750 teachers he contacted had sent him assignments.

My meetings with the teachers taught me that, even in L1 situations, teachers across the disciplines were concerned about the declining English standards of their students. Of course, like their counterparts in the Faculty of Science at the University of Kelaniya in Sri Lanka, these teachers, too, had strong views of what language skills the students needed and how they should be taught. Were these concerns (complaints, actually) a result of a generation gap, or the result of a somewhat elitist attitude to higher education? Just as the District Quota System in Sri Lanka had opened university education to rural students barely proficient in English, the open admission policies of The University of Texas allowed almost any high school graduate to enter university. In fact, the teachers' views had some justification. Probably as a result of open admissions, the dropout rate at Texas for undergraduates was well over 50% at the time of my research.

My teaching assistantship at Texas placed me in the rank of an assistant instructor and required me to teach first year writing courses in the English Department. Did my dual and somewhat unusual role as a non-native speaker teacher/researcher of writing open doors which otherwise may have remained shut? In fact, many of the teachers in engineering were of the view that their non-native speaker students' writings were heavily plagiarised 'cut and paste jobs' (see Braine, 1988b), and, during my visits, pulled out reports written by these students to prove their point. What they did not appear to realise was that students were often required to compose lengthy (five to six thousand-word) reports with no more guidance than a one-page hand-out, with the required first-year writing course as their only preparation.

The research was not without its lighter moments. Perhaps the most memorable was an assignment from a physics course titled *Writing: A tool for intelligent life*. The course syllabus affirmed that '[s]ince the elements of style stand most easily revealed in a literary context, fiction [would] form a large component of the assigned reading'. Readings were to be chosen from Rudyard Kipling, Jonathan Swift, Winston Churchill, Robert Oppenheimer, Joseph Conrad and George Orwell, among others. As part of the coursework, students would be asked to 'rewrite, in more bearable style'

---

[2] See Braine (1995) for detailed data.

articles from standard scientific journals which, according to the syllabus, 'are full of abominable writing'. Apparently the physics teachers had a low opinion of style in their own field!

The Chinese University of Hong Kong

When I joined The Chinese University of Hong Kong in 1995, I entered a somewhat surreal world. As Britain's last major colony, Hong Kong was passing through another nervous, uncertain phase in its history. To support its immensely successful service-based economy, Hong Kong needed to maintain a high standard of proficiency in English.[3] As a result, English teaching was enjoying a boom which attracted teachers from every corner of the globe. Staffed by a truly international faculty, the tertiary institutions paid a great deal of attention to their students' English language enhancement. Unlike in the United States, where cash-strapped universities were downsizing academic departments and cutting funding for research, Hong Kong universities were generous in awarding research grants. My proposal to analyse the writing tasks of undergraduate courses in the engineering and science faculties, which was essentially a replication of my doctoral research, was funded.

By necessity, the needs analyses methodology in Hong Kong had to be different from that of Texas. The Chinese University did not have a WAC programme, and the official timetable and course descriptions contained in the students' handbook gave no indication of the quantity of writing required in courses. In fact, formal writing courses were confined to the English Department and the English Language Teaching Unit. As a result, instead of narrowing the research to a few selected teachers, a mass-mailing approach (which Horowitz [1986b] had used rather unsuccessfully in his needs analysis) had to be adopted.

With the help of two undergraduate student helpers, I began the project in January 1996. First, we sent letters to 223 teachers in the engineering and science faculties who were listed in the timetable as teaching in English or in Cantonese and English, inviting them to participate in the project by sending us their course syllabi and assignments. Within a week, 80 had replied, citing their reasons for being unable to participate: some were too busy, others were not teaching that semester/year, and the rest did not give writing assignments in their courses. In response to follow-up requests, phone calls

---

[3] For a description of the status of ELT in Hong Kong during this period, see Flowerdew, Li, and Miller (1998).

and e-mail messages, only 5 teachers from engineering and 4 from science agreed to participate in the project. Despite requests through e-mails and telephone calls, 134 teachers did not respond at all.

Because the response was so poor, I contacted the Deans of the two faculties. One announced my project to heads of departments at a meeting, and I was asked to contact the heads directly to obtain the data. However, during visits to two heads of departments, I was given syllabi from courses that the heads themselves taught; they did not appear to have information relating to other teachers of their departments or were reluctant to share the syllabi with me. In lieu of writing assignments, I was also given two student reports written about ten years earlier.

My meeting with the other Dean was revealing. I was informed that most teachers did not have course syllabi (also referred to as course outlines) because the syllabi were gradually developed as the courses were being taught. I also learned that instead of creating writing assignments or prompts, most teachers simply prescribed exercises from textbooks.

Because data was not forthcoming from traditional sources, my student helpers suggested another indirect but obvious source: students enrolled in engineering and science courses and the Internet. Through informal networks and at casual meetings, the student helpers sought course syllabi and writing assignments from students. Some teachers in engineering had homepages for their courses on the Internet, and we downloaded a few course syllabi. We also contacted the administrative assistants of all the departments, knowing that each department was required to keep teaching materials on file for a University-wide Teaching and Learning Quality Process Audit that was conducted a few months earlier.

Despite five months of effort, the results were disappointing. From the Faculty of Engineering, I collected only 35 course syllabi, 29 writing assignments and 62 student reports. The data collected from the Faculty of Science was even more disappointing: 25 course syllabi, no writing assignments and 22 student reports. Although 60 course syllabi were eventually collected from both Faculties, they were not appropriate to needs analysis because syllabi do not provide sufficient information on the types of writing done in academic courses. Only writing assignments (prompts), because they can be classified on the basis of locus, length, genre, cognitive demand and rhetorical specification, can provide reliable information on the writing needs of students. But, as stated earlier, only 29 assignments were collected from engineering, and none from science. Of these assignments, which came from two engineering courses, 22 contained only instructions for laboratory experiments and were too succinct for detailed analyses.

Although most teachers were reluctant to share their syllabi or writing assignments, they were generous in sending us reports written by their students. Entirely unsolicited, these reports poured in, one teaching assistant sending 19 nearly identical reports written by students in a course. In the end, these student reports were helpful, because a close analysis did provide insights into the writing demands of the courses. In almost every academic department in engineering, students are required to write lengthy project reports, especially in their final year. So, we began to collect reports written by our student informants.

Why were teachers in engineering and science reluctant to share their writing assignments? At first, this seems surprising because most of these teachers had received their post-graduate degrees in North America, where writing is encouraged across the curriculum. Nevertheless, the term post-graduate is crucial here. Even in North America, emphasis on writing instruction is placed at the under-graduate level, with required writing courses being offered usually during freshmen and junior years. Except at a few institutions, post-graduate students receive little or no assistance with their writing, often being allowed to 'sink or swim' when completing their theses and dissertations. Thus, it would not be surprising to learn that most teachers in engineering and science faculties, having completed their undergraduate degrees at Asian institutions, had received no instruction in writing, and in turn placed little emphasis on it. As the Dean suggested, they would assign homework tasks from textbooks instead of composing assignments on their own; in fact, there may be few or no writing assignments given at all.

As Spack (1988) noted, another reason may have been the teachers' reluctance to allow an English teacher to see their 'poorly written or poorly designed texts' (p. 33). This may have led to the unsolicited supply of numerous student reports. However, one teacher from engineering, who sent course syllabi, general instructions and test papers from all three courses he taught, requested me to comment on and correct his use of English in the material.

In retrospect, could the initial use of a questionnaire, a data gathering method popular in Hong Kong, have opened the door to better co-operation from subject-area teachers? Or could the selection of a smaller sample of teachers have helped? I have since learned that in Hong Kong EAP circles, only teachers from business were considered 'friendly' to English teachers and co-operative in EAP research. However, this information came too late for my research.

In 1996, the university's fortnightly newsletter sought opinions of teachers from different faculties on the language needs of their students. A teacher from business wrote about the importance of English language skills for her students. A teacher from engineering took the opposite view, arguing that natural language was a second language for engineers, because they only needed quantitative skills and knowledge of software and hardware. Students knew their priorities and natural language was not one of them. The teachers, for their part, could extract meaning from the students' disorganised writing; as long as they got the correct answer, faulty English did not matter. Respectable engineers did not talk to people who could not understand them; only sales engineers, who apparently are not a respectable breed, did (Ng, 1996).

To end this section on a positive note, the Dean of Engineering obviously did not share this teacher's view. Alarmed at the poor language skills of his students, the Dean has made *Technical Communications*, a course offered by the university's English Language Teaching Unit, a requirement for all engineering majors and also provided funding for the courses. In discussions with the Unit, the Dean emphasised that his main concern was the lack of communication between engineers and those from other backgrounds, and that he wanted the courses to emphasise general rather than technical writing. Deans in business and the social sciences have followed suit, requiring their students to take writing courses and funding relevant courses offered by the Unit.

Conclusion

The three case studies reflect the development in needs analyses from the use of questionnaires to analysis of authentic material. The 1970s analysis in Sri Lanka relied entirely on the rather impressionistic responses by teachers and students to questionnaires. The analysis in Texas, because of its more focused nature and the realisation of the importance of using authentic materials, collected and analysed writing assignments. Because this approach proved to be a success, the same method was tried in Hong Kong, but with disappointing results.

Twenty years ago, the concept of EAP or the importance of taking learner needs into consideration in course design could not be taken for granted. In fact, Corbluth (1975) was no exception in being critical of ESP, stressing the importance of the general educational and cultural roles of English language teaching and cautioning teachers not to yield completely to the new ideology. Twenty years later, although the occasional slingshot may still be fired at EAP by critics of the communicative approach, EAP has become a significant aspect of English language teaching worldwide.

If the teaching of English has seen a transfer of expertise, methodology, and technology from the powerful Centre to the less developed Periphery, EAP could be viewed as a transfer in the reverse order – from the Periphery to the Centre. In its infancy, the most rapid growth of ESP/EAP was seen in the Middle East and the Far East, fueled mainly by the British Council and to a lesser extent by organisations such as RELC in Singapore.[4] Needs analysis techniques used successfully in the Periphery in EFL contexts are now adapted and used routinely for research and course design in the Centre in ESL contexts.

---

[4] The single North American exception was the Trimble, Selinker, and Lackstrom team at the University of Washington, and their pioneering work in English for Science and Technology (EST) in the 1960s and 1970s.

13 The curriculum renewal process in English for academic purposes programmes

Fredricka L. Stoller

'Successful organisations are biased towards action and they avoid stultification by developing and changing rather than remaining routinised and standardised' (White, 1988: 138). English for Academic Purposes (EAP) programmes are no different from other organisations. Although some EAP programmes change little over time, seemingly content with the comfort and security of the status quo, many EAP programmes view change as a natural and integral part of programme life. In such programmes, curriculum renewal represents one effective way of responding to the evolving needs of students and faculty, to the shifting circumstances of the educational programmes themselves, and to new insights from the professional literature. Curriculum renewal that is grounded in sound decision making and a thoughtful consideration of the factors impacted by reform can ensure programme integrity, viability, responsiveness and competitiveness.

The challenges of curriculum renewal are complex. Because curriculum reform is best advanced through the collaborative efforts of faculty, students and administrators, the process of reform requires a working environment characterised by participatory decision making, opportunities for experimentation and open lines of communication (see Christison and Stoller, 1997). Curriculum reform also necessitates a responsiveness to internal and external changes (e.g. changes in student enrolment patterns, faculty hiring practices, institutional mandates), making timely access to information critical. Adding to the complexity of the process is the critical need to understand the linguistic, academic and acculturation needs of EAP students in general terms and, whenever possible, in terms more specific to the educational settings and academic disciplines to which the EAP students will be transitioning. Comprehending students' needs requires a strong programmatic commitment to on-going needs analyses, systematic course and programme evaluation, familiarity with current research on language learning and language teaching in

EAP contexts and an understanding of current issues related to curriculum design. Similar in importance is the need to recognise the cyclical nature of curriculum development and to comprehend the processes associated with the implementation of change and innovation.

Despite the complexities associated with curriculum reform, many EAP programmes are actively engaged in the process, motivated by the desire to meet the needs of their students, to nurture the professional development of their faculty, and, in many cases, to remain competitive in the language programme market. To develop this discussion of curriculum renewal further, I shall review the professional literature in four areas: EAP student needs, EAP curriculum design, the more general curriculum development process and the process of innovation diffusion. The literature review will be followed by a case study that highlights the role of faculty and student feedback in the EAP curriculum renewal process.

EAP student needs

Most professionals involved with EAP curriculum development and instruction agree that the primary goal of EAP programmes should be to prepare students for the demands required of them in subject-matter classrooms (Jordan, 1989, 1997). One formidable challenge that curriculum designers face involves the identification of the linguistic, academic and acculturation demands of subject-matter classrooms, recognising all the while that expectations vary in different institutions, in different academic disciplines and at different levels of education (e.g. entry level courses and more advanced courses). Professionals in the field have approached the task of determining students' immediate and future needs in different ways. Some have surveyed subject-matter instructors across a range of educational contexts and academic disciplines to determine course expectations and requirements (e.g. Ferris and Tagg, 1996a, 1996b; Horowitz, 1986b; Johns, 1981). As an example, Ferris and Tagg (1996a, 1996b) studied the views of college and university professors on the difficulties that second language (L2) students have with listening and speaking tasks in their classrooms. They found that lectures are becoming less formal and more interactive, giving rise to new expectations from students. As a result of their study, Ferris and Tagg recommend that EAP programmes expose students to a variety of lecture and interaction formats, help students understand the importance of communication skills in academic contexts, and assist students in developing the confidence to participate in class by asking and responding to questions and engaging in class discussions.

Other EAP researchers have surveyed L2 students enrolled in subject-matter courses to ascertain their perceptions about the relative importance of language skills and classroom tasks for academic success (e.g. Christison and Krahnke, 1986; Ferris, 1998; Ostler, 1980). Ostler's early study, as an example, showed that students felt the greatest need to develop the ability to read textbooks (indicated by 90% of respondents), followed by the need to listen and take notes (84%), ask questions in class (68%), write research papers (58%) and read academic journals and papers (58%).

Although sometimes overlapping with the previously mentioned studies, others have analysed specific skills demands in mainstream classrooms (see Waters, 1996, for a review of research studies), focusing on reading and writing (e.g. Chiseri-Strater, 1991; Ginther and Grant, 1996; Haas, 1994; Leki, 1995b; Spack, 1988), speaking and listening (e.g. Ferris and Tagg, 1996a, 1996b; Flowerdew, 1994a; Mason, 1994; Mendelsohn and Rubin, 1995), and study skills (e.g. Jordan, 1997). It is evident from these studies that there is no single conception of academic literacy across the disciplines – thus the term 'academic literacies' (Chiseri-Strater, 1991; see also Johns, 1997a), referring to the fact that reading and writing assignments are shaped by individual academic disciplines, courses, professors and students.

A number of professionals have extended skills-related discussions to contrast skills-based instruction in language programmes with skills expectations in mainstream classrooms (e.g. Atkinson and Ramanathan, 1995; Leki and Carson, 1994, 1997; Shih, 1992). For example, Leki and Carson (1997) compared writing assignments in L2 classes with those assigned in content classes. They discovered that L2 classes place a greater emphasis on linguistic and rhetorical forms (resulting in 'non-text-responsible writing') than on the display of content knowledge ('text-responsible writing'), the latter being the primary criterion for success in non-language classes. Leki and Carson make a strong case for incorporating text-responsible writing into language classes to prepare students for the writing demands of mainstream courses.

Other comparison studies examine textbooks and instructional materials currently being used in EAP courses to determine how they correspond to non-language course work (e.g. Flowerdew and Miller, 1997; Murphy, 1996; Shih, 1992). These analyses reveal a mismatch between many EAP materials and the discourse experiences students are likely to encounter in mainstream courses. For example, Murphy (1996) points out that current listening and reading materials tend to be organised around unrelated series of topics, limiting students' opportunities to learn content in depth and incrementally over a period of time, as they will have to do in mainstream courses. The same materials are even more constricting because they rarely integrate reading and listening activities, despite the fact that the two skills are so often linked in non-language courses. Flowerdew and Miller (1997) conducted a study to determine how commercially available L2 listening textbooks interface with authentic lecture experiences typical of non-language classes. Their study revealed that EAP listening textbooks neglect a range of listening skills required of students in mainstream classes.

Just as Flowerdew and Miller have analysed authentic lectures to reveal the most effective ways to prepare EAP students for authentic listening experiences, other professionals have analysed different forms of discipline-specific written and oral discourse to discover the difficulties that EAP (or English for Specific Purposes) students might encounter when faced with processing the discourse of mainstream courses (e.g. Conrad, 1996; Johns, 1997b; Swales and Feak, 1994). These systematic text and genre analyses have revealed the realities of discipline-specific courses, with significant implications for the development of instructional materials for targeted EAP groups.

EAP curriculum design considerations

Discussions of EAP curriculum design vary in large part because of different organising principles and varied perspectives on language learning, language teaching, and language. Some models of EAP curricula emphasise the need for students to interact with content in cognitively demanding ways and in ways similar to those in which content is used in target language situations. EAP professionals assuming such a stance advocate using academic subject matter (i.e. content) as the basis for curriculum design. These professionals have explored the role of content learning and its relationship with language learning in discussions of content-based instruction (CBI) in EAP contexts. This work is best represented by studies reported in Adamson (1993), Benesch (1988), Brinton, Snow and Wesche (1989), Kasper (1997), Snow (1993a), Snow and Brinton (1997), Snow, Met and Genesee (1989) and Wesche (1993). These studies reveal three prototype models for CBI: sheltered instruction (i.e., a content course taught by a 'language sensitive' content specialist to a segregated group of learners, thereby 'sheltering' the second language learners from native speaking students); adjunct instruction (i.e., a set of two courses – a content course taught by a content specialist and a language support course taught by a language professional – that share the same content base and co-ordinated assignments); and theme-based instruction (i.e., a language course structured around topics or themes that form the backbone of the course curriculum and provide the basis for language skills instruction). In sheltered and adjunct models, content is relatively predetermined; in theme-based models, content is often selected by the language teacher or students (cf. Stoller and Grabe, 1997, who argue that most instruction is theme-based; thus sheltered and adjunct instruction are not alternatives to theme-based instruction but rather comprise two methods of theme-based instruction).

Similar to the adjunct model just described is Johns's (1997a) notion of linked courses for academically oriented students. Johns's linked courses are actually part of a larger-scale integrated curriculum in which language-minority university students enrol in a block of courses that reinforce one another. The informal and formal collaboration among course instructors often results in more language-sensitive instruction on the part of discipline-specific instructors.

Instead of using academic content as the springboard for EAP curriculum design, some EAP professionals advocate curricula that are structured around real-world academic tasks (see Carrell and Carson, 1997; Crookes and Gass, 1993a, 1993b). According to Carson, Taylor and Fredella (1997):

task-based EAP instruction expands on the CBI focus on language as a vehicle for learning content by then using content as a vehicle for task mastery. Task-based EAP instruction . . . requires mastery of content, but it is the task that focuses the way that language learners will read/write/listen/ speak about content.

(Carson, Taylor and Fredella, 1997: 367)

Although increasing numbers of EAP professionals now contend that content-based and task-based approaches to curriculum design represent viable responses to the real-world needs of EAP students, we still need to consider the ways in which language skills are addressed in EAP courses. The literature is expansive in this area and just a few representative articles will be reviewed here. For example, Carrell and Carson (1997) make a strong case for integrating extensive and intensive reading to prepare students for the tasks and texts that they are likely to encounter in academic courses. Through intensive reading, students can improve their reading skills and strategies; through extensive reading, they can learn to 'orchestrate, coordinate, and apply intensively acquired skills/strategies over the larger texts and multiple reading sources that are required in all academic course work' (p. 47). Murphy (1996) proposes a 'comprehension-for-learning' curriculum that integrates reading and listening to prepare EAP students for the exigencies of mainstream courses where students must integrate what they hear during a lecture (or class discussion) with what they have already read or what they are going to read. Hirvela (1997) persuasively argues in favour of integrating 'disciplinary portfolios' into EAP writing instruction, wherein students analyse and reflect upon the writing practices within their own disciplinary communities.

Conversely, Benesch (1996) considers the target situation as the site of possible reform. In Benesch's view, the focus of EAP courses should be to empower students to challenge their traditional, subservient roles within the hierarchy of mainstream academia (cf. Johns, 1995). Although driven by differing goals and political orientations, professionals involved with Project LEAP (Learning English-for-Academic-Purposes; Snow, 1992, 1993b, 1994; Snow and Kamhi-Stein, 1996; Tricamo and Snow, 1995) also view the target situation as the appropriate site for curricular reform. Project LEAP personnel assist discipline-specific university instructors in scaffolding their teaching to reach their linguistically and culturally diverse students more effectively.

It is evident from this discussion of EAP curriculum design that there is no single template for an effective EAP curriculum, largely due to diverse perspectives on language and content learning and diverse instructional settings. There are strong cases to be made, however, for using academic content or academic tasks as foundations for curriculum development. It is surprising that many EAP programmes (at least in the United States) continue to endorse the discrete-skills paradigm that came into vogue in the 1970s; these programmes are resisting the change toward more content- and task-based approaches despite their students' well-defined academic aspirations and their urgent need to prepare for the content-learning demands of mainstream courses (see Hafernik, Messerschmidt and Vandrick, 1996).

Curriculum development processes and innovation diffusion

Curriculum development is often represented as a dynamic system of interrelated elements. The on-going cycle of planning (e.g. needs analyses, setting of goals and objectives), development, implementation, and evaluation (of courses, materials, students, teachers, administrators and the programme as a whole), in essence defines the curriculum development process. This potentially never-ending cycle allows programmes to fine-tune themselves, adapt to new conditions, respond to internal and external mandates, apply new findings in the field, innovate, and develop consensus among EAP faculty, administration and students (see Brown, 1995).

EAP programmes that actively and systematically engage in the on-going development cycle usually experience some degree of curricular change and innovation as a result. Although much of the literature on *change* and *innovation* uses the terms interchangeably, it is useful to make a distinction between the two. Change, often identified as one of the most stable features of organisational life, results in an alteration in the status quo but not necessarily in improvements. Innovation, on the other hand, results from deliberate and conscious efforts that are intended to bring about new and improved practices (Hamilton, 1996; Nicholls, 1983). Consequently, while change is inevitable in EAP programmes, innovations are desirable. Many factors come into play in the innovation diffusion process, though here I limit myself to a set of guiding principles that can stimulate innovative EAP practices.

1 EAP faculty play a significant role in bringing about curricular innovation. EAP programmes that encourage and reward creativity, initiative, commitment, professionalism and professional development create a working environment that stimulates innovative practices.

2 EAP programmes interested in creating an environment conducive to innovation must recognise that managing innovations is a complex process. The adoption of an innovative proposal involves an extended (and sometimes complicated) decision-making process.

3 EAP programmes must be willing to fail on some attempts at innovation in order to succeed on others. According to Rogers (1995), 75% of all innovations fail.

4 The responsibility for innovation must be shared and should not be left to chance. Innovations cannot sustain themselves without a team of steadfast supporters who are willing to champion the innovation from the early introductory and developmental stages through implementation and diffusion.

5 Innovations are not equal. Although all innovations can be seen as improvements in the status quo, they share few other similarities. Their visible differences are obvious to us all; for example an innovation in computer-aided instruction is clearly distinct from the introduction of 'disciplinary portfolios' in an EAP writing class. What we do not often consider, however, are the 'invisible'

characteristics that can so easily sway potential adopters' opinions. The extent to which innovations are accepted by potential adopters is strongly influenced by perceived attributes of innovations. Some attributes (e.g. visibility, trialability, feasibility) lead to positive attitudes, whereas others (e.g. complexity) can create immediate barriers. Because subjective perceptions are often more powerful than objective viewpoints, it is important to find out how potential adopters view proposed innovations.

6 EAP programmes, like other work place environments, often have personnel who are content to maintain the status quo, rather than entertain new alternatives, simply to preserve the balance and predictability of the work environment. Innovators must strive to alleviate the fears of resisters and stimulate their willingness at least to consider innovative proposals.

Curriculum renewal, in large part, is dependent on a programme's ability to innovate. The adoption of these six principles allows EAPs to nurture a working and learning environment that is receptive to the on-going curriculum development process and the dialogue that is required to stimulate innovations.

A case study

Curriculum renewal involves interplay between what we know about EAP student needs, EAP curriculum design, the nature of curriculum development, and innovation diffusion. Inextricably linked to these factors are responses to new perspectives in the field, changing student populations, institutional mandates, new faculty interests and research, and feedback solicited in a regular and systematic way from students and faculty. A longitudinal case study (1987–1997) of the EAP programme at Northern Arizona University (NAU) illustrates this interplay. To frame the study, I will describe the EAP curriculum at NAU and then focus on the ten-year process of soliciting feedback from students and faculty as an example of an effective mechanism for identifying aspects of an EAP curriculum that merit modification. I will conclude by summarising some of the changes (and innovations) that have been implemented over the years.

Description of EAP curriculum

NAU's EAP curriculum can be characterised as a hybrid curriculum, combining an integrated-skills, content-based approach with

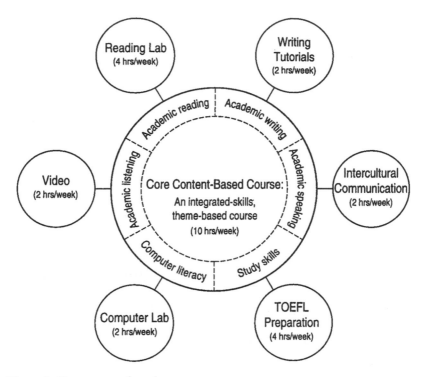

Figure 1 Core content-based course

discrete-skills instruction (see Stoller, 1999). Students, mostly international students who have been provisionally admitted to the university, receive 26 hours of instruction per week, from seven instructional modules (see Figure 1).

As suggested in Figure 1, the Core course is considered central. The other six modules are designed to reinforce and augment the skills, tasks and strategies introduced in the Core class. The modular approach is appealing because it provides full-time students with a comprehensive course of study and part-time students, who might also be concurrently matriculated in mainstream classes, with the opportunity to enrol in select modules that best match their individual needs. It should be noted that this curriculum presupposes a curriculum-wide commitment to vocabulary development and grammar improvement. Thus, all instructors use their classes to promote vocabulary growth and to provide contextualised instruction in, and feedback on, English structure.

Core class

The Core class is designed to simulate the demands of regular courses and to offer systematic and scaffolded language- and content-learning support. It is organised around units (of themes and topics) that normally run three weeks or approximately 30 hours. (For a more detailed discussion of *themes and topics*, in addition to *transitions* and *threads*, see Stoller and Grabe, 1997.)

Reading lab

The close relationship between academic success and efficient reading, supports the need for a focused reading skills module. The Reading Lab combines sustained silent reading, teacher-guided instruction, individualised reading (which allows students to work at their own level and their own pace with texts from their own academic disciplines) and out-of-class pleasure reading. This combination of activities accommodates intensive and extensive reading in addition to explicit instruction in strategic reading (see Janzen, 1996; Janzen and Stoller, 1998; Stoller, 1995).

Intercultural communication

The Intercultural Communication (IC) course focuses on speaking and listening skills development, as well as cultural adaptation. Two types of participants enrol in IC: EAP students and proficient speakers of the target language. Class participants develop increased intercultural sensitivities through a series of experiential crosscultural and human relations training activities while improving their speaking and listening abilities (see Maggio and Gay, 1986; Weeks, Pedersen and Brislin, 1982). Participants actively explore issues that are relevant to their immediate social and academic lives, including cultural adjustment, culture shock, stereotypes, and the dynamics of verbal and non-verbal communication.

Video

This class is designed to expose students to varieties of spoken English and help them improve their listening comprehension with authentic language materials. Each session is organised around a single videotape; some complement themes being explored in the Core class and others introduce new subject matter. The use of videotapes not only provides students with authentic listening practice, but also provides a natural springboard for speaking and writing practice, aiding students in transferring information learned from one medium to another (i.e., from a video to a written or spoken 'text'). Because of the ease with which focused speaking instruction can be integrated into this course, Video is designated as the curricular module in which students receive systematic feedback on pronunciation.

Computer lab

Computer Lab students improve their word processing skills and are introduced to other computer literacy skills that will make them more competitive in regular classes. Listening, reading and writing tasks become truly purposeful as students learn new computer skills, including the use of electronic mail, various software programmes and the Internet.

Writing tutorials

Because of the importance of writing in most academic courses, this hybrid curriculum is structured to address students' individual writing needs by means of one-on-one or small-group tutorials. The emphasis of the tutorials usually evolves over time as student needs change. In writing tutorials, more advanced students benefit from being introduced to the writing conventions of their intended academic majors (see Johns, 1997a).

TOEFL preparation

The TOEFL preparation course emphasises test-taking strategies, the intricacies of English grammar, vocabulary building, reading comprehension and rate building, and listening discrimination.

The seven curricular modules described here characterise the basic framework of NAU's EAP curriculum. The curriculum was initially designed more than a decade ago to reflect views espoused in the literature, the past experiences of the principal curriculum designer, institutional and professional expectations, and the hypothesised needs of the target student population. Over the last ten years, the curriculum has undergone both minor and major changes, some of which have evolved into significantly larger innovations. The longitudinal study that follows documents some aspects of that change and innovation process.

Longitudinal study

The goal of the study was to collect data systematically from a variety of sources and in a number of different ways, to reveal the perceived effectiveness of the EAP curriculum and to identify specific aspects of the curriculum that merited modification. It was anticipated, from the outset, that changes and innovations would be implemented in the EAP curriculum as a result of study findings at yearly intervals during the ten-year period under investigation.

Subjects

Four groups of subjects participated in the study. The first group included L2 students enrolled in the EAP programme (N = 306). The second group included a subset of the first group, specifically EAP students who were about to exit the EAP programme, having completed their English language studies (N = 211). The third group, in actuality a subset of the second group, included past EAP students who had completed their first full semester of regular university course work (N = 40). The fourth group included EAP instructors (N = 44), all of whom were graduate teaching assistants working on Master's degrees in Teaching English as a Second Language (TESL) or PhDs in Applied Linguistics.

Data collection

Data were collected by means of four instruments; each instrument, described below, targeted a different group of subjects:

- End-of-semester written course evaluations were completed by all EAP students. The evaluation forms, modified each semester by EAP instructors, solicited quantifiable and qualitative information that focused on the effectiveness of each EAP course in relation to its goals and objectives, aspects of the course that the students liked or thought should be changed, and students' perceptions of their own language improvement based on their enrolment in the course.
- Semi-structured exit interviews were conducted by the programme director with students who were just completing the EAP programme. Fifteen-minute interviews were guided by set questions.
- Semi-structured interviews were conducted by the programme director with a subset of past EAP students who were invited to make an appointment to discuss their first semester in regular

university classes. Students were requested to leave copies of the syllabi for all of their classes with the director for programme files. The 15–30 minute interviews were structured around set questions.

• End-of-school-year faculty meetings, with instructors and the programme director in attendance, were devoted to a formal critique of the EAP curriculum and suggestions for curriculum reform. The agenda for the meeting followed the format indicated in Appendix A.

Curricular modifications resulting from student and faculty input

Over the last decade, the EAP curriculum at NAU has undergone many transformations, many of which have stemmed from one or more of the data sources described above. Faculty and student input have provided the impetus for many of the changes and innovations, though it is virtually impossible to match up a given change with a specific data source because most changes were gradual and evolutionary. (See Stoller, 1995, 1997, for a discussion of impetuses for change in intensive English programmes.) Some of the changes that have occurred over the last ten years have stemmed from faculty action-research projects and others from experimentation with new instructional techniques that later became regular components of the curriculum. Others have involved broadening the scope of curricular goals and objectives so that instructors and students have more options available to them. Others have entailed the redefinition of courses, the redistribution of curricular elements and the purchase or adoption of new materials. Twelve changes, which are considered innovative in the NAU context, are summarised below to illustrate the breadth and scope of innovations that can be linked to faculty and student input.

1 Early on, the programme's Core class used L2 textbooks that were billed as content based. Because the programme had a commitment to extended content learning, faculty found it necessary to spend innumerable hours searching for content materials to augment limited textbook content. Instructors spent so much time searching for compatible content that they hardly had time to develop exercises to make them accessible for their students. Thus, it was suggested at a faculty meeting that we rethink our textbook adoptions. We ended up adopting informational readers (i.e., non-fiction, non-narrative readers) written for high school

first language (L1) learners (e.g. Greenhaven Press and Lucent Books). Using these content-rich resources freed up faculty to use their professional expertise to develop instructional tasks that made the content accessible to L2 students.

2 The adoption of content-rich resources led to well-developed thematic units that resulted in substantive language and content learning in the Core class. Despite this fact, faculty and students felt that the Core curriculum was fragmented, with few connections among the disparate themes being explored. After some experimentation, the use of 'threads' (i.e., abstract, broad concepts) – to create linkages across themes and foster greater curricular coherence – became a regular approach to course design. As an example, the concept of 'responsibility' was used to link themes as disparate as civil rights (responsibility to uphold civil rights for all citizens), pollution (responsibility to control pollution), demography (responsibility to regulate family size), the solar system (responsibility to conduct ethical research) and Native Americans (responsibility to protect endangered cultures). (See Stoller and Grabe, 1997, for a more in depth discussion of threads.)

3 Linked to our adoption of textbooks designed for L1 students were the difficulties students experienced processing authentic and densely organised texts. As a possible solution to this problem, instructors piloted the use of graphic organisers (e.g. Venn diagrams, time lines, grids, flow charts, comparison/contrast tables), which later became a standard scaffolding device throughout the curriculum (see Mach and Stoller, 1997).

4 The original teacher guidelines for the Core class specified that thematic units were to conclude with two culminating activities, one oral and the other written, that obliged students to synthesise and extend information learned from multiple content sources. Instructors felt restricted by the wording of the guidelines and proposed broadening the scope of the requirement so that students could exhibit what they had learned in different modes. This led to experimentation with public poster sessions (Esposito, Marshall and Stoller, 1997), formal, public debates (Mach, Stoller and Tardy, 1997) and oral presentations in K-12 classrooms as alternative culminating activities.

5 Past EAP students, having completed one semester of regular courses, consistently commented on the heavy reading loads that they had to endure in mainstream classes. Reading Lab instructors were not convinced that the teaching of strategies (e.g. summarising, asking questions, predicting and checking predictions,

rereading) was translating into better student reading abilities. One instructor piloted a new Reading Lab course that changed the orientation of instruction, emphasising the training of strategic readers rather than the teaching of discrete strategies (Janzen, 1996; Janzen and Stoller, 1998). Elements of that pilot have now become standard features of the Reading Lab.

6 Students reported that in some skill areas they did not notice appreciable improvement at the end of the course, even though they had worked very hard. Faculty proposed the use of multi-skill portfolios (rather than the standard writing portfolio) to help students chart their progress in speaking, listening, reading, writing and vocabulary.

7 Faculty grew increasingly frustrated with students' obsession with the TOEFL course. The course was modified over time to include what we now call 'real-world activities' that make explicit connections between TOEFL and real-world language demands. Through the adoption of *Consider the Issues* (Numrich, 1995) for the TOEFL course, as one example, we expose students to authentic radio broadcasts (from National Public Radio) that help them improve their listening skills for the TOEFL, future university courses, and non university-related listening.

8 When the programme set up its first computer laboratory, students most often entered the programme without knowing how to type or use computers. Thus, initial instruction focused on keyboarding and word processing. As the years passed, students arrived with these skills in hand and grew impatient with the course. The focus of computer lab instruction has since changed to emphasise the use of computers for information searches (via the Internet) and communication (via e-mail).

9 For a number of years, the International Communication (IC) instructor commented that native speaker participants (MA-TESL students) were missing class, primarily during mid-term and final-exam periods. To encourage better attendance and more attentive participation, the EAP programme director worked with MA-TESL faculty to create a mechanism for giving MA-TESL students practicum credit for their participation in IC.

10 The need for more explicit attention to vocabulary building was voiced by students from all three student-respondent groups as well as instructors throughout the years. After tinkering with different approaches to vocabulary development, instructors began experimenting with an adaptation of Green's (1993) Word Wall approach. (See Eyraud, Giles, Koenig and Stoller, 2000, for details.)

11 Instructors voiced concerns that students did not fully comprehend the connection between the EAP curriculum and mainstream classes. The need for 'reality checks' led to the regular incorporation of a number of activities into the curriculum, including (a) a class-visitation project (which required students to plan and then visit mainstream classes in their intended academic departments) (b) the regular review and evaluation of course syllabi (collected from past EAP students returning for interviews) (c) guest speakers (to expose students to native speakers who were not sensitised ESL teachers), and (d) panel discussions led by past EAP students who were now immersed in regular coursework. It is important to note (in part because of budgetary matters that concern most language programme personnel) that the guest speakers (student club presidents, graduate teaching assistants from a range of disciplines, some instructors) and past EAP students who visit class do so without any form of compensation; if their busy schedules permit it, they usually agree to participate after being invited by the director of the EAP programme.

12 Core instructors complained that they were overburdened with responsibilities. Explicit pronunciation instruction was therefore removed from the Core class and incorporated into the Video course. To complement the new pronunciation goals for the Video course, a dialogue journal replaced the more traditional written journal, providing the instructor with an additional opportunity for providing regular, systematic and individualised feedback on pronunciation.

Conclusion

These twelve innovations represent a sampling of the curricular changes that have been implemented over the lifetime of the Northern Arizona University EAP programme. Reflective of the past, we are currently engaged in a series of new changes and are likely to continue fine-tuning our programme in response to the needs of our students, faculty and home institution. It should be noted that the overall success of these innovations has been judged by in-house action research projects, end-of-course evaluations, and interviews with students and faculty. Although our claims of sustained programme competitiveness and effective teaching and learning cannot be backed by empirical comparisons with other programmes, we do not believe that this belittles our efforts.

The actual changes reported here are far less important, however, than the process of curriculum renewal that has taken place at NAU and that can take place in any EAP programme that is receptive to change. Curriculum renewal is a complex process; it is dependent on an understanding of EAP student needs, EAP curriculum design, the curriculum development process and innovation diffusion. Although a grasp of these issues at intellectual and practical levels is critical, we should not underestimate the value of a responsiveness to student and faculty input. Their feedback can add to the vitality of an EAP programme and lead to innovations that will meet student needs, promote faculty development, and sustain programme competitiveness. Curriculum renewal that is based on the 'pulse' of an EAP programme – represented by student and faculty needs and perceptions, in addition to participatory decision making, consensus building, and an openness to experimentation – can contribute to the vibrancy and effectiveness of the programme as a whole.

Appendix A

End-of-school-year faculty meeting agenda

1 Critique of the current programme.
   (a) What aspects of the curriculum do you think are particularly critical for our students?
   (b) What aspects of the curriculum should we change? Why? How?
2 Recommendations for the future.
   (a) Identify one curricular innovation that you implemented this year that should become a regular part of the curriculum. Be prepared to provide a rationale for your recommendation.
   (b) Based on your students' linguistic, academic and acculturation needs, what do you wish we had done this year that we did not?
3 Other recommendations for next year.

14 Team-teaching in EAP: Changes and adaptations in the Birmingham approach

Tony Dudley-Evans

Introduction

The question of whether EAP teaching should be 'common-core' or subject specific has always been controversial. In the early days most EAP materials (e.g. Herbert's *The Structure of Technical English, The Focus Series*) assumed a homogeneous group of students from one discipline, and concentrated on linguistic features of communication in that discipline. Subsequent materials (e.g. *Reading and Thinking in English*) took account of the fact that many EAP groups are, in fact, heterogeneous with students from a range of disciplines and focused on study skills that were considered to be important whatever discipline one was studying. This position was justified theoretically by the argument that the most important aspects of communication in academic contexts are common to all disciplines and that ESP teaching should not be concerned with teaching 'specialised varieties' of English but with the common features (Hutchinson and Waters, 1987). In recent years the increasing evidence from discourse and genre analysis that there is, in fact, significant variation between disciplines in the way that they structure their discourse, both in writing (Myers, 1989; Dillon, 1991) and in academic lectures (Olsen and Huckin, 1990; Dudley-Evans, 1994c), has strengthened the case for the inclusion of some specific work in an EAP programme. The case can also be made on pedagogic grounds. Brinton, Snow and Wesche (1989: 1) argue that simply 'contextualising' EAP lessons is not enough and that the basis of EAP teaching should be the authentic texts that students have to handle. Brinton *et al.* advocate the concurrent teaching of academic content and relevant language and skills, and suggest that this concurrent teaching provides a format in which 'students can respond orally to reading and lecture and reading materials', and which 'recognises that academic writing follows from listening and reading, and thus requires students to

225

synthesise facts and ideas from multiple sources as preparation for writing' (Brinton *et al.*, 1989: 2).

EAP and team-teaching at the University of Birmingham

The long-established EAP programme at the University of Birmingham has always combined the common-core approach with specific courses in key departments with large numbers of international students on post-graduate courses. Following Blue (1988) I shall refer to a common-core EAP programme as English for General Academic Purposes (EGAP) and a specific programme as English for Specific Academic Purposes (ESAP). At Birmingham there are EGAP courses in listening, writing and speaking, but also ESAP courses in departments focusing on the skills that are the most relevant at particular stages of the academic course, ie., listening and reading in the early part of the first semester and academic writing in later stages. The justification for the inclusion of a ESAP component in the course was always that students seemed better able to transfer the generalised skills taught in the EGAP course if they also received more specific teaching related to their actual subject tasks, i.e., the tasks that they are confronted with every day of their course, through an ESAP course. As mentioned in the introduction, this essentially pedagogic justification has been reinforced by the results of genre analysis showing that there are significant variations in the discourse of different disciplines.

The ESAP work at Birmingham has involved liaison with the actual departments on the basis that the EAP teacher can only deliver such work effectively if he or she has the active co-operation of subject teachers. I have categorised this liaison into three levels of co-operation, *co-operation, collaboration* and *team-teaching* (Dudley-Evans and St John, 1998). The first level, co-operation, involves seeking information from the department about the content of the courses, the tasks required of students, the expectations of the department and its related discourse community about the nature of communication in the subject. The second level, collaboration, involves the working together of the language teacher and the subject teacher outside the classroom to devise specific activities in the ESAP class that run concurrently with the subject course and help students cope with that course. The third level, *team-teaching*, involves the language and subject teachers working together in the same classroom. The aim at Birmingham has been to go beyond just co-operation to develop collaborative and team-taught ESAP teaching.

The original team-teaching work reported in Johns and Dudley-

Evans (1980) and Dudley-Evans and Johns (1981)[1] concentrated on helping international students on two particular Master's courses, the MSc in Transportation and the MSc in the Conservation and Utilisation of Plant Genetic Resources. The team-taught sessions involved the working together of a language teacher and a subject teacher and concentrated on listening comprehension of lectures and the writing of examination answers. The team-taught sessions were either a follow-up tutorial on a specific lecture in which the subject teacher at the tutorial was always the actual person who had delivered the lecture, or a session in which the subject teacher would bring a possible examination question for which a suitable answer would be discussed and then written up in the session.

I do not propose to outline the procedures for the sessions as these were extensively reported on in the papers referred to above, and more recently in Dudley-Evans and St John (1998). But it is worth reminding ourselves of the roles played by the three types of participant in the sessions, the students, the subject teacher and the language teacher. The main role of the language teacher is to prepare the material for the session in co-operation with the subject teacher and to run the session. The subject teacher acts as an advisor entering the discussion to clarify points about the subject and to evaluate the students' contributions. Are they correct in their answer to the question raised by the language teacher? What further detail do they need to add to make their answer complete? The students have the opportunity to raise questions and to clarify points about the subject with the actual subject teacher. Swales (1988a) summarises the triangular relationship in Figure 1.

In many ways the role of the language teacher is that of the intermediary seeking to interpret on behalf of the students what the subject teacher meant in his or her lecture or in an examination question. The language teacher will respond to the questions but also suggest questions that students might put to the subject teacher. The language teacher will also bring in the subject teacher to the discussion to answer questions or clarify issues when this seems necessary.

It is this concern with the relationship between the three parts of the triangle that I feel is the key to success and the longevity of this kind of teaching. I have suggested that there are three main reasons for the success of the team-teaching done at the University of Birmingham:

---

[1] The first of these two papers, i.e., Johns and Dudley-Evans (1980) can also be found in John Swales's *Episodes in ESP* (1988) with an introductory commentary by Swales.

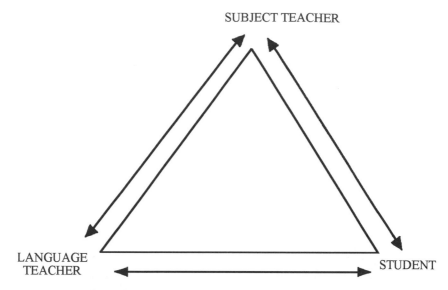

Figure 1 Teacher roles

1 the roles of the subject teacher and the language teacher are, as far as possible, clearly defined;
2 the demands made on the time of each subject teacher are relatively limited as one lecturer will normally only be asked to do one or two sessions in one 10/11-week term;
3 the subject teacher and the language teacher respect each other's expertise and professionalism.

Another key part of the success of these sessions is the way in which they help NNS students adopt a more active role in following the course. At first, international students appear to find the way in which a language teacher is asking questions or giving advice on communication about the subject very strange. Similarly, they initially fail to understand the nature of the interaction between the language and the subject teacher. But, as they become used to the sessions, they seem to become much more comfortable about asking their own questions and raising queries about content or the way in which content is presented. This clearly helps develop students' rhetorical awareness of the subject.

Recent developments

The focus of the team-taught sessions has moved away from lecture comprehension towards writing, either texts required as part of the

Master's course, i.e., classroom genres (Johns, 1995) such as examination answers, project reports or the dissertation, or authentic genres that students will have to write once they enter (or re-enter) professional life. These authentic genres include project bids, executive summaries and managerial reports, and involve developing a persuasive argument for a particular course of action.

The main reason for this shift of focus is that these courses have been placing increased emphasis on written tasks using both classroom genres and authentic genres in the assessment of students. In the International Highway Engineering course (it has changed its name from Transportation) and also in the Masters in Development Administration written communication is now an integral credit-bearing part of the course attended by native speakers as well as non-natives. The preparation for writing examination answers has also been extended to other departments offering Master's courses mainly geared towards international students, such as the MBA courses in International Business (MBA IB) and International Banking and Finance (MBA IBF and Development Finance courses run by Accounting.[2]

I will give two examples of exercises used recently with the International Highway Engineering MSc group, one concerned with a classroom genre, the examination answer, and another concerned with an authentic genre related to professional life.

Examination question

The Highways lecturer produced the following question, which was one that she had devised herself based on the material that she was using in the lecture course that she was giving at that time. The subject matter was thus reasonably familiar to students.

Describe the main types of data collected at the inventory stage of a Road Maintenance Management System (RMMS), discussing the typical procedures adopted for the acquisition of the required data at this stage.

The first part of the discussion focused on the meaning of the question noting that the question has two parts, a 'describe' section and a 'discuss' section. It was also noted that the answer to the discussion section would carry a higher weighting in the marks, approximately 60%.

The content of the answer was then teased out from the students by the language teacher with the subject teacher evaluating the points

---

[2] Sadly no team-taught courses are now run in Plant Biology as a result of changes in the English level of students accepted for the Master's courses.

Table 1. *Horizontal negotiation*

System	Advantage	Disadvantage
Manual with subsequent transfer to computer	Simple Inclusive	The transfer is expensive and inefficient
Use of lap-top computer	Quicker More efficient	None
Use of video camera	Quicker Cheaper	Does not provide as much detail as other methods

suggested by students. It emerged that the answer, as with so many others, seemed to work most effectively as a discussion of the advantages and disadvantages of each system, and the discussion of the content led to the summarising matrix shown in Table 1. This matrix was devised by the language teacher on the whiteboard to summarise the points made by the students and the subject teacher.

The next stage was to consider whether the information in the table should be written up in the actual answer following a vertical or horizontal path through the matrix. For example horizontal negotiation (Johns, n.d.) involves dealing with each system at a time, outlining the advantages and disadvantages; vertical negotiation deals with the advantage of each system and then the disadvantage as demonstrated in Table 2. In this case it was agreed that horizontal negotiation was more appropriate, as it facilitated the evaluation of each system and the reaching of a conclusion about the most appropriate procedure to be adopted. This is, in fact, the more normal form of writing up such information.

The benefits of the class are, I believe, clear. The students gain from the revision of the material and from the discussion of the most effective means of presenting the information. They are able to generalise from the discussion of the meaning of the question and the tactics for answering it to other examination questions. The subject teacher sees at first hand any difficulties that students are having with the content and its presentation. In this case she was very interested by the discussion of the use of the matrix as a summarising technique and commented that she found the discussion of the advantages and disadvantages of horizontal or vertical negotiation extended her own

Table 2. *Vertical negotiation*

System	Advantage	Disadvantage
Manual with subsequent transfer to computer	Simple Inclusive	The transfer is expensive and inefficient
Use of lap-top computer	Quicker More efficient	None
Use of video camera	Quicker Cheaper	Does not provide as much detail as other methods

understanding of the answer she was looking for. For the language teacher the main benefit is the opportunity to go into authentic content without getting out of his or her depth, and to help the students and the subject teacher devise appropriate strategies for structuring information.

An example related to professional work

I have noted that one of the major developments in the programme is that the English class now also focuses on writing tasks that are still considered part of the academic course, but in fact relate more to the kind of writing that students will have to carry out once they enter professional life, e.g. technical and managerial reports, bids for contracts and other such persuasive documents. It is recognised that some of the graduates will not have to do this in English, or that even those who will use English may need to adopt a very different style in their own country from that favoured in Britain or the USA. Nonetheless it has been found that these tasks are welcomed by students and are seen as a model to inform any future professional writing that they have to carry out in their own country after entering a job. In other words, they may write them in a very different style in their country but they are able to make the appropriate adaptations more effectively if they are aware of what is done in the UK. The tasks also provide useful input into some of the writing required on the course. This writing is in fact often influenced by professional writing and we have noticed that there is increasing convergence between so-called academic writing and professional writing on postgraduate courses

Table 3. *Compaction test results*

Test no. 12	Standard Compaction	Test no. 13	Heavy Compaction
Moisture content %	Dry Density Mg/m	Moisture content %	Dry Density Mg/m
4	–	4	2.00
6	1.90	6	2.12
8	1.99	8	2.17
10	2.08	10	2.15
12	2.06	12	2.08
14	1.96	14	1.98

such as Highway Engineering, which has a post-experience and training orientation rather than strictly academic orientation.

The example used the following brief:

Exercise

Your brief is to give an appropriate compaction specification (maximum dry density and moisture content) for a material which is available from a borrow pit and which will be used somewhere in the highway structure.

Notes/information
1 The job is called Nata-Maun Road, Botswana.
2 The material has already been classified by BS 1377 'Soils for Civil Engineering Purposes Tests nos. 1 to 7', and has been described as a brown clayey gravel with sand inclusions, well graded with a PI of 5. The natural moisture content is 12%.
3 Compaction test results are available (BS test nos. 12 and 13).

Suggested layout
Title
Extent of investigation
Description of sample and location in the highway
Test methods to be used
Tables of results
Calculations
Comments on test method
Summary of results with appropriate comments and/or explanation
References

This example is discussed in detail in Dudley-Evans (1995). The key points are that students were asked to plot a graph of the results before they discussed the method and the results. The task thus had a validity from the subject point of view. Once this had been done, the discussion concentrated on the strategy that the writer should adopt in order to convince the potential readership, i.e., senior management with a technical background. The discussion focused on whether an 'executive summary' briefly outlining and justifying the main recommendation was needed, and whether the main recommendation also needed to be included in the introduction to the report. This second point about the introduction was raised by the language teacher following findings by Swales and Najjar (1987) that a significant number of academic introductions, even if they have an abstract, include a brief summary of the main findings of the research reported.

It was decided that an executive summary was needed, but that the recommendation about the appropriate compaction specification should not be included in the introduction, but only in the summary of results at the end of the report. It would of course be included as the main point of the executive summary.

Discussion

I would like to focus on two issues arising from this update of the team-teaching work at the University of Birmingham. The first is the question raised by a 'critical' view of EAP. I have found that the ideas of critical linguistics (e.g. Pennycook, 1997b; Benesch, 1996) force EAP teachers to reconsider some of the issues that have been taken for granted in EAP, and what effects EAP teaching will have. I am particularly interested in what critical linguistics has to say about the description I have provided here and elsewhere of the relationship between the three elements of the triangle of the students, the subject teacher and the language teacher, and the question of whether the issue of 'institutional power' has been neglected in the discussion of these relationships. The second is the question of how applicable this team-teaching model for subject language co-operation is for other situations, especially outside the countries of the UK, the USA, Australia and New Zealand.

Power and the relationships

I have emphasised the benefits of the team-teaching approach for each element of the triangle, and, in particular, the need for mutual respect between the subject and language teacher. Benesch (1996 and 1999) makes particularly interesting comments suggesting that EAP approaches, and by implication the team-teaching work described here, are too 'accommodationist'. By this she means that the work is too accepting of the established ways of the departments and is too much concerned with making students aware of the department's practices and too little concerned with helping students question those practices and be aware of their own rights. In Benesch (1999) she describes how a collaboration under the American adjunct model[3] (which did not involve team-teaching) led to modifications in the teaching of the department she was collaborating with and sensitising students to their rights within the academic context.

The situation – an undergraduate course in the Psychology department at a university in New York with a large number of international students – is one where the lecturer is or appears to be willing to help students with difficulties in following the lecture course. However, he is not prepared to do so at the expense of falling behind in the syllabus. As Benesch puts it, the course is dominated by the need for 'coverage', i.e., completing the syllabus. The teaching and learning are 'regulated by the tradition of the textbook-driven lecture course, a manifestation of institutional control' (Benesch, 1999). Benesch was, however, able to show students how to ask questions when they had not fully understood a particular point, and this did change the nature of the interaction in the classroom. Students had been made aware of their rights and this affected the nature of the relationship between them and the lecturer.

The main question arising from Benesch's very interesting description is how far generalisations can be made from one undergraduate course, however effective the particular approach adopted by the EAP teacher may have been in that situation. The assumption that Benesch makes seems to be that power, or the control of what happens during the course, resides entirely with the subject lecturer as the representative of the department. In a situation such as that at the University of Birmingham described here, like so many other British universities, departments are very dependent on the income of international students, especially those following postgraduate courses or research. This means that power does not reside so uniformly with the department and the subject lecturer. Course

---

[3] The American adjunct model involves the students enrolling simultaneously in two related courses, one a subject course and the other a language course. The two courses share the content and assignments and the main aim is to help the students on the language course cope with the subject course and its assignments. There is no team-teaching and the teaching fits into my *collaboration* category.

content on programmes with large numbers of international students has been modified to meet their different academic background and needs, and teaching methods varied to match the learning styles of international students. This certainly leads to change, but it also raises questions about whether this 'marketisation' of a postgraduate course has led to a dilution of the academic standards and content of the course. It is my (perhaps over-optimistic) observation that the need to find a balance between academic content and the need to provide a practical post-experience course has been a healthy tension and that the resulting courses do provide a good balance between the two.

Another key aspect of how the triangular relationship has developed is the way in which the role of the language teacher, as a person knowledgeable about communication in disciplines, has been widely accepted by departments and their advice on issues such as wording of examination questions, preparation of students for the writing of dissertations, and assessment of oral presentations has been actively sought.

All of this means that power in these situations is much more difficult to define and a much more fluid affair than those who adopt a critical stance seem to imply. Certainly in the team-taught sessions the control of the session is taken by the different components of the triangle at different times; the initial stages are usually controlled by the language teacher's agenda, but students can change the agenda to meet their own problems. And it is not uncommon for the subject teacher to take over control of the session at certain points if he or she wishes to make a point or to amplify a point he or she has made in a lecture.

All of this indicates that the situation described here is very different from the 'coverage-dominated' undergraduate course described by Benesch. It seems that the economic power of the students has spilled over into the academic sphere and has brought about healthy changes in approach and attitude on the part of the department to the course content, the teaching methods used and the preparedness to accept a directly interventionist role for the EAP teacher.

The team-taught sessions have also had an effect on the behaviour of the subject lecturers. The language lecturers involved have always fought shy of commenting directly on the subject lecturers' performance in lectures or on the standard of their questions, as this could affect the trust between the two sides, the importance of which I have emphasised in this paper. However, the effect of seeing students' difficulties with particular points covered in a lecture or with the phrasing of an examination question does undoubtedly change the way that the subject lecturers present certain points in their lectures and write their examination questions.

Transfer of the team-teaching approach to other situations

It is clear that it is much easier to establish the type of collaboration with subject specialists and the team-teaching described in this paper in a British university. Both teachers are native speakers and established members of the university teaching staff and it is not difficult to establish the relationship and respect needed to make these sessions work. A quite frequent reaction to this approach on the part of EAP teachers working either in a non-English medium situation, or an English-medium situation where the majority of subject teachers are non-native speakers is that it would be very difficult to establish the trust needed to get the sessions going. Our experience in Singapore (Dudley-Evans, 1984a) was that, although it was possible to get the co-operation of subject teachers,[4] there was always the suspicion that the language teacher's hidden purpose was really to evaluate the quality of the subject teacher's English and to report back to the institution on this. This hardly led to the situation of trust that we regard as essential to the success of such teaching.

Nonetheless there have been reports of successful team-teaching operations outside Britain. De Escorcia (1984) describes a programme of English for Economics in Colombia in which there was close collaboration between the subject teacher and the language teacher in the selection of relevant sources for reading material in English for the EAP class. Chamberlain (1981) describes the formation of language-discipline teams in the teaching of Namibian refugees in Zambia. He notes the need for respect of the rather different priorities of the subject teacher and the language teacher. More recently, Vukadinovic (1998) reports on a team-teaching experiment in Slovenia where the language teacher co-operated with subject teachers in the department of Chemical Education and Informatics. Most of the work involved integrating the language classes with the subject classes so that the two ran in parallel. In the laboratory students concentrated on designing and carrying out their experiments, while the English class focused on writing a Teacher's Guide for the experiments carried out in the laboratory and on

---

[4] These teachers were all NNSs. The term 'non-native' is, however, difficult to define in Singapore, where many use English widely but have another language as their mother tongue.

preparing an oral presentation on the experiments. The subject and language teachers mostly worked together outside the classroom in the preparation of the course outline and the teaching materials, only collaborating directly in the classroom on the assessment of students' oral presentations.

The models described by De Escorcia and Vukadinovic both rely rather more on integration of the English course with the subject course than on actual team-teaching. The English teacher finds out what exactly is being taught on the subject course and then relates the activities of the English class to the subject syllabus. These activities run concurrently with the subject course. As both authors note, this increases the relevance of the English class, enables a number of 'grey areas' to be covered (e.g. the structure of a laboratory report) that might not be taught by either party and, more generally, reduces the problem of the isolation of the EAP teacher from what the students are actually doing.

These models seem to be a practical and effective means to making subject language collaboration work in non-English medium situations. They are still informed by the original work on team-teaching described by Dudley-Evans and Johns (1981), but make sensible and practical adaptations to that approach. We recognise that the Birmingham team-teaching approach is something of an ideal model that cannot necessarily transfer to other situations. Indeed, in Birmingham itself, the collaborative model is used in other departments and actual team-teaching only occurs on an occasional basis (typically in the run-up to examinations).[5]

Conclusion

In this paper I have described the team-teaching approach adopted as part of the EAP programme run at the University of Birmingham in the UK and outlined some of the new directions that work has taken in recent years. I have also argued that an approach based less on actual team-teaching in the classroom but on collaboration outside the classroom and integration of the EAP course with the subject course may be a more appropriate and effective model for other situations, especially outside the UK

Although there are differences between a team-teaching and collaborative approach, both share a spirit of inquisitiveness about

---

[5] It is also worth noting that the American adjunct model for content-based second language instruction (see Brinton, Snow and Wesche, 1989) follows similar patterns to the collaborative approach of De Escorcia and Vukadinovic.

the subject course, a desire to make the EAP course relevant to that subject course and a willingness to question constantly whether the EAP course is truly meeting the needs of students. Where the EAP course is isolated from the subject course, there will always be the danger that it will become too detached from what students are doing in their subject courses. EAP has been noted for its vitality and innovation, but the more it becomes separated from the subject content, the greater the danger is that it will lose its dynamism.

15 Does the emperor have no clothes? A re-examination of grammar in content-based instruction

Donna M. Brinton and Christine A. Holten

Introduction

The appearance of content-based instruction (CBI) on the language teaching scene is often traced to Mohan's, 1986 text, *Language and Content*. In this text, Mohan laid out the then quite revolutionary premise that language should and could not be taught in isolation from content, and that authentic content provided the richest and most natural context for language teaching to occur. Today, this premise is widely accepted, and the approach itself enjoys wide popularity.

To better understand the approach, let us examine the following three definitions of CBI:

(1) A content-based curriculum is simply one in which the basic organisational unit is a theme or topic, rather than the more customary grammatical patterns or language functions. The goal of this is to provide meaningful contexts for language learning instead of focusing on language as an object of study. At the foundation of this approach is the Krashenesque notion that acquisition is best promoted when language is presented in comprehensible and interesting communicative contexts. However, we diverge from Krashen and side with recent first language trends in reading and writing across the curriculum in the belief that instruction in higher-level language and study skills is warranted . . . and that such intervention can and does make a difference. (Bycina, 1986: 13)

(2) . . . we define content-based instruction as the integration of particular content with language-teaching aims. More specifically . . . it refers to the concurrent teaching of academic subject matter and second language skills. The language curriculum is based directly on the academic needs of the students and generally follows the sequence determined by a particular subject matter in dealing with the language problems which students encounter. The focus for students is on acquiring information via the second language and, in the process, developing their academic language skills. (Brinton, Snow and Wesche, 1989: 2)

(3) Discipline-based language instruction, and the broader 'content-based' approach to which it belongs, are part of a trend at all educational levels aiming at the development of use-oriented second and foreign language skills. Content-based language teaching is distinguished first of all by the concurrent learning of a specific content and related language use skills in a 'content driven' curriculum, i.e., with the selection and sequence of language elements determined by the content . . . Essential to all content-based language teaching is a view of language acquisition which emphasises the incidental internalisation of new knowledge by the learner from rich target language data, while focusing on the meaning being communicated . . . In content-based language teaching, the claim in a sense is that students get 'two for one' – both content knowledge and increased language proficiency.

(Wesche, 1993: 57–58)

There are interesting similarities in the above definitions, which can be summarised as follows:

1 The goal of CBI is to provide a meaningful context for language teaching to occur.
2 The organisation of a CBI course centres around content.
3 Content drives the curriculum, i.e., it is the starting point for decisions about what is taught.
4 Language and content are taught concurrently.
5 Comprehensible input, provided through the content materials, leads to language acquisition.

Far more interesting, however, are the differences exhibited between Bycina's (1986) definition and the Brinton, Snow and Wesche (1989) and Wesche (1993) definitions. As noted in (5) above, all three definitions agree that comprehensible input, presented in the form of authentic content, fosters acquisition. The definitions do not agree, however, on the extent to which overt language instruction should occur in CBI, with Bycina on one extreme taking a strong stand for such 'intervention' to occur and Wesche on the other extreme arguing that 'incidental internalisation' of new language occurs through exposure to content. Neither the Brinton, Snow and Wesche nor the Wesche definitions contain reference to the need for explicit attention to form.

Language vs. content

As is revealed in the above definitions, inherent in CBI is a tension between language on the one hand and content on the other. Thus, while from the theoretical point of view it is argued that content presents an ideal vehicle for language to be presented, the practitioner is often left to his or her own devices to decide when, how, and even whether this presentation of language should occur during the act of teaching. The difficulty faced by the practitioner is compounded by (1) the fact that many commercial ESL/EFL teaching materials that take a CBI approach gloss over the teaching of grammar (Master, 2000) and (2) CBI teacher training is often deficient in providing guidance in this area (Brinton, 2000). Further, in English for Academic Purposes (EAP) settings, the practitioner is often faced with the task of assisting students to understand difficult content. The result is that far too often in the battle between language and content, content wins out (Holten, 1997), and the majority of time in the classroom is devoted to helping students comprehend the content.

Eskey (1997) summarises this curricular tension, stating:

any courses built around a content-based syllabus . . . have their limitations and generate certain specific problems . . . The first is the problem of relating language form to language function and content in this kind of syllabus. This is the old accuracy/fluency problem, and content-based courses tend to come down hard on the side of fluency. Content and function flow rather smoothly together, being complementary aspects of language as a system for communication, but attending to grammar in any systematic way is difficult within communicative paradigms. One major reason may be the absence of insightful theoretical work on the relationship between grammatical form and discourse function . . . It seems to me that on the issue of how to teach linguistic forms, or how to insure that they will be learned, we don't really even know the right questions to ask.

(Eskey, 1992/1997: 139)

A counter-argument to Eskey's claim that CBI does not easily lend itself to teaching grammar is found in Master (2000), who argues that:

Content-based instruction is an ideal means of assuring the integration of [form-focused instruction]. By dealing with grammar within the context of understanding content, many of the original criticisms of the grammatical syllabus are satisfied: students no longer deal with decontextualised sentences or spend years learning isolated rules that inhibit their spoken fluency.   (Master, 2000: 94)

Having made this strong argument, however, Master presents several caveats that are more in line with Eskey's original claim. First, according to Master (p. 98), there is a limited range of grammatical items that lend themselves to exploitation in CBI (e.g. patterns linked to rhetorical structure such as compare/contrast, logical connectors, forms of subordination, gerunds and infinitives, and verb tenses). Additionally, Master documents (98–99) the serious lack of CBI student texts and teacher training materials that directly address grammar teaching, noting the related reluctance of authors to use sufficient and appropriate metalanguage in their explanations. In other words, the problem of teaching grammar in CBI involves both a limited range of items usually covered and the limited explanation of those items that *are* covered. Master notes (p. 102) that 'in allowing content to dictate what elements of grammar are covered in class, [we are] debilitating our students in those areas that are not likely to be focused upon'. Master concludes his article (102–103) by suggesting several ways in which grammar teaching can be more successfully integrated into CBI. The first of these has to do with the teaching materials themselves, which must include more systematic treatment of grammar. Since one cannot depend on materials for a complete solution to the problem, however, Master's second solution places responsibility on the teacher. This responsibility entails using content as a point of departure for focusing on grammar. However, to insure more exhaustive coverage of grammar in CBI, the teacher needs to expand the grammar explanation beyond the structure found in the content materials, and then link back to the content by demonstrating how particular ideas could be expressed using a greater variety of grammatical structures.

CBI in an EAP setting

In an effort to understand where focus on form fits into a content-based curriculum, we examined what practitioners and students have to say. We reviewed end-of-quarter instructor reviews of curriculum and student end-of-term course evaluations from our ESL programme for matriculated students, the ESL Service Courses at UCLA. We also interviewed selected instructors in the hope of clarifying why an effective way to focus on grammar and vocabulary within a content-based curriculum still eludes us.

As is no doubt true in most programmes, the ESL Service Course curriculum has undergone numerous changes over time, and is strongly influenced by current EAP theory and practice. CBI has had a long-standing influence on the curriculum. In 1979, the adjunct model of instruction was introduced into specially-designated sections of the Service Course curriculum via the university's Freshman Summer Programme (see Brinton, Snow and Wesche, 1989, for a description of this curriculum). However, due to the logistical difficulties involved in establishing adjunct courses at a large university such as UCLA, this curricular option was not pursued outside of this special programme. Nonetheless, the faculty remained committed to the basic premise of content-based instruction, and in 1990 a modified version of CBI was introduced into the first three courses of the university's four-course required ESL sequence. In this model, the simulated adjunct model (see Valentine and Repath-Martos, 1997), content is imported into an ESL class via authentic video lectures from undergraduate content-area classes. These video lectures form the core of the content unit, and are supplemented by authentic content-area reading and writing assignments along with related readings (e.g. excerpts from popular sources and from literature), language and skill-area instruction, related discussion activities, visuals, etc.). (See Weigle and Jensen (1997) and Holten (1997) for further information on the simulated adjunct model.)

Adopting the simulated adjunct model in the first three courses of our required sequence has proven a very effective way to deliver ESL instruction for academic purposes to the undergraduate students who enrol in the ESL Service Courses at our institution. It has worked so effectively primarily because it suits the needs of the two divergent populations that we serve in these courses: (1) US residents and citizens who have completed some portion of their education at US high schools and/or community colleges before entering UCLA and (2) international students who hold an I-20 student visa. In the decade or so since we adopted content-based syllabi in all of our courses, we have fine-tuned our approach, seeking more authentic lecture materials, incorporating longer, more challenging reading passages, and adjusting the balance given to the four skills. But one curriculum development problem has remained intractable: what place should overt language instruction have in a content-based syllabus and what form should that instruction take?

Dissatisfaction with the grammar and vocabulary component in our content-based courses is a recurring theme both in the end-of-course evaluative comments made by ESL students enrolled in them, and of instructors' written reviews of curriculum after teaching a content-based course. Especially striking is the fact that almost every review of curriculum written by an instructor over the last four years has mentioned something about the question of how best to address grammar in CBI, no matter what course in the ESL sequence the instructor has taught.

The instructors' call for more attention to grammar came largely in response to the needs and wishes expressed by the students in their classes. Some instructors suggested that grammar work be approached in a more overt way, one that would be more salient for the students:

The needs which are not addressed, at least as I taught the course, include basic grammar, vocabulary . . . Of course, these skills are developed, but they are not addressed in a systematic way, and many of my students expressed a desire for some more systematic, explicit 'teaching' of grammar, and vocabulary . . .

If there were more time, I would like to add more grammar. Although the students grumble about grammar work when they have to do it, this is the first thing they ask for more of, if you ask them.

Another instructor worried about the validity of a curriculum that seems, on the face of it, not to address the very factors that placed the students into an ESL course in the first place:

This has been said before – but what about grammar? We place students in classes based on language proficiency, yet beyond correcting errors in compositions, we never directly teach anything to help them in this area.

According to the views of several instructors, the inclusion of grammar and vocabulary teaching may in fact be a utopian ideal, i.e., an unattainable goal in a CBI framework. As one instructor wrote, 'In a perfect world, ideally, more materials to integrate skills of grammar and language into the content work and to support their use in discourse context would help.'

In their end-of-course evaluations, the students were less vocal and less consistent than the instructors in their calls for more instruction in grammar and vocabulary. However, in the four years of evaluative comments we examined, requests like the following appeared with some frequency.

We need some correction to the grammar in our journal. I think that the level of our English grammar is also important, not only the content.

And they tended to comment positively when they did receive the kind of grammar instruction that they found helpful.

The instructor is very concerned about our grammar. In every homework she would correct my mistakes and inform me on what I should focus on. I've learned a few things that I probably would never have known if she hadn't done this.

She is very good in helping me to find grammar errors on my paper. I think that ESL students want to learn more grammar and sentence structures so that they can write and understand English better.

Tensions over language instruction

These kinds of explicit comments and advice from both teachers and students about the kind of language instruction they want are a curriculum designer's gold mine. Both our instructors and our students have done everything short of writing materials for us. Given this great advice, why are we still struggling with how to incorporate grammar and vocabulary work consistently into UCLA's CBI courses? Some tentative answers can be found when we examine how the tension over grammar instruction manifests itself. In our setting, we experience it in two ways: (1) disagreement over what approach to take to grammar instruction, and (2) avoiding grammar instruction.

One of the unspoken tensions that we have experienced in supervising TAs and developing CBI curriculum is 'how' to incorporate grammar and vocabulary work into any given lesson plan. It is not simply a matter of adding 'more grammar' to the curriculum; rather, it is a matter of which approach to grammar instruction to adopt. Do you adopt a commercial text with grammar explanations and exercises and use it as a side light to the CBI curriculum? Do you let students' written production drive your decisions about what to teach, basing grammar lessons on error analysis and then teaching students to edit their work for those particular structures? Do you let the grammar structures and lexicon used in the CBI reading materials drive your decisions? Or do you let the writing task drive your decision, anticipating key grammar structures and vocabulary items that students will need in completing writing assignments?

A reasoned combination of the above approaches is probably best, but in our own setting we have been unable to reach agreement about which combination of approaches to adopt. This lack of consensus is evident in the following instructor comments from the questionnaires and reviews of curriculum:

the grammar features that grow out of the materials are not necessarily the ones which students need the most. Therefore, I think the editing of one's own grammar will always be the most targeted and necessary component in these courses in which time is at such a premium. Also, even though the grammar textbooks are not related to the content, I feel . . . that when I see an error pattern that is clearly relevant to all students, a good grammar text does work well.

. . . It is important to touch on grammar, but I think in an integrated fashion – in other words, drawn from the content and student-produced materials, rather than rigidly (i.e. prescribed curriculum, with set topics) or in a parallel, yet unrelated fashion (i.e. with some sort of grammar text assigned in addition to but apart from the content text of the course).

I think error correction using students' papers is . . . good . . . But I think there's got to be other ways without resorting to traditional grammar books. Right now, I'm working on an approach to dovetailing some

*grammar work with editing strategies based on error correction as a start,
but giving students some general grammatical principles they can actually
take home with them.*

*I don't find general grammar lessons to be useful, but anything that can be
tied to the work that students must do for this or other classes is great, since
it is relevant and practical to the students.*

*There were supplementary grammar books which I found largely
unsatisfactory. The most effective exercises were the ones that TAs teaching
the courses had developed and which were integrated into the content.*

From these comments it is clear that each of the instructors favours a
slightly different approach or combination of approaches to incorporating grammar in CBI. The only common denominator seems to
be that of relevance, i.e., making sure that whatever grammar is
covered addresses student-produced grammar errors.

Deciding an approach to grammar instruction that fits with CBI
and meets students' needs is further complicated by the fact that
students have opinions about the types of grammar instruction that
they find helpful and comfortable – and these opinions, like those of
the instructors, differ. Students' strongly held, but often conflicting,
opinions about what constitutes grammar instruction confound the
decisions faced by materials developers and lesson planners.

*I like it when the instructor corrects my mistakes in every homework and
informs me on what I should focus on.*

*In the course work, I would expect more grammar (even repetition of the
same topic) and vocabulary.*

*More standardised grammatical exercises (as opposed to editing exercises)
could be adapt[ed] to make the material covered more organised.*

*I had problems with the grammar, I did not quite get the 'hang' of it.
Maybe start at a lower level or spend a bit more time on the grammar.*

The avoidance phenomenon

Tension over form-focused instruction evinces itself in another, even
more curious way: TAs in our programme tend not to spend time
doing overt grammar instruction even when such lessons are made
available to them by their supervisors. By design, CBI curriculum
forces instructors to serve three 'masters': content, skills and language. But our TAs struggle with how to serve all three in the time
allotted, a dilemma evident in the following comments:

*I would like to have more time in the curriculum to work on these grammar
issues . . . but . . . I spend so much time getting through the content, the
other aspects of the course, such as grammar, get pushed aside.*

I feel that there is so much really difficult conceptual content to cover that there is little time for grammar.

I would like to make a suggestion that we should spend more time on language . . . I tried to incorporate [this] into the curriculum, but I found that we have too many things on the content to cover linguistic skills. Actually, I had no time to touch on the tenses and other important grammatical items.

Perhaps the sentiments of our TAs can best be summed up by the following comment: 'More grammar, but there is no time!'

These TAs are often given both lesson plans and materials for integrating grammar into the content unit they are teaching. The lesson plans, ostensibly, are guides for how to integrate and balance work on skills, content and language. In practice, however, when hard instructional decisions have to be made between the three 'masters', the first thing that is usually jettisoned from the lesson plan is grammar and vocabulary work. For example, we have seen TA lesson plans where the grammar section has been crossed out (apparently because the TA did not intend to teach this part of the weekly lesson plan or ran out of time to do it). Similarly, in weekly level meetings, TAs have balked at teaching the grammatical point outlined by the supervisor, rationalising their decision based on lack of adequate time to cover grammar. And finally, we have received a report from a researcher observing one of our CBI classes that the content-based grammar lessons in the assigned textbook were not systematically covered by the TA, and that when grammar was addressed, it seemed to be done covertly rather than overtly (Kusuyama, 1998). This research, in fact, confirms one of our long-held suspicions that our TAs are uncomfortable with grammar instruction featuring teacher-fronted explanations and form-focused exercises (not including editing exercises) because they do not see the relevance of these activities for their students.

When we asked instructors in our questionnaires to estimate the amount of time they spend teaching grammar, they reported a range from 10–25% (with the average amount of time spent being 15%). The time spent on skills and content, on the other hand, comprised the remainder of the instructional time. In other words, while in descriptions of the content-based curriculum in the ESL Service Courses overt language instruction, skill development and content are described as receiving roughly equal emphasis, the reality is that grammar and vocabulary do indeed get short shrift.

Sources of tension

Eskey (1997) suggests two possible reasons underlying the unresolved problem of how best to deliver form-focused instruction: (1) the communicative emphasis underlying the CBI instructional paradigm in itself and (2) the lack of research on the interrelationship between form and content. The interviews and teacher and student comments that we reviewed, however, seem to indicate that the source of the problem is not theoretical or empirical, but pedagogical. That is, the source of the problem lies with the players in the CBI classroom: the students, the teachers and the university context itself.

The factors that most confound decisions about grammar instruction in our situation are those of student proficiency and expectations. Similar to most programmes, students placed in the same course in our programme are commonly at different proficiency levels and even the same student exhibits varying proficiencies across the four skills. Students themselves recognise and comment on this:

The pace of the class was slow. Problem is that all of us are on different levels and it's hard to work with all of us.

The post-course student comments seem to suggest that student proficiency influences student expectations in language courses. In our data, students enrolled in the lower-level courses made fewer comments about wanting more focus on grammar and vocabulary while students at the higher levels were more dissatisfied about not receiving enough overt grammar instruction.

In addition, our courses serve both international students and US resident students, populations whose prior grammar instruction varies widely, and therefore, whose needs and expectations are different. Anyone who has ever taught grammar in a class mixed with international and US resident students knows the tightrope one walks in every grammar lesson: Will I bore the international students with basic explanations of rules and forms that they already learned in junior high school? will the US resident students find basic grammar explanations demeaning or will they simply be 'lost'? As was shown in a recent study of the decisions instructors make about teaching grammar, a teacher's 'beliefs about students' expectations [have] a powerful influence' on the instructional choices and approaches she or he adopts (Borg, 1998: 16).

Like Master (2000), we agree that the rich language context provided by CBI reading and listening materials offers great potential for bringing life to grammar lessons for both popula-tions. But how to balance explanation, application and commu-nicative practice across the four skill areas in a way that will meet both the needs and expectations of a complex student population is not always self-evident, no matter how experienced the instructor.

This brings us to the second factor that makes focusing on form in CBI difficult: teachers who lack relevant training. Most courses in pedagogical grammar have barely enough time to teach participants the forms and functions of the most important grammatical struc-tures in English and to impart some idea about how to teach these communicatively. They lack the time to teach students how to exploit these in a CBI instructional framework: how to mine a content-area text (written or oral) for potential grammatical and lexico-grammatical items to teach; how to explain and practise structures within the rich content in which they were found; or how to achieve a proper balance between letting content or letting student error patterns drive the selection of grammar structures to be taught.

In addition to the issues related to language and language peda-gogy per se, instructors in a CBI context often lack training in how to prioritise tasks and 'kill two birds with one stone'. Serving three masters simultaneously requires that a content-based instructor con-stantly make choices, but how to make these is often not included in teacher training.

The final source of difficulty when instructors must choose between grammar, skills and content in the CBI classroom, is the university setting itself. To put it simply, many ESL instructors suffer from 'content envy.' In the university, where most CBI instruction takes place, those who are content-area experts are respected, while those who teach ESL or writing are relegated to the position of 'handmaiden' to the perceived 'real' professors (Gold-stein, Campbell and Cummings, 1997). In a world that values content, it is difficult for an instructor to choose to focus on language. Complicating the situation is the fact that students themselves may place a lower value on the acquisition of language skills, and may not adequately realise the need in their discipline for advanced academic language proficiency. Because they frequently resent required language and writing courses, we constantly strive in the EAP curriculum to make these required classes more palatable by highlighting interesting issues raised in the content or by empha-sising skills whose transferability to their content courses is trans-parent.

A framework for the systematic integration of grammar in CBI

The problem of how and when to focus on form has its origins in the classroom, so the solutions must begin there also. For this reason, we would like to suggest pedagogical guidelines for integrating grammar into the CBI classroom systematically.

1 *Our primary job is to teach language.* One of the most useful pieces of advice that we have ever received is never to lose sight of the fact that we are primarily language teachers. This may seem self-evident, but it is not always so transparent to instructors faced with difficult decisions concerning how best to use precious instructional time. Since it is doubtful whether ten or fifteen weeks of instruction can really impact a student's overall language proficiency, teachers often choose to spend class time equipping students with skills and strategies that will help them compensate for developing language proficiency. But the fact remains that what placed them in ESL courses in the first place were gaps in language proficiency. And not to address these directly seems an abdication of responsibility.

2 *The only way to content is through language.* If you are not convinced of this, think for a moment about how much instructional and studying time is spent on teaching new vocabulary in a lower division biology or political science class. While it is important that students understand a concept central to the content of a given CBI unit, language instructors can help them achieve this comprehension through focusing primarily on the language rather than the content.

3 *Students need a two-pronged approach to grammar and language instruction.* They need to learn to see and edit the errors they produce. At the same time, they need guidance in expanding their grammatical and lexical repertoire based on how language works in the content texts. Our experience tells us that this will not happen 'incidentally', as early definitions of CBI suggested. Academic texts, for instance, contain more than adequate examples of the various meanings of modal auxiliaries. Nonetheless, students exposed to these examples in a CBI curriculum often remain confused by the shades of meanings that modals add to sentences and they tend to circumvent using them in their own writing. If we address the grammatical gaps in their speaking and writing as well as structures they avoid, their overall fluency in English will improve as will their academic speaking and writing. The common denominator in balancing approaches must be to link form and function.

Conclusion

Does the emperor have no clothes? Our research and experience tells us that the emperor does have clothes; in other words, CBI is a highly effective method of delivering EAP instruction. But we would recommend that the emperor needs better 'wardrobe coordination'. As we have found in reviewing instructor and student responses, CBI curricula need more systematic and principled attention to language instruction. Ultimately, if we allow content alone to drive our language teaching agenda (or alternatively, if we allow student error patterns to dictate what grammar is taught), we are doing our students a disservice. We also recommend that the emperor seek 'fashion consultation'. It is unrealistic for us to expect instructors schooled in communicative language teaching approaches to achieve the very difficult balance that is inherent in CBI between skills, content and language. Just as we, as ESL teachers, are remiss if we do not address students' grammar needs, we are remiss as ESL teacher trainers if we do not train teachers new to this approach to integrate language and content systematically.

16 The specialised vocabulary of English for academic purposes

Averil Coxhead and Paul Nation

It is useful for teaching and learning to divide the vocabulary of English into four groups.

1 The high frequency words. These consist of around 2,000 word families. They are wide range high frequency words that are an essential basis for all language use. They include most of the 176 function words of English. Typically they provide coverage of around 80% of the running words in academic text. The classic collection of these is Michael West's (1953) *General Service List of English Words* (GSL).

2 The academic vocabulary. This consists of 570 words (Coxhead, 1998) that are reasonably frequent in a wide range of academic texts, but are not so common, although they do occur, in other kinds of texts. Because they provide coverage of around 8.5%–10% of the running words in an academic text, they are very important for learners with academic purposes. They make the difference between 80% coverage (one unknown word in every five running words) and 90% coverage (one unknown word in every ten running words).

3 Technical vocabulary. This differs from subject area to subject area. For any particular subject it consists of probably 1,000 words or less. It could provide coverage of up to 5% of the running words in a text.

4 The low frequency words. These consist of words that are typically very narrow range and low frequency. Because of the topic of a particular text a small number may occasionally be quite frequent within that text. In general, they consist of words that occur once or twice and then will not be met again for a long time. Of the 86,741 different word types in the 5,000,000 running word corpus used in the Carroll, Davies and Richman (1971) count, 40.4% occurred only once in that corpus.

When learners have control of the 2,000 words of general usefulness in English, it is wise to direct vocabulary learning to more specialised areas depending on the aims of the learners. First, it is possible to specialise by learning the shared vocabulary of several fields of study, for example academic vocabulary. Next the specialised vocabulary of one particular field or part of that field can be studied. This paper looks at ways of clearly setting vocabulary goals for special purposes courses and suggests ways in which those goals can be reached. Because many courses focus on learners who will do academic study in English, we will look first at academic vocabulary.

Academic vocabulary

Academic vocabulary is variously known as sub-technical vocabulary (Cowan, 1974; Yang, 1986; Anderson, 1980), semi-technical vocabulary (Farrell, 1990), specialised non-technical lexis (Cohen, Glasman, Rosenbaum-Cohen, Ferrara and Fine, 1988), frame words (Higgins, 1966), and academic vocabulary (Martin, 1976; Coxhead, 1998). The division of the vocabulary of academic texts into three groups of general service or basic vocabulary, sub-technical vocabulary and technical vocabulary is a commonly made distinction (although it ignores low frequency vocabulary with no technical or sub-technical features). Dresher (1934) made such a three-part distinction when looking at mathematics vocabulary for native speakers. Other writers have independently made a similar distinction. Typically academic vocabulary lists include words like **assume, achieve, concept, community, proportion** which are common in academic texts.

There have been several studies that have investigated the vocabulary needed for academic study. Two of them (Campion and Elley, 1971; Praninskas, 1972) assumed that learners already know a general service vocabulary and these studies looked at academic texts to see what words not in a general service vocabulary occur frequently across a range of academic disciplines. Two other studies (Lynn, 1973; Ghadessy, 1979) looked at the words that learners of English wrote translations above in their academic texts. There were considerable overlaps between these four lists and they were combined into one list, the University Word List (UWL), by Xue and Nation (1984) (also in Nation, 1990). This combined list of academic vocabulary was designed so that it consists of words not in the GSL (West, 1953), but which occur frequently over a range of academic texts. The UWL vocabulary, which contains over 800 word families, accounts for 8.5% of the running words in academic texts. Its low coverage of non-academic texts shows its specialised nature. It provides 3.9% coverage of newspapers, and 1.7% coverage of fiction

(Hwang, 1989). Here are some words from the UWL (Xue and Nation, 1984): **acquire, complex, devise, fallacy, goal, imply, intelligent, phase, status.**

The UWL has been replaced by the Academic Word List (Coxhead, 1998). This list of 570 words is based on a 3,500,000 token corpus of academic English which is divided into four groupings of Arts, Science, Law and Commerce, with each grouping consisting of seven sub-groupings such as psychology, mathematics, history, etc. Both range and frequency were used in choosing words for the list, with all word families in the list occurring in all four groupings, in 22 of the 28 sub-groupings, and at least a 100 times in the total corpus. The frequency of each of the words in the list was compared with their frequency in a 3,500,000 corpus of novels. This was done to see which words in the list were truly academic words and which were general service words not in West's (1953) GSL. The list appears to provide slightly better coverage of academic text than the UWL even though it contains fewer words. The list is divided into ten sub-lists each based on range and frequency criteria.

The importance of academic vocabulary

There are several reasons why academic vocabulary is considered to be important and a useful learning goal for learners of English for academic purposes.

1 Academic vocabulary is common to a wide range of academic texts, and generally not so common in non-academic texts. One of the earliest studies to look at this is typical of the many small-scale studies that followed it. Barber (1962) compared three academic texts ranging in length from 6,300 to 9,600 tokens. Barber's f.nding that there were academic words common to the texts influenced a lot of thinking about English for Specific Purposes. Several subsequent studies have confirmed that it is possible to create an academic vocabulary common to a range of academic writing (Campion and Elley, 1971; Praninskas, 1972; Hwang, 1989). There has been little research comparing the frequency of specific academic words in academic and non-academic texts (Cowan, 1974), but the studies that have done this (Coxhead, forthcoming) show a sizeable contrast in frequency.

2 Academic vocabulary accounts for a substantial number of words in academic texts. There are two ways of measuring this: by looking at the number of tokens (coverage) academic vocabulary accounts for, and by looking at the number of types, lemmas or

word families. Sutarsyah, Nation and Kennedy (1994) found that academic vocabulary (the University Word List) accounted for 8.4% of the tokens in the Learned and Scientific sections (Section J) of the *LOB* and *Wellington Corpora*, and 8.7% of the tokens in an economics text. Coxhead (forthcoming) found that her academic word list (AWL) covered 10.2% of the tokens in her 3,500,000 running word academic corpus. These are substantial percentages given that a general service 3rd 1,000-word list would only cover around 4.3% of the same corpus.

Farrell (1990: 31), using a different classification of general service, semi-technical and technical vocabulary, found that out of 508 lemmas occurring more than five times in his corpus of electronics texts, 44% of the lemmas were semi-technical, and 27.7% technical. Sutarsyah, Kennedy and Nation (1994) found that in a 295,294 token economics textbook, there were 1,577 general service word families, 636 University Word List families, and 3,225 other families which included technical words and low frequency words.

The coverage of each of the sub-lists in Coxhead's AWL shows how even the specially selected Academic Word List contains words with a wide range of frequencies.

Table 1. *Coverage of the sub-lists of the Academic Word List*

Sub-list and number of words	% coverage	Number of tokens per 350-word page
1 60 words	3.6	12.6 words per page
2 60	1.8	6.3
3 60	1.2	4.2
4 60	0.9	3.2
5 60	0.8	2.8
6 60	0.6	2.1
7 60	0.5	1.8
8 60	0.3	1.1
9 60	0.2	0.7
10 30	0.1	0.4
Total 570	10.0	35.0

3 Academic vocabulary is generally not as well known as technical vocabulary. In a small-scale investigation of difficulties found by second language learners reading academic texts, Cohen, Glasman, Rosenbaum-Cohen, Ferrara and Fine (1988) found that non-technical vocabulary like **essential, maintain, invariable** was more

often unknown than technical vocabulary. Cohen *et al.* identified
the following problems with such vocabulary in addition to simply
not knowing the words.
(a) It was sometimes used with a technical meaning and some-
    times not, and learners were not always aware of this.
(b) Learners were often not aware of related terms being used to
    refer to the same thing. That is, they did not pick up instances
    of lexical cohesion through paraphrase.
Anderson (1980) also found that sub-technical terms were the
words most often identified as unknown by her learners in
academic texts. In addition, many learners get low scores on the
UWL section of the Vocabulary Levels Test (Nation, 1990).
4 Academic vocabulary is the kind of specialised vocabulary that an
English teacher can usefully help learners with. This is in contrast
to technical vocabulary where the teacher can often do little
because of the teacher's lack of background knowledge of the
subject, the need to learn technical vocabulary while learning the
content matter of the technical field, and the mixture of specialist
disciplines within the same group of English students. From this
perspective, an academic vocabulary list represents an extension of
the general service vocabulary for learners with academic purposes. That is, it is a list of words that deserves a lot of attention in
a variety of ways from both the learners and teacher no matter
what their specialist area of academic study.

The nature and role of academic vocabulary

There have been attempts to study the role that academic vocabulary
plays in an academic text. At one level the Latinate nature of the
vocabulary adds a tone of formality and learnedness. It is this aspect
that Corson (1985, 1997) describes in his work on the lexical bar.
Some writers have also tried to examine the kinds of language
functions and notions that the academic vocabulary represents.
Strevens (1973) suggests a classification of 'those concepts which are
general to science and technology but not typically present in non-
scientific English. These concepts reflect and convey the philosophy
and methodology of science' (p. 226).

Discrimination and description imply concepts of *identity* and *difference,*
processes, states, changes of state, quantification;
Classification implies concepts of *taxonomies* and the *co-occurrence of*
features;
Inter-relation implies concepts of *causality, influence,* and *interaction;*

Explanation implies concepts of *evidence, intuition, hypothesis, experiment, models, theory;* etc.   (Strevens, 1973: 226–227)

Martin (1976) classifies academic vocabulary into (a) the research process (b) the vocabulary of analysis, and (c) the vocabulary of evaluation. These categories correspond to parts of a typical report of experimental research.

In a fascinating and insightful paper addressing the same problem, Meyer (1990) suggests that there is a process of delexicalisation or grammaticisation going on in English where words which used to carry a full lexical meaning are now becoming more like function words. These include words like **affecting, barring, concerning, fact, process, matter** whose jobs in some other languages are done by function words or inflections.

English has a large number of lexical items that are on the verge of sliding down on the lexicality scale towards uses that are more conditioned and thereby closer to the use of grammatical morphemes. This process is characterised by semantic bleaching, a tendency towards more formulaic uses and the formation of lexical classes that seem more closed than the fully open classes at the top of the lexicality scale.

(Meyer, 1990: 4)

Meyer classifies academic words into three major categories:

1 Vocabulary relating to the domain of the text and the linguistic acts performed in it. This includes words like **argue, examine, survey, recommendation** which tell us 'what the authors are doing in their texts and what they ascribe to other authors' (Meyer, 1990: 5).
2 Vocabulary describing scientific activities. This includes words like **analyse, examine, survey, implementation**. They relate closely to the categories described by Strevens (1973) above.
3 Vocabulary referring to the subject matter of scientific activities. This includes technical vocabulary but is by no means restricted to that. Meyer describes three main groups as examples:
   (a) Lexical expression of tense, aspect, modality, etc.: **current, present, recent, ability, impossibility, likely**.
   (b) Classification of states of affairs: **change, development, process, structure, quality.** Meyer notes that many of these words seem to be taking on the role of classifiers, that is, general words to characterise a group of related items or state of affairs. Classifiers can fulfil the functions of acting as short-hand anaphoric items, acting as a general term to be elaborated on later, and acting as a kind of proper name for something already defined.

(c) Relations between states of affairs: this is a very diverse group. It can include quantitative changes **expansion, increase, decline, reduction,** causal relations **arising, affecting, contribute,** set inclusion **include, comprise,** and many others.

The academic vocabulary of texts allows the writer to 'generalise over complex states of affairs, and to report and evaluate linguistic acts and scientific activities' (Meyer, 1990: 9).

Viewed from this perspective, academic vocabulary performs important roles in helping academics do what they need to do. The 'context-independent' vocabulary is an important tool of the writer in doing learned and scientific things.

Testing academic vocabulary

Because the AWL is such a useful prerequisite for coping with academic texts, it is important for teachers and learners to know how well this vocabulary is known. Tests of the AWL are still being developed, but there are several tests of the UWL which have been widely used and carefully studied. There are tests of receptive knowledge (Nation, 1990; Beglar and Hunt, 1999) and measures of productive knowledge (Laufer and Nation, 1995; Laufer and Nation, 1999). The tests are easily administered and provide a quick way of seeing if special attention needs to be given to academic vocabulary.

Learning academic vocabulary

Specialised word counts have several values. Firstly, they provide a useful guide for teachers to help them decide which vocabulary to focus on in reading, writing, listening, speaking, and testing activities. Secondly, they can act as a checklist and goal for learners. Learners can go through such lists, mark the words they do not know and set about learning them. In this way these very important words are brought to the learners' conscious attention and learning can proceed from there.

For learners studying English for academic purposes, academic vocabulary is a kind of high frequency vocabulary and thus any time spent learning it is time well spent. The four major strands of a language course – meaning focused input, language focused learning, meaning focused output, and fluency development – should all be seen as opportunities for the development of academic vocabulary knowledge, and it is important that the same words occur in each of these four strands.

1 There should be listening and reading activities that encourage the learning of academic vocabulary. This can involve the intensive and extensive reading of academic text, and listening to lectures and discussions. If learners are not familiar with academic vocabulary, then its introduction in this way would need to be controlled so that there is not too heavy a vocabulary burden (Worthington and Nation, 1996). For learning through meaning focused input learners need to be already familiar with at least 95% and preferably 98% of the running words in the texts.

2 There should be language focused activities such as direct teaching, learning from word cards and word analysis. Academic vocabulary is largely of Latin or Greek origin and so learners can use word part analysis to help learn the vocabulary (Farid, 1985). The direct study of academic vocabulary is a way of quickly gaining some knowledge of these words. The same words need to be met again in the other three strands to strengthen and enrich the knowledge gained from direct study. Table 1 shows that some academic vocabulary occurs relatively infrequently and direct study would help establish these words because learners may not be doing a large enough quantity of reading to have it established by repetitions in the texts (Worthington and Nation, 1996).

3 Because academic vocabulary is useful in speaking and writing, learners need the opportunity to use it in meaning focused output activities, that is, in speaking and writing in academic contexts. Corson (1995: 149) argues that using academic (Graeco-Latin) vocabulary helps users by letting them put their knowledge on display. They 'show that they can operate within the meaning systems associated with the school's culture of literacy'. Productive use of academic vocabulary is an important component of academic success. This can be encouraged through the presentation of prepared formal talks, discussions based on texts, reviewing the literature of a topic and writing summaries and critical evaluations of articles.

4 Being able to use words fluently is a part of vocabulary knowledge. Being able to access words quickly means that more processing time is available for concentrating on what to say rather than how to say it. Fluency is encouraged by repeated opportunity to work with texts that are within the learner's proficiency. One way that fluency can be encouraged is through the use of issue logs, an idea developed by Nikhat Shameem and Alison Hamilton-Jenkins at the English Language Institute at Victoria University of

Wellington. Each learner chooses a topic to follow and become an expert on over several weeks during a pre-university English course. These topics might be terrorism, a current conflict, global warming or the political events in a particular country. Each learner regularly finds and reads newspaper reports on their topic, listens to TV and radio news and writes a weekly summary of recent events related to their topic. They present a weekly oral report to members of their small group who discuss their report. These activities involve the learners using the four skills of listening, speaking, reading and writing with repeated attention to the same topic area. They thus soon bring a lot of background knowledge to their reading and discussion – ideal conditions for fluency development.

Knowing academic vocabulary is a high priority goal for learners who wish to do academic study in English. After gaining control of the 2,000 high frequency words, learners then need to focus on academic vocabulary. Knowing the 2,000 high frequency words and the AWL will give close to 90% coverage of the running words in most academic texts. When this is supplemented by proper nouns and technical vocabulary, learners will approach the critical 95% coverage threshold needed for reading.

Technical vocabulary

The motivation for distinguishing technical vocabulary from other vocabulary is similar to that for distinguishing the academic vocabulary from the general service words, that is, to distinguish a group of words that will be particularly useful for learners with specific goals in language use, such as reading academic texts in a particular discipline, writing technical reports or participating in subject-specific conferences.

Having distinguished such a group of words it is possible to see how they affect language learning goals, particularly the number of words that need to be known to be able to cope effectively with language in use. The approach taken here is to use percentage of text coverage as an indicator of this. Having distinguished such a group of words it is also possible to examine how they would be learned and the role of teaching in the learning process.

Distinguishing technical vocabulary from other vocabulary

In essence, a technical word is one that is recognisably specific to a particular topic, field or discipline. There are degrees of 'technical-ness' depending on how restricted a word is to a particular area. These degrees can be shown by classifying technical vocabulary into four categories, with category 1 being the most technical and category 4, the least. The examples in each category are taken from the fields of law, applied linguistics, electronics, and computing.

Category 1

The word form appears rarely if at all outside this particular field.

Law – jactitation, per curiam, cloture
Applied Linguistics – morpheme, hapax legomena, lemma
Electronics – anode, impedance, galvanometer, dielectric
Computing – wysiwyg, rom, pixel, modem

Category 2

The word form is used both inside and outside this particular field but not with the same meaning.

Law – cite (to appear), caution (v.)
Applied Linguistics – sense, reference, type, token
Electronics – induced, flux, terminal, earth
Computing – execute, scroll, paste

Category 3

The word form is used both inside and outside this particular field, but the majority of its uses with a particular meaning, though not all, are in this field. The specialised meaning it has in this field is readily accessible through its meaning outside the field.

Law – accused (n.), offer, reconstruction (of a crime)
Applied Linguistics – range, frequency
Electronics – coil, energy, positive, gate, resistance
Computing – memory, drag, window

Category 4

The word form is more common in this field than elsewhere. There is little or no specialisation of meaning, though someone knowledgeable in the field would have a more precise idea of its meaning.

Law – judge, mortgage, trespass
Applied Linguistics – word, meaning
Electronics – drain, filament, load, plate
Computing – print, programme, icon

Words in category 1 are clearly technical words. They are unique to a particular field in both form and meaning. Yang (1986) and Becka (1972) suggest that these words could be found by computer analysis using figures based on frequency and range. Someone who knows these words is likely to have knowledge of that field that goes well beyond knowing the words. Indeed, it is likely that these words can only be learned and really understood by studying the field. They could not sensibly be pre-taught.

Words in category 2 are clearly technical words if the more general meaning of the word when used outside the field does not provide ready access to its technical use.

Words in categories 3 and 4 are less obviously technical because they are neither unique in form or meaning to a particular field. The words, particularly in category 4, are readily accessible through their use outside the field. A glance at a list of category 4 words is sufficient to quickly identify what field is being examined. Murphey (1992) in a study of pop songs found that the word **love** was extremely frequent, in fact among the top ten words along with **the, be, you**. **Love** is probably not a technical word, although it meets the criterion for category 4, because pop songs are not considered an area of technical knowledge. Sutarsyah, Nation and Kennedy (1994) in a study of an economics text found that a group of around 30 words that were obviously related to the field of economics accounted for over 10% (one in every ten) of the running words in the text. These were words like **cost, demand, price** (see Table 2). These words occurred in the economics text with at least seven times the frequency with which they occurred in the similarly sized general academic corpus.

Over half of the 34 words from Table 2 are in the first 1,000 of the West's GSL and four-fifths are in the GSL or UWL.

Categories 2 and 3 indicate that range based on form alone is not sufficient to make sensible decisions between what are technical words and what are not. In many cases, meaning must also be considered. The cline which exists from categories 2 to 4 raises the question of whether a technical word needs to have a technical meaning, that is, a meaning which is different from its uses outside a

Table 2. *Words in the most frequent 1,000 words of an economics text*
that occur much more frequently than in the general academic corpus

Word family	Frequency in the economics text	Frequency in the general academic corpus
Price	3080	90
Cost	2251	91
Demand	1944	102
Curve	1804	83
Firm	1743	41
Supply	1590	86
Quantity	1467	53
Margin	1427	24
Economy	1353	172
Income	1183	96
Produce	1237	167
Market	1104	110
Consume	955	70
Labour	1004	131
Capital	907	50
Total	946	114
Output	861	50
Revenue	763	10
You	866	118
Profit	733	27
Production	772	84
Average	777	90
Goods	705	21
Product	749	106
Trade	621	85
Buy	521	35
Wage	522	75
Monopoly	454	13
Percent	450	41
Million	445	42
Household	360	41
Equilibrium	328	21
Choice	339	39
Elasticity	333	34
Total frequency	34,594	2,322

Words not marked are in the first thousand words of the GSL (19 out of 34 words)
Words marked *word* are in the second thousand words of the GSL (3 words)
Words marked **word** are in the UWL (6 words)
Words marked *word* are not in the GSL or UWL (6 words)

particular field, and if so how different the meaning needs to be. The cut-off point distinguishing technical words from non-technical words could come after category 2, 3 or 4.

Making lists of technical vocabulary

There are two systematic ways of developing lists of technical vocabulary – one is through the use of technical dictionaries, and the other is through the use of corpus based frequency counts. Technical dictionaries can be regarded as technical vocabulary lists, but they do not contain frequency information that would be helpful in assessing the relative usefulness of the words, and they give little indication of how the words were chosen to go in them.

Using a dictionary

Using a dictionary to create a technical vocabulary list involves all the methodological problems of sampling, defining what is actually being counted (i.e., what is counted as a word) and classification described in Nation (1993). There is also the problem of the choice of the dictionary, because working from a dictionary means that the base data has been compiled by someone other than the researcher and the principles underlying its compilation are not likely to be described or apparent. Does the dictionary adequately represent the field which is being examined? Is the dictionary up-to-date? Is it as complete as possible? Does it reflect a US or UK bias?

Using a corpus-based frequency count

It is possible to use an existing frequency count that distinguishes range figures from frequency figures (the best example is the American Heritage Word Book [Carroll, Davies and Richman, 1971]), or to carry out a range and frequency count comparing a general corpus with a specialised corpus (see Sutarsyah, Nation and Kennedy, 1994). It is possible to dispense with the general count as some studies have done (Farrell, 1990), but then there is greater dependency on intuitive judgement. Frequency based studies of technical vocabulary usually produce the following findings.

1 A small group of highly topic related words (**current, fig., voltage, circuit, . . .**) occur very frequently accounting for at least 10% of the running words in the corpus.
2 Several of the words in this high frequency group are in West's *GSL of 2,000 Words* or the UWL with related meanings (**circuit,**

field, energy, plate, connected, supply, positive, flow, . . .). Few of the words 'are really "technical" in the sense of being completely unknown in general language' (Farrell, 1990: 37–38).

3 A few of the highly frequent words stand out as reflecting the nature of the discourse (fig., if, we [the most frequent pronoun]).

4 Several words are clearly technical in form and meaning but have a very low frequency of occurrence in the corpus. This would make it difficult to distinguish technical words purely on the basis of frequency.

5 Several technical words have very low range *within* a specialised corpus (Farrell, 1990: 30). This means that the occurrences of a particular technical word are not spread evenly through a text, but cluster in a particular chapter or section. This reflects the occurrence of some proper nouns in novels, with some characters appearing for a short time and then never being mentioned again.

Learning technical vocabulary

Several writers (Cowan, 1974; Higgins, 1966; Barber, 1962) consider that it is not the English teacher's job to teach technical words. 'Learning these words is an automatic consequence of studying the discipline that uses them' (Cowan, 1974: 391). However, the use of general service words and academic words as technical words (**resistance** in electronics; **wall** (cell wall) in biology; **demand** in economics) means that the English teacher may be able to make a useful contribution to helping the learners with technical vocabulary. Strevens points out that:

The learning of special vocabulary [technical words] seems to be less of a problem to the learner than it may appear to the English language teacher. The scientist has acquired a conceptual framework into which new terminology fits relatively easily, compared with the puzzlement of the Arts-trained teacher when faced with such terms.

(Strevens, 1973: 228)

Godman and Payne (1981: 37) argue that a technical term 'is dependent for a full appreciation of its meaning on the meaning of the other terms in the cluster of which it is a member'. This is perhaps another way of saying that knowing a technical word involves knowing the body of knowledge that it is attached to.

Flowerdew (1992: 208) notes that definitions in science lectures to non-native speakers 'are often organised in systematic patterns, as a function of the logical/discourse structure of the subject matter/lecture'. For example, in a lecture entitled 'Characteristics of living organisms', 'definitions of the various basic functions of life, such as respiration, reproduction, locomotion, excretion, form the framework of the overall lecture' (Flowerdew, 1992: 208–209). This discourse role of definitions underlines the point that knowing the technical vocabulary is very closely related to knowing the subject area.

Considering the large numbers of technical words that occur in specialised texts, language teachers need to prepare learners to deal with them. Flowerdew's (1992) research on definitions in academic lectures confirms that academic discourse contains large amounts of deliberate definition. It is worth checking to see how well learners recognise that definition is occurring and how well they interpret the definition. Bramki and Williams (1984) and Williams (1985) have also described the clues that show that a writer is defining a word and it is worth spending time with learners finding examples of definition in technical texts so that learners become easily able to recognise and interpret this 'lexical familiarisation'.

Although English teachers are not usually well equipped to work with technical texts and the technical vocabulary they contain, they can help learners get accustomed to the idea that different uses of words may have a shared underlying meaning. The 'wall' of a living cell shares important features with the 'wall' of a house. Visser (1989) devised the following kind of exercise to deal with this. The learners can work individually or in pairs on the exercises.

Table 3. *Shared meaning exercises*

Interpret /intɸ+ˈprɒt/ verb	Interpret /intɸ+ˈprɒt/ verb	What is the core meaning of this word?
If you **interpret** something in a particular way, you decide that this is its meaning or significance. *Even so, the move was interpreted as a defeat for Mr Gorbachev. . . The judge says that he has to interpret the law as it's been passed . . . Both of them agree on what is in the poem, but not on how it should be interpreted.* How would you interpret the meaning of this sign?		If you **interpret** what someone is saying, you translate it immediately into another language. *The woman spoke little English, so her husband came with her to interpret. . . Three interpreters looked over the text for about three or four hours and found that they could not interpret half of it.* Interpret this sentence into your language: 'I really like chocolate cake.'	

These exercises are easy to make and, as well as improving knowledge of particular words, they get learners used to the idea that words 'stretch' their meanings. The sample sentences come from the COBUILD dictionary.

The main purpose in isolating an academic vocabulary or a technical vocabulary is to provide a sound basis for planning teaching and learning. By focusing attention on items that have been shown to be frequent, and in the case of academic vocabulary of wide range, learners and teachers can get the best return for their effort.

The research on academic vocabulary is encouraging, although much still remains to be done. It has been shown that it is possible to devise lists of academic words which are small enough to be feasible learning goals and which provide enough coverage of academic text to make them a very valuable part of a learner's vocabulary.

Research is needed on the way the particular words behave in certain subject areas and the general discourse functions of academic vocabulary. For example, it may be interesting to take an academic function, like defining or referring to previous research, and see what role academic vocabulary plays in this. This research would confirm or question the value of courses for academic purposes for students from a variety of disciplines, and would suggest how attention could be most usefully directed towards academic vocabulary.

17 Language learning strategies and EAP proficiency: Teacher views, student views, and test results

Matthew Peacock

Introduction

Student use of second language learning strategies – conscious or unconscious methods of helping and accelerating learning – has received a considerable amount of attention in the twenty years or so since Rubin's influential 1975 article on the 'Good language learner' called for research in the area. Oxford and Burry-Stock (1995: 4) report that 40 to 50 studies (many unpublished) involving more than 8,000 learners have been done using the prime data-collection instrument on strategy use, Oxford's SILL (Strategy Inventory for Language Learning, 1990), alone. Many of these studies have found strong links between strategy use and target-language proficiency, and this has increased interest in the topic of what strategies are used by better learners.

Cohen (1998: 4) defines second language learning strategies as processes consciously chosen by students that result in action 'taken to enhance the learning or use of a second language . . . through storage, retention, recall, and application'.

Oxford, in her SILL, divides the 50 common strategies on the questionnaire into six categories, as follows (the complete list of strategies can be seen in Oxford, 1990):

Memory

(remembering more effectively), e.g. 'I review English lessons often.'

Cognitive

(using all your mental processes), e.g. 'I use the English words I know in different ways.'

Compensation

(compensating for missing knowledge), e.g. 'To understand unfamiliar English words, I make guesses.'

Metacognitive

(organising and evaluating learning), e.g. 'I plan my schedule so I will have enough time to study English.'

Affective

(managing emotions), e.g. 'I try to relax whenever I feel afraid of using English.'

Social

(learning with others), e.g. 'I practise English with other students.'

I suggest that learning strategy research is worthwhile because students do differ in achievement and we should investigate what factors affect this. There is a lot of evidence that strategies affect proficiency and moreover, as Oxford and Nyikos assert (1989: 291) 'Unlike most other characteristics of the learner . . . strategies are readily *teachable*.' Researchers should examine the use of individual strategies, so that teachers know precisely what strategies to teach learners or to embed in tasks and materials. There have been recent calls for such research: Green and Oxford (1995: 267) note that 'Few largescale SILL studies . . . have looked at variation in the level of use of individual items, and even fewer have looked for individual item variation in terms of both proficiency level and gender.'

While there is strong evidence of a link between strategy use and EFL proficiency, few studies have focused specifically on EAP or compared results among students from different academic disciplines. I suggest that there is a need for such research because of the large number of students around the world studying in English-medium universities, for example in Hong Kong and other parts of Asia. The City University of Hong Kong (where this study took place) has more than 17,000 NNS students. The EAP courses they normally take in the first year focus more on helping them in their studies than in their future careers. Strategy use for these and other EAP learners must be as useful and important as it appeared to be among the EFL learners in previous strategy research. I suspect that too many EAP learners rarely use the best strategies or a sufficiently wide range of strategies (as Ehrman and Oxford say is true of ESL learners in general [1989: 1]). We need to draw up a list of the attributes of the good EAP learner.

I also suggest that teacher opinion on the relative usefulness of the fifty strategies listed on the SILL by Oxford is a neglected resource in strategy research, and that these teacher opinions have implications for curriculum design and teaching practice. Learner opinion, too, is normally expressed only through self-report on the SILL and further research is needed here. Finally, I propose that interdisciplinary strategy use should be investigated among EAP students, as it is likely that discipline affects strategy choice – it certainly affects learning styles as we shall see below. Interdisciplinary differences could be a factor of considerable importance to EAP teachers, who may have to tailor courses for particular groups of students.

In this chapter I shall first provide an overview of some of the larger-scale empirical studies that have used the SILL to investigate the relationship between strategy use and proficiency (literature on the teachability of language learning strategies will be discussed below, in my conclusions). I shall then describe the methodology and results of the present research. Implications for teaching EAP will be discussed at the end of the chapter.

Literature review

Green and Oxford (1995) investigated the self-reported strategy use of 374 tertiary-level students of ESL as a required subject in the University of Puerto Rico and found significantly greater strategy use among more proficient students in four of Oxford's six broad SILL categories – Cognitive, Compensation, Metacognitive and Social. There were no significant differences in the other two categories – Memory and Affective. They also report significantly higher strategy use among females in four categories: Memory, Metacognitive, Affective and Social strategies. They do not report interdisciplinary results.

Ku (1997) surveyed 335 college students in Taiwan. She reports that the strategies most often employed were from the Compensation category, followed (in descending order) by the Cognitive, Metacognitive, Memory, Social and Affective categories. She also reports higher strategy use overall among more proficient students and among females, but does not give separate results either for the college students or for individual strategies, or report the statistical significance of her findings.

Mullins (1992; cited in Oxford and Burry-Stock, 1995: 10, 13), researching 110 Thai university EFL students, found high use of the Compensation, Cognitive and Metacognitive strategies, and medium use of the Social, Memory, and Affective strategies. There was a positive correlation between the use of Compensation and Metacognitive strategies and proficiency.

Ehrman and Oxford (1995) used the SILL to collect data on strategy use from 262 NS government employees (age and gender not reported) studying different foreign languages at the Foreign Service Institute (FSI) of the US State Department. All subjects were also given a proficiency test. Ehrman and Oxford do not give separate results for individual strategies – only categories. The most frequently used strategies were from the Compensation category, followed by Social and Cognitive ('generally used'), then Metacognitive, Memory and Affective strategies ('sometimes used'). Only the compensation strategies correlated (weakly) with proficiency (r = .21, p<.05, Spearman's rho). Ehrman and Oxford also conducted an earlier study (1989) on strategy use with another 78 FSI students (48 NNS, 30 NS; 41 male, 37 female) using a previous, 121-item, version of the SILL. These 121 individual strategies were grouped into categories that corresponded only roughly with those used on the more recent 50-item version. The most frequently used strategies were from the Compensation category, followed by Cognitive, Affective, Metacognitive, Memory, Social, Self-management and Independent strategies. Females reported significantly (p<.05) greater strategy use than males in four categories: Cognitive, Metacognitive, Compensation and Self-management.

Oxford and Nyikos (1989) researched strategy use among 1,200 American university students (95% NS; around half were male) studying foreign languages, also using the 121-item version of the SILL. They categorised strategies differently; the category most frequently used by students were what they term 'Formal rule-related practice strategies', then 'General study strategies', and finally 'Conversational input elicitation strategies'. They report higher strategy use among more proficient students; in females; and among humanities students rather than science and engineering students.

Few SILL studies mention interdisciplinary strategy use. The literature on learning styles, however, does refer to differences by field of study. Reid (1987: 94), researching 1,388 students in university ESL classes in the USA, found visual learning to be a major learning style among science students, and minor for humanities majors; and engineering and computer science students to be significantly more 'tactile' than humanities students. Melton (1990: 41) found 'kinesthetic learning' significantly more popular with English literature than medicine/science majors among 331 university students in China. Finally, Chu, Kitchen and Chew (1997: (5) report that business students had a significantly stronger preference for group learning over engineering students, and engineering students a significantly stronger preference for individual work over science students, among 318 university ESL students in Singapore.

Some conclusions can be drawn from the research published to date (also refer to Rubin, 1987; Oxford and Crookall, 1989; Vann and Abraham, 1990; LoCastro, 1994: Gu, 1996; and Kern, 1989). First, much of the research is confined to describing the broad categories of strategies that students use rather than the individual strategies. The most frequently used categories seem to be Compensation, Cognitive and Metacognitive. Second, there is often a positive association between the use of certain strategies and proficiency. The categories most often linked with proficiency appear to be Compensation, Metacognitive and Cognitive. Third, strategy use is often higher in females (but so is proficiency – this will be discussed below). Fourth, there is a lack of published research on what strategies EAP students use or recommendations for what they should use, and also little on the interdisciplinary use of strategies.

Research method

Research questions

The project aimed to investigate the following five research questions:

(1) What language learning strategies do City University EAP students use?
(2) Does strategy use differ by discipline?
(3) What strategies are associated with higher or lower levels of proficiency?
(4) What strategies do EAP teachers believe to be the most useful for EAP?
(5) What strategies do EAP students believe to be the most useful for EAP?

Subjects

Seven City University EAP classes (all taught by me) took part in the study[1] – a total of 140 learners, 80 male and 60 female. Their

[1] This project was supported by Research Grant number 9030640 from the City University of Hong Kong.

average age was 20, ranging from 18 to 24. They were all first-year Hong Kong Chinese students from the Departments of Science (40 students), Maths (40) and Engineering (60) taking the compulsory EAP course 'English Communication Skills'. I selected these classes for the study so I could compare strategy use across disciplines.

The 43 teachers who took part were all staff in the Department of English.

Data-collection procedure

Data on the first three questions were collected from all 140 students using a self-report questionnaire and a comprehensive proficiency test. The links between major subject of study (physics, computing mathematics, or engineering), gender, strategy use and proficiency were also checked in order to evaluate variations between disciplines and by gender. Data on question four, teacher views on the most useful strategies for EAP, were gathered using a modified version of the SILL, on which teachers were asked to rate each of the 50 strategies for usefulness on a scale of one to seven. It was completed by 43 EAP teachers in the Department of English. For question five, student opinions on the best ways to learn English were collected through a semi-structured interview.

Four data-collection instruments were used:

(1) A self-report questionnaire for learners on language learning strategy use.
(2) A teacher version of the same questionnaire.
(3) A comprehensive proficiency test.
(4) A semi-structured interview sheet for learners.

Instruments (1) (2) and (3) collected quantitative data, while instrument (4) collected qualitative data. Data collection was deliberately broadened from just the student version of the SILL (instrument [1]), as I believe it is necessary to back up quantitative self-report data from students (such as those from the SILL) with data from other sources. Most studies using the student SILL have not done this.

(1) Learner self-report questionnaire – the SILL

At present, the prime data-collection instrument used for researching learner use of language learning strategies is the 50-item SILL[2]

---

[2] I wish to thank Rebecca Oxford for her permission to use the SILL for this project.

(Oxford, 1990). The SILL asks learners about the frequency of their use of these language learning strategies. It has a Likert-scale format: learners are asked to report on a scale of one to five how often they use each of the 50 strategies. The choices are: | never or almost never | usually not | somewhat | usually | always or almost always |.

I gave the SILL to all 140 students (one for each learner) during 1997/98, after getting their permission to involve them in the study. Students were told that it was not a test and that there were no right or wrong answers. The questionnaires were filled out in class and handed back on completion, so the response rate was 100%. The forms were not completed anonymously (students wrote their student numbers on the form) to let me check the association with proficiency test scores.

The internal consistency reliability of the SILL using Cronbach's alpha was computed at .9150 based on my entire 140-person sample (for further discussion of the reliability of the SILL, see Oxford and Nyikos [1989: 292]).

(2) Teacher questionnaire – a teacher version of the SILL

The teacher version of the SILL contains the identical list of 50 strategies on the student version. However, the instructions are different – I asked teachers to rate the 50 strategies for 'usefulness for Hong Kong tertiary-level EAP learners' on a scale from 7 ('very high usefulness') to 1 ('very low usefulness'). I replaced the five-point scale with a seven-point scale because teachers are skilled in this assessment. This new teacher version of the SILL was prepared by me for this project. I propose that the teachers' knowledge and experience made their voices worth listening to, and that the teacher version of SILL is a useful instrument to add to the armoury of the learning strategies researcher.

The teacher version of the SILL was completed by 43 teachers in early 1998. The internal consistency reliability of the teacher version of the SILL using Cronbach's alpha was computed at .9387 (N = 43).

(3) Comprehensive proficiency test

The test had four parts: listening comprehension (dictation, 20% of total marks); grammar (30 multiple-choice questions on a variety of structures, 30%); reading comprehension (a passage followed by ten multiple-choice questions, 20%); and essay writing (a 120-word essay – students were asked to agree or disagree with the statement 'I learn more when I study with classmates than when I study alone' – 30%). All 140 students took this 90-minute test during 1997/98. It was administered by me during class.

(4) Semi-structured interview sheet (selected learners)

The aim of these five-minute semi-structured interviews was to collect qualitative data to back up and assist interpretation of the data obtained from the SILL. Learners were asked for their opinions on the best way to learn English. A total of 70 learners were interviewed (the 35 most proficient and the 35 least proficient learners, according to proficiency test results). Learners were interviewed one by one after each class as time allowed, and answers were recorded in note form. It was not possible to interview all the students due to time constraints.

Analysing the data

Descriptive statistics (mean scores, frequencies and standard deviations) were computed for all SILL items, and for all tested proficiency scores. Responses on the student version of the SILL were recoded into three broader categories for the purposes of analysis – 'Always or usually true', 'Somewhat true', and 'Never or usually not true'. Associations between student use of strategies and the following variables – proficiency, discipline, and gender – were checked via one-way analysis of variance. Significance levels were set at $p<.05$, non-directional. All interview data were tabulated and categorised.

Results

Results on my five research questions will be listed in order.

(1) What language learning strategies do City University EAP students use?

Results on the first research question, taken from the SILL, indicate that students always or frequently use 18 of the 50 strategies, primarily from the second and third of Oxford's six categories – Cognitive (using all your mental processes) and Compensation (compensating for missing knowledge). These 18 strategies are listed in Table 1 in rank order. The strategy used most often by students is

Table 1. *Strategies always or usually used by students (N = 140)*

Rank	Strategy	Strat. Type
1	If I can't think of an English word, I use a word or phrase that means the same thing.	C
2	To understand unfamiliar English words, I make guesses.	C
3	If I do not understand something in English, I ask the other person to slow down or say it again.	F
4	I pay attention when someone is speaking English.	D
5	I encourage myself to speak English even when I am afraid of making a mistake.	E
6	I try to find out how to be a better learner of English.	D
7	I try to relax whenever I feel afraid of using English.	E
8	When I can't think of a word during a conversation in English, I use gestures.	C
9	I first skim an English passage (read over the passage quickly) then go back and read carefully.	B
10	I write notes, messages, letters or reports in English.	B
11	I notice my English mistakes and use that information to help me do better.	D
12	I find the meaning of an English word by dividing it into parts that I understand.	B
13	I practise the sounds of English.	B
14	I try not to translate word-for-word.	B
15	I look for words in my own language that are similar to new words in English.	B
16	I use new English words in a sentence so I can remember them.	A
17	I watch English language TV shows spoken in English or go to movies spoken in English.	B
18	I read English without looking up every new word.	C

A = Memory strategies D = Metacognitive strategies
B = Cognitive strategies E = Affective strategies
C = Compensation strategies F = Social strategies

ranked number 1 in the table, the second most often used is number 2, and so on.

Table 2 shows the ten strategies *least* often used by students, in rank order. The strategy used *least* often of all by students is number 50.

Table 2. *The ten strategies least frequently used by students (N = 140)*

Rank	Strategy	Strat. Type
41	I make summaries of information that I hear or read in English.	B
42	I try to learn about the culture of English speakers.	F
43	I plan my schedule so I will have enough time to study English.	D
44	I ask for help from English speakers.	F
45	I ask English speakers to correct me when I talk.	F
46	I use flashcards to remember new English words.	A
47	I give myself a reward or treat when I do well in English.	E
48	I physically act out new English words.	A
49	I talk to someone else about how I feel when I am learning English.	E
50	I write down my feelings in a language learning diary.	E

A = Memory strategies   D = Metacognitive strategies
B = Cognitive strategies   E = Affective strategies
C = Compensation strategies F = Social strategies

(2) Does strategy use differ by discipline?

Two broad differences in strategy use were found among students from different disciplines. The physics students used significantly (p = .037) fewer Cognitive strategies than did the computing mathematics or engineering students, and the computing mathematics students used significantly (p = .038) fewer Metacognitive strategies than did the physics or engineering students.

Differences in strategy use by gender

Males reported significantly (p<.05, N = 140) higher use of three strategies than did females:

I use the English words I know in different ways.
I try to guess what the other person will say next in English.
I try to find as many ways as I can to use my English.

(3) What strategies are associated with higher or lower levels of proficiency?

Table 3 gives proficiency test results for all students:

Table 3. *Proficiency test results (N = 140)*

Section	Mean Score	s.d.	Min.	Max.	N
Listening comprehension (20 pts.)	13.04	1.95	8	19	140
Grammar (30 pts.)	20.79	3.30	11	28	140
Reading comprehension (20 pts.)	14.01	2.85	4	20	140
Writing (30 pts.)	20.32	2.38	13	25	140
TOTAL (100 pts.)	68.27	7.00	42	85	140

Table 4. *The five learner strategies positively associated with proficiency*

SILL Item	Strategy	Sig.	N	Strat. Type
8	I review English lessons often.	.0265	140	A
27	I read English without looking up every new word.	.0185	140	C
29	If I can't think of an English word, I use a word or phrase that means the same thing.	.0482	140	C
30	I try to find as many ways as I can to use my English.	.0457	140	D
50	I try to learn about the culture of English speakers.	.0035	140	F

Sig. = significance   N = number
A = Memory strategies   D = Metacognitive strategies
B = Cognitive strategies   E = Affective strategies
C = Compensation strategies   F = Social strategies

Results on my third research question reveal a statistically significant ($p<.05$, $N = 140$) *positive* association between five individual strategies and proficiency. This means that the students who used these five strategies more frequently were significantly more proficient than those who used them less. These five strategies are listed in Table 4.

My results also reveal a statistically significant ($p<.05$, $N = 140$) *negative* association between four individual strategies and EAP proficiency. This means that the students who used these four strategies more frequently were significantly *less* proficient than those who did not. These four strategies are listed in Table 5.

Table 5. *The four learner strategies negatively associated with proficiency*

SILL Item	Strategy	Sig.	N	Strat. Type
21	I find the meaning of an English word by dividing it into parts that I understand.	.0489	140	B
28	I try to guess what the other person will say next in English.	.0240	140	C
41	I give myself a reward or treat when I do well in English.	.0031	140	E
46	I ask English speakers to correct me when I talk.	.0333	140	F

Differences in proficiency by discipline

There were no significant differences in proficiency between disciplines.

Differences in proficiency by gender

Females did significantly ($p < .001$, N = 140) better than males on the proficiency test. The mean score for females was 71%, and for males 66%.

(4) What strategies do EAP teachers believe to be the most useful for EAP?

Teachers (N = 43) rated 15 strategies as having high or very high usefulness for EAP, primarily from Oxford's second and fourth categories – Cognitive and Metacognitive. These 15 strategies are listed in Table 6 in rank order. The strategy ranked highest (most useful) by teachers is ranked number 1 in the table, the second most useful is number 2, and so on.

Table 7 shows the ten strategies rated *least* useful by teachers, in rank order. The strategy rated *least* useful of all by teachers is number 50.

(5) What strategies do EAP students believe to be the most useful for EAP?

The learner interviews, in which the 35 most proficient and the 35 least proficient learners were asked for their opinions on the best way

Table 6. *Strategies rated 'very high / high usefulness' by teachers*
(N = 43)

Rank	Strategy	Strat. Type
1	I read for pleasure in English.	B
2	I try to find as many ways as I can to use my English.	D
3	I write notes, messages, letters or reports in English.	B
4	I watch English language TV shows spoken in English or go to movies spoken in English.	B
5	I pay attention when someone is speaking English.	D
6	I look for opportunities to read as much as possible in English.	D
7	I notice my English mistakes and use that information to help me do better.	D
8	I ask questions in English.	F
9	If I can't think of an English word, I use a word or phrase that means the same thing.	C
10	I think of relationships between what I already know and new things I learn in English.	A
11	I read English without looking up every new word.	C
12	I start conversations in English.	B
13	I encourage myself to speak English even when I am afraid of making a mistake.	E
14	I ask for help from English speakers.	F
15	I look for people I can talk to in English.	D

A = Memory strategies   D = Metacognitive strategies
B = Cognitive strategies   E = Affective strategies
C = Compensation strategies F = Social strategies

to learn English, yielded useful data. Table 8 displays the results. Some learners gave more than one answer. Each entry in the table indicates one mention by one learner – for example, 21 of the most proficient learners recommend 'practise a lot' as the best way to learn English, whereas only 17 of the least proficient learners did so. Activities mentioned by only one learner are not shown.

Discussion

In this section I will discuss and compare the results presented in the previous section. One aim of this study has been to try to answer the general question 'What are the most useful strategies for EAP

Table 7. *The ten strategies rated least useful by teachers (N = 43)*

Rank	Strategy	Strat. Type
41	I ask English speakers to correct me when I talk.	F
42	I remember new English words or phrases by remembering their location on the page, on the board, or on a street sign.	A
43	I look for words in my own language that are similar to new words in English.	B
44	I talk to someone else about how I feel when I am learning English.	E
45	I use flashcards to remember new English words.	A
46	I notice if I am tense or nervous when I am studying or using English.	E
47	I use rhymes to remember new English words.	A
48	I make up new words if I do not know the right ones in English.	C
49	I write down my feelings in a language learning diary.	E
50	I physically act out new English words.	A

A = Memory strategies D = Metacognitive strategies
B = Cognitive strategies E = Affective strategies
C = Compensation strategies F = Social strategies

Table 8. *Interview – 'What is the best way to learn English?' (N = 70)*

	35 most proficient learners (top 25%)	35 least proficient learners (bottom 25%)
Practise a lot	21	17
Live in target-language country for a while	8	3
Read English-language newspapers frequently	7	9
Talk to foreigners / make foreign friends	5	2
Get as much speaking practice as possible	4	2
Watch English-language television frequently	3	2
Go to EFL classes	2	4
Increase effort to learn	2	0
Use English outside the classroom	0	5
NO ANSWER	0	4
Overcome shyness	0	4
Play games in English / language games	0	3

students?' I shall approach the answer to this question by comparing results on my five research questions.

The 18 strategies used by students (Table 1) came primarily from the Cognitive and Compensation categories. Apparently my students did not often use the other 32 strategies on the SILL, and indeed often gave low or very low scores for them. These low scores lead me to suggest that 'Fakability (social desirability)' (see Oxford and Burry-Stock, 1995: 11) seemed to be not acting as an intervening variable in this study. Fakability, or giving positive answers to please the teacher (in this study that would mean giving mostly high scores on the SILL), is a common criticism of the SILL and a potential problem for validity with data from the instrument.

The 15 strategies rated by teachers as having high or very high usefulness for EAP (Table 6) came primarily (9 out of 15) from the Cognitive and the Metacognitive categories (moreover *all* of the top 7 were from these categories). Examination of the standard deviations of scores on individual items on the teacher version of the SILL indicates that there was a considerable degree of agreement among the 43 teachers. While I cannot show that the teachers were correct in naming which strategies are most useful for EAP, I propose that their knowledge and experience made them skilled in this assessment. There is some evidence for this skill: three out of the five strategies positively associated with proficiency were among those rated by teachers as having high or very high usefulness (see Tables 4 and 6).

The match between the strategies recommended as useful by teachers and the strategies always or usually used by students was only 7 out of 15 (in other words, only 7 out of the 15 strategies highly recommended by teachers [Table 6] were among those often used by students [Table 1]). This is not a very close match; my students did not, in the main, use the strategies recommended by their teachers. This study did not investigate the reasons for this. One possible reason for my learners' choice of strategies might be that they come from a culture that values rote learning and memorisation (see Richards and Lockhart, 1994: 55). However, I believe this is not true of my learners: my learners did not use (Table 1) the few SILL strategies connected with these methods, nor did they mention them during interviews (Table 8).

I conclude that the Cognitive and the Metacognitive strategies may be the most useful for EAP, and that the students in this study did not use many of the Metacognitive strategies. However, this finding, plus the fact that most of my students did not use the strategies that appear to be associated with better proficiency, implies a need for teacher attention to the promotion of strategy use among students (this will be further discussed below).

Three other factors are common to the list of 15 strategies rated by teachers as having high or very high usefulness (Table 6). First, no fewer than five out of the six strategies ranked highest for usefulness involve additional student study outside the classroom. I suggest that teachers encourage and assist their students to increase their involvement in this area. Second, they emphasise students being more active learners[3] (this is also true of the strategies positively associated with proficiency – see Table 4). Third, they involve students taking the initiative in speaking. Teachers might also encourage their students to increase their involvement in these two areas.

It is noteworthy that the top six 'best ways to learn English' suggested by the most proficient learners during interviews (Table 8) also involve additional study outside the classroom (just as five out of the top six strategies recommended by teachers did). This adds further weight to the notion that students should increase their involvement in this area, and that teachers should encourage this.

The interview results were useful and I believe that more teachers should be collecting their students' opinions on how they learn best and on what they want to do in class and perhaps incorporating the results in classroom tasks and materials (for suggestions on this see Yorio, 1986: 671). When students' perceived needs and wishes are not met the result can be frustrated and disappointed students.

My research design did not allow me to investigate the possible reasons for the two broad differences in strategy use found between students from different disciplines (physics students using significantly fewer Cognitive strategies, and computing mathematics students using significantly fewer Metacognitive strategies). But as these are the two categories of strategies that I have proposed are most useful for EAP, I suggest that these findings may be worthy of EAP teacher intervention, and also of further research. My research design also did not allow investigation of the slightly higher use of strategies by males than females. However, it is interesting to note that the differences in strategy use by discipline and by gender were evidently *not* a result of higher proficiency – the males were significantly *less* proficient than the females, and there were no differences in proficiency by discipline. There must have been reasons for the differences other than levels of proficiency. These findings are interesting because

---

[3] This finding reflects Rees-Miller's comment (1993: 680) in her review article on learner training that 'above all . . . the good language learner is an active participant in the learning process'.

they run counter to one argument on the causality of strategy use, which is that while the use of strategies might lead to better proficiency, better proficiency might enable higher strategy use (see Skehan, 1989: 92, 97[4]).

Conclusion

I noted in my literature review above that strategies are teachable. I believe that strategies training is important, because I agree with Richards and Lockhart (1994: 63) that an 'important aspect of teaching is to promote learners' awareness and control of effective strategies and discourage the use of ineffective ones'. A number of researchers have successfully attempted strategies training in the classroom – Wenden (1986), O'Malley (1987), Kern (1989), Oxford, Crookall, Cohen, Lavine, Nyikos, and Sutter (1990), Chamot (1993), Dornyei (1995), Nunan (1996), and Bejarano, Levine, Olshtain, and Steiner (1997). Ellis and Sinclair (1989) and Wenden (1986) make detailed and useful suggestions for strategies training.[5] It is probably not necessary to train learners in strategy use openly. Interested EAP teachers can identify the strategies that are associated with proficiency with their students and embed those strategies in teaching tasks, materials and curricula. They should also evaluate the success of this strategy training.

Learners who can use a wide range of appropriate strategies have a greater degree of self-sufficiency and are developing as autonomous learners. This is particularly important for EAP learners, whose time in the EAP classroom is limited. Their need in this area is further highlighted by the fact that the teachers in this study, as well as the most proficient learners, highly recommended independent study outside the classroom.

My findings suggest the following areas for future research. What strategies do students use – and what strategies are associated with proficiency – in other EAP contexts, and other academic disciplines? Do students in different academic disciplines use different strategies (and if so, why, and what are the implications)? What strategies do other EAP teachers recommend, and do they match the strategies used by their students? Can useful strategies be effectively taught, and is the acquisition temporary or permanent? Can they be taught unconsciously (implicitly, perhaps embedded in tasks and materials),

---

[4] Skehan says that perhaps only a longitudinal research design can investigate this argument.

[5] Rees-Miller (1993: 685, 687), however, advises caution in this training because of differences among learners.

or is conscious attention to strategy type and form necessary? Does the effectiveness of strategy training vary by academic discipline? I also propose that researchers check the difference, if any, between what strategies students are actually using and what they self-report using. They could also observe, in the classroom, the links between increased strategy use and enhanced learning.

Finally, I suggested in my introduction that we need to draw up a list of the attributes of the good EAP learner. Table 4 (strategy use / proficiency association) contributes to the list – we can say that good learners review English lessons often, read English without looking up every new word, use a word or phrase that means the same thing when they can not think of an English word, and try to find as many ways as they can to use their English. Another answer based on the present study is to list the top eight or ten strategies rated as very useful by the 43 EAP teachers (see Table 6) – this answer is certainly based on a great deal of teacher knowledge and experience.

I suggest that much more work is needed on the important task of describing the attributes of the good EAP learner. The question is important because EAP teachers might be able to develop and promote those attributes if they are known.

18 Issues in EAP test development: What one institution and its history tell us

Fred Davidson and Yeonsuk Cho

Introduction: contexts and mandates in EAP testing

The testing of English for Academic Purposes (EAP) is a special case of a more general phenomenon in education: assessments which answer educational mandates within given instructional contexts. A mandate is the justification for a test, and the context is the environment or setting in which a test operates. There may be (and often are) many test mandates within a given context. In a typical EAP test setting, the context is usually an institution of tertiary education at which there are a number of students for whom the institution's lingua franca is a foreign language. This triggers a number of reactions by the institution, including (typically) an array of EAP instructional courses and some sort of EAP assessment. If more than one EAP test evolves, it is likely that each addresses a different mandate. Our home institution is a case-in-point. We have three mandates for EAP assessment: assessment of written mode ability of newly-matriculated non-English speaking students (which is the focus of this paper), the assessment of speaking of the same newly-matriculated students, and additional oral testing of non-English speaking students who will serve as instructors at the university during their post-graduate career. All three mandates function within the context of our campus: each is shaped by the unique mix of political, social, curricular and logistical constraints at our university.

In this paper we seek to narrate the evolution of the assessment of EAP during intake testing at our campus, with particular focus on mandates for testing in the written mode. We shall explain the history of this particular context and explore the particular mandate(s) for our test as they rose and changed over the past fifty years (or so). This will allow us to discuss various general issues of EAP theory and practice, of general educational testing, and of language testing.

We shall first describe our context: the University of Illinois at Urbana-Champaign (UIUC) and its international student population. Then, we shall describe three major historical eras of the EFL testing at UIUC, each of which followed a major model of EAP instruction and/or practice in educational assessment.[1] In the first era, a structuralist model of language ability dominated UIUC EFL tests during a time when no particular strong model of language testing, test quality control or test development existed there – this corresponds to Spolsky's (1978) prescientific era of language tests. The second era also yielded an EFL test which adhered to a language ability model (albeit a new communicative model), but more importantly, concerns of psychometric quality control were implemented. Finally, the third and present era continues the psychometric quality controls implemented in Era Two and attention to a language model (as in both Eras One and Two) while adding an accountability-oriented, criterion-referenced, specification-driven test development procedure. Each era thus retains the persona of the previous era, but responds to new influences.

The context: ESL students at the University of Illinois at Urbana-Champaign

In 1867, the US government provided a 'land grant' for a university in east-central Illinois. Located approximately 200 km south of downtown Chicago, what was then called Illinois Industrial University grew to become a major academic institution in the central part of the US. Today, 'The [UIUC] campus includes some 200 major buildings on 1,470 acres, serving more than 2,000 faculty members, 26,000 undergraduates and 10,000 graduate [i.e., post-graduate] and professional students' (<www.uiuc.edu/admin2/about.html>). In the most recently completed academic year, 1998–99,[2] there were 3,245 international students enrolled at UIUC (Office of International Student Affairs, 1998).

---

[1] In one sense, all three eras were 'EAP' testing, because all three concerned a common academic context and a similar mandate. However, only the third era (and to some extent the second) correspond to 'EAP' in the modern technical sense of the term.

[2] UIUC's academic year is divided into a sixteen-week fall semester, a sixteen-week spring semester, an intensive three-week 'Summer Session I', and a longer eight-week intensive 'Summer Session II'. The test discussed in this paper is given at various dates throughout the year, with large administrations at the start of the fall, spring, and Summer Session II terms. ESL service courses which depend on the test's results are offered in those same three terms. (Generally, there are no Summer Session I ESL classes.)

An 'international student' is generally a non-Illinois resident who is not a citizen or legal permanent resident of the US and who attends UIUC on a US government student visa. International students are required to take the TOEFL prior to coming to campus, and if the TOEFL result is below a certain value, they are also required to take the examination that is the focus of this essay: the UIUC English as a Second Language Placement Test (EPT). There is a campus-wide TOEFL value set for all students of 550 for admittance and 613 for exemption from the EPT.[3] Academic units (e.g. particular degree-granting departments like Mathematics or Chemical Engineering) may raise the upper number but may make no other changes to this campus mandate. On average, some 500 new international students are mandated to the EPT each academic year. Of that number, about three-quarters are required to take some form of EFL written-mode enhancement course. Some students are required to take course sequences that would last over two or three academic semesters while others can complete the requirement in a single academic term. Students who were not required to take the EPT or those who work up and through their EPT required courses may enrol in a set of elective ESL courses.

The earliest documented evidence of the testing of academic English of international students at UIUC is 1907, where some action was apparently taken by campus administration: 'The Secretary of the Senate referred to the Senate's action on October 7th 1907, with reference to the admission requirements in English and Rhetoric of students from foreign countries, and asked whether the Senate's action on this matter was final. The President ruled that it should be so considered.' (Minutes of the UIUC Senate meeting 14 February 1910.) The minutes or records of the 1907 meeting itself cannot be located at the UIUC archives, so the precise details of this early debate are unfortunately lost.

The earliest mention of a suite of EFL instructional courses for international students is in the *University of Illinois Catalog 1946–47*, which lists programmes of study and course descriptions for classes offered at the campus. That is, there is an historical record of the testing of international students at UIUC some forty years before there is discussion of any overt or special service programme to provide follow-up instruction to such students. At first glance, this may seem odd. However, it is important to recall

---

[3] The equivalent values also apply on the new computer-based TOEFL score scale. This entry cutscore is one of several topics addressed by a new campus Task Force, convened in the 1999–2000 school year.

that EFL as a teaching industry did not really surface in the US until after World War II. Programmes such as those at the University of Michigan (where Lado worked) grew most rapidly in the late 1940s and the following decade (Spolsky, personal communication).

The first era: a structuralist model of language

It is not possible to discuss second/foreign language testing apart from studies in linguistics and Second Language Acquisition (SLA). Studies in linguistics have informed the field of SLA and in turn, have had direct impact on language test design. This is true of the first ESL assessment at UIUC, which came at a time when second language pedagogy was dominated by structuralism. Testing under this model typically involved a multi-item assessment instrument, where each item measured control of a particular discrete language focus.

ESL instruction began in the fall of 1947, when the structuralist school of language teaching was prevalent. Precise records of a separate UIUC ESL testing programme at that time have not been located. We know that by about 1950, the nascent UIUC ESL programme used Lado and Fries' tests from Michigan. The Michigan tests continued through the mid-1950s, and gradually, the UIUC ESL faculty began to write tests of their own (Mary A. Hussey, letter). These early UIUC ESL tests were very similar in form to the Lado and Fries Michigan measures and were, in effect, measures of knowledge of particular discrete linguistic structures or certain lexical items. Although 'SLA' as a term did not exist at that time, in effect, the dominant theoretical model of ESL pedagogy at UIUC came from the second language acquisition theories developed at the University of Michigan. So, too, did the dominant testing model; in fact, there is some documentary evidence that UIUC-developed tests paralleled Michigan tests as late as 1964.

The Michigan-inspired structuralist focus of the first UIUC-authored ESL test is clearly evident in some sample items from 'The Brennan Test' (authored by and named for Helen Brennan, founder of the ESL Division at UIUC, and dating from the 1950s [see Figure 1]).

The Brennan test contained 100 items, for which students were allowed forty minutes. Through the 1950s and into the 1960s, the Brennan test was revised and altered, first by Professor Mary Hussey and then by Professor Mary Hussey and Susan Taylor. Both the Hussey and Hussey/Taylor tests continued to have discrete-point structural sections.

[correction question type]
Mr. Jones (teach) my English class yesterday.

[question transformation type]
What language _____?
Mary speaks English.

[sentence construction type]
was not   The movie _____.
interesting
enough

[multiple-choice grammar and usage type]
I studied English (A–for) two years.
                  (B–during)
                  (C–since)

Figure 1 Sample UIUC ESL testing items from the first era

Throughout this period, an essay exam was usually included in EAP testing at UIUC. Both the Michigan testing system and the locally-developed UIUC tests (Brennan, Hussey, and Hussey/ Taylor) typically included a timed writing sample. From the inception of formal ESL teaching in 1947 until the start of Era Two described below, a writing task was often included in the EFL testing of newly-matriculated students. Records are unclear about the precise role these essays held in the intake testing; we believe that the structuralist multi-item test dominated the entry decision-making, and it seems that the influence of the essay seemed to vary. This may reflect the reduced role of EFL composition studies during structuralism and doubts about its quality in the early days of language testing (see Harris, 1969, especially pp. 69–71). However, it is interesting to note that direct assessment of writing is a secondary thread through the fabric of EFL testing at UIUC. It existed in Era One; Era Two saw no composition measure but there were proposals to return to it; finally, in the present test, composition returned to dominate the assessment practice; perhaps this reflects the face validity of a composition task, which is an activity quite common in academic settings.

Following is a sample writing prompt from the 1960s:

COMPOSITION TEST

This is a test of your ability to write in English. You will have *25 minutes* to write a composition on the subject given below. Your composition will be graded mainly on *grammar* and *organisation*.

Write your composition on the paper provided. Do not copy your composition. If you want to make a change, draw a line through the part that you want to change, and continue writing.

'An Important Historical Person in my Country'

In your composition, you should (1) *describe* the person and the time during which he or she lived, and (2) *explain* why you believe that person is an important person in the history of your country.

Figure 2 Sample Composition Test Prompt from the first era

Throughout the first era, there was variation in the amount of instructions, precision of the prompt, and detail of the rating guidelines. We take this flexibility to reflect changes in the structure of ESL courses as well as feedback from ESL teachers and the campus.

In addition, the ESL assessments from 1947 through the 1950s and 1960s included the testing of listening comprehension. These tests were also patterned after the Michigan Test of Aural Comprehension. For example, the 1964 Hussey exam required students to listen to spoken sentences and then circle a picture response that corresponded to the sentence.

In summary, the first era of EAP testing at UIUC was dominated by attention to a structuralist model of language ability. It was also dominated by influence from the University of Michigan ESL programme; the Michigan tests were actually employed in the early years, and later those tests served as models on which UIUC tests were constructed.

The second era: psychometric concerns

Structuralism/behaviourism in language testing received much criticism for its heavy reliance on surface levels of linguistic control. Contrastive analysis of first and second language differences in grammar, lexis and phonology predominated through the late 1970s, when the modern era of communicative competence (arguably) began (Savignon, 1972; Savignon, 1983; Canale and Swain, 1980;

Bachman, 1990). The notions of integrative testing (Carroll, 1961) and communicative competence helped to put an end to discrete structuralist language teaching, and the EPT also entered a new era which reflected this paradigm shift: language tests had to reflect integrated command of a wide array of language skills.

In 1978, Lyle Bachman arrived at the UIUC campus and began oversight of the EPT. He was very concerned with two new notions in language testing. First, he redesigned EAP testing at UIUC. Evidence also indicates that he coined the name: 'ESL Placement Test' or 'EPT'. Bachman's EPT included a new structure test and replaced the composition measure with two new tests: a cloze and a dictation, which were thought to be (at least) equally integrative measures to a composition but of greater psychometric quality (again, see Harris, 1969: 69–71).

The second change instituted by Bachman was careful attention to the statistical psychometric qualities of the EPT; we believe this is a far more critical alteration of EAP assessment at UIUC than simple change of test content, and it is this quality control which causes us to date the 'second' testing era from Bachman's arrival. The records show that Bachman exhaustively analysed test materials in order to document the test's validity and reliability. For example, in a letter to campus departments (November, 1980), the following statistical information was provided:

Table 1: *Statistical Information about the EPT in the second era*

	Mean	SD	Reliability	SEM
Structure	49.99	10.00	.969	1.761
Cloze	49.99	9.99	.776	4.728
Dictation	50.09	10.01	.948	2.283
Total	50.04	8.74	.912	2.592

There is no evidence prior to Bachman's arrival of formal acknowledgement of measurement error in the EPT (Standard Error of Measurement or 'SEM'). Doing so is now commonly advised in the accountability-centred ethic that governs modern psychometrics (see Standard 2.1, APA, 1985).

In addition, records show that fundamental language testing research was begun on the EPT during his era. Bachman (personal communication) instituted formal needs analysis as a basis for test design, and coupled various innovations to the scholarship of the time (e.g. the use of cloze and dictation testing). In effect, Bachman's work reflected the systematic data-based approach to test development prevalent nationally and internationally by the mid-1980s. We can find no records of data-driven empirical research on the EPT prior to his arrival.

Perhaps this is not surprising. Language testing is indeed often given a 1961 birthdate, but it did not reach legal mature activity until the Language Testing Research Colloquium began in 1978 and the journal *Language Testing* appeared in the early 1980s. What is more, by the early to mid 1980s, techniques for assessment of composition had improved greatly due to very active study of ESL writing assessment. Prior to his departure, Bachman was planning to reintroduce an essay test, and so the essay exam actually introduced in Era Three was a very logical step.

The third (and present) era: language modelling, psychometrics and classroom content

The current EPT is also concerned with rich, integrative measurement of established statistical quality. Operational quality control and foundational language testing research both continue in the EPT arena, but a new competitor has entered the game: content evidence of validity to academic classroom activities. Language ability in the third EPT era is defined in terms of the tasks seen to be most important in academic ESL. To illustrate this point, we will focus on the writing component of the EPT.

A direct writing measure was reintroduced to the test shortly after the arrival of Fred Davidson at UIUC (at the beginning of fall semester, 1990). Records indicate that a composition was part of the ESL testing during the first era. It was removed, but records also show that towards the end of the second era, a composition was to be reintroduced. What, then, distinguishes the second from the third era? How, precisely, has content validation to classroom tasks actually transpired? We believe Era Three is most clearly differentiated from earlier eras by the now-dominant role of detailed test specifications.

A test specification is a blueprint for test items or tasks. From a specification, many equivalent tasks can be written for piloting and possible inclusion in an operational test. Specifications can be written at many levels of detail; by analogy, a blueprint for a new house could be general and rough (showing major walls and features) or very detailed (showing the precise placement of electrical outlets and the exact routing for plumbing). We can find no specifications at all for the tests written during the first era, and the specifications during the second era that do exist in our files are written at a very high level of generality which do not reflect details of actual classroom EAP tasks. By contrast, the present EPT composition task is supported by a test specification which is detailed and which approximates the tasks students actually perform in UIUC classes. This specification is available for public review on the Web (see the 'Specbank' at <http://www.uiuc.edu/ph/www/fgd>). It has been continually refined and developed to assure its validity against academic tasks at UIUC.

The EPT specification given here follows a format first made popular by Popham (1978). The process by which such a specification is written is elaborated in Lynch and Davidson (1994). Students are exposed to prompt materials (video plus passage) which are developed from this specification; students then write compositions based on that prompt material, and the compositions are scored by trained raters according to the rating guidelines given as a supplement in the specification.

The specification serves as an efficient and hopefully vigilant way to concentrate and focus the interests of test users on the quality of the test. Refinements to the test become situated as changes in the test specification: the version given on the Web is its seventh generation since 1991. The specification is basically a criterion-referenced test, and its criteria are the skills needed to function in EFL at UIUC. These criteria are the product of consensus dialogue among many interested influences in an era of heightened accountability: ESL teachers, academic units, test developers, feedback from piloting and trialling, and communicative language teaching pedagogy and theory.

There is much of Era One in Era Three. From the inception of ESL at UIUC up to the late 1970s, whenever a composition task was used as part of entry and placement testing, it was assessed by raters who had actually taught in the classes into which students might be placed. This model continues in the present system: in order to be a rater one must have taught in the course sequence for which one reads papers – either the graduate courses or the undergraduate courses. Unlike Era One, the EPT raters are now monitored for psychometric quality control. Unlike Era Two, EPT ratings (and the prompt material) are now anchored via a detailed specification to tasks thought to reflect actual classroom tasks at UIUC. The specification functions as a rallying point or locus for communication among parties interested in the EPT. Constant monitoring of operational reliability and validity (as established in Era Two) can be tracked to and reflected in changes in the specification.

Conclusion: the *realpolitik* of the UIUC EPT

The context of the EPT is quite similar to that of 1947:[4] assessment of academic English ability of newly-arrived international students who do not meet the pre-admission standard (a given TOEFL score). Times have changed, however, and so the mandate for the test continues to evolve. Several changes are under consideration for the EPT in the coming years. First, we are curious whether the test's validity could be improved if we moved to special-field testing. We take to heart the warnings provided by Clapham (1996) about difficulties in special-field testing; however, a serious on-going worry is that most of the validation of the EPT video-reading essay has been via the content of the ESL classes as opposed to the English demands in students' fields of study. The current specification reflects on-going dialogue with ESL teachers, and via that avenue, to needs elsewhere at UIUC. This is rather indirect. The next step in the content validation evidence of the video-reading essay is to work more directly with academic units at UIUC. Studies are underway on topics such as: is it feasible to develop special-field EPT video/reading tasks? Are there alternate task-types that more accurately reflect the special-ised ESL that students need while studying at UIUC? Is special-fields testing logistically feasible at UIUC? We next plan to liaise directly with units to see whether the EPT could be altered to take student academic discipline and background knowledge into consideration.

A key dilemma of the EPT is its frustrating score turnaround mandate. We are obliged to provide results to the University, to departments, and to students within about 24 hours of completion of the exam. In most cases, students who are required to take ESL classes do not in fact begin instruction for six, eight or even ten days. There is a window of opportunity for additional reassessment (perhaps in the form of a portfolio) by which writing ability could be more accurately assessed, and students possibly re-placed in the ESL course sequence. A major study is underway on this question (Cho, forthcoming).

We also must constantly attend to creation of alternative and equivalent forms of the video-reading prompt material. At present, there are four forms of the test. Continued cyclical use of those forms engenders a certain 'cottage industry' at the campus: students know

---

[4] The context and elements of the mandate of the current era are also strikingly similar to that of 1907, when EAP testing was first discussed in the UIUC Faculty Senate, and the same fundamental ethics of EAP – though it did not bear the name 'EAP' at that time – were resonant.

what kind of topic they are likely to encounter at the test. It would be better to have about a dozen forms to ensure test security. Fortunately, if we accept the present specification as fairly stable, then generation of new test forms is a straightforward exercise.

There is also much to be gained if we could develop a discrete multi-item test of sufficient difficulty and with sufficient evidence of content validity (again, to academic tasks at UIUC). There is, at present, a multiple-choice grammar test which we use as a tie-breaker for close decisions on the essay, and we hope to phase out many poorly-performing items from that test in favour of items with greater content relevance to academic performance. The leading candidate is a new component to the EPT which measures reading and listening comprehension of the essay and video; this would form a new section to the test. We are presently trialling this test (Pyo, forthcoming).

Much of the true experimental work on the test happens in testing classes and seminars, in independent projects, in Master's theses, and in doctoral dissertations. The EPT really has no recurring research and development budget; rather, the funds designated for the test are virtually all dedicated to administration, scoring and processing of test results. The revision and analysis of the EPT in recent years has relied on a series of marriages-of-convenience between the needs of the test and the interest of graduate students. For example, Liu's 1997 dissertation made major advances in refinement of the test specification and (thence) generation of equivalent forms of the video/reading prompt material. As another example, a recent validity study (Steward, 1999) explored the writing features which best describe student essays at each of the four rating levels. We recently completed a study (Cho, 1998; at the suggestion of many ESL instructors) on the feasibility of a multiple-choice test of awareness and repair of plagiarism. The gist of that study is that plagiarism was a trait that cannot be measured in our context: it is better assessed through a direct writing task (if in fact it can be detected there at all). There is a small but intriguing proposal in a language testing class: could the EPT be delivered on computer, and if so, would it be possible to have discrete tasks of acceptable content validity and high difficulty – tasks which are not feasible in a paper-and-pencil mode? Ideas like that surface from time to time; sometimes they evolve and get piloted, often they die back into the archives of the test and the memories of its cast of characters.

The *Realpolitik* of ESL at UIUC impinges on the test in interesting ways. One strong present pressure is special-field testing. This mandate comes from many sources, but most actively from academic units that wish to tailor not only the fulfilment of the ESL course requirements but also the determination of those requirements. Many degree-granting programmes feel that the single most important activity that their international students should pursue is study in the content field. ESL – although acknowledged as a central campus mandate – is seen as a burden. Even if we decide that special-field testing is not workable at UIUC, a heightened spirit of accountability shall continue to shape EPT research and development.

The EPT has reacted and continues to react to changes in the *realpolitik* of academic English instruction at UIUC. Era One of EAP tests at UIUC reflected the influence of the University of Michigan and of a structuralist model of language teaching and assessment, and therefore were not really EAP tests at all. Era Two saw a movement toward an integrative test model (in the form of the dictation and the cloze tests) in addition to a discrete structure test component, but more importantly, it was a time when psychometric quality control entered the test design. One hallmark of sound psychometric test development is the use of needs analysis, which was pursued in Era Two; hence, it can be said that the beginnings of EAP assessment at UIUC began in that era. Era Three – the present time – is characterised by serious EAP outreach to the actual academic tasks that ESL students must perform while studying at the campus; this outreach includes but goes beyond simple content analysis of the language students will use. We see the development of the EPT as a dialogue among many interested parties, and the validity of the test is thus a larger argument than simple grounding in that content (a concern voiced by Fulcher, 1999).

In truth, each era flowed seamlessly from one to the next. In truth, each influenced the next. And in truth, elements of each remain and retain influence in subsequent times. For example, the present composition and rating system recalls the essay test used in Era One. The structure test in Era Two echoed the structuralist model dominant in Era One. And the psychometric quality monitoring established in Era Two are as important if not more important today.[5] The current EPT is the sum and total of the UIUC EAP assessments that have preceded it. It is a historical entity. Without an understanding of how testing originated and evolved at this particular setting, we cannot explain what this test is or what it is to become.

---

[5] Following are some routine analyses run on regular EPT data: inter-rater reliability, comparison of placement rates from one administration to the next, comparison of EPT results to further testing in the ESL courses, etc.

19 Teaching writing for academic purposes

Dana R. Ferris

The study and teaching of second language writing has gained status as a sub-discipline of both applied linguistics and composition studies over the past decade (Silva, Leki and Carson, 1997). In addition to the emergence of an entire journal devoted to the topic (the *Journal of Second Language Writing*), a number of books and articles have been published which focus on a wide range of general and specific issues related to the description of second language writers and texts, the teaching of L2 writing, and the preparation of L2 writing teachers (e.g. Belcher and Braine, 1995; Byrd and Reid, 1997; Carson and Leki, 1993a; Connor, 1996; Connor and Kaplan, 1987; Connor and Johns, 1990; Ferris and Hedgcock, 1998; Grabe and Kaplan, 1996; Hamp-Lyons, 1991c; Harklau, Losey and Siegel, 1999; Johnson and Roen, 1989; Kroll, 1990; Leeds, 1996; Leki, 1992; Purves, 1988; Reid, 1993; Tannacito, 1995; Zamel and Spack, 1998).

Though there are many theoretical and practical issues that emerge from these sources, some are particularly salient to the endeavour of teaching L2 writing for academic purposes: (1) how L2 writers are similar to / different from L1 writers; (2) variation across differing L2 populations (e.g. immigrant vs. international students); (3) the controversy over discipline-specific or general-purpose academic writing instruction; (4) teacher response (written or oral) and peer feedback; (5) error correction and grammar instruction for L2 writers; and (6) issues surrounding assessment and grading in L2 writing. In this chapter, the current thinking on each issue will be reviewed in turn. This will be followed by a report on a study which touches upon several of those issues.

L1 and L2 writers: similarities and differences

In early studies of L2 writing, leading scholars argued that L2 teachers and researchers should be guided by the insights of L1

298

composition theorists, in particular to embrace the tenets of the 'process approach' to composition instruction (Zamel, 1982, 1985, 1987). Others, however, have argued that L2 writers are so distinct from native English speaking writers that L2 writing teachers need to examine all aspects of their composition instruction to be certain that their unique needs are met (e.g. Goldstein and Conrad, 1990; Leki, 1990a; Patthey-Chavez and Ferris, 1997; Ramanathan and Kaplan, 1996; Reid, 1994; Silva, 1988, 1993, 1997; Silva, Leki and Carson, 1997; Zhang, 1995).

It appears to be true that many composition approaches and techniques introduced in L1 settings are also appropriate and beneficial for L2 writers. For instance, many American college and university ESL writing instructors have successfully introduced invention and pre-writing techniques, multiple-drafting and revision, peer response and portfolio assessment into their courses. On the other hand, it has also been clearly demonstrated that L2 student writers are quite distinct from their L1 peers. A review of research by Silva (1993) illustrates quite convincingly that texts by L2 authors vary from those produced by native speakers across almost every imaginable dimension (e.g. lexical variety, syntactic choices, cohesion and coherence, global rhetorical structure, etc.). As early as 1985, Ann Raimes concluded that while L2 writers essentially have the same needs as their L1 counterparts, they need 'more of everything' (p. 250). More recently, Silva (1997) argued that 'the ethical treatment of ESL writers' requires that such students be offered a variety of placement options (e.g. mainstream or sheltered writing classes), teachers trained and expert in meeting their needs, and materials and techniques which are appropriate given their linguistic and cultural backgrounds.

Differences across L2 populations

It is also important for theorists and teachers to understand that significant differences exist across L2 contexts and populations. As noted by Raimes (1991), 'there is no such thing as a generalised ESL student' (p. 420). It is not possible here to discuss all of the 'varieties' of L2 student writers, but one important distinction worldwide, between student writers who are long-term residents in English-speaking countries and international (visa) students, has recently begun to receive increased attention (Ferris and Hedgcock, 1998; Harklau *et al.*, 1999; Byrd and Reid, 1997). Specifically immigrant (or long-term resident) and international student writers may differ in their motivations and attitudes towards developing writing skills in English, in their responses to writing class expectations such as multiple-drafting, revision and peer feedback, and in their knowledge and command of formal English grammar.

The focus of instruction: discipline-specific vs. general purpose instruction

One of the most persistent and controversial issues in L2 writing is the debate over the purpose of EAP writing classes. Should teachers aim to develop generalised academic writing skills in their students, hoping that these skills and strategies will transfer to subsequent writing tasks across the curriculum? Or should they focus instead on teaching students how to analyse and imitate the norms of the specific discourse communities to which students hope to gain admission? This debate dates back (at least) to two, 1986 (a,b) articles by Horowitz, in which he raises objections to the process approach in academic settings and offers some insights about the nature of writing tasks across the curriculum.

One of the most persuasive arguments for the generalist view is made by Spack (1988). She asserts that academic discourse communities are too diverse to cover adequately in a writing course and that the writing in some disciplines is so poor that we should not encourage our students to emulate it. Most significantly, she points out that English writing teachers are not equipped to analyse the content and discourse of various disciplines in order to teach their students how to write in those content areas. Today there appear to be more adherents to Horowitz's position, at least if one examines recent scholarly publications in L2 writing. Ironically, however, the majority of ESL writing classes follow the more generalised approach recommended by Spack, at least in American academic settings. This discrepancy may be due largely to the related problems of teacher preparation to teach writing in the disciplines and of institutional resources (i.e., lack of funds to offer a range of specialised writing courses).

Response to student writing

Over the past ten years, considerable attention has been paid by researchers to issues surrounding response to student writing, including teacher commentary on students' ideas and organisation, oral feedback given during teacher–student conferences, and peer feedback. Early L2 research on teacher feedback (Cumming, 1985; Zamel, 1985) suggested that teacher commentary on ESL student writing was highly focused on student errors, negative, appropriative and inconsistent (but see response to Zamel by Silva, 1988). Recent research on teacher response to student writing has included surveys of student opinion (Cohen, 1987; Cohen and Cavalcanti, 1990; Ferris, 1995a; Hedgcock and Lefkowitz, 1994; Leki, 1991b; Radecki and Swales, 1988) and discourse analytic examination of the nature of teacher commentary and its effects on student revision (Ferris, 1997; Ferris, Pezone, Tade and Tinti, 1997; Goldstein and Conrad, 1990; Patthey-Chavez and Ferris, 1997). These studies have reported that students value teacher feedback and that they attempt to utilise it in their revisions, but that sometimes students avoid or ignore teacher commentary or use teacher suggestions to make changes that actually weaken their papers (or at least do not improve them).

There has been a great deal of attention given over the past decade to the nature and effects of peer feedback in the L2 writing class. Peer response is a practice enthusiastically advocated by some (e.g. Ferris and Hedgcock, 1998; Mittan, 1989), while others express caution about its appropriateness for culturally diverse students (e.g. Leki, 1990b; Nelson and Carson, 1998; Zhang, 1995). Studies of peer response have ranged from surveys and interviews assessing student attitudes (Carson and Nelson, 1996; Leki, 1990b; Mangelsdorf, 1992, Mendonca and Johnson, 1994; Zhang, 1995) to discourse analytic examinations of the nature of the interactions during peer response sessions and/or the stances taken by students (Lockhart and Ng, 1995; Mangelsdorf and Schlumbarger, 1992; Mendonca and Johnson, 1994; Villamil and deGuerrero, 1996). Finally, a group of studies has examined the effects of peer feedback on student revisions (Berger, 1990; Connor and Asenavage, 1994; Mendonca and Johnson, 1994; Nelson and Murphy, 1993). These studies have reported conflicting findings, and have utilised widely different methodologies. Given all of this activity and conflicting views, only a few generalisations can be made: (1) students appear to enjoy peer feedback and to find it valuable, though they would not support the abandonment of teacher feedback in favour of peer response; (2) students engage in a wide variety of interactions and assume a range of personae during peer feedback sessions, and these differing styles may influence the effects of the feedback and the attitudes of the participants towards peer response; and (3) students are more likely to consider the suggestions made by their peers in constructing revisions if teacher feedback is not given simultaneously.

The role of error correction and grammar instruction in EAP writing classes

Two lines of research have examined the importance of student accuracy in EAP writing tasks. The first, known as 'error gravity research', has examined university instructors' tolerance of errors in student writing (Janopoulos, 1992; Santos, 1988; Vann, Lorenz and Meyer, 1991; Vann, Lorenz and Meyer, 1984). The second has looked at students' perceptions of the importance of grammar feedback on their writing (Cohen, 1987; Ferris, 1995a; Hedgcock and Lefkowitz, 1994; Leki, 1991b; Radecki and Swales, 1988). Though methodologies and results vary, it is clear that both instructors and students perceive accurate writing to be important in academic settings. The more difficult question is how best to help students improve their accuracy. Though research is scarce and inconsistent on this point (see Ferris, 1999; Truscott, 1996), there is consensus that error feedback is most effective when it is selective, prioritised and indirect (noting location of errors rather than making overt corrections), and that students should be encouraged to develop independent self-editing skills (Bates, Lane and Lange, 1993; Ferris, 1995b, 1995c; Ferris and Hedgcock, 1998; Frodesen, 1991).

Assessment of student writing

Experts on L2 writing assessment have focused on two major issues: the impact of time limits on student writing (and especially of whether L2 students can be assessed fairly in timed writing situations) and models for evaluation (holistic, analytical and portfolio grading) (Ferris and Hedgcock, 1998; Grabe and Kaplan, 1996; Hamp-Lyons, 1990, 1991c; Reid, 1993). In general, most experts favour direct writing assessment (evaluation of actual student writing rather than multiple-choice tests that get at students' knowledge about writing). As for time limits, L2 writing teachers express a great deal of concern over whether students can ever be assessed fairly when they have to write under time pressure. Though this is a concern in L1 writing assessment as well, the burden seems especially heavy on students composing in their L2.

Holistic scoring has been widely used for large-scale writing proficiency examinations on university campuses and for the Test of Written English (TWE). It is efficient and relatively cost-effective; nonetheless, researchers express serious reservations about its reliability as a scoring method (see Hamp-Lyons, 1991c). Analytic scoring is more appealing to many teachers for classroom evaluation, as it is more precise and gives more information to the students. Portfolio assessment is growing in popularity in both L1 and L2 composition programmes. It offers the significant benefits of emphasising student progress and effort over time and communicating important values about revision to the students. However, both analytic scoring and portfolio grading can be extremely cumbersome to administer and very labour-intensive for teachers. While all three evaluation approaches have their benefits and drawbacks, portfolio assessment seems the most true to the principles of process-oriented writing instruction that many modern teachers value. Within that framework, analytic scoring seems to offer greater reliability and more helpful information than holistic scoring, which may be best reserved for large-scale test administrations for which the other models are not practical.

To summarise, writing researchers and theorists examining the development of student writing skills for academic purposes have focused on the nature of the students (differences between L1 and L2 writers and between international and immigrant student writers), the nature of instruction (discipline-specific or general purpose; the role of reading in the writing class; the use of computer-assisted writing) and the nature of feedback (teachers' written and oral commentary, peer response, error correction and assessment). In the second part of this chapter, I will describe an original study designed to investigate several of these issues (response to student writing, error correction and the effects of differences in student ability and assignment type on teacher feedback) in an academic writing context.

The study

Background

This case study was designed to follow up on the issues raised by an earlier large-scale quantitative study (Ferris, 1997; Ferris *et al.*, 1997). In this study, my associates and I examined over 1,500 teacher comments made on 110 first drafts written by 47 ESL students enrolled in three different sections of a sheltered ESL freshman composition course at a large public university in Northern California. The effects of the teacher's comments were then traced in 110 student revisions. Two different analytic models (see Ferris, 1997) were used to examine the sample: (1) a model used to describe and categorise the characteristics of the teacher commentary and (2) a model used to assess the effects of the teacher feedback on the student revisions. The most significant findings of the study were as follows:

(1) The teacher's commentary addressed a variety of goals and took different linguistic forms.

(2) Significant differences in feedback type were found across the two semesters of data collection, different assignment types, point of semester at which feedback was given and student ability levels.

(3) Many of the teacher's comments led to positive changes in the revisions. Approximately 26% were not utilised by the students (when 'positive' comments are excluded from consideration), and 19% of the teacher's comments led to changes with negative or mixed effects on the student revisions.

(4) Across the entire sample, the most problematic comments (leading to changes that had negative or mixed effects on the revisions) were requests for information or indirect requests (directives given in question form) and comments in which the teacher gave information to the student (without telling him/her how to respond to the information). The most helpful comments (leading to changes with positive effects on the papers) were direct requests in statement form and summary comments about grammar problems.

Research questions guiding the present study

The quantitative study left some unanswered questions. Though it was clear that the students in general paid attention to teacher feedback and attempted to address it in their revisions, there were a number of teacher comments which were apparently avoided or ignored by the students. While, the majority of the 'no change' comments were either positive comments (no change expected) or 'give information' comments (changes expected sometimes but not always), there was a significant minority of teacher statements or questions to which the students did not respond. In addition, students sometimes made changes inspired by teacher feedback which actually weakened the papers or at best had mixed effects. In the large-scale quantitative study, it was impossible to pinpoint the reasons behind these observations. To address these unanswered questions, it was decided therefore to undertake an intensive qualitative analysis by looking at a subsample of students and texts and using a case study approach. This examination was guided by the following research questions:

(1) What caused students to utilise teacher feedback successfully?

(2) What caused students to make teacher-influenced revisions which weakened, rather than strengthened, their papers?
(3) What caused students to neglect teacher commentary altogether?
(4) What was the apparent impact of student and classroom variables on the response and revision process?

Participants

The teacher

The instructor was an experienced and highly regarded teacher of ESL composition who had been in the field for about ten years. She was well trained in both L1 and L2 composition theory and practice, having completed four separate graduate courses on the theory and teaching of writing. The instructor used several different types of feedback in her classroom. Students received feedback from peers in small assigned writing groups at least once and sometimes twice during the drafting and revision stages; they also received written feedback from the teacher on two separate drafts of each essay. The majority of the teacher comments were about the writers' ideas and organisation, but she also made summary comments in her endnotes about two or three prevalent patterns of grammatical errors in the students' papers, paired with underlining several examples of each error type in the text.

The students

The eight subjects were selected from one of the three classes in the original study. From a coded master list of students, eight students were randomly selected: four who had been identified by the teacher as 'strong' writers and four who were described as 'average' or 'weak' writers. All eight of the students were between 18–22 years old; there were three women and five men. Two of the students (both in the 'strong' group) were international students, while the others were long-term residents of the United States (length of residence ranging from 6–13 years). Five of the eight (one strong student and all four weak students) had taken one or more ESL writing courses at the same university or at a local community college.

The writing course

The writing course was a sheltered freshman composition class for ESL students at a large public university. Students could be placed in the freshman composition course either through obtaining a qualifying score on the in-house placement test for ESL students or having passed the previous course in the composition sequence. It was a graded three-unit course which counted towards graduation and fulfilled the freshman composition requirement. In-class activities included discussion of readings, instruction on reading and writing strategies, grammar mini-lessons, pre-writing and revision activities, peer response, student-led discussions and oral reports. The students had four major essay assignments, with the fourth being a library research paper.

Data collected

Six papers written by each student (two drafts each of three different essay assignments, for a total of 24 paired drafts or 48 papers) were obtained from the original corpus (Ferris, 1997; Ferris *et al.*, 1997). In addition, the teacher provided background information about the students, copies of specific essay assignments and her observations about the strengths and weaknesses of each of the eight students.

Data analysis

Building on the quantitative analysis already completed for the original study, the 48 student texts – first drafts with teacher comments plus revisions – were examined carefully in an effort to determine why some teacher suggestions appeared to be more helpful to students than others (i.e., were assessed as having positive effects rather than negative or mixed effects) or why some comments were disregarded or avoided altogether (i.e., those comments which had led to 'No Change' categorisations in the revisions). In addition, the effects of student ability levels (Table 1) and of the different assignment types (Table 2) on the response-and-revision process were assessed.

Findings

The teacher comments and student revisions fell into three categories: (1) comments leading to effective revisions; (2) comments leading to ineffective revisions; and (3) comments which were not addressed at all by the students. These three categories are discussed in turn and are followed by an assessment of how the different assignments and student ability levels affected the types of feedback received and the amount and characteristics of revisions made by the students.

Table 1. *Characteristics of teacher commentary and student revisions (differences across students)*

Variable	Stronger Writers N = 4 (12 papers)		Weaker Writers N = 4 (12 papers)	
Total Comments				
All three papers	212		144	
Mean per paper	17.7		12	
Comment Types	*Totals*	*% of Total*	*Totals*	*% of Total*
Ask for Information	50	23.5	38	26.4
Request	52	24.5	42	29.2
Give Information	34	16.0	24	16.7
Positive	66	31.1	42	29.2
Grammar	10	4.7	10	6.9
*Revision Effects**				
No Change	24	16.4	40	39.2
Negative	10	6.8	6	5.9
Mixed	44	30.1	36	35.3
Positive	68	46.6	30	29.4

*Calculated with 'positive' comments removed from total. For stronger group, N = 146. For weaker group, N = 102.

Comments leading to effective revisions

The comments which appeared to influence successful revisions broke down into three general types: (a) specific questions asking for information from students' personal experiences (b) requests for summarised or paraphrased information from another author's text, and (c) comments which called for relatively simple changes at the word- or sentence-level.

Specific questions asking for additional personal information

First, among the comments which influenced effective changes, there were a number of examples of comments in which the teacher asked for more detail about the writer's personal experiences – information or analysis known only to the writer. In general, the students did a competent job of providing the requested information and incorporating it skilfully into the revisions.

Table 2. *Characteristics of teacher commentary and student revisions (differences across assignments)*

Variable	Assignment 1		Assignment 2		Assignment 3	
Total Comments						
All papers	132		132		102	
Mean per paper	16.5		16.5		12.8	
Comment Types	Totals	% of Total	Totals	% of Total	Totals	% of Total
Ask for Information	42	31.8	22	16.7	24	23.5
Request	30	22.7	42	33.3	20	19.6
Give Information	16	12.1	16	12.1	24	23.5
Positive	38	28.8	40	30.3	28	27.5
Grammar	5	4.6	8	6.0	6	5.8
*Revision Effects**						
No Change	30	31.3	22	22.9	14	23.3
Negative	8	8.3	4	4.2	4	6.7
Mixed	24	25.0	18	18.8	38	63.3
Positive	36	37.5	48	50.0	18	30.0

*Calculated with 'positive' comments removed from total. For Assignment 1, N = 96. For Assignment 2, N = 96. For Assignment 3, N = 60.

Requests for summary or paraphrase of another author's ideas

A second type of comment requested summaries or paraphrases of another author's viewpoints. In this writing class, all of the essay assignments required the student writers to respond to other authors' texts in some manner. Because of this, the teacher often asked the students to summarise the authors' ideas before launching into their own discussion. The students generally were able to address these types of comments quite effectively in their revisions.

Comments suggesting revisions at the word or sentence level

Finally, the student writers were most effective at utilising teacher commentary when the changes required to address the feedback were fairly simple, requiring only minor word- or sentence-level revisions.

In summary, teacher feedback could be most often traced to effective student revisions in this sample when the comments requested specific information known to the writer or specific information from assigned readings or when the requested changes were at the word- or sentence-level in the discourse.

Comments leading to ineffective revisions

On the other hand, a number of the teacher comments led to revisions which were not skilfully executed and which, if they did not actually weaken the papers, also did not improve them much (if at all). The student writers in this sample attempted to address the vast majority of the teacher's comments (nearly 75%), at least to some degree. However, it did not necessarily follow that the changes made in response to teacher feedback improved the paper or that the revisions were well done. In general, these ineffective revisions followed from teacher questions, but unlike the questions discussed previously, these questions were broader and dealt more with students' logic or argumentation than with specific details from students' lives or from other authors' texts.

In addition to the less successful changes which resulted from teacher comments about logic or argumentation, students also sometimes had trouble with rhetorical or organisational changes. One example of this problem (not shown because of length) came from the final paper of one of the weaker students, where the teacher suggested that he move two sentences to a later point in the same paragraph, which he obediently did. However, he did not make any necessary adjustments to the syntactic structure of the sentences he moved or to other parts of the paragraph to make the text flow coherently.

Comments not addressed in the revisions

As already discussed, the vast majority of the teacher's comments were addressed by the students in this case study, though some influenced more effective revisions than others. However, there were also examples of comments which the students apparently did not address at all in their revisions. For instance, both strong and weak students at times deleted material that had been in their first drafts and about which the teacher had made suggestions. Without talking to the students themselves, it is hard to know whether these deletions were a natural consequence of the overall revision process or whether they represented an avoidance strategy – in other words whether problematic sections were deleted simply because the student did not know how to 'fix' them according to the teacher's criticism. In the case of the stronger students, the former explanation seems likely, as they did major overhauls of their papers on all three essay assignments. On the other hand, weaker students more or less kept their original essay structure and simply deleted problematic sentences from the revisions. In general, however, such deletions strengthened the students' essays, since problematic sentences or sections disappeared from the revised versions.

In some weak students' papers, there were a number of examples of teacher comments which the student writer simply did not deal with at all in the revisions. In other words, they made no changes to the relevant sections, despite the fact that the teacher had called attention to problems there.

However, other cases (all from the same weak student) were different. The teacher was directive and specific in the first two comments, telling the writer that he needed to incorporate more information from his sources and tie his ideas more closely to his thesis. In the third comment, she pointed out an inconsistency to his logic. Though the three comments were somewhat different from one another in content and style, what they had in common was that, to address any of them, the student needed to make major changes to his ideas and organisation to incorporate the teacher's suggestions. Since this student was generally diligent in responding to teacher feedback that was less cognitively and rhetorically demanding and required fewer sweeping changes, it seems likely that he was not sure what to do with these comments, and therefore simply chose not to deal with them.

Student variables and contextual factors influencing the results

In addition to examining the effects of different types of teacher comments across the sample, the examination of work by students of differing ability levels and across a variety of essay assignments allows some speculation as to the effects of individual differences and the writing tasks on the response-and-revision process in this context. The quantitative trends (the statistical summaries given in Tables 1 and 2 and the qualitative analysis of the teacher comments and student revisions, taken together, suggest several generalisations about the effects of these student and classroom variables.

First, there were clear differences among the eight students as to their utilisation of teacher commentary. The stronger writers were able (and apparently willing) to take suggestions from their teacher and use them to recast entire paragraphs and sometimes even whole sections of their papers. The weakest of the strong writers and the strongest of the weak writers exhibited similar patterns in that they responded effectively to certain types of feedback (specific requests for information or for summaries of assigned readings) and less successfully to more open-ended questions which challenged the validity of their arguments rather than asking for specific details. The weakest writers, on the other hand, sometimes ignored such higher-order questions altogether in constructing their revisions. It is impossible to know in such cases whether they did not understand what the teacher was asking or were not competent to incorporate her suggestions effectively.

Second, the students' revisions were more effective on the first two assignments, in which they analysed readings from their textbook. The final assignment (on the 'Baby Jessica' case) was the most difficult in that students had to synthesise information from several readings and write on a topic with which they had little personal experience. Also, the teacher's feedback was considerably different on the Baby Jessica papers: Her comments were longer, more informative (e.g. pointing out a fact of the case that the writer had missed) and more abstract, forcing the student writers to grapple with problems of logic rather than providing readily accessible information about their own experiences or about class readings. As a result of both the assignment being more difficult and the teacher's responses being harder to cope with, the students were more likely on this assignment to avoid problems by deleting them.

Implications

As noted previously, there is evidence from both L1 and L2 composition research that student writers take their teachers' comments very seriously and make sincere attempts to consider and utilise suggestions and criticisms in formulating revisions (Ferris, 1995a, 1997; Hedgcock and Lefkowitz, 1994; Straub, 1997). This generalisation may be seen as both good news and bad news for composition instructors. It is good news because teacher feedback on student papers, whether oral or written, is a valuable opportunity to provide individualised, text-based, contextualised instruction beyond what is possible within the writing classroom. If teachers are going to spend a lot of time and effort writing comments on student papers, it is gratifying to know that student writers are paying attention to it.

On the other hand, with such power comes responsibility. This study, together with the larger discourse analysis which preceded it, clearly showed that teacher commentary had a great deal of influence on student revisions. There are some who might argue that this much teacher influence is a bad thing, as it crosses the line between student ownership and teacher appropriation (Brannon and Knoblauch, 1982; Sommers, 1982; Zamel, 1985). Should teachers back off and give less feedback or somehow communicate to their students to pay less attention to it in order to foster increased independence in self-evaluation and revision?

This study also demonstrated that teacher feedback in some instances led to student revisions which did not improve the papers and sometimes even weakened them. Knowing this – that students will generally at least attempt to utilise teacher commentary but that they may not always do so effectively – writing instructors had better consider carefully what they say to students, knowing that their suggestions, and sometimes even their very words (see Patthey-Chavez and Ferris, 1997) will likely appear in some form in the next draft of students' essays. If teachers ask student writers, via their comments, to do something that they are unable to accomplish successfully, but knowing they will try to do it anyway, have teachers helped or harmed their students' writing development? If a student is unwilling or unable to address a particular comment in a revision, is that comment necessarily a 'bad' one? Can teacher feedback foster the development of critical thinking skills without any tangible evidence of this development on student revisions? And if so, is this rather abstract goal a valid focus for teacher energy and student attention? Is there room for teacher commentary which may facilitate students' long-term growth as writers and thinkers without leading to any visible short-term improvement, or does such feedback simply clutter up the response-and-revision dynamic? These are difficult issues.

It seems likely that little will be accomplished by knowingly giving feedback that is over students' heads, whether rhetorically or linguistically, but hoping that the students will somehow 'learn' from it. In such instances, the teacher commentary will more likely frustrate students and/or be ignored. On the other hand, the mere fact that a student does not address a teacher's suggestion in revision hardly means that the teacher's comment was 'bad' or 'unsuccessful' – it may simply mean that the writer has chosen to go in a different direction with his or her text, which is a healthy sign of independent thinking, not a cause for alarm. When teacher feedback is avoided or ignored, only the student writer can tell us why. Similarly, it is quite possible, and even likely, that teacher feedback can help students think more clearly and critically long before they are able to produce evidence of such improved thinking in their texts. Thus, we should not assume that feedback which is unaddressed by students is somehow 'wasted' or harmful or that it has not helped the students' development.

The balance, then, is to construct commentary that helps students to think without overwhelming them and to assess students' responses to feedback more precisely (i.e., not only by examining their revision products). Specifically, if students (especially weaker writers) avoid sweeping challenges to their logic but respond effectively and concretely to specific micro-level suggestions, perhaps the challenging questions can be paired with straightforward suggestions as to how the answers to the questions could be successfully integrated into the student's emerging text. In one example, the teacher wrote the following comment: 'You might consider what some psychologists have said about the impact of this situation on Jessica'. To make this suggestion more concrete, the teacher perhaps could have said this instead: 'In our readings, there were several statements from psychologists about what the effect on Jessica might be if she were returned to her birth parents. You might add a paragraph here which summarises this information and discusses whether or not these expert opinions support your argument.' This revised comment still challenges the student to think further about his or her argument but is more concrete about what specific actions the student should take to find and incorporate the information. As to assessing why students do or do not incorporate teacher suggestions into their revisions, a pedagogical tool I have advocated elsewhere (Ferris, 1997, 1999) is the 'revise-and-resubmit' cover letter, in which students explain, when submitting a revised letter, how they have addressed the feedback they have received (or why they have chosen not to). This exercise has three benefits: (1) it requires students to take feedback seriously and to think reflectively about their own writing and revision; (2) it gives teachers insights into their students' writing processes, strengths and weaknesses; and (3) it gives instructors information about the clarity and helpfulness of their own written commentary.

By the same token, voicing such philosophical questions about teacher response and its effects on student revision does not absolve writing instructors of their dual responsibility to make their feedback as effective and clear as possible and intentionally to help students to understand it and utilise it successfully. In the case of some students' inability to move or rearrange text successfully, the teacher could have gone beyond saying 'Move the two sentences to the end of the paragraph' and reminded or helped the student to make the rhetorical and syntactic adjustments needed to make the revised paragraph flow smoothly. Hairston (1986) comments that 'as writing teachers we have expected students to revise their work, but we have not really taught them how to go about it' (p. 121).

What can be concluded from this in-depth analysis and from the larger-scale quantitative descriptions of response and revision which preceded it, is that writing researchers need to be much more precise in the ways they look at teacher commentary and its effects. It is simply not adequate, for instance, to tell teachers to use questions rather than statements or imperatives. As this study demonstrates, not all questions are equally effective or accessible to all students.

Further, teacher commentary and students' ability or willingness to utilise it in revision will vary depending upon the abilities of the students and the nature of the writing task. Teacher response to student writing is an interaction filled with complexity and possible communication breakdowns. Nonetheless, this study also illustrates the importance of teacher commentary and, for good or ill, its potential power.

20 Reading academic English: Carrying learners across the lexical threshold

Tom Cobb and Marlise Horst

The ESP reading problem

With the growth of English as the lingua franca of work and study, many non-English speakers find themselves needing to attain some level of proficiency in English in order to function in jobs or courses. However, they may have limited time to devote to language learning, and little interest in knowing English outside the work or study context. Responding to these circumstances, English for Specific Purposes (ESP) curriculum designers have attempted to reduce the time frame of learning through domain targeting. They attempt to identify and teach the lexis, syntax, functions and discourse patterns most commonly used in a domain (for chemistry students, test tubes, passive voice, clarification requests and laboratory reports). This approach has given waiters, tour guides and airline pilots enough English to function in their domains after relatively short periods in the classroom. But it runs into complications when the specific purpose is to read extended texts in a professional or academic domain.

It now seems clear that the cross-domain generalities of English (pronoun system, verb tenses, basic vocabulary, etc.) can be introduced and practised within a subset of the language. Simple reading tasks such as understanding signs and instructions can be undertaken knowing only the English used in a particular job or profession. But does this hold true for reading longer texts? Consider the position of the learner who knows the grammar of English and the technical terms of a domain: text analysis shows that these terms are typically rather few (Flowerdew, 1993c), roughly 5% of tokens (Nation, 1990). Function or grammar words account for about 40% more, so the density of unknown words for this learner amounts to 55%, about one word in two. Is knowing half the words an adequate basis for reading comprehension?

Reading as guessing

Until recently, it was widely assumed that L2 reading could proceed from a minimal knowledge base, at least in the sense of linguistic knowledge. Early post-behaviourist analyses of L1 reading (e.g. Goodman's 1967 'guessing game' theory) emphasised the naturalness of reading, and assigned a major role to inference and prediction drawing on general world knowledge. Decoding, vocabulary size, syntactic distinctions or other aspects of linguistic knowledge previously emphasised were now assumed to play a minor role. When asked if his analysis applied equally to L2 reading, Goodman (1973) pronounced the theory 'universal'. It was imported into ESL methodologies by leaders in the field, including Coady (1979), and quickly assumed a dominant position at the expense of other analyses of the reading process (Weir and Urquhart, 1998). The implications of guessing theory for ESP reading seemed clear: if guessing is a major part of reading, then knowing half the words in a text should be enough to get the guessing underway.

But there were two problems with guessing theory. First, there was little evidence for it and strong evidence against it (Gleitman and Rozin, 1973; Stanovich, 1980). Second, the theory was probably harmless enough in L1, where children, whatever their teachers' theories, made their guesses from a well-developed linguistic knowledge base. But if L2 readers were not taught vocabulary and syntax, then they really were guessing as they read, from whatever world knowledge they happened to possess. If L2 readers turned out not to be very good at the guessing game, reading theorists knew why: poor L2 readers had never learned to read naturally in their L1. Hence the remedy for poor L2 reading was to instruct learners in the high-level skills they should have developed reading their first languages.

Course designers in the 1980s apparently believed that many L2 readers needed such remediation, since coursebooks were mainly devoted to skills like guessing words in context and finding main ideas in paragraphs (Bernhardt, 1990), with no evidence that learners were unable to exercise these skills adequately in L1 (Bernhardt, 1991), or that problems exercising them in L2 were not caused by lack of L2 vocabulary and syntax. The skills approach to L2 reading relied on dubious assumptions, but without detailed comparisons of L1 and L2 reading outcomes, it was difficult to refute. The guessing approach to L2 reading, its sudden arrival and lengthy retreat, are reviewed by Grabe (1991).

Rethinking the problem

In the context of the increasing demand worldwide for English academic reading skills, and the common experience of English instructors worldwide that 'most students fail to read adequately', Alderson (1984: 1) articulated the central question about L2 reading as follows: is weak L2 reading a language problem or a reading problem? If it is a reading problem, then poor readers are poor readers in any language and there is little an English course can do for them other than remediate their general reading skills. If it is a language problem, then it stems from missing L2 knowledge related to reading (lexis, syntax, discourse patterning) that an L2 reading course could help students acquire and learn to use.

Alderson concluded that while it is possible for weak L2 reading to stem from weak L1 reading, the odds are greater that it stems from inadequate L2 knowledge, and furthermore, that strong L1 reading is no guarantee of strong L2 reading. Evidence for this included the fact that good L1 readers do not invariably become good L2 readers even after lengthy exposure to L2 texts (Clarke, 1979; Cooper, 1984). Therefore, some form of focused instruction seems necessary to turn good L1 readers into good L2 readers, something more than exposure to L2 texts aided by inferences from world knowledge. But what form of instruction? Alderson argued, setting the research agenda for the following decade, that the next step was to specify kinds and amounts of knowledge that constitute a 'threshold of linguistic competence' (Cummins, 1979) or 'critical mass' (Grabe, 1986) that allow the transfer of L1 skills to L2.

The question for ESP learners and their course designers was then as follows: What kinds of linguistic knowledge underpin L2 reading, and how much of it must learners acquire to read academic texts in their disciplines? (Or, perhaps how little, given that English is a means to an end.)

Locating thresholds

Alderson's (1984) call for thresholds attracted the interest of ESL researchers. Empirical confirmation continued to pile up showing that reading skills do not magically transfer from one language to another, particularly where two writing systems are involved (Koda, 1988). Alderson's hunch that weak L2 reading is normally a language problem was confirmed in several multiple regression analyses, including one by Bossers (1991) in which L2 knowledge level predicted L2 reading level four times better than did L1 reading level at all but advanced levels. The nature of the linguistic knowledge affecting reading skill has been specified as knowledge-based ability rather than knowledge per se, for example the large, well-connected lexicon underpinning rapid lexical access (Segalowitz, Poulsen and Komoda, 1991).

Progress has also been made on defining pedagogically usable thresholds. Cummins (1979) believed that research would identify distinct thresholds for different kinds of language knowledge and language tasks. For the task of academic reading, the main knowledge type of interest is lexical. Word knowledge is the key ingredient in successful reading in both L1 (Freebody and Anderson, 1981) and L2 (Cooper, 1984), contributing more to L2 academic reading success than other kinds of linguistic knowledge including syntax (Saville-Troike, 1984).

The search for a lexical threshold to reading proceeded in two complementary directions, comparing comprehension measures to either the absolute number of words learners know or else to the proportion of tokens they know in a particular text. Looking at absolute knowledge, Laufer (1992) compared Israeli university students' recognition vocabulary sizes to their reading comprehension scores, and found that minimal comprehension correlated reliably with knowing the 3,000 most frequent words of English. Looking at proportion of words known in a particular text, Hirsh and Nation (1992) determined that an unsimplified text can be comprehended when 95% of tokens are known, or there is approximately one unknown word per two printed lines. But is knowing the 3,000 most frequent words the same as knowing 95% of the words in particular texts? Clearly, one frequency-based threshold would be more pedagogically useful than a separate threshold for every text.

Nation and colleagues have worked long and hard to show that 3,000 words account for 95% of tokens in most texts, provided they are the right 3,000 words. Starting from the interesting discovery that the 2,000 most frequent word families of English reliably account for roughly 80% of tokens in a text in any domain (Carroll, Davies and Richman, 1971), Nation (1990) argues that reading in English depends on learners knowing these 2,000 words (like ache, admire, accuse and advise), which are most accessible in the form of West's (1953) General Service List (GSL). But the GSL itself hardly constitutes the entire lexical threshold, since 80% of words known (two words unknown per printed line) is far from 95% (one per two lines). However, attempts to close this gap by simply moving down the frequency list become unuseful shortly after the 2,000 mark (the next 1,000 words merely add another 3–4%, and so on).

In a research project begun long before the call for thresholds, independent research groups in several developing countries noticed that the GSL alone did not empower students with adequate reading ability, and so searched for a specification of the additional words that would prepare learners to read academic texts in English. Xue and Nation (1984) put this research together, producing the University Word List (UWL), an 800-family list of words found in academic texts across disciplines, which, when added to the GSL, reliably account for 90% of tokens. Coverage at this level has been confirmed by analysis of text corpora in a variety of disciplines using the computer programme VocabProfile (Hwang and Nation, 1994).

Sutarsyah, Nation and Kennedy (1994) argue that the GSL and UWL are the minimum lexical knowledge base for reading in any academic domain. These two lists constitute a general English for Academic Purposes (EAP) vocabulary syllabus that takes a learner to the outer edge of reading in a specific domain. At that point, an ESP vocabulary course would take over, the syllabus of which could be identified by extracting GSL and UWL terms from a corpus of domain texts, leaving a residue of terms which characterise the domain. In the case of economics, this residue amounts to 450 word families, accounting for a further 5% of tokens. In other words, systematic study of these three lists – containing just over 3,000 words – brings the learner to the 95% mark. For the remaining 5% of low frequency terms that inevitably crop up in any domain, often carrying crucial information (Kucera, 1982), learners have crossed 'the threshold where they can start to learn from context' (Nation, 1997: 11) as they do in reading their first languages.

So here is a strong hypothesis about the location of a lexical threshold, the point in L2 acquisition where learners will access their L1 reading skills. However, locating a threshold and carrying learners across it are two different things. The discussion to this point is about a syllabus not a method, about what to teach not how. As Sutarsyah *et al.* (1994) conclude, 'there is a need for courses that focus on the vocabulary of these two important lists' (p. 48).

Can 3,000 words be taught?

Designing a course to introduce learners to 3,000 words represents a challenge, and few courses attempt to do it. If the normal pace of classroom acquisition is about 550 words per year (Milton and Meara, 1995), then learning 3,000 words is a labour of some five years. Course books focus almost exclusively on the first 1,000 words of English (Meara, 1993), and techniques to accelerate the pace of lexical growth have usually proven unsuccessful. For example, looking up lists of words in a dictionary has been shown to produce inert knowledge that 'does not increase comprehension of text containing the instructed words' (Nagy, 1997: 73). Useful lexical knowledge which transfers to the comprehension of novel texts seems to depend on meeting new words in rich natural contexts (Mezynski, 1983). However, given the haphazard nature of acquisition from context (Haynes, 1993; Laufer and Sim, 1985), this type of learning requires a lengthy period of time (Nagy, Herman and Anderson, 1985), well beyond the time normally allotted for an EAP course.

Thus, L2 vocabulary acquisition is beset by a logical problem, as noted by researchers over the years. Carroll (1964) expressed a wish that some form of vocabulary instruction could be devised that would mimic the effects of natural contextual learning except more efficiently. Krashen (1989: 450) echoed the sentiment 25 years later: 'vocabulary teaching methods that attempt to do what reading does – give the student a complete knowledge of the word – are not efficient, and those that are efficient result in superficial knowledge'. In Pinker's (1989) terms, it is a learnability paradox: you learn words by meeting them in natural contexts, but to make sense of the contexts you need words.

The next section will revisit these same issues closer to the ground.

ESP in Oman

One of the main test-beds for ESP concepts from 1975 to 1985 was the Arab Middle East, particularly the Gulf states. This was so for a number of reasons (Swales, 1984b). In brief, sudden economic development fueled by oil and the need to produce an educated middle class quickly through training in English, led to a number of interesting experiments in domain-targeted curriculum design. There was an ambiance of 'no time to lose' that fit well with notions of accelerated learning.

One promising experiment in ESP unfolded at Sultan Qaboos University (SQU) in Oman (Adams-Smith, 1984; Cobb, 1996; Flowerdew, 1993a), where the approach was to integrate English language and content instruction. Coming on-stream a decade after other countries in the area, Oman was in a position to profit from educational experiments conducted elsewhere. A curriculum development team with experience in similar projects in the region was assembled (Beretta and Davies, 1985; Scott and Scott, 1984; Stevens and Millmore, 1987) a year before the University opened in 1986. When classes started, English language instructors taught first-year students in classic ESP fashion; they attended and followed up physics lectures, prepared students for the language of their chemistry experiments, and attended biology laboratories to help cut up frogs and write up results. Advanced courses were developed for engineering and medicine. If an ESP approach to academic study was ever going to succeed, it should have succeeded in Oman.

But language learning at SQU in its first decade was hardly a great success. One problem was that students arrived from secondary school much less proficient in English than course planners had expected. Tested on entry with the IELTS, most students were several bands below entry level for a British university (Flowerdew, 1993a). On the bright side, this was a real test of 'ESP from the beginning' that would demonstrate whether it was possible to achieve competence in a foreign language through domain targeting, by-passing the lengthy route through general English.

The Omani students' main weakness was in reading English texts. Between 1987 and 1990, the scientific texts used in both language and content courses were continually simplified and shortened so the students would have some hope of comprehending them (Flowerdew, 1993a). The main source of the problem appeared to be the students' lack of vocabulary. Arden-Close (1993: 251) observed chemistry lectures extensively in this period, and reported that the professors saw the students' language problems 'as almost exclusively vocabulary problems'. Flowerdew (1992) observed that content-course lecturers spent an inordinate amount of class time explaining the meanings of scientific words.

However, it was not only scientific words the students did not know. Arden-Close's (1993) research indicates where the main vocabulary problems lay. He observed numerous interchanges in which science lecturers unversed in language issues attempted to communicate with students. In one discussion, a chemistry lecturer backs up further and further in a search for common ground. Attempting to get across the idea of a 'carbon fluoride bond', he tries a succession of analogies: teflon pans, a tug of war, an assembly line – to no avail. Apparently, *pan*, *war*, and *line* (all in the GSL) were simply unknown. In another discussion, a biology lecturer discussing 'hybridisation' seeks an everyday example in dogs, switches to the local case of goats, realises he does not know the names of the different breeds in Oman, and finally resorts to mixing colours. But alas, 'a lot of them don't know their colours yet' (p. 258). There was apparently no common lexical ground to retreat to.

Support for this anecdotal evidence was provided by testing the recognition vocabulary sizes of first-year students with Nation's

(1990) Levels Test starting in 1993. After a year of study, students typically had recognition knowledge of about 900 words at the 2,000-word (GSL) level, fewer than half. Given that 80% of the words in any text derive from this level, these students faced more than one unknown word in two.

Students at SQU may have been starting from an unusually weak position, yet there is other evidence from ESP ventures in the developing world indicating that students' main vocabulary problems are at the general not technical level. English scientific terms are often already known in the first language, as concepts awaiting new labels or even loan-words. If unknown, they are often inferable from diagrams, glossed and emphasised in lectures, and have stable meanings from one context to another. None of this is true of the high frequency words that scaffold the technical terms. Problems with general or sub-technical terms have been identified in Malaysia (Cooper, 1984), Bahrain (Robinson, 1989), Papua New Guinea (Marshall and Gilmour, 1993), and Israel (Cohen, Glasman, Rosenbaum-Cohen, Ferrara and Fine, 1988). In the Israeli study, subjects translated both technical and general terms from a text, with 85% success for technical terms but only 32% for sub-technical (from the second thousand words of the GSL, *perceive, pattern, efficient*, or the UWL, *assertion, variable, diversity*).

After six years of ESP-from-the-beginning, the University decided to shift policy and give the students a year of general English before starting their academic subjects. The first step was to find a suitable placement test to establish their level of general English. It was now recognised that an instrument measuring very elementary levels was required. The choice fell on the Preliminary Test of English (PET), Cambridge University's (1990) most basic proficiency test, which confirmed that the students' level was indeed very low (mainly Bands 1 and 2). It was decided also to use the PET as an exit test, which the students were required to pass at a fairly high level (Band (4) before beginning their academic subjects. To meet this objective the students would study general English for one year using such coursebooks as *Headway* (Soars and Soars, 1991), with supplementary vocabulary work in *A Way With Words* (Redman and Ellis, 1991) – general English coursebooks rather than EAP texts. But after a year, many students still had difficulty with the PET, especially its reading section.

The students' needs had been correctly identified at a more basic level, but the courses chosen to address them made no claim to meet the urgent needs of academic learners. Typically, the students would get through one coursebook in a three-volume set designed for a more leisurely pace of learning. In terms of vocabulary, the words introduced were few and not always the most useful; no coverage of the full vocabulary of general English was attempted. However, this vocabulary can be targeted no less than that of a domain, by focusing on the GSL and UWL. And the contexts in which these words are presented need not be the shopping and dating experiences of *Headway*; words like *pan*, *war*, and *line* can be presented in subject-area contexts (as the chemistry lecturer attempted to do with his carbon fluoride bonds).

The vocabulary of general English can be targeted, but delivering it is another matter. To review, 3,000 words are far more than are normally learned by students in a year, and far more than can be easily contextualised by course writers, especially since stable learning requires meeting each word at least five times (as determined by Saragi, Nation and Meister, 1978), or eight times (according to an on-site study by Horst, Cobb and Meara, 1998). Abbreviating the process by learning wordlists and translation equivalents results in static knowledge unlikely to increase comprehension of novel texts. The remainder of this chapter describes the development of an instructional strategy to tackle these problems, which is to insert an EAP vocabulary course into the general course described above. Its objective is to introduce academic learners to large numbers of general English words in authentic contexts, so that they remember the words and can interpret their meanings in novel contexts. The course is a corpus-based lexical tutoring system: corpus analysis had helped frame the problem of ESP reading, so it seemed plausible that corpus-based tutoring might help solve it.

Design and test of a lexical tutor

Students were predisposed to participate in an intensive vocabulary acquisition experiment. They knew the test they needed to pass was based on a word list, the 2,387-word Cambridge Lexicon (Hind-marsh, 1980), roughly equivalent to the GSL. They were aware of how few words they knew, assessing vocabulary weakness to be their main problem with English. Checks were undertaken to be sure that devoting class time to experimental vocabulary acquisition would actually address the students' immediate needs. Four versions of the PET were checked against the Hindmarsh list with VocabProfile, and found to exploit the list quite fully but to contain few off-list items. Also checked against the list were the students' general English coursebooks, none of which included even half the words on this list, even in courses three volumes long (see Cobb, 1996, for details; Meara, 1993, for a similar finding).

System design

One way to ensure that students systematically encounter hundreds of words in context and at an accelerated pace is to present the words in a computer concordance. A concordance programme linked to a suitable corpus can present large numbers of words to students in ways that escape the learning paradox outlined above. First, a concordance programme is essentially a word list in context, and so might blend the efficiency of list targeting with the richness of multicontextual learning. Second, a concordance makes the five-encounters requirement simple to verify. Third, a concordance might overcome the unreliability of contextual learning, since with a number of contexts available learners can search for ones that make sense, doing in minutes what takes years in natural exposure.

On the other hand, a concordance is difficult to read; its texts are reduced in size and coherence; there is little opportunity for the normal flow of natural reading; the on-screen text-to-space ratio breaks established standards of text design; and there is no guarantee that the transfer of learning that has been established for meeting multiple contexts on paper (Mezynski, 1983) is replicable on a computer screen.

Several attempts to interest SQU students in learner-oriented concordances such as Microconcord (Oxford, 1993) were met with indifference. However, two studies had shown these students getting useful information from concordances, one a gap-filling activity where they worked with concordance print-outs (Stevens, 1991b), the other a text-manipulation activity where they accessed concordances on-line (Cobb, 1997). It was concluded that the lack of interest in concordancing derived from difficult texts and unwieldy interfaces while the medium itself had benefits. Thus, work was begun on the design of a corpus and interface for learners with an elementary level of linguistic and computational knowledge.

Corpus development involved scanning and collecting texts from the students' language course, particularly those dealing with business, and eliminating lexical items that did not fall within the PET list (involving some rewriting). Then, the PET list was checked against the corpus to ensure that every word appeared at least five times (involving additional rewriting). The result was a 50,000-word collection of texts, many of which the students were already familiar with. Corpus-building procedures are further discussed in Cobb (1996).

Interface development followed directly from observations of students' efforts to use Microconcord. Keyboard entry clearly posed an obstacle, most of the students being poor typists and spellers. The concordance output did not make different kinds of textual information visually salient, and the interface did not make it clear what learners were supposed to do in a concordancing session – which words to investigate, or what to do with lexical information they had assembled. It became clear that a concordance interface for the early stages of vocabulary acquisition should do the following:

identify which words to investigate and make them easily accessible;
provide a means for learners to take away lexical information in hard copy (or else most of the lab hour was spent transcribing from the screen);
build in motivation for considering each word in several sentence contexts.

These desiderata were realised as follows: the concordance was mouse driven, eliminating keyboard problems; lists of to-be-learned words were linked to the interface, so that clicking on them drove the concordance searches, and different types of information appeared in different fonts and colours; motivation for looking at several contexts was piggybacked to the desire for hard copy – students collected and sent words to a linked database for print-out at the end of concordancing sessions, with at least one example sentence from the corpus for each word (a stipulation coded into the programme). The assumption was that learners would look through concordance lines for a comprehensible example sentence for their print-outs, rather than selecting one that made no sense. The software platform chosen for this project was Apple's Hypertalk, the search engine at its centre was developed by Zimmerman (1988), and interfaces were designed by Cobb (1996). The programme was called PET·2000.

Using PET·2000

The students' reading course was expanded to include the vocabulary module. The entire 2,387-word list was installed in the concordance interface, and the students were assigned roughly 200 words from the list to be learned every week (e.g. all the words starting with 'C'). The list was available only on computer, and one lab-hour per week was set aside for this work for 12 weeks. About 20 of each week's words were randomly selected for weekly classroom quizzes. The students' task was to look through the 200 new words each week, decide which ones they did not know, send these to their databases with one or more examples from the corpus, add definitions if desired in English or Arabic, and print up the session's work as an instalment in a growing personal glossary. Students added an average of 100 words (SD = 14.5) per session. The fiction was that learners were lexicographers constructing dictionaries, following the constructivist principle of modelling learners on experts (Cobb, in press). The learner-lexicographers worked individually or in groups. They reported normally checking several contexts before selecting one for their database, and the user tracking routine confirmed that fewer than half the examples selected were simply the first one listed in the concordance.

Testing the tutor

The learning effects of PET·2000 were assessed at a point when the students had been learning English for about five months. Four intact groups at two proficiency levels were randomly selected for testing (participants had already been assigned to groups randomly by the institution). The first level consisted of two groups (n = 17 each) of lower intermediate students (with an average vocabulary size of 1,200 words). The second consisted of two groups (n = 12 each) of intermediate students (with an average of 1,500 words). At each level, groups were randomly assigned to experimental and control conditions. Experimental group participants used the concordance software as described above to search through contexts. Control group participants used a modified version of the software to send items with no examples to their databases for subsequent annotation with L1 translations from (off-line) dictionaries. All groups spent roughly the same amount of time on their PET·2000 work, 45 minutes per student per week for 12 weeks, with low and non-systematic variance according to the programme's time records.

Measures

Participants were pre- and post-tested using a two-part measure. The first part was the Levels Test at the 2000 level, a test of basic meaning recognition, which asks students to select brief definitions for 18 randomly selected GSL words (also appearing on the PET list). The second was a gapped passage, which asked examinees to fit 15 supplied words from the same list to gaps in two novel GSL-constrained texts of about 250 words each. The two parts were intended to assess two kinds of lexical knowledge: definitional knowledge of decontextualised words, and the more complex knowledge required to integrate a learned word into an extended novel context. At pre-test, class means were statistically equal on both measures within each level.This test was given two weeks after the beginning of the training period, in March 1995, and then again two weeks after the end. The pre-test was given after training had already begun to allow a technology habituation period; since learning rate and volume were issues, it was important to measure learning only when the procedure was functioning smoothly. Thus, any learning gains measured by the test were produced in a period of only two months. No feedback was given after either testing session, and there was no indication that participants remembered the test in any detail when they encountered it a second time. The hypothesis was that all students would make substantial but similar gains on the definitional measure, but only concordancers would make significant gains on the novel text measure.

The study followed a repeated measures factorial design, the factors being 2 (Treatments) × 2 (Skill Dimensions) × 2 (Levels) at two points in time (pre- and post-training). Pre-test and post-test scores for each treatment were entered into a separate repeated measures analysis of variance (ANOVA), with test scores as dependent variables, and level and treatment as independent variables. If the experimental prediction was borne out, there should be a significant time-treatment interaction on the novel text measure but not on the definitional measure.

Results

On the definitional measure, there was a significant main effect for time, $F(1,54) = 6.74$, p<.05, showing mean post-test scores (75.91) were higher than pre-test (69.53) by about 6.4%. However, this effect was unrelated to treatment. On the novel text measure, there was a similar but larger main effect for time, $F(1,54) = 19.48$, p<.001, showing mean post-test scores (74.03) were higher than pre-test (64.84) by almost 10%. On this measure there was also a significant time-treatment interaction, $F(1,54) = 6.24$, p<.05, showing differential contributions to the gain by treatment condition. Table 1 shows the components of this finding, indicating significant differences as established by a post hoc Tukey HSD test of multiple comparisons, a $(1,56) = 10.69$, p<.001.

At the lower intermediate level, both groups made significant gains on the Levels Test, the control group gaining about 7% (representing 140 new words) and the experimental group 9% (180 words), not significantly different from each other. Nonetheless, a gain of 9% on the 2,000 level represents a gain of 180 words in a period of two months, or 1,080 if continued for a year. This is roughly double the

Table 1. *Mean pre-post and gain scores by task, condition and level*

	Definitions Task						Novel Text Task					
	Control			Experimental			Control			Experimental		
	Pre	Post	Gain	Pre	Post	Gain	Pre	Post	Gain	Pre	Post	Gain
Lower Intermediate												
M	65.24	71.94	6.7*	65.53	74.4	8.87*	60.24	62.76	2.52	60.65	74.12	13.47**
SD	15.38	13.41		12.40	13.81		19.33	17.08		17.80	15.00	
Upper Intermediate												
M	75.17	79.58	4.41*	75.67	79.92	4.25*	71.42	77.08	5.66	70.75	86.83	16.08**
SD	11.18	12.23		10.80	12.00		12.14	10.66		12.35	8.90	

*$p<.05$ **$p<.001$

550-word baseline found by Milton and Meara (1995), and reinforces the longstanding claim of both Meara (1980) and Nation (1982) that learners in language courses may often be lexically underchallenged. Of course, learning vast numbers of words quickly would be of little use if the knowledge were not transferable to a novel context, so it is encouraging that concordancers gained 13.47% on this measure as well.

The upper intermediate students made smaller gains on the Levels Test, probably because with 75% of words known at pre-test there were few opportunities for further definitional learning at the 2,000 level. However, there were still opportunities for other types of learning. Over the two-month training period, concordancers gained 16% on the transfer measure.

Complementing these quantitative measures were observational and anecdotal impressions from both students and content area instructors. In the following year, when PET·2000 graduates had started working on the UWL, a content area instructor wrote a letter to the Language Centre commending staff for whatever they were doing that for the first time enabled students to read their economics texts.

Further work

With corpus-based tutoring shown to be an effective means of accelerating EAP vocabulary growth, the next step is to build the UWL into the interface, attached to a second or expanded corpus, and following that, to incorporate domain-specific wordlists and corpora into the system. Work is under way to develop a purpose-built UWL corpus using the principles discussed above, i.e., eliminating any terms beyond the GSL and UWL, and assuring that all 800 terms of the UWL are represented at least five times.

The long-term objective is to produce a set of wordlists and corpora, possibly with Internet delivery, that will allow a student anywhere to locate and cross the lexical threshold into L2 reading in a profession or subject with the smallest delay.

21 Incorporating reading into EAP writing courses

Alan Hirvela

Introduction

While reading has been an especially rich area of research for both L1 and L2 reading specialists over the past three decades and has produced a wealth of valuable studies and insights, it remains an enigma for reading researchers. For all we now know about reading, it is still, says Mackey (1997), an experience that is 'complex, untidy, and inevitably partial' (p. 428) as well as 'invisible and private' (p. 430).

These observations are particularly important with respect to the reading practices and experiences of L2 readers, as well as to researchers' and teachers' quest to understand those practices and experiences better. Reading in a second language is clearly a complex and difficult undertaking for many students, plus, as Carson and Leki (1993b) have stated, 'reading can be, and in academic settings nearly always is, the basis for writing' (p. 1). In particular, university students frequently perform the act of composing from source texts. Hence, as Spack (1988) has indicated, 'perhaps the most important skill English teachers can engage students in is the complex ability to write from other texts, a major part of their academic writing experience' (p. 42). Thus, Grabe (1991) sees the need for 'reading and writing to be taught together in advanced academic preparation' (p. 395). Meanwhile, students having writing problems may actually be experiencing reading problems. The act of composing from sources starts with the reading of those texts. Difficulties in reading them impact significantly on writing about them, since students are writing in response to what they have read and how they have read it. Finding ways to incorporate reading effectively into EAP writing courses is essential, then, if we are to establish a meaningful link between reading and writing in EAP writing instruction.

330

The 'texts debate' in EAP reading/writing instruction

A major point of contention in EAP is what kinds of texts should be used in EAP instruction. EAP specialists such as Horowitz (1990) and Johns and Dudley-Evans (1991) have challenged the 'wide-angle' approach described most notably by Hutchinson and Waters (1987) which advocates using a variety of text types in line with what Widdowson (1983) calls a 'scale of specificity' of learners' needs, i.e., some learners have narrower, more pragmatic needs, while others have broader needs. In this view, texts should be selected in accordance with where students fall along the scale of specificity. Another important issue is the enduring and often divisive controversy over the use of literary vs. non-literary or academic texts. Historically, in ESP and EAP there has been strong sentiment against literature. Indeed, as Strevens (1977) noted in the formative years of ESP's development, it arose partly as a reaction against 'the earlier assumption of language teaching as a handmaiden of literary studies' (p. 89). More recently, Kasper (1995a, 1995b, 1995/96, 1997) has conducted research comparing students' performance in reading where some groups read literary texts and others academic texts. Her research shows not only that students reading non-literary texts outperformed those who read literature, but that there was a strong preference among the students for non-literary texts. Lipp and Wheeler (1991) have likewise reported student preferences for non-literary texts. However, a number of practitioners have spoken in favour of literature in L2 writing instruction (e.g. Gajdusek, 1988; Hirvela, 1990; Oster, 1985; Parry, 1996; Spack, 1985; Vandrick, 1997). A common theme in their work is that literature-based reading and writing experiences offer students valuable preparation for the wide range of academic literacy requirements found at the undergraduate university level. Interesting and compelling arguments have been made on both sides of the materials/texts issue.

The study

The purpose of the study discussed in this chapter was to add insight into the texts debate so as to deepen our understanding of how reading can be more effectively linked to writing in EAP writing courses.

Methodology

This was a quantitative and qualitative study of mainly first-year university undergraduate students enrolled in an academic writing course for non-native speakers of English at a large American research university. The course precedes the first-year composition course required of all undergraduates. It focuses on such common elements of EAP writing instruction as summarising, paraphrasing, direct quotation, synthesising material from source texts and writing responses to source texts. The three sections of the course offered in the spring session of 1998 were the sites for the data gathered during the study. For each of their writing assignments the students were required to read one or more source texts and then incorporate them into their writing. Both non-literary and literary texts were used as source texts.

Data gathering occurred in three phases. In the first phase, students were asked to complete a description and self-assessment of their attitudes toward reading and writing in their native language (L1) and in English. In the second phase, they were asked, at the end of the course, to complete a questionnaire asking for their responses to the kinds of texts they read and to the reading-writing tasks they were asked to perform. Of the 38 students who participated in the first two phases of the study, 34 (95%) were Asian (mainly Chinese, Korean, Indonesian and Japanese) and 24 (63.2%) were taking their first composition course in the United States and had only recently arrived from their home countries. The study's third and final phase consisted of interviews of three students. These students twice participated in semi-structured interviews aimed at exploring their reactions to the course's texts and activities.

Materials (texts)

For their first major reading/writing assignment, the students were assigned George Orwell's well-known autobiographical essay, 'Shooting an elephant'. This is a combined non-literary/literary text that introduced students to some rhetorical features common in non-literary texts and narrative features often found in literary texts. The students then read and wrote about a short story, 'A Family Supper', by Kazuo Ishiguro, for their second composition. Here, as with the Orwell essay, they wrote a paper responding to the text. For their third and final composition, the students were asked to read three academic texts (from professional journals) about the topic of student journal writing. One text, by Linda Lonon Blanton (1987), came from the *ELT Journal*; another, by Michael Carroll (1994), came from the *TESOL Journal*. The third, by Nancy Duke Lay (1995), was from the journal *Teaching English in the Two-Year College*. In their paper, students synthesised important material from the three articles

Table 1. *Attitudes towards reading in the L1 and in English*

Language	Like	Mixed Feelings	Dislike
L1	31	1	6
English	16	6	16

and then discussed their own thoughts about the value of journal writing. They also wrote a collaborative, or group, paper for which they read six newspaper articles on the topic of examinations and their value to learning. In this paper they objectively synthesised relevant information and quotations from the source texts.

Results

Phase one: student self-assessment of L1 and L2 reading and writing

As explained earlier, at the beginning of the course the students were asked to complete a questionnaire requesting comments on their feelings about reading and writing in their L1 and in English. By examining how the students viewed themselves in terms of their literacy practices and preferences, the study could then more effectively investigate their attitudes toward the texts and the reading-writing assignments in the course. Responses to questions about whether they enjoyed reading and writing in the L1 and L2 were coded into three categories – like, mixed feelings, and dislike – and reported in Table 1.

Of special interest here is the strong popularity for reading in the L1 (31 of 38 students, or 81.6%) and the fact that this number was nearly twice as high as that for reading in English. The equal number of students liking and disliking reading in English is also worth noting, as is the fact that only 16 (42.1%) of the students showed clear-cut enjoyment of reading in English.

Table 2 reports students' feelings about writing. Here, clearly, there is an overall reaction against writing, whatever the language, with 23 of the 38 students, i.e., 60.5%, expressing dislike for writing in the L1 and 26 students, or 68.4%, disliking writing in English. Of considerable interest here is the contrast with the students' attitudes toward reading. For instance, only 6 students (15.8%) expressed dislike for reading in the L1 and, as pointed out earlier, 16 or 42.1%, did not like reading in English.

Table 2. *Attitudes towards writing in the L1 and in English*

Language	Like	Mixed Feelings	Dislike
L1	12	3	23
English	7	5	26

Students' written comments on the kinds of texts and some of the subjects they enjoyed reading were also interesting. For instance, regarding L1 reading, 17 students said they liked reading novels, 10 indicated that they enjoyed reading newspapers and magazines, and 6 said they liked reading comics/cartoons. As for reading in English, 8 students listed novels among their preferred reading, 6 said they liked to read magazines, 4 indicated an interest in short stories, 3 mentioned comics/cartoons, and 2 wrote positively about newspaper reading.

Phase two: attitudes towards text types and reading/writing activities

In this phase of the study, students completed an eight item 'Survey of Student Attitudes/Preferences' at the end of the course. Each item consisted of a statement concerning the four texts or text types used in the course. The four texts and their text types were: Semi-Literary Essay (Orwell's 'Shooting an Elephant'), Short Story/Literary (Ishiguro's short story, 'A Family Supper'), Newspaper Articles/Non-literary (six newspaper articles about examinations), and Academic Articles/Non-literary (three articles about student journal writing from professional journals). Students were asked to respond to each statement about the texts using a four point scale by which they ranked the texts. The questionnaire was completed by 38 students, but some questions were left unanswered. Hence, the actual number of responses varied from between 34 and 37.

The tables in this section report the number of students who selected each text type as well as the mean scores for each text type. Texts are identified either by a key noun included in the title or one reflecting the text type.

Of particular interest here is the ranking of the two literary-type texts as the least difficult in the light of the common perception among teachers that non-native speaking students find such texts too difficult to read. This could, of course, be at least in part because of the particular texts involved; other texts might have resulted in

Table 3. *Which text/text type was considered most difficult to read*

(1 = most difficult to 4 = least difficult)

Text	1	2	3	4
'Elephant' (semi-literary essay)	3	8	7	18
'Supper' (literary)	5	6	15	10
Newspaper Articles	22	10	3	2
Academic Articles	8	11	11	4

Mean Scores	
Newspaper	1.59
Academic	2.32
Literary	2.83
Essay	3.11

different rankings. Still, the literary rankings are interesting in the context of the non-literary/literary texts debate. Also of interest is the ranking of newspaper articles as most difficult, as well as the considerable gap between that text type's mean score and the mean scores for the other text types. The number of students ranking them most difficult (22) is also noteworthy.

Here, the fact that the literary text and the semi-literary text, respectively, were regarded as the most enjoyable to read, and by a considerable margin over the non-literary texts, is of particular interest. So, too, is the numbers of students who selected them first: 19 for the short story and 16 for Orwell's essay. These responses are in stark contrast to the first choice numbers for academic articles (2) and newspaper articles (1). The results raise interesting and important questions about the degree to which student enjoyment of texts and text types should be factored into EAP course and syllabus design, a topic discussed later in this chapter.

Here, it is interesting to see that the academic articles were regarded as most helpful, though there was not a significant degree of difference between this text type and the others. That the literary text was seen as least helpful, and that so few students ranked it first (4) compared to the other texts, must be noted. On the other hand, the clustering between it and Orwell's essay as well as the newspaper articles in terms of mean scores, suggests that this may not be an important distinction.

Table 6 shows a decided preference for the literary and semi-literary texts, respectively. These responses are similar to those for

Table 4. *Which text/text type was most enjoyable to read*

(1 = most enjoyable to 4 = least enjoyable)

Text	1	2	3	4
'Elephant' (semi-literary essay)	16	14	2	4
'Supper' (literary)	19	11	4	2
Newspaper Articles	1	5	14	16
Academic Articles	2	5	16	12

Mean Scores	
Literary	1.69
Essay	1.83
Academic	3.09
Newspaper	3.25

Table 5. *Which text/text type was most helpful in developing academic reading ability*

(1 = most helpful to 4 = least helpful)

Text	1	2	3	4
'Elephant' (semi-literary essay)	11	6	12	7
'Supper' (literary)	4	11	11	8
Newspaper Articles	9	10	5	12
Academic Articles	14	8	7	7

Mean Scores	
Academic	2.19
Essay	2.42
Newspaper	2.56
Literary	2.68

Table 4 ('most enjoyable to read') and so would seem to show a real level of appeal for such texts, at least in the case of the texts involved in this study. If stimulating students' interest in the L2 is a priority, these results suggest literary-type texts may deserve more consideration in text selection than appears to be the case at present. Also of note are the numbers for first ranking of each text, with the short story far more popular at 21 first choices than the others, especially newspaper articles at 3 and academic articles at 2. That so few

Table 6. *Which text/text type was most interesting to read*

(1 = most interesting to 4 = least interesting)

Text	1	2	3	4
'Elephant' (semi-literary essay)	11	17	2	5
'Supper' (literary)	21	10	3	2
Newspaper Articles	3	1	17	15
Academic Articles	2	7	13	13

Mean Scores	
Literary	1.61
Essay	2.03
Newspaper	3.17
Academic	3.63

students found the academic articles interesting to read is especially intriguing in the EAP context.

The considerably greater interest in the literary-type texts is once again of particular note here, both in terms of their mean scores and the number of students ranking them first (19 for the short story and 12 for Orwell's essay). In the case of each of these texts, the students were writing about a character or a dilemma motivating the text. Whether the students' real preference was for the task or texts is difficult to determine. However, in a separate course evaluation form, the students rank ordered the three major types of writing they performed in the course: writing response essays (about Orwell's essay and the short story), an objective synthesis paper (based upon the newspaper articles) and a synthesis-response paper about the academic journal articles. Of these major reading/writing assignments, students ranked the synthesis assignment as most difficult (with a mean score of 1.62 on a three-point scale), the synthesis-response paper as second most difficult (mean: 1.68), and the response papers as least difficult (mean: 2.70). In other words, they felt more comfortable with the writing involving the literary texts. But the question remains: which came first, the text or the assignment type? The rather lukewarm response in Table 7 to writing about the academic articles (mean: 2.78) should be noted, because this was, in many ways, the most EAP-like assignment.

Perhaps not surprisingly, these results mirror those in Table 7, i.e., the texts that were the least enjoyable to read were the most difficult to write about, and vice-versa. It should also be pointed

Table 7. *Which text/text type was most enjoyable to write*

(1 = most enjoyed to 4 = least enjoyed)

Text	1	2	3	4
'Elephant' (semi-literary essay)	12	16	4	5
'Supper' (literary)	19	11	1	5
Newspaper Articles	1	3	16	17
Academic Articles	6	6	14	10

Mean Scores	
Literary	1.78
Essay	2.05
Academic	2.78
Newspaper	3.32

Table 8. *Which text/text type was most difficult to write*

(1 = most difficult to 4 = least difficult)

Text	1	2	3	4
'Elephant' (semi-literary essay)	3	3	13	16
'Supper' (literary)	5	2	12	17
Newspaper Articles	21	10	4	0
Academic Articles	7	21	3	4

Mean Scores	
Newspaper	1.51
Academic	2.11
Literary	3.14
Essay	3.20

out that the students wrote about the newspaper articles in a collaborative or group writing format, an experience many of them found difficult for various reasons. Still, the comparative comfort the students felt toward writing about texts of a literary bent is quite interesting, particularly in light of the objections to literature noted in the discussion of the Table 3 responses. These results would seem to offer interesting insight into the question of how much students actually struggle with and are uncomfortable with literary texts.

Table 9. *Which texts would students recommend for future use in ESL (i.e., general English) composition courses*

(1 = most recommended to 4 = least recommended)

Text	1	2	3	4
'Elephant' (semi-literary essay)	12	11	4	8
'Supper' (literary)	11	12	8	4
Newspaper Articles	4	5	14	13
Academic Articles	10	7	9	9

Mean Scores	
'Supper'	2.14
'Elephant'	2.23
Academic	2.49
Newspaper	3.19

Here, again, we see a favourable reaction to the literary-type texts, with the academic articles also fairly strongly recommended. An explanation for the positive response to the Orwell essay and the short story may well be that students liked and saw value in the narrative structure of the texts. At the same time, they presumably saw pragmatic value in using texts like the three journal articles, with their formal academic text characteristics. The rather negative reaction to the newspaper articles could be read, as before, as a response to how they were used in the course (i.e., in the collaborative assignment) or to the texts themselves.

These results are of considerable interest from an EAP perspective. The clustering around the 2.50 mean score, as well as the minimal difference in mean scores among the four texts/text types suggest that the students saw essentially equal value in all four choices. Orthodox EAP thinking would likely assert that the academic articles would be of greatest value, and that students would not be inclined towards the more literary-type texts. For new undergraduates like these students, there appeared to be value in a mixed assortment of texts rather than a focus only on purely academic ones, thus raising an important question about whether a sole or heavy concentration on one text type is advisable in EAP academic literacy courses. The results reported for the literary-type texts in Tables 4, 6, 7 and 9 likewise raise this question and appear to provide valuable input into the text selection issue.

Table 10. *Which texts would students recommend for EAP-type writing courses*

(1 = most recommended to 4 = least recommended)

Text	1	2	3	4
'Elephant' (semi-literary essay)	10	8	9	9
'Supper' (literary)	10	11	4	11
Newspaper Articles	8	9	10	10
Academic Articles	7	8	13	7

Mean Scores	
'Supper'	2.44
'Elephant'	2.47
Academic	2.57
Newspaper	2.59

Phase three: interviews

This phase of the study was designed to 'flesh out' or investigate responses made in the study's second phase by focusing more intently on three students enrolled in the course. Each of these students participated in two semi-structured interviews, one shortly after the mid-term point in the course, when they had read and written about the two more literary texts – Orwell's essay and Ishiguro's short story – and the second as they were completing the course and thus had read all of its major texts and worked on the major reading-writing assignments. The interview questions focused on their responses to the four different texts/types and to the course's major reading-writing assignments. The interview data from each student's interviews are presented in three sets, with each focusing on one of the students.

Interview Set #1
In-Kyung was a 22-year-old female Korean student majoring in Chinese. She had been in the United States about seven months and had taken some pre-admission intensive English courses prior to beginning her undergraduate study at the research site. She was extremely fond of reading in her native Korean and also enjoyed writing in the L1. She did not like reading and writing in English.

During the first interview, where the focus was on Orwell's essay and the short story, she generally made a clear distinction in her responses to the two texts. With regards to reading and the value of the texts for EAP purposes, she favoured Orwell's essay. In her view, that essay *'is more suitable for an academic course because it's logical and organised and helps develop reading skills and vocabulary'*. In contrast, the short story *'is more killing time kind of reading'*. The clear and *'straightforward'* rhetorical structure in Orwell's essay was more useful for her in developing her academic reading ability. She found the short story *'not logical'* in its structure and felt that this was not useful in the academic context. However, with regards to academic writing she preferred the short story. The story *'was more thought-provoking'*. It has an ambiguous ending in which readers are left uncertain about its outcome, whereas Orwell's message is clear in the conclusion of the essay. In-Kyung's feeling was that the essay has *'a clear ending, so there's not much to write about'* in contrast to the various interpretations possible with the short story. (Here it must be remembered that with both texts the students were writing a response essay, so the response element was perhaps a major factor in how they viewed the texts.)

The second interview focused on responses to the non-literary texts. In-Kyung found both the newspaper articles and academic journals hard to read, but she favoured the journal articles for both reading and writing purposes. Regarding the texts, she remarked that the academic articles *'were more in an explanatory mode'* and so *'easier to understand and therefore easier to write about'*. She also liked the combination of synthesis and response in this assignment. In contrast, she often struggled with the newspaper articles because they dealt with examinations in the American context, and she felt she lacked the background knowledge necessary to understand the articles fully. However, she felt the focus on synthesis writing with both the newspaper and journal articles was quite helpful for students.

In looking at the course and its texts as a whole, she felt that the short story provided the most enjoyable reading experience for her, while the most enjoyable and meaningful for writing purposes was the set of three academic journal articles. She also indicated a preference for the synthesis writing over the response papers.

Interview Set #2

Reem, a 23-year-old woman from Saudi Arabia, was a native speaker of Arabic who had been in the United States for nearly five years. This was her first writing course since her arrival in America. She was pursuing a major in the Computer Information Systems Department. Writing in English was not of great interest or appeal to her, but she did like to read in English.

Her responses during the first interview were much like those of In-Kyung in Interview Set #1. Like In-Kyung, she found the short story a more enjoyable text to read and write about, and she, too, found the Orwell essay easier to read. The *'cultural background was easier compared to the Japanese background in the story'*, and she felt it *'was more straightforwardly written than the short story'*. Orwell's essay was *'clearer all the way through and that made it easier to read'*. Ishiguro's story was *'difficult because it was not clear'*. However, the short story *'was more interesting because it was going around the point'* and so *'it felt more like a mystery, with a totally different mood'*. Regarding which kinds of texts should be read in a course like this one, she expressed a preference for both the essay and the short story, especially as opposed to textbooks. In her view, *'textbooks would be boring in this kind of class'*. She saw value in the story-telling aspect of both texts.

Reem's responses during the second interview differed considerably from In-Kyung's. Though, like In-Kyung, she believed that the newspaper articles were more difficult to read and write about, she preferred that difficulty. As she explained, *'the greater difficulty meant I learned more about reading'*. This was true, too, with regards to the Orwell and Ishiguro texts, i.e., the newspaper articles were still the most helpful for her in developing her reading ability. She also felt that the newspaper articles were best among the four text types used in the class with regards to academic reading and writing instruction because *'they provided more new information'* to the students, especially *'cultural knowledge'*. She was non-committal about the academic articles, mainly because she felt she had not had enough time to read them as thoroughly as she had the other texts.

As for the course's writing experiences, she, like In-Kyung, preferred the synthesis-based assignments, in particular the objective synthesis paper based upon the newspaper articles. In her words, *'the synthesis writing was more valuable even though it was more difficult than the response papers'*.

Reem's comments present interesting similarities and contrasts with In-Kyung's remarks. Of particular interest is her belief in the greater value of more difficult texts and writing assignments.

Interview Set #3

The final participant in the interviews was Wan-hua, an 18-year-old female student from Taiwan majoring in Chemistry. She had been in the United States for two and a half years and had studied at another college prior to coming to the research site. She had also studied for nearly a year in an American secondary school. She considered herself an '*active*' reader in Chinese and enjoyed writing in her L1. However, she did little reading in English outside of assigned school reading.

Wan-hua's experiences and responses reported in the first interview regarding the literary type texts were much like those reported earlier. That is, she found Orwell's essay easier to read than Ishiguro's short story but felt the short story was more enjoyable to read. As she explained, Orwell's essay was '*not hard to understand, but it was boring and I couldn't keep focused on it*'. In contrast, she liked the '*indirect, Asian style*' of Ishiguro's story and felt she could rely on her Chinese background somewhat in understanding the characters and their actions. She also said that the ambiguity of the story's ending was '*an asset*' for her as a reader. However, this ambiguity made it more difficult to write about; the essay was simpler, with its '*main idea so clear and easy to respond to*'. As for the suitability of the texts in developing academic reading and writing skills, she had no preference between the two: '*Both of them are good for stimulating students' interest and working in English*'. Like Reem, she felt that the fact that the two texts had '*no resemblance to textbooks*' made them especially appealing to students. She did, however, feel that Orwell's essay, with its straightforward rhetorical style, '*helped me to reinforce my knowledge of how English articles are organised*'.

The second interview revealed that Wan-hua responded much like the other two participants in her reactions to the two text types. She, too, found the newspaper articles more difficult to read, and at the same time stated that they were more useful for her and other students in developing academic reading ability. The journal articles were more interesting to read, she said, but they were '*too easy*' in terms of their organisation. She noted that she '*read each one once and then just scanned them after that*'. Like In-Kyung, though, it was her view that the academic articles were more useful in developing academic writing ability. The newspaper articles were helpful '*in learning about American culture*', but the journal articles were '*more relevant to her writing needs*'. Regarding the course texts and assignments, she most enjoyed reading the short story and found the synthesis-response assignment based on the academic articles the most valuable one for herself.

In Wan-hua's responses, we once again see interesting distinctions made in feelings about the texts and assignments. Literary reading continued to be the most enjoyable, while non-literary reading and writing had greater pragmatic value for her. As with the comments from the other two interview participants, her responses offer valuable insight into EAP writing instruction and ways of locating or incorporating reading in such courses.

Discussion

Phase One of this study revealed the following points relevant to EAP reading-writing instruction: the students were very positive about reading in their native language, only mildly enthusiastic about reading in English, and did not like writing in either the L1 or the L2. These results are important to bear in mind while interpreting the Phase Two and Phase Three results of the study.

One point that emerges clearly in Phase Two and Phase Three is the students' greater level of enjoyment in reading the literary-style texts than the non-literary texts, a result that is especially interesting to consider in view of what Kasper, and Lipp and Wheeler, cited earlier, have reported about student preferences for non-literary texts. When the positive feelings about the literary texts are juxtaposed against the students' lukewarm (at most) feelings about reading reported in Phase One, it could be surmised that the inclusion of some literary texts in EAP writing courses would stimulate students' interest in reading and perhaps contribute to the development of both their reading and writing, as a study by Janopoulos (1986) indicated. Here it is especially worth noting the Table 9 and 10 results, where the students favoured, by a small margin, the use of literary-style texts in general English and EAP courses.

Furthermore, it was explained earlier that the students ranked the response writing assignments as the least difficult of the three writing experiences in the course. Given the students' apparent antipathy toward writing in the L1 and the L2, it may be that literature-based response assignments are a helpful starting point in EAP writing courses in the sense of beginning to open up the writing experience for students. If, as we have seen in Tables 4 and 6, they experience greater enjoyment and interest in reading literary over non-literary texts, the combined reading and writing experience involving literary texts may serve as a more positive entry point into EAP writing than the more strictly academic reading materials and writing assignments endorsed in orthodox EAP. In other words, the literature-based reading and writing could operate in the 'wide-angle' mode discussed by Hutchinson and Waters and the broader end of Widdowson's 'scale of specificity', while the synthesis writing about non-literary texts fulfils 'narrow angle' needs on that end of Widdowson's scale.

The study's results also show that the students saw considerable pragmatic value in the writing involving the non-literary texts and the synthesis-based papers. Both the Table 10 results and the interview data suggest that the students made some distinction between what they enjoyed reading and writing and what they saw as useful for academic purposes. However, as we see clearly in Table 10, where the students clustered around all four text types with regards to which they would recommend for EAP courses, that distinction between enjoyment and practical value did not lead to a clear-cut preference on the students' part with regards to teaching and learning materials. What the students seem to be calling for in these responses is a *balance* in what they are asked to read and to write about. The students appeared to see some kind of value in all the materials they used in the course. These are extremely interesting results when contrasted with what orthodox EAP pedagogy and most EAP writing textbooks advocate: a concentration on non-literary, 'academic' texts that link students concretely with academic reading and writing practices in the university setting. As students move from course to course over their years of undergraduate study, what they are asked to read and write may well vary considerably, particularly since they may be required to take a variety of courses outside their chosen discipline or major. Hence, exposure to the balance of texts and writing assignments that the students in this study seemed to prefer, may be the most appropriate approach in undergraduate EAP writing courses.

When they read a variety of text types, students are exposed to an assortment of rhetorical styles and are provided ample opportunities for the kind of interactive reading approach generally supported in reading-related research and pedagogy. Based on what the students in this study indicated, there is value in such exposure. Providing an array of reading experiences through both literary and non-literary text types will enable students to gain additional practice in using different reading strategies and create more opportunities for EAP teachers to discuss a host of such strategies. At the same time, writing about both literary and non-literary texts opens students up to writing in a variety of repertoires.

Regarding this chapter's primary interest – the question of how to incorporate reading into EAP writing courses meaningfully – the approach emerging from this study is one that says reading can be included effectively in such courses when it occurs through employing different text types that not only activate students' interest in reading, but also satisfy their desire for academic experiences in reading and writing. A movement among text types, essentially along the lines of a 'scale of specificity' that Widdowson speaks of, might make reading an effective source of both reading and writing activity. Perhaps students can begin at one end of this scale of specificity – the broad end, involving literary texts and writing in response to them – and move toward the narrow end, where they focus on non-literary texts and write papers that use the texts in ways other than response. In such an EAP setting, students can experience something of the array of reading and writing experiences, or academic literacies, they will encounter in their entire undergraduate curriculum.

The results of this study suggest, then, that there is room for a variety of text types and writing experiences in EAP writing courses, and that reading can be made a meaningful part of such courses within this kind of broader framework. Perhaps the best way to incorporate reading into EAP writing courses is by using various kinds of texts as source texts that students can respond to in a variety of writing formats.

Conclusion

This study explored a setting in which students read and wrote about both literary and non-literary texts and reported their responses to these texts and assignments. Their responses indicate that they found value, albeit of different kinds, in both the literary and non-literary texts. However, it must be pointed out that this study was relatively small in scale, and no firm conclusions or recommendations can be made on the basis of such a limited sample of students. On the other hand, the results do add to our emerging knowledge of how EAP students feel about different kinds of reading and writing situations. It would be interesting and valuable now to explore other EAP settings in which students read and write about both literary and non-literary texts so that we can better understand which kinds of texts we should use in EAP writing instruction and how we can enrich the reading dimension of such courses through our choice of texts and of writing assignments in response to them.

22 The development of EAP oral discussion ability

Peter Robinson, Gregory Strong, Jennifer Whittle and Shuichi Nobe

Introduction

Findings from research into effects of EAP instruction undertaken in one programme cannot be automatically assumed to generalise to others, given the powerful influence of learner variables such as cultural background and L1, and institutional constraints such as programme goals and resources, on the development of communicative L2 ability. At the least, research into the effectiveness of EAP instruction can serve as one component of an individual programme evaluation. This was the primary aim of the research we report on in this chapter. However, research findings may also prompt teachers and administrators in comparable EAP settings to ask similar questions, and embark on similar projects – one consequence we hope will follow from the research reported here.

We begin this chapter by summarising findings from previous EAP needs analyses that have focused on speaking requirements of university level students in a variety of settings. We then identify component skills contributing to a particular academic speaking task that emerges as important from this survey – small group discussion – relating these skills, where possible, to findings from SLA research. These include conversational management skills such as turntaking, as well as paralinguistic skills such as appropriate use of eye contact, gaze direction and gesture, all of which need to be integrated in successful performance of EAP discussion tasks. Following this we describe two dominant approaches to EAP course design, skill- and task-based approaches, and report the results of a one-semester effect of instruction study which operationalised skill and task-based approaches to developing EAP discussion ability in a Japanese university. Finally, we discuss our findings, drawing conclusions about which approach is best suited to developing discussion ability at our own university, and suggesting issues for future research into the effectiveness of EAP speaking instruction in programmes similar to ours.

Developing EAP speaking skills: needs, research and pedagogy

Compared with research into other skill areas there has been relatively little research into the development of EAP speaking at the university level. Most EAP research has concentrated upon methods for increasing academic literacy, principally writing (e.g. Horowitz, 1986b; Leki and Carson, 1994, 1997) or on methods for improving academic listening (e.g. Flowerdew, 1994a; Mendolsohn and Rubin, 1995). Those researchers who *have* addressed the issue of developing academic speaking have tended to focus on problems of non-native pronunciation and the organisation of classroom presentations by international teaching assistants (e.g. Rounds, 1987; Williams, 1992). However, most needs analyses of ESL students in academic environments have established the importance of holistic, interactive speaking tasks such as small group oral discussion, supporting our decision to focus on this aspect of EAP speaking ability in this chapter.

Ostler (1980) surveyed ESL learners at the undergraduate and graduate levels at one university and found that they felt they lacked the proficiency required for the listening and speaking tasks in their courses. Ostler reports that the ESL students thought note-taking, asking questions and participating in discussions were the most important skills in their academic studies. Johns (1981) surveyed both ESL learners and instructors at one university on the relative importance of academic skills in reading, listening, writing, and speaking. While participants rated the receptive skills of reading and listening as more important than writing and speaking, Johns concluded that more specific and practical activities were needed in all four skills to prepare ESL students for an academic environment. Other evidence suggesting that ESL learners in university environments need to improve their speaking ability comes from a study conducted by Johns and Johns (1977). They cite numerous reasons for the difficulties ESL students experience when participating in academic seminars. These include students' lack of confidence in their ability to express themselves, and in the quality of their ideas, and in their inability to formulate ideas in English and to respond quickly in a discussion.

Additional surveys of ESL learners indicate students are intimidated by formal academic presentations and by both large and small group discussions (Ferris and Tagg, 1996a; Spack, 1994). Mason (1994) found that even students with high TOEFL scores (between 550 and 600) felt that their linguistic resources were inadequate for the academic tasks that they faced at university. The graduate students in this ethnographic study reported that the academic listening/speaking skills in their courses required them to participate in discussion groups and in collaborative class projects. In a larger EAP survey, conducted at four different tertiary institutions in California, Ferris and Tagg (1996b) asked 234 content-area instructors from a number of disciplines about the types of listening and speaking tasks they expected of their college/university students, as well as what university ESL classes could do to help their students with the oral/aural tasks they face. Ferris and Tagg hypothesised that professors would be very concerned with their ESL students' speaking ability, and more specifically with formal presentation skills and class participation skills. As in a previous study (Johns and Johns, 1977), Ferris and Tagg found that academic tasks varied across institutions and academic disciplines. Instructors teaching larger classes, for example, were less likely to require class participation or small group assignments than teachers of smaller classes. They also found that professors required a variety of tasks besides the ability to take notes from lectures. Business professors, for example, were particularly interested in the ESL students' abilities in leading discussions, participating in debates and completing assignments that required communication with native speakers. In general, however, respondents were very concerned with their students' ability to interact with others in the classroom. There were many statements about ESL students' perceived inability or unwillingness to participate in class discussions, or to ask or respond to questions. Ferris and Tagg concluded that EAP teachers should prepare their students for the interactive nature of US classrooms and help them to overcome their discomfort with small-group discussions and group projects.

In a subsequent study, Ferris (1998) analysed data from surveys of ESL students at three different tertiary institutions in California to complement data already gathered from subject-matter instructors in the previous study. The 476 subjects who responded to the questionnaire reported that courses they were taking often required class participation and small-group interaction. Although there was a lack of agreement between the instructors and the learners about the needs of ESL students, as well as the ranking of aural/oral skills, both students and instructors surveyed felt ESL students could benefit from further development of their academic speaking abilities.

While this brief review reveals a clearly perceived need for the development of academic discussion ability among both students and teachers in a variety of EAP settings, there has been little research into its acquisition. Reacting against input-based methodologies for

L2 teaching, SLA researchers have, in recent years, increasingly argued for the importance of output, particularly speaking, as a means of confirming and disconfirming learner hypotheses about L2 syntax and vocabulary use (e.g. Long and Porter, 1985; Swain, 1995). However, such research has overwhelmingly concentrated on the development of sentence-level lexical and grammatical knowledge rather than discourse ability and been concerned with dyadic, transactional tasks (see, e.g. Pica, Kanagy and Falodun, 1993; Yule, 1997) rather than group interaction during discussion and argumentation.

One exception to this has been SLA research into turntaking and ethnic identity. Sato (1982) found that Japanese, Korean and Chinese students took fewer 'self selected' turns in classroom conversation than non-Asian students. Hazel and Ayres (1998) also found that American participants were more likely to self select turns in conversation than Japanese participants who preferred 'other selection', or waiting to be nominated to speak. However, an Asian, non-Asian dichotomy in turntaking behaviour is too simplistic. Duff (1986) found that turntaking in Chinese-Japanese dyads was dominated by Chinese students. This research confirms our own observations of incoming Japanese undergraduates to our English programme. They expect turns to be nominated for them by others in the group and are unwilling to take the floor themselves. This leads to a ritualistic, circular manner of passing on the turn to the next person during a discussion (so each person has equivalent participation rights). Such behaviour is unnatural by Western standards, and will not serve our students well in the cut and thrust of interactive discussion in non-Japanese academic or business contexts, which many of them intend to work or study in on exit from our programme.

Nonverbal aspects of EAP discussion ability: eye contact and gaze direction

In addition to the obvious necessity for appropriate use of phrasal language to perform such functions as agreeing, expressing an opinion, etc., the contribution of nonverbal activity (e.g. eye gaze, facial expressions and hand gestures) to successful participation in academic discussions is also extremely important but has, to date, been almost completely ignored by EAP researchers. Without being aware of it, instructors interacting with international students are often influenced by their use of, and response to, nonverbal cues for oral interaction and participation, and cross-cultural differences in nonverbal behaviour patterns can often lead to misunderstanding or even communication breakdown. One option for EAP pedagogy is to train students to use nonverbal communication skills properly in future intercultural encounters. The issue addressed in the study reported below is whether awareness of nonverbal and verbal aspects of participation in group discussions is best developed through teacher-led explicit instruction in microskills, or through learner-led noticing activities during whole task practice. In what follows, studies of eye contact and gaze direction in particular are reviewed for the contribution they can make to EAP discussion skill development.

An oral academic discussion should be interactive. It is something we do with, not to, our listeners (Adler and Rodman, 1997). Knowledge of the functions of gaze and the factors which influence gaze patterns is indispensable for successful interactive communication. Some functions of gaze are: regulating the flow of the conversation via floor-taking signals, monitoring feedback, influencing audience evaluation and expressing emotions (Knapp and Hall, 1997). People gaze less while talking than while listening (Argyle and Ingham, 1972), but gaze communication is effective as a floor-apportionment signal when the speaker comes to the end of a thought or an idea unit, especially in conversation between strangers (Kendon, 1967; Beattie, 1978a, 1978b). Although speakers can signal listeners to assume the speaking role at these junctures by using gaze, the speaker also uses these glances to obtain feedback, to see how the speaker is being perceived, and to see if the listener will let the speaker maintain the floor (Knapp and Hall, 1997). Speakers can judge listeners' reactions by reading, for instance, their facial expressions. If the listener is gazing at the speaker, it is usually interpreted as a sign of attention to and involvement with what he or she is saying. Of course, monitoring occurs while the speaker maintains the floor, too.

In mainstream Euro-American culture, listeners seem to judge speakers who gaze more as being more positive (e.g. truthful, mature) and judge speakers who gaze less as more negative (e.g. defensive, unconfident) (Beebe, 1974). The same verbal message is regarded more favourably with more gaze than with less gaze (Exline and Eldridge, 1967). Moreover, audiences prefer speakers who glance long and evaluate less favourably those who gaze infrequently and with shorter glances (Kendon and Cook, 1969). Thus, the messages communicated by eyes vary depending on the amount, the duration, and the quality of gaze, and this is very useful when one wants to make a favourable impression in an oral academic setting in English.

In much of the United States, as suggested in the previous paragraph, direct eye contact is believed to reflect honesty and sincerity (DeVito, 1998). However, this does not necessarily apply to other cultural groups. For instance, many Japanese often interpret this as a lack of respect (i.e. rude, threatening and disrespectful) (McDaniel, 1997). The Japanese rarely gaze at the other person's face during interaction, and then only for very short durations (Axtell, 1990). Direct gaze is normally avoided, except for particular situations (e.g. unless a subordinate is reprimanded by a superior) (McDaniel, 1997). Along with such differences in overall gaze patterns across cultures, there are also universal interactive functions of gaze. A particular point of discourse is often emphasised by gazing (Mehrabian and Williams, 1969). Both listeners and speakers have a tendency to avert gaze when they are trying to process difficult or complex ideas. The speaker's fluency also affects gazing patterns. During fluent speech, speakers tend to look at listeners much more than during hesitation (Beattie, 1978a, 1978b).

In summary, eye contact and gaze direction perform many significant functions (e.g. regulating the flow of conversation, monitoring feedback) and becoming aware of L2 rules for this aspect of nonverbal communication contributes significantly to the development of oral discussion skills. The issue we now turn to is how to organise instructional programmes and teaching methodology to best develop awareness of this, and other aspects of discussion ability for our EAP students.

Syllabus design and focus on form in developing EAP discussion ability

Choice of syllabus entails two fundamental pedagogic decisions: what is to be taught, and in what *sequence*. A useful distinction in conceptualising options in syllabus design was made initially by Wilkins (1976; see also Long and Crookes, 1992; Nunan, 1988b; White, 1988) and refers to the learner's role in assimilating the content provided during group instruction and applying it individually to real world language performance and interlanguage development. *Synthetic* syllabi involve a focus on specific elements of the language system, often serially and in a linear sequence, such as grammatical structures, language functions or reading and speaking microskills. The easiest, most learnable, most frequent or most communicatively important (sequencing decisions can be based on each of these ultimately non-complementary criteria, and on others) are presented before their harder, later learned, less frequent, and more communicatively redundant counterparts. These syllabi assume the learner will be able to put together, or synthesise in real world performance, the parts of the language system (structures, functions, skills etc.) that they have been exposed to separately in the class-room.

Articles describing methodologies and materials for teaching EAP usually imply, and occasionally explicitly state, a preference for synthetic syllabi. In some cases the teaching of speaking is repre-sented as a series of exercises in delivering oral presentations. Accompanying these are proposals for (assumed-to-be-complemen-tary) language-focused syllabi which categorise and sequence the phrasal exponents of language 'functions' that typify rhetorical modes, such as statement of thesis, main idea or topic, and general-ising and illustrating (e.g. Mangelsdorf, 1989; Meloni and Thompson, 1980). In other cases the development of academic speaking is conceptualised by the syllabus designer as the teaching of micro or subskills (e.g. Brown, 1995). Balcom and Kozar (1994), for example, describe some of these as: being able to defend points of view, respond to questions, ask for clarification, express a comment, agree or disagree and provide constructive criticism. However, the analysis of communicative activities into component subskills which can be taught and assessed separately has been under attack for some time, particularly in the field of L1 reading instruction and assess-ment. Hambleton and Murphy (1992: 6), for example, comment that: 'the practical activity of becoming a reader is hindered or even prevented by instruction and assessment that focus on discrete skills with the assumption that practice in such skills will somehow combine to create competence in the holistic skill of reading'.

In contrast to synthetic syllabi, *analytic* syllabi do not divide up the language to be presented in classrooms but involve holistic use of language to perform communicative activities. One version of an analytic syllabus is adopted in task-based approaches to language teaching in which pedagogic tasks (not aspects of the language system) are selected as the units of syllabus design and sequenced according to such criteria as increasing complexity and authenticity (see Long, in press; Robinson, 1998a, 1998b; Skehan, 1998). The learner's role in these syllabi is to analyse or attend to aspects of language use and structure as the communicative activities require them to, in line with: (a) their developing interlanguage systems; (b) preferred learning style and aptitude profile; and (c) to the extent that they are motivated to develop to an accuracy level which may not be required by the communicative demands of the task. Additionally, interventionist teacher techniques can be used during or following task performance to draw learners' attention to aspects of task performance that are non-target-like, but are judged to be learnable and remediable (see Doughty and Williams, 1998; Long and Robinson, 1998). For these reasons researchers have argued that analytic approaches to syllabus design, accompanied by focus on form techniques, are more sensitive to SLA processes and learner variables than their synthetic counterparts and do not subvert the overall focus on meaning and communication encouraged during classroom activity.

A study of oral academic discussion skill development

The present study attempts to operationalise a task-based approach to the development of EAP discussion ability in which students performed academic oral discussions, then during or following task participation were encouraged to 'notice' (Robinson, 1995; Schmidt, 1990) aspects of their verbal and nonverbal performance that could be improved. Two groups operationalised this approach – one in which the post task noticing activities were frequent and structured (Group (2), and one in which the activities were less frequent and less structured (Group (1). This latter group approximated experiential learning through exposure and task practice alone while the former group implemented a greater number of interventionist teacher-led noticing activities. We expected learning in both of these groups to be strongly influenced by learners' inductive learning abilities.

We contrasted teaching operationalising this approach with teaching following a more familiar and traditional synthetic EAP syllabus in which students were explicitly taught a series of academic discussion microskills (e.g. being able to use phrases for agreeing and disagreeing, rules for turntaking, etc.) and were encouraged to practise them, largely in isolation from integrative whole task practice (Group (3). In contrast, we expected this group to be influenced by learners' deductive learning abilities.

The students

The analytic or task-based approach and the synthetic approach to syllabus design were compared over one semester at Aoyama Gakuin University (eight classes delivering instructional treatments, and one class each for pre and post-testing). Three classes of 19, 20 and 21 intermediate level students participated in the study. The students were English majors in the first term of their freshman year. This was the first of two years in an integrated language skills programme that combines six hours of weekly instruction in speaking, listening, writing and reading. On exit from the programme students complete the final two years of their undergraduate degree by taking specialist content courses in linguistics, communications and/or literature.

Upon entering the programme, the students take a language placement test and are grouped according to three different levels of ability. The curriculum is organised into themes at each of these levels and students undertake a variety of tasks and activities such as writing journals and essays, reading and reporting on newspaper articles, doing book reports and oral presentations and participating in small group discussions. Needs analysis surveys of the students indicated that they wanted to do much more speaking in class and that they were frustrated because they felt unable to communicate with native speakers. At the same time, their specialist content teachers indicated that the most of the students had little ability to participate in discussions, even in Japanese.

The treatments

In the analytic or task-based approach, students in small groups worked on a weekly cycle of task (whole group oral discussion), and then post-task activities that included self-reflection on their task performance, and/or group discussion of comments they made about their own and each other's performance using taped audio and video recordings of their group discussions. Group 2 performed more of these than Group 1.

In the initial classes a limited number of awareness-raising activities were used by both task-based classes to orient students to the features of turntaking, eye contact, gesture and language use, that they could profitably attend to and comment on throughout the rest of the semester in subsequent post-task noticing activities. These activities involved watching sample videos of EAP discussions illustrating these features, and then doing group exercises on them.

Throughout the rest of the semester, at the beginning of each class, students in the task-based classes were randomly assigned to discussion groups of three or four persons. These groups sat together and watched other groups performing discussions, noted the features of those discussions, and rated each group's performance. Selections from audio and video recordings of their own discussions were later transcribed or analysed by each group and were used to find examples of successful and unsuccessful phrasal or turntaking language, or discussion performance, etc. They compared their observations with those of their classmates. To ensure that both task-based classes used topics of similar interest and difficulty, a discussion text 'Impact Issues' was used. About 45 minutes was spent on discussion activities during each week of the eight-week treatment.

In contrast, students in the class following the synthetic, skill-based syllabus (Group (3) were explicitly taught exponents of language used in discussions for soliciting opinions, expressing agreement, interrupting to make a point, etc. The appropriate expressions were shown to the students and they rehearsed and memorised them on a weekly basis in pairs, applying them to follow up practice activities. There was little opportunity for whole task discussion practice. No video or audio recordings of their own discussion performance were made and analysed. Pedagogy largely involved individual and pairwork. The teacher followed a syllabus that specified which language functions and discussion strategies would be taught each week and adopted a traditional presentation, practice, production methodology (see Willis, 1996, for further discussion and exemplification of the contrast between this and task-based teaching methodology).

The Rating Instruments

The pre-test and post-test consisted of videotaped group discussions of five minutes in length. The pre-test videos were filmed during the first class session, and the post-test videos were filmed at the end of the semester. The individual students in each discussion were scored by three experienced North American native speaker raters (mean length of ESL experience over ten years) who underwent a training session when they practised use of the rating instrument. The rating instrument operationalises many of the verbal and nonverbal components of academic discussion ability described earlier in this chapter. They then spent several hours rating the randomly presented videos, with no knowledge of which were pre-tests and which were post-tests. The three ratings, from one to five on a five-point scale, for each of four categories (turntaking, eye contact and gesture, language use, content) were averaged. Interrater reliability was .76.

Results

The three groups were equivalent in performance on the pre-test. Results of the repeated measures ANOVA (Group x Category x Pre-Post-test) of the rating averages show no significant differences for the factor Group, but significant differences for Category and for Pre-Post-test (p<.01). As can be seen in Figure 1, all groups improved

Discussion scores

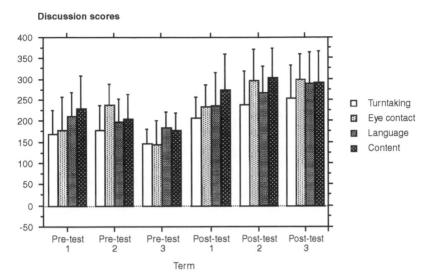

Figure 1 Pre- and post-test discussion scores for groups 1, 2 and 3

from pre to post-test, with higher ratings in the areas of content and language than in turntaking, eye contact and gesture. A priori planned comparisons revealed a significant difference on the post-test between task-based Group 1 and the superior skill-based Group 3. Task-based Group 2 and the skill-based Group 3 were equivalent.

Discussion and conclusion

Both structured task-based teaching, incorporating focus on form activities, and skill-based teaching are equivalent, with skill-based teaching having advantages over the unstructured, experiential, task-based group who were given fewer opportunities to notice, analyse and discuss recordings of their own discussion performance. The success of the skill-based group is possibly due in some part to transfer of training and expectations from prior language learning experience, since the skill-based approach is most similar to our students' previous English learning experience in Japanese high schools where explicit instruction and deductive learning, following a presentation-practice-production methodology, are heavily favoured. Longer term studies of the effects of our different kinds of instruction are needed. Nonetheless, the results suggest that structured focus on form, where teachers provide many activities for directing learner attention to aspects of their task performance that differ from native speaker norms, plus extensive whole task practice is equivalent to carefully targeted and sequenced microskills teaching.

Our findings also suggest that nonverbal aspects of discussion abilities – particularly turntaking – appear to be the least susceptible to instruction over the short term, in all conditions. It is not clear yet whether these aspects are best acquired incidentally, over a longer period, compared to verbal aspects which may benefit more from an explicit intentionally directed focus of learner attention and subsequent rehearsal and memorisation, as they received in the skill-based group. There also may have been cultural factors influencing the rating of turntaking and gesture. As mentioned previously, Hazel and Ayres (1998) found that there was a distinction between the turntaking behaviour of Japanese and American students participating in discussions in small groups of four persons. Of the eight groups videotaped, and then rated, the American students in mixed groups of American and Japanese took significantly more turns than did the Japanese. Consequently, the tendency for Americans to avoid silences may have affected the raters' judgement of the turntaking ability of the students in the present study, or they may have misinterpreted or overlooked examples of culturally based turntaking behaviours. Jungheim (1995), for example, noted differences between 14 native speakers of English and 22 Japanese non-native speakers of English in the interpretation of gestures used to select and nominate turns in English native speaker discussions.

Clearly the use of raters in evaluating speaking performance introduces a source of unreliability into evaluating speaking performance. In testing oral language ability, inter-rater reliability is an important gauge of the validity of a test (Bachman, 1990). The means of achieving greater inter-rater reliability include training raters in assessing test candidates, and using raters of similar background and experience, as was done in this study. However, Douglas and Selinker (1993) note that although raters may even agree on scores, they may do so for different reasons. For these and other reasons (Norris, Brown, Hudson and Yoshioka, 1998; Robinson and Ross, 1996) it has been argued that performance and criterion-referenced tests, in the sense of a yes or no judgement of whether a task outcome was achieved, are the most appropriate means for assessing task-based instruction. However, the nature of the academic discussion task targeted in the present study did not lend itself to such a decision about the success of the performative outcome.

One related practical concern regarding the assessment procedure adopted in this study is to ensure a fair and accurate assessment of the different groups, made more difficult in this case by the use of videotaping for pre- and post-test assessments. There must be careful consideration of such details as stationary cameras and microphones, camera distance from the student groups, the placement of students so that their faces and upper bodies are entirely visible in order to assess eye contact and gesture, and where to situate groups in the room so that natural light from windows does not affect the filming. Discussion lengths, preparation time and the use of notes while speaking, must also be uniform between groups. In the latter case, students referring to notes will speak more confidently, but use less eye contact and gesture. The use of notes must therefore be controlled for in pre- and post-test video recordings.

In conclusion, while focus on form research has begun to show positive results for improvement in structural aspects of language use at the lexical and grammatical level, its effect on pragmatic and discourse level phenomena has so far been little examined. However, these are extremely important to the development of EAP speaking and other abilities. Research into developing effective pedagogic focus on form techniques for the manipulation of learner attention to these aspects of language development while maintaining an overall communicative task focus, we think, promises much in the long run for EAP pedagogy and the development of oral academic task ability. However, determining appropriate techniques for delivering focus on form in this domain is not unproblematic. In our study, the task-based group who were provided with most structured opportunities to analyse and compare their own discussion performance performed better than the group who simply practised the task with few structured noticing activities. The incidental learning of discussion skills by learners in this latter group was significantly less effective than the explicit learning of skills encouraged during the skill-based treatment – a similar finding to those obtained in more controlled laboratory settings (e.g. DeKeyser, 1995; Robinson, 1997) for acquisition of second language grammatical knowledge. The generalisability of findings from these laboratory studies, and our own classroom study, must continue to be demonstrated and cannot yet be assumed, but we see in the combination of these two modes of research the prospect of establishing an empirical basis for decisions about the optimum learning conditions for EAP students as well as for students in other language learning programmes.

23 Second language lecture comprehension research in naturalistic controlled conditions

Steve Tauroza

In the last twenty years, a large number of research studies have attempted to collect data on second language (L2) lecture comprehension in controlled conditions (see Chaudron, 1983; Chaudron and Richards, 1986; Chaudron, Loschy and Cook, 1994; Chiang and Dunkel, 1992; Dunkel, 1988a, 1988b; Dunkel, Mishra and Berliner, 1989; Dunkel and Davis, 1994; English, 1986; Flowerdew and Tauroza, 1995; Hansen and Jansen, 1994; Olsen and Huckin, 1990; Rost, 1994; Tauroza and Allison, 1994). In these studies, however, the subjects were given a lecture-like experience rather than observed while in a normal lecture. Tauroza (1998) analysed the studies to determine the extent that the lecture experience in the studies matches the way that students experience authentic lectures. From this review, it was apparent that many of the earlier studies were of questionable validity because the lecture experience presented to the subjects was clearly different from the way in which most students experience authentic lectures.

In this chapter, techniques for simulating authentic lectures in controlled conditions will be described. Following this, a recent research study that uses these techniques will be reported. This study will show that data can be collected in conditions that are both controlled and completely naturalistic. However, before moving on to these issues, it is pertinent to consider the following questions regarding the value of conducting research in controlled conditions: *Given the problems relating to validity, why not simply forget about using controlled conditions in L2 lecture comprehension research? Would it not be better to take an ethnographic approach and observe what students do in actual lectures as, for example, Benson (1988) did? Why not rely on students reporting their experiences of actual lectures as Flowerdew and Miller (1992) did?*

Literature review

Limitations of the ethnographic approach in L2 lecture comprehension

Ethnographic studies typically use techniques that do not interfere with the event or experience that is under investigation. With regard to research on lecture comprehension, studies taking an ethnographic approach usually rely on students' notes and/or self reports in order to arrive at what the students have understood (see Benson, 1988; Clerehan, 1995; and Flowerdew and Miller, 1992). However, there is not a clear relationship between student notes and comprehension (see Chaudron, Loschy and Cook, 1994 and Dunkel, 1988a for overviews of this issue). For instance, students do not note down everything they comprehend. Typically, they omit information that seems irrelevant, obvious and/or easy to recall. In addition, as comprehension and note-taking in lectures are real time activities, students are limited in what they can note down by time restraints. Due to lack of time, students may omit to note something that they have comprehended even though they regard it as relevant. Therefore, lecture notes inevitably provide an incomplete indication of what the note-taker has comprehended.

This incompleteness makes it difficult to interpret data, particularly in studies that investigate the effects of specific linguistic features on comprehension. For instance, in a study of students' comprehension of phrases containing the contracted negative particle, it would be difficult to assign a specific explanation for omissions concerning phrases containing negative particles because the omissions may have been due to: (a) the students misunderstanding the phrases containing the negative particle (b) the students judging the contents of the phrases insufficiently important to merit recording, or (c) the students having insufficient time to note down the information. It would be possible to interview students afterwards about the reason why they omitted mentioning the phrase but students would probably find it difficult to recollect clearly why they had omitted mentioning one brief phrase in a lecture excerpt lasting twenty minutes or more.

There are also limitations to the value of using self-report of degree of comprehension as subjects are prone to overestimate how much they have comprehended. Regarding self-report of factors that cause comprehension problems, such reports provide us with valuable insights into what listeners perceive as a source of difficulty.

However, listeners' perceptions can be distorted or totally erroneous. For instance, Flowerdew and Miller (1992) have shown that L2 learners consider fast speech a major cause of comprehension problems they encounter in lectures. However, a growing body of research indicates that this perception is probably an illusion on the part of listeners. Studies by Anderson-Hsieh and Koelher (1988), Cheung (1994) and Dahl (1981) show that learners perceive speech as relatively fast when other factors unconnected with speed make the message difficult to comprehend. Therefore, although studies that use subjective reports are useful because they give us information about listeners' beliefs, there remains the need for further investigations to assess the relationship between belief and reality.

It is clear from the above that using an ethnographic approach to investigate the effects of specific linguistic features on lecture comprehension has difficulties. This is not to say that an ethnographic approach is always impractical or of little value. The approach is very useful for a variety of types of studies, for instance, those focusing on broader issues such as Clerehan's (1995) study of differences between L1 and L2 students note-taking practices, or McKnight's (1994) investigation of the relationship between lecture course notes and student performance in end-of-year examinations. As noted above, studies using self-report, as in Flowerdew and Miller (1992), are very useful for what they reveal about students' beliefs and perceptions. However, studies featuring controlled conditions are preferable for investigating the effects of specific factors on L2 lecture comprehension because they allow a focus on the factor under investigation and produce generalisable findings.

In the following section, research studies on L2 lecture comprehension are reviewed in order to identify key factors that L2 lecture comprehension researchers should incorporate in their methodology in order to collect data in a naturalistic manner in controlled conditions.

Studies on L2 lecture comprehension in controlled conditions

Since the early 1980s, most studies on L2 lecture comprehension have focused on one of two areas; either note-taking (Dunkel, 1988a, 1988b; Dunkel, Mishra and Berliner, 1989; Chaudron, Loschy and Cook, 1994) or discourse markers and organisation (Chaudron and Richards, 1986; Olsen and Huckin, 1990; Dunkel and Davis, 1994; Flowerdew and Tauroza, 1995; Tauroza and Allison, 1994). Other issues have been studied sporadically, such as: kinesics (English,

1986), the effects of speech modification/simplification (Chaudron, 1983; Chiang and Dunkel, 1992), the effects of prior knowledge and language proficiency (Chiang and Dunkel, 1992), the testing of L2 lecture comprehension (Hansen and Jansen, 1994) and research methodology (Rost, 1994).

However, there were serious problems in the research methodology of many earlier studies. They claim to focus on L2 lecture comprehension and yet they tested their subjects in conditions that bore little resemblance to normal lecture conditions. This is clear when we consider fundamental characteristics of the lecture experience and consider the mismatch between these characteristics and the lecture experience the subjects were given in some of the above studies.

Fundamental characteristics of lectures

When students attend lectures in Anglophone universities today, they typically undergo the following experiences:

1. They are required to combine information coming from both visual and aural sources

Surveys in the UK (King, 1994) and Australia (Isaacs, 1994) indicate that lecturers normally present a mass of information visually during lectures. In 14 engineering lectures in an English university, King (1994) found that 206 slides and 56 transparencies were used (over 18 per lecture on average) in addition to handouts and blackboard notes. Isaacs (1994) surveyed the lecture techniques of 64 academics in a large Australian university. Of his sample, 94% reported that they either always or often used a blackboard and/or overhead projector in their lectures. In addition to using the blackboard and overhead projector, Isaacs' respondents also made use of hand-outs, slide projectors and the whiteboard.

2. Students usually hear a lecture presented in 'conversational style' (see Dudley-Evans and Johns, 1981) rather than listen to a lecturer reading aloud from notes

Although no recent formal survey has been conducted on the style of presentation preferred by lecturers, Flowerdew and Tauroza (1995: 441), commenting on Dudley-Evans and Johns's (1981) distinction between the 'reading' and the 'conversational style' of lecture presentation, observed 'the literature is fairly clear-cut in seeing the conversational style as by far the most common, especially where

second language listeners are concerned'. The 'literature' they referred to includes various contributors in Flowerdew (1994a) as well
as DeCarrico and Nattinger (1988).

3. In lectures, students are required to process stretches of discourse lasting 15 minutes or longer

In a corpus of 31 lectures delivered by 22 lecturers in Hong Kong (see
Tauroza, 1994), none of the lecture monologues were interrupted by
interactive exchanges (questions/requests for clarification) more frequently than once every 15 minutes.

These characteristics are important for research on L2 lecture
comprehension as there is evidence that (1) visual aids assist comprehension (Mueller, 1980; Ruhe, 1996) (2) L2 learners process oral and
written texts in different ways (Lund, 1991), and (3) the ability to
concentrate (focus attention) varies over time (Buzan, 1995); as
attention is a factor in comprehension, we can assume that the
amount of time listeners are required to attend will affect their levels
of comprehension.

It is clear that researchers of the lecture comprehension process
should ensure that their subjects receive visual as well as aural
information, have the lecture presented in conversational style and
listen to a stretch of discourse that is at least 15 minutes long. In
Table 1, we can see the extent that the lecture experience in 14 recent
studies of L2 lecture comprehension matches the way that students
experience authentic lectures.

The simulations of the lecture experience used in the first six
studies listed in Table 1, from Chaudron (1983) to Dunkel and Davis
(1994), did not match the basic characteristics of real life lecture
comprehension. The subjects heard the listening passages as though
they were blind, listened to written text read aloud, and did not hear
any uninterrupted passage that lasted more than ten minutes. Therefore, although the studies provide information about what L2
listeners comprehend in specific circumstances, the extent that the
findings are relevant to the lecture comprehension process is
doubtful.

The studies listed in the middle of Table 1, English (1986), Hansen
and Jensen (1994), and Rost (1994), provided subjects with some of
the basic characteristics of real life lectures but not all. Therefore,
there are doubts about the validity of the methodology used in these
studies. (Rost, 1994: 111–112) highlights such doubts when discussing the validity of his study). The final five studies listed in Table
1 provided subjects with a lecture-like experience that featured all of

Table 1. *Basic features of typical lectures versus the lecture experience in L2 research*

	Visual input	Unscripted	Length
Chaudron, 1983	N	N	< 1.5
Chaudron and Richards, 1986	N	N	1.5
Dunkel, 1988a	N	Y/N*	1.5–3
Chiang and Dunkel, 1992	N	N	7–9
Chaudron, Loschy and Cook, 1994	N	N	6–7
Dunkel and Davis, 1994	N	N?	7–10
English, 1986	Y	Y	8–12
Hansen and Jensen, 1994	N	Y	3–5
Rost, 1994	Y	Y?	2–4
Dunkel, 1988b	Y	Y?	23
Dunkel, Mishra and Berliner, 1989	Y	Y?	23
Olsen and Huckin, 1990	Y	Y	16
Tauroza and Allison, 1994	Y	Y	16
Flowerdew and Tauroza, 1995	Y	Y	24–26

Key
1. Visual input Y = Listeners heard the passage and saw the speaker/visual aids.
2. Unscripted   Y = Lecture delivered in conversational style with features of normal speech (fillers, hesitations, false starts). A question mark indicates that the author/s did not specifically state whether the lecture was read from a script or not. In such cases, I have indicated the likely category based on whether the features of normal speech were present or absent in the transcript of the lecture.
3. Length   Duration of lecture in minutes (where more than one passage was used the maximum and minimum times are given).
* = The study investigated the effects of styles of delivery (conversational versus reading aloud). Hence, one passage was scripted and the other was not.
? = The authors of these studies did not explicitly state whether the lecture was scripted or not. The tentative categorisation is based on an analysis of the lecture transcripts. If normal features of speech such as nonverbal fillers and/or false starts appeared in the transcript, it was classed as probably being unscripted. If no such features appeared in the transcript, it was classed as probably scripted.

the basic characteristics of real lectures, and the results of such studies can be interpreted with fewer doubts about research validity.

To illustrate how data can be collected on L2 lecture comprehension in conditions that are both controlled and naturalistic, a recently completed research study will be described. The study focuses on the effects of prompting learners to predict prior to the presentation of lecture materials. The materials had routinely featured as lecture input on courses at the institute where the subjects studied. The lecture comprehension experience of the subjects matched the characteristics of real lectures.

Prediction and the comprehension of academic presentations

During the last decade, the teaching of listening strategies has been recommended for helping learners deal with listening problems and as a means of developing their LC abilities in general (see O'Malley, Chamot and Küpper, 1989; Rost, 1990, 1997). Although researchers have identified types of strategies that are used more frequently by successful listeners than unsuccessful listeners (see O'Malley, Chamot and Küpper, 1989), little evidence demonstrates that teaching L2 learners strategies enhances comprehension. Therefore, it was decided to investigate whether having L2 learners use a strategy prior to listening to lecture materials would aid their comprehension.

The strategy selected for investigation involved listeners making predictions regarding the contents of lectures. This strategy was chosen because it has long been regarded as a key strategy in successful listening, for example, Brown claimed: 'The most important work that a listener can do . . . is to predict what a speaker is likely to be going on to say.' (1978: 278).

Brown assumed that such predictions would provide the listener with a framework of ideas that the incoming information could be checked against so that 'the text becomes a sampling exercise for the student where he has to listen to see if what he predicted in fact does occur'.

This strategy is a way of encouraging listeners to activate relevant schemata regarding the subject matter before listening. Brown (1978) emphasised the importance of this function of prediction when she stated 'What is crucial is the stimulating of [the listener's] own relevant experience.'

Findings by Tudor and Tuffs (1991) lend support to this view. They concluded that such activity aided comprehension, particularly the activation of text relevant schemata.

Vogely (1995) points out that teachers need to know **how** to induce learners to listen strategically as well as **what** strategies should be taught. As there are various techniques to encourage students to predict, it was decided to see if the two following techniques led to better comprehension:

1 Students receive a lecture title and spend a few minutes thinking about (predicting) the possible issues that would be covered in the lecture prior to listening to it.

2 Students receive an indication of the specific points in a lecture and spend a few minutes predicting what would probably be said about the points.[1]

Both techniques appear to be efficient and practical ways of letting students activate relevant schemata prior to listening and enhance their comprehension. However, there appears to be no empirical data in support of the effectiveness of either technique. Therefore, the following methods were used to investigate whether teaching students the techniques improved comprehension and also whether one of the techniques for prompting predictions was superior; that is, whether students' comprehension was better following general predictions based on the lecture title as opposed to predictions regarding specific points in the lecture.

Methodology

Subjects

The subjects were first year undergraduate students at the City University of Hong Kong. They were majoring in either English for Professional Communication or Teaching English as a Second Language. They were all L1 Cantonese speakers with proficiency ranging from 530–575 TOEFL. The subjects were required to take a course aimed at enhancing their ability to comprehend lectures and films. During this course the investigation of the effects of predicting prior to listening to lecture materials took place.

Materials

The input materials were video excerpts on topics related to their study and had featured in lectures for first-year students in previous years. The excerpts were between 17 and 25 minutes long. The topics dealt with were:

---

[1] The information regarding the comparative benefits of the two types of prediction is of value because if it is found that predictions based on the specific points in the lecture outline lead to greater comprehension than general predictions based on the lecture title, lecturers could be informed of this finding and encouraged to provide their L2 students with lecture outlines and time to go over them before the lecture.

Session 1: 'Humans as information processors', which examined how people react to information overload, a 17-minute excerpt from a lecture given in an introductory course on information systems.

Session 2: 'Before Babel', which looked at evidence for the existence of a common origin for the world's languages, a 22-minute excerpt from a BBC programme *Horizon*.

Session 3: 'An English-speaking world', which gave an overview of the roles and functions of English as an international language, a 25-minute excerpt from a BBC programme *The Story of English*.

The videos were displayed on a screen so all subjects could see them clearly. To assess the subjects' comprehension in each session, they received questions to which they provided short answers in note form while watching. The questions focused on key information in the lecture. (Examples of questions in Sessions 1 and 2 are in Appendices A and B.) There were questions regarding 17 items of information in Session 1 and 14 items per session in Sessions 2 and 3.

Procedure

The subjects were divided into two groups matched for proficiency. Subjects who could not be matched were excluded from data analysis. There were 30 matched subjects in each group for Sessions 1 and 2 and 25 for Session 3. The groups will be referred to as A and B.

All the subjects watched the input in three different sessions at fortnightly intervals, one topic each week. The activities of each group in the sessions are summarised in Table 2.

In the first session, on 'Humans as information processors', Group A were given the lecture title and questions on the contents of the lecture and prompted to make specific predictions prior to listening (see Appendix A for the hand-out that the subjects received). Group B received the lecture title and questions but were not prompted to do anything prior to listening.

In the second session, about whether the world's languages sprang from one common source, Group B received the following, which included prompts to encourage them to predict the themes that would be covered in the lecture (marked in bold on the sheet):

Table 2. *Group activities*

	Group A	Group B
Session 1:	Predicted specific points based on questions	Not prompted to do anything
Session 2:	Not prompted to do anything	Predicted themes from title
Session 3:	Predicted specific points based on questions	Predicted themes from title

Extensive listening: academic listening

Before Babel

- You will watch a video about the findings of research involving comparative and historical linguistics. The video is called 'Before Babel'.
- The Babel legend is found in the Bible. According to the legend, there was a time when all the people of the world spoke the same language. In this period, the people who lived near the town of Babel decided to build a tower so high that it would go up to heaven. God became very angry at this and, to defeat their plans, he made them speak different languages so that the builders working on the tower could not understand each other. Therefore, they could not co-operate and work on the tower stopped.

From what you know about the subject area (comparative and historical linguistics), the title of the video and the legend of the tower of Babel, what do you think the video will be about?

Note your ideas below regarding the general theme. Also note down any particular points that you feel may be mentioned.

The subjects had five minutes to reflect on the possible themes and make notes. They then received a sheet containing the questions they had to respond to (see Appendix B). At the same time as Group B received the questions, Group A received the questions as well as the information given five minutes earlier to Group B; that is, the information shown above minus the text marked in bold. Both groups were allowed two minutes to read through the questions before watching the lecture.

In the final session, on 'An English-speaking world', Group A received the questions and were prompted to predict their answers in a similar way as in Session 1. Group B received the lecture title and were prompted to make predictions about the themes in a similar

Table 3. *Results*

Session 1: Predictions based on specific points
(N = 30 per group; maximum score possible: 17)

	Mean	SD
Predictions (specific):	11.7	1.66
No predictions:	11.5	1.68

The difference between the scores of the groups was not statistically significant ($t = 0.46$; p < .645).

Session 2: Predictions based on lecture title
(N = 30 per group; maximum score possible: 14)

	Mean	SD
Predictions (title):	5.2	2.36
No predictions:	6.2	2.09

The difference between the scores of the groups was not statistically significant ($t = 1.68$; p < .098).

Session 3: Predictions based on lecture title versus specific points
(N = 25 per group; maximum score possible: 14)

	Mean	SD
Predictions (title):	7.6	2.32
Predictions (specific):	8.9	1.92

The difference between the scores of the groups was statistically significant ($t = 2.19$; p < .034).

way as in Session 2. Both groups were allowed five minutes for this. Group B then received the questions and were allowed two minutes to read them before watching the lecture.

Results

Mean scores and standard deviations for the groups in each session are reported in Table 3 along with the results of statistical analysis of the scores using t-tests (bi-directional) for independent samples.

Discussion

The results show that when subjects predict about specific points in a lecture they comprehend more than when their predictions are based on the general topic. However, neither strategy is of more benefit than allowing students to use their own listening approaches.

Regarding what students did when not required to make predictions, it was observed that around 80% of the subjects underlined key words in the questions. Subsequent questioning revealed that only around 10% of them had been encouraged by their teachers to do this. Apparently, the majority of the students had spontaneously developed a listen-for-key-word strategy. Presumably, they use the strategy whenever they are given lecture outlines or questions on key points prior to a lecture. Given that the students use the strategy on their own initiative, it is clear that they consider focusing on key words to be of benefit. The results indicate that allowing students to listen for key words is as good as having students predict lecture contents based on specific points.[2]

Before reviewing the aspects of the study that make it a good example of a quasi-experimental investigation conducted in naturalistic controlled conditions, we will consider why the predictions regarding the specific points were of more use to the subjects than the predictions regarding general themes. The predictions regarding the specific points were based on the questions regarding key points of information in the lecture (these questions performed a similar function as outline lecture notes), whereas the predictions regarding general themes were based on the lecture title. The questions provided the subjects with greater information about the lecture contents than the lecture title. Although both groups eventually received the questions, the subjects who made predictions about specific points had much more time to reflect on the questions and digest their implications than the other subjects. Therefore, in the same way as students would have more prior knowledge about a lecture when they receive outline notes as opposed to just the lecture title, the students making predictions regarding the specific points had probably assimilated a greater degree of information about the lecture contents than the students making predictions based on the lecture title; the latter had only sufficient time to read through the questions before the lecture, whereas the former had this time plus time to reflect on the questions and their likely answers. Although there is some controversy over the role of prior knowledge as an aid to L2 listening comprehension,[3] the additional time to reflect on the prior information is the most likely reason why the predictions based on specific points were more helpful than the predictions based on

---

[2] The initial analysis of a follow-up experiment indicates that this remains true even when students have practised the specific-point prediction technique for three months.

[3] The findings of Markham and Latham (1987) and Long (1991) indicate that prior knowledge aids comprehension, whereas Jensen and Hansen (1995) found only a trivial effect for prior knowledge.

the lecture title. This conjecture is supported by Chiang and Dunkel's (1992) finding that prior knowledge improves scores on listening comprehension tests when it relates directly to the information required by the questions.

Final comments: creating naturalistic controlled conditions in research on L2 lecture comprehension

Recently there have been a number of articles emphasising the value of using either authentic materials or more naturalistic materials in courses that aim to develop L2 academic listening comprehension (see Flowerdew and Miller, 1997; Mendelsohn, 1998; and Raphan, 1996). This chapter has sought to highlight a similar value in having naturalistic conditions when studying L2 lecture comprehension. In the first part of this chapter, it was shown that L2 lecture comprehension researchers who wish to collect data in a relatively naturalistic manner while using controlled conditions should ensure that:

1 Their subjects can see the speaker clearly as well as any visual aids.
2 The lecture is delivered in a conversational style rather than read from a script.
3 The lecture discourse should be longer than 15 minutes; showing lectures in their entirety is optimal.

The study reported above incorporated those features. Regarding Point 1, care was taken to ensure that the video was projected on a large screen. Furthermore, the task that the subjects completed while viewing, taking brief notes in response to questions regarding the key points of information, was designed so that it was not dissimilar from the note-taking that students might do when given outline notes. This allowed the students to view the visual component naturalistically. Other tasks designed to assess comprehension, such as filling in blanks on lecture transcripts, would interfere with this as it would require subjects to follow the printed text while they listened rather than looking at the lecturer.

Finally, the study sought to incorporate features that might affect how students attend to lectures, for example the topics of the lecture excerpts were all relevant to the subjects' degree programmes.

Research methodologies incorporating the above features will reduce the size of the gap between L2 lecture comprehension research that uses an ethnographic approach and studies that collect data in controlled conditions. This will lead to fewer doubts about the validity of studies that use controlled conditions to collect data.

Appendix A

Hand-out (with the first five questions) given to Group A in Session 1 on 'Humans as Information Processors' (Group B were given the lecture title and the questions but not the text shown in italics below).

Name .... Student No. ....

Humans as Information Processors

You will watch a 17-minute video of the beginning of a lecture on 'Humans as Information Processors'. *Before you hear the lecture, you will have 5 minutes to read through the attached questions. As you read each question, note down on this sheet of paper what you think may be the answer. Obviously, you will only be guessing regarding many of the questions. When you listen to the lecture, note down your answers on the sheet with the questions on it.*

1.

2.

3.

4.

A.

B.

C.

5.

1. What is the primary objective of an information system?

2. What is the most significant difference between a computerised system and an information system?

3. What can a study of humans as information processors help us to do?

4. The lecturer says that humans have five sensory receptors. List three of them:

A.

B.

C.

5. What is the 'major processor' in humans?

Appendix B

Questions given to all subjects in Session 2 on the 'Before Babel' video.
'BEFORE BABEL'

1. How many languages are there around the world?

2. One linguist, Merritt Ruhlen, uses a tree as a metaphor. In the metaphor, what do the following parts of the tree represent:
   a) the branches
   b) the leaves

3. What did Sir William Jones discover?

4. What must you find in order to say that different languages form a family?

5. The narrator says that the Indo-European family of languages stretches between two countries. What are the two countries?
   a)
   b)

6. In the process of language change, what parts of speech (speech sounds) change most rapidly?

7. According to Professor Labov, what do these changes lead to?

8. Traditionally, how have linguists worked when comparing languages?

9. How has Professor Joseph Greenberg's technique differed from the traditional/classical approach?

10. Which are the elements (the categories) of a language that are most stable over time? (List out of 3)
    a.
    b.

11. What did Greenberg's technique reveal?
    Spelling of proper names used in the video:
    Sanskrit (an Indian language)
    Nigeria (a country in West Africa)

24 Designing tasks for developing study competence and study skills in English

Alan Waters and Mary Waters

Any consideration of how to design appropriate activities for helping students to study successfully in English has to be based on an understanding of two fundamental factors, namely, (i) what effective study involves, and, (ii) what an effective approach to learning to study entails – conceptions, in other words, of the underlying 'what' and 'how', respectively, of this area of the design of activities. Obviously, numerous other factors also play an important role in the design process, such as sequencing, variety, feasibility, level and so on, but ultimately, everything depends on whether the materials have validity in terms of the underlying view of studying and learning to study on which they are based. Unless these concepts are sound and appropriate ones, the materials, however technically well-developed, will simply be misdirected.

In what follows, therefore, we will first of all briefly consider the main 'messages' of research about the nature of effective study. We will then present a rationale for an approach to helping students master such study processes. The remainder will focus on how these concepts can be taken into account in an overall framework for the design of study development activities.

The nature of effective study

There is general agreement in the EAP research literature (see, e.g., Dunkel, 1988b; Johns, 1981; Braine, 1989, etc.) that effective study involves the successful use of techniques such as how to take notes, skim and scan, construct a bibliography and so on – in other words, a command of what are commonly referred to as study 'skills'. However, a significant number of other research studies, both from outside as well as within EAP, show that there is also an additional – and more fundamental – dimension to effective study. Just as research into the learning process has led us to distinguish, on the one hand, between the visible or tangible level of learning – the psycho-motor domain – and, on the other, the covert, underlying level, made up of the cognitive, affective and other domains, the study process also needs to be seen in terms of its deeper (and, as will be argued, more fundamental) features, as well as its more 'surface' or study 'skills' aspects.

For example, Marton (1975), in a well-known and influential investigation, compared the study patterns of successful and less successful university students in terms of two main information-processing strategies. These were, on the one hand, the 'deep' approach, involving an active focus on determining 'what the discourse was about', 'learning through the discourse' and so on, and on the other, the more passive 'surface' approach, concerned with 'the discourse itself', 'learning the discourse' and the like. Students who used the former strategy were significantly more successful in terms of learning outcomes, both qualitatively and quantitatively, than those using the latter.

Perry (1975), in an enquiry into how students progress in their study patterns over the course of their degree programme, showed that students experiencing learning difficulties in the earlier years of the studies did so primarily because of their 'absolutist' attitude to knowledge, i.e., they tended to view it in an 'either-or', 'black-and-white' way. Studying was seen as mainly to do with the accretion of factual knowledge. However, students who experienced greater success in the later years of their studies did so as a result of having developed a much more 'relativistic' attitude to knowledge. From this perspective, information was seen as a 'moving target', a provisional construct, in need of constant reinterpretation.

Gibbs (1985) refers to a number of investigations (e.g. Fransson, 1977; Entwistle and Wilson, 1977; Biggs, 1976; Perry, 1977, etc.) into the relationship between level of confidence and approaches to study. All of these studies showed that when student confidence was low, this increased the tendency for 'surface' information-processing strategies to be used. In other words, cognitive processing abilities are not enough on their own: the right kind of 'emotional intelligence' (Goleman, 1996) is also needed for successful study.

Similar evidence has been produced by studies conducted within the field of EAP. For example, Olsen and Huckin (1990), in their research into academic lecture comprehension, found that failures in their subjects' understanding appeared to be because of the use of an 'information-driven' listening strategy (i.e., one that simply strives to absorb facts), rather than a 'point-driven' one (i.e., whereby the listener is actively involved in attempting to impose an overall framework of meaning on the data).

Benson (1991), in an investigation of a post-graduate student's approach to academic reading, concluded that effective academic reading demanded not just a process of comprehension but also of learning. In other words, in order to succeed academically, the student must be adept at not only absorbing facts ('learning to read') but gradually linking them to his or her existing framework of knowledge and, ultimately, arriving at a new synthesis of information based on his or her own ideas and those in the readings ('reading to learn').

Hawkey (1982) investigated the way in which cognitive/affective and social factors appeared to affect the 'EAP success' of post-graduate students studying in a variety of UK universities and other institutions. He found that measures of cognitive/affective traits (e.g. 'radicalism', field independence, etc.) and social factors (attitude, motivation, etc.), when combined with language measures, predicted the presence of necessary language ability more strongly than language measures alone. He therefore concludes that:

TL [target language] level is a powerful but not sufficient predictor of C2 [second culture] EAP success . . . My evidence is that selection (and, therefore, assessment) should be on the basis of UK academic awareness as well as TL level. (*ibid*: 443)

Numerous other studies involving similar findings could be adduced. However, it is hoped that these representative examples will be sufficient to show that successful study, in addition to its study skills aspect, also involves an underlying dimension – what may be referred to as study 'competence' (Waters and Waters, 1992), made up of elements such as deep-level information-processing strategies, relativistic attitudes to knowledge status, appropriate emotional balance, an information-driven approach to understanding, the ability to read to learn, 'academic awareness' and so on.

Figure 1 demonstrates how this distinction can be represented. As this diagram indicates, studying can be seen as consisting of two main levels, namely a study skills level and a study competence level.[1] The study *skills* element is made up of individual techniques of study, such as note-taking, skimming/scanning, using a bibliography and so on. The *competence* aspect is a general capacity for study, consisting of attributes of the kind identified in the research studies discussed above such as self-confidence, self-awareness, the ability to think critically and creatively, independence of mind and so on.

---

[1] Although the two levels have been shown separately for the sake of clarity, in reality, of course, the division is less clear-cut.

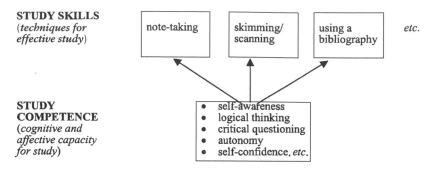

Figure 1. *Study skills and study competence: their relationship in successful study (based on Waters and Waters [ibid.])*

Furthermore, as the arrows in the diagram indicate, the competence level is the foundation on which mastery at the study skills level rests. Thus, for example, being able to ask critical questions is an integral part of study techniques such as revising an essay draft, searching for references, examining statistical data and so on. *It therefore follows that, in activities for helping students to study effectively, the focus needs to be first and foremost on building up the necessary study competence.* A knowledge of the techniques of study is obviously vitally important also, and this therefore needs to be a major focus of study development materials. However, in order to learn how to study successfully, study skills have to be acquired within a framework of study activities that concentrates in the first instance on building up the underlying cognitive and affective capabilities on which effective study is based.

A methodology for learning to study

In the light of this conception of the study process, let us now come to the second of the two main questions with which this paper began, viz: what might constitute an appropriate overall approach to helping students master both study skills and competence of the kind that have been identified?

Clearly, an essential criterion is that the processes of the study learning approach itself should not conflict with those of the approach to study it is attempting to facilitate. Thus, mere 'transmission' of information about the necessary skills and abilities, and mechanical, discrete practice in their use, will be inappropriate. Instead, the learning processes need to be ones which will both try to teach and simultaneously mirror the nature of the approach to study being advocated. The problem-solving task (Bruner, 1975) seems to us to be the best methodological vehicle for this purpose. By posing study problems rather than simply providing ready-made answers right from the start of the learning-to-study process, the basic constituents of effective study become not only the object of the learning but also its means.

This is likely to occur because a problem-posing approach has the potential to:

- *encourage independence of mind*: the learners have the opportunity to develop the habit of thinking for themselves;
- *foster self-awareness*: in the course of trying to solve problems, learners increase their awareness of themselves as students, their existing strengths and weaknesses, what capabilities they already have, what other ones they need to develop further;
- *increase self-evaluation skills*: wrestling with problems creates the necessity and enhances the ability to critically evaluate the quality of possible solutions;
- *build up self-confidence*: problem-solving is the essence of what study involves, and so exposure under 'controlled conditions' to a simulated version of it will make learners more likely to perceive that they will have the ability to eventually cope successfully with the real thing;
- *develop flexibility and adaptability*: instead of one set way of studying, there is scope in problem-solving for learners to develop a range of approaches, suited to their own learning styles and personalities;
- *improve capacity for learning in general*: solving any one problem helps to develop the ability to solve problems of other kinds.

For all these reasons (and, as for the list of attributes of the study process in the previous section, others could be readily adduced), we see the problem-solving task as the 'weapon of choice' when it comes to attempting to develop in the student a practical grasp of what competence-based study involves.

An activities-design framework

These conceptions of the study and learning-to-study processes can be translated into an EAP activities design framework, consisting of three main types of problem-solving task, viz. **Direct Study Competence Tasks**, **Indirect Study Competence Tasks** and **Skills Transference Tasks**.

By **Direct Study Competence Tasks** are meant activities which focus on increasing the student's awareness of and ability to handle aspects of study competence. The realisation of study skills through study competence is addressed only indirectly in tasks of this kind.

In **Indirect Study Competence Tasks,** the surface concern is with developing the student's practical mastery of study skills. However, as an essential part of this process, tasks of this kind are also concerned with helping the student see how the effective use of study skills depends crucially on the development and deployment of the necessary study competence.

Skills Transference Tasks consist of a series of study problems linked together in the form of a life-like study cycle. The students first of all use their knowledge of study competence and skills to try to solve the problems. They then reflect on the process in order to discover what it tells them about their present study level – in terms of both its competence and skills aspects – and what targets for further progress they may need to set.

Sample tasks

In what follows, examples of each of these types of task are presented and discussed.

1. Direct study competence tasks: an example[2]

DOES IT FOLLOW?
Logical thinking is an important skill when dealing with facts.

Task 4.1 Misha and Daniel have been conducting a wide-ranging survey into perceptions of differences between married working men and women in the UK, as part of a Sociology assignment. Here are some of the results they obtained:

	% Men			% Women		
Question	Yes	No	No opinion	Yes	No	No opinion
1. Do you help with the housework?	24	71	5	93	2	5
2. Have you ever been discriminated against in your job because of your sex?	5	87	8	56	20	24

---

[2] This and the remaining examples are taken from Waters and Waters (1995).

3. Are women better than men at looking after children?	82	13	9	78	7	15
4. Are men better than women at studying scientific subjects?	85	11	4	65	27	8
5. Are men better than women at studying non-scientific subjects (languages, etc.)?	67	17	16	56	41	3
6. To what extent have you fulfilled your life's ambitions?	65	31	4	19	73	8
7. Is your wage lower than that paid to a member of the opposite sex doing the same job?	2	88	12	85	13	2

>>> a. Do these statements follow *logically* from the statistics above? Please note that you are not required to question the validity or reliability of the statistics. Rather, your task is to assess whether the conclusions drawn from the statistics are sound or not.
   1. More men should help with housework.
   2. Better legislation is needed against sexual discrimination at work.
   3. Women are generally better than men at looking after children.
   4. Women lack self-confidence in their ability to study.
   5. Women have far fewer satisfying career opportunities than men.
   6. Women should be paid higher wages.
>>> b. With 2 or 3 other students, discuss your answers. Did you find this task easy or difficult? Discuss.

Although the first part of this activity (Task 4.1) involves the student in skimming and scanning tabular information – a type of study skill – the overall focus is, of course, on developing a central aspect of study competence, namely, logical thinking. The students have to decide whether or not the sample conclusions drawn from the statistical data are justified in terms of the reasoning underlying them. However, because of the problem-solving nature of the task, it also involves the development of other aspects of study competence as well. For example, deciding on whether the statements are logical or not requires students to question their knowledge of and therefore clarify their existing level of understanding of the concepts involved in solving the problem, i.e., it increases self-awareness. They also gain experience in applying concepts in order to draw conclusions,

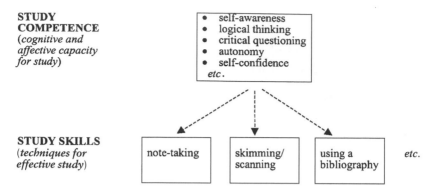

STUDY COMPETENCE *(cognitive and affective capacity for study)*
- self-awareness
- logical thinking
- critical questioning
- autonomy
- self-confidence
etc.

STUDY SKILLS *(techniques for effective study)*   note-taking   skimming/ scanning   using a bibliography   *etc.*

Figure 2. Study skills and study competence: their relationship in learning to study (direct study competence tasks)

making independent judgements about the quality of their answers, and interpreting and clarifying the meaning of the various types of information they have to process – all further, important attributes of a general, well-developed study competence. This process continues in the second main part of the activity (Task 4.1b), where students are involved in the use and development of aspects of study competence such as reflection, discussion, group work and inductive thinking. In this way, the activity as a whole develops students' study competence both in terms of its direct focus and indirectly, through the learning methods being deployed.

The relationship between study skills and study competence in learning to study is embodied by tasks of this kind as shown in Figure 2.

2. Indirect study competence tasks: an example

CHECKING RELIABILITY AND VALIDITY

The findings of research need to be both reliable and valid. This means that they are not biased, do not rely on unclear definitions, and are not pre-determined by the researcher. In other words, if someone else wanted to check the information, they should be able to do the same thing and get the same result.

Reliability refers to whether or not the findings are constant and unchanging – and do not depend on what sample is chosen, who the researcher was, or how the questions are interpreted. In other words, you can rely on the results to describe the population accurately.

Validity refers to whether or not the results describe what they say they describe. In other words, do the methods used affect the results, and what populations can the results realistically be attributed to?

One important way of ensuring reliability and validity is to select a representative sample. There are several other factors to take into account as well.

Task 2.1 Check the language

Often interviews, questionnaires, and records are subject to different interpretations which will bias the results.

A group of EFL students want to find out what a typical English family's eating habits are. They decide that the best way to determine this is to write a multiple-choice questionnaire.

English Eating Habits Questionnaire

1. What do you like to have for breakfast?
   - a. bacon and eggs
   - b. toast with jam
   - c. coffee
   - d. cornflakes
2. What do you usually eat for dinner?
   - a. meat
   - b. chicken
   - c. fish
   - d. eggs
3. How often do you eat potatoes for supper?
   - a. every day
   - b. frequently
   - c. seldom
   - d. never
4. Which food do you think is the best?
   - a. Chinese
   - b. Italian
   - c. English
   - d. French
5. Does your family sit down and eat together?
   - a. yes
   - b. no
   - c. sometimes
   - d. only on Sunday
6. Which of these statements do you agree with?
   - a. British people do not like foreign food.
   - b. British cooking is boring.
   - c. British tea is old-fashioned.
   - d. British people eat too much fried food.
   - e. Convenience food is good for you.

>>> With 2 or 3 other students, use their questionnaire to answer the
following questions:
1. Are there any words that could have more than one meaning?
2. Are any of the questions open to more than one interpretation?
3. Will the answers on the questionnaire bias the responses given to
the questions?
4. What assumptions do the writers of the questionnaire make
about English eating habits?
5. How could this questionnaire be improved to make it more
reliable?

Task 2.2 Making sure the language is reliable

>>> a. With another student, select one of the topics below (or one of your
own if you prefer). Write a short questionnaire to use to find out the
needed information.
1. Attitudes to speaking English
2. Typical family life of the members of the class
3. How to make the best use of the weekend
4. Opinions on women–men equality
5. Attitudes to pets

>>> b. Exchange questionnaires with another pair of students and answer
the questions. With 2 or 3 other students, discuss any problems that
occurred. Do you think the questionnaires would produce reliable
and valid results if they were given to a representative sample? You
may wish to use the check questions in Task 2.1 to help guide the
discussion.

>>> c. With 2 or 3 other students, discuss the advantages of testing the
method of doing the research before conducting it.

In this activity, the main focus is on some of the study skills needed
for conducting basic research, such as assessing the validity and
reliability of research instruments and questionnaire writing.
However, because of the problem-solving nature of the tasks, the
students also have to make use of a number of aspects of the related
underlying study competence in order to develop their knowledge of
these skills. Thus, carrying out Task 2.1 involves critical questioning,
logical thinking and self-confidence in decision-making. Task 2.2
requires the students to put principles into practice, formulate appropriate questions, present and critically evaluate each other's ideas,
make logical deductions and so on. Thus, although the overall
intention is to increase the students' understanding of a number of
research-related study skills, the activity is designed in such a way
that development of these areas is simultaneously linked to getting
the students to deploy (and further develop, in an incidental fashion)
the related aspects of study competence, both as part of the direct

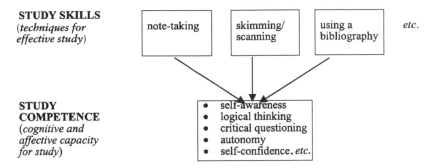

Figure 3. Study skills and study competence: their relationship in learning to study (indirect study competence tasks)

focus of the activity, and indirectly, as a function of its problem-posing structure.

This kind of learning task embodies the type of relationship between study skills and study competence shown in Figure 3.

3. Skills transference tasks: an example[3]

COMMUNICATION AND THE MEDIA

You have enrolled in a course entitled 'Communication and the Media'. Sections of this course are presented in which you are expected to participate as a student of the subject. As well as learning about the relationship between communication and the media, you will be expected to step back and evaluate how well you are applying the study skills you have learned to the tasks in hand.

1 DEFINING *COMMUNICATION* AND *MEDIA*

Dr White is your lecturer in charge of the Communication and Media course. You have just arrived in class, and you have your pencil ready to take notes. She is about to speak.

[TAPE]

Task 1.1 Did you take notes of the aims of the course? Do you feel it important to write down the aims of a course? Discuss this with a partner.

Task 1.2 What did Dr White say the aims of the course were? (If you did not take notes, try to remember what she said.)

---

[3] Please note that the input sections and the final set of tasks in this activity have been omitted because of reasons of space.

With a partner, compare your answers. How did they differ? Are her aims clear? If not, what questions might you wish to ask Dr White?

Task 1.3 How does Dr White define the terms *media* and *communication*? Are these definitions you usually use for these terms? Your teacher will lead a seminar discussion on these issues.

>>> a. With 2 or 3 other students, discuss different kinds of media and methods of communication you are familiar with. Which kinds would you include in your definition of *media* and *communication*? See if your group can agree on clear definitions of both terms.

>>> b. Take part in the seminar.

Task 1.4 With a partner, discuss how well you feel you were able to understand the lecture and participate in the small-group and seminar discussions in Task 1.3. You may wish to consider the following questions:

1. Was I able to follow the main ideas of the lecture?
2. Did I take notes on the main ideas?
3. Was I able to understand the important vocabulary?
4. Did I get lost in the details?
5. Did I listen to and evaluate the logic and underlying messages in addition to surface meanings and words?
6. In the discussion, did I stick to the point?
7. Did I summarise ideas and present my own ideas clearly?
8. Did I listen to other speakers and use their ideas to modify or substantiate my own thinking?
9. Did I use my critical thinking skills, or did I simply accept what was said?

2 THE MEDIUM IS THE MESSAGE

You have been asked to read several articles on the impact of choice of language and media on the message conveyed.

Task 2.1 Read the following articles to help you develop your position regarding the following question:

Does the choice of language or media significantly affect communication? Give reasons and examples to justify your position.

[ARTICLES 1–3]

Task 2.2 With a partner, discuss the position you have taken. How did you use the articles to support your position? What other information influenced your position? What kinds of additional information would have been helpful?

Task 2.3 With 2 or 3 other students, discuss the topic. You may wish to choose a discussion leader to report the conclusions of the group to the whole class in the next task.

Task 2.4 A class take part in a seminar discussion of the topic with your teacher. Present and discuss the conclusions different groups reached.

Task 2.5 How well do you feel your group was able to discuss the question?

>>> a. On your own consider the following questions:
1. Did everyone listen to each other's point of view?
2. Were your notes adequate?
3. Were you able to summarise others' points of view?
4. Do you agree with the conclusion your group reached? If not, why not?
5. Do you feel the discussion could have been improved? If so, how?

>>> b. With a partner, compare your answers.

3 ADVERTISING AND THE MEDIA

You have now been asked to read the following articles on the topic of advertising and the media. You expect to have an examination on this topic at the end of term, and therefore you wish to make sure you understand and remember the information.

[RELATED READINGS AND FURTHER TASKS]

4 THE IMPACT OF MEDIA ON COMMUNICATION

You have been asked by Dr White to complete a project on some aspect of communication and the media.

Your project should not be more than 1,000 words and needs to include some outside reading or research. Your research may be in either English or your own language.

You may wish to include pictures, graphs, drawings, examples and any other information that supports your position. You may present your project as either an essay or a poster.

You may work in groups of 2 or 3, or on your own.

You may choose a topic of your own, or you may wish to develop one of the following topics:

1. Look at several newspapers in your country and compare the way they cover various news items. How does the language and presentation vary? What underlying messages are being conveyed? Do you consider the coverage reasonable and fair? Discuss.

[FURTHER POSSIBLE TOPICS and RELATED FOLLOW-UP TASKS]

5 UNIT ASSESSMENT

Task 5.1 Did you enjoy completing the tasks in this Unit? Why or why not? Were the ideas challenging? Did you find the tasks too difficult or easy? Were the problems mainly to do with language (i.e., the kind of English used) or content (the ideas being presented)?

Task 5.2 Look at the Study Skills Profile at the end of the book. Use it to assess how well you were able to complete the task assigned. What study skills were needed to successfully complete the tasks? What study skills do you need to concentrate on to become a more successful student?

In this activity, the overall focus is on giving students opportunities to experience the 'two-way traffic' flow that exists between the study skills and study competence levels in the real-life study process. They are also asked to reflect on the implications, in terms of assessing their current levels of mastery and, as necessary, their consequent personal targets for further development. At the study skills level, thus, the activity provides opportunities for practice in the skills involved in note-taking, seminar participation, speaking and listening, skimming and scanning for information and so on. At the study competence level, taken as a whole, the various study- and meta-study tasks require the full range of aspects of what this element in the study process entails: thus, for example, Task 1.1 involves self-assessment (of study priorities and of study approach); Task 1.2 requires critical questioning; Task 1.3 calls on logical thinking; Task 1.4 asks for self-reflection, and, in the process, encompasses a wide range of other aspects of study competence; and so on. In this type of activity, thus, there is a constant movement between the study skills and study competence levels of the study process, and the latter aspect is once again brought into focus both directly and also indirectly, through the use of a problem-solving approach to learning to study.

The relationship between study skills and study competence in tasks of this kind is shown in Figure 4.

Taken together, thus, the three types of study learning activities described above – **Direct Study Competence Tasks, Indirect Study Competence Tasks,** and **Skill Transference Tasks** – provide a basic framework for guiding the design of study development materials. Such a framework allows the development of both the study skills and the study competence levels of the study process to be addressed, but does so in such a way as to give due weight to the latter, while at the same time ensuring that its integration with the study skills level – and the need to also address the development of understanding and practical ability in this element as well – are both properly achieved. Furthermore, the sequence which has been adopted in presenting the three main types of tasks is the same one that we recommend should

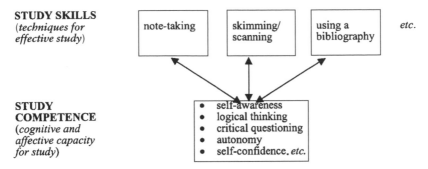

Figure 4. Study skills and study competence: their relationship in learning to study (skill transference tasks)

underpin the design of the study development course as a whole. By focusing first of all on the development of the study competence element, the learner is given a foundation in the approach to study that is needed as a basis for work on developing study skills. This, in turn, should make it possible to develop further the learner's study competence simultaneously, in the manner illustrated in Example 2 above. Finally, as a result of the preceding stages, the student should be in a good position to benefit as fully as possible from experiences involving a life-like integration of the two study levels, and opportunities to reflect on the process.

Conclusion

As the findings of research into the study process of the kind discussed at the beginning of this chapter indicate, learning to study effectively needs to be seen primarily as a process of making a certain turn of mind personally meaningful in relation to handling academic data, rather than as merely a matter of exposure to and practice of a repertoire of study techniques. Materials for helping students learn how to study successfully therefore need to be designed with this purpose in mind, both in terms of their content and in terms of the kind of learning processes they stimulate. In this chapter, we have tried to show how this can be done, in terms of a variety of activity types, which, taken together, can be seen to form a basic overall framework for the design of courses for developing a sound grasp of both study competence and study skills.

25 Promoting EAP learner autonomy in a second language university context

Tony Lynch

Part 1: Review of the literature on autonomy

Autonomy in language learning

Introduction

It is now a decade since the publication of five key books that have contributed to popularisation of the concept(s) of independence and autonomy in language learning: they dealt with self-instruction (Dickinson, 1987), learner strategies (Wenden and Rubin, 1987), applications of autonomy (Brookes and Grundy, 1988; and Holec, 1988), and the learner-centred curriculum (Nunan, 1988a). After something of a lull in the early 1990s we have recently seen edited collections on independence and/or autonomy (a special issue of *System* 23/2, 1995; Broady and Kenning, 1996; Pemberton, Li, Or and Pierson, 1996; Benson and Voller, 1997a), on self-access learning (Gardner and Miller, 1994, 1999), and a book-length treatment of learner-centredness in language education (Tudor, 1996). Like *authentic*, *communicative* and *student-centred*, the concept of autonomy 'has rapidly achieved a moral status backed by dominant beliefs in liberal progressive education' (Pennycook, 1997c: 39).

The terms *independence* and *autonomy* are broad and elastic – and indeed often seem to overlap (cf. Brookes and Grundy, 1988). In this chapter I will be using the single term *autonomy* to cover both. The autonomy literature now embraces learning and communication strategies, self-directed learning, self-access centres, learner-centredness and collaborative learning. However, the concerns of those writing about learner autonomy can seem rather narrow from the perspective of someone teaching EAP students in a second language context. Autonomy is often described in terms of learners' degree of freedom to select, practise and act within the confines of the language teaching institution, rather than their capacity to continue to learn English in their daily interaction with the academic discourse community. This is a point I will return to later in this chapter when I discuss the PROFILE project at the University of Edinburgh.

Definitions

Many papers have been devoted to terminological ground-clearing, e.g. Little (1990), Dickinson (1995), Benson (1996, 1997) and Broady and Kenning (1996). The range of meanings of *autonomy* reflects the provenance of 'our' idea of learner autonomy, which draws on a variety of disciplines. Gremmo and Riley (1995) trace it to ideas in ancient philosophy, political science, psychology and sociology, and also link it with contemporary assumptions about rights of participation, expressed in movements as diverse as campaigns for minority rights, the counter-culture(s) of the late 1960s, and continuing education. But five generally accepted senses of autonomy in language learning have now emerged:

1 **situations** in which learners study entirely on their own
2 a set of **skills** which can be learned and applied in self-directed learning
3 an inborn **capacity** which is suppressed by institutional education
4 the exercise of **learners' responsibility** for their own learning
5 the **right** of learners to determine the direction of their own learning (Benson and Voller, 1997b: 1–2)

The nature of autonomy

A great deal of the discussion of what autonomy is and how it can be fostered has revolved around whether it is essentially **psychological** or **social**. Early ideas on strategy identification and training in second language learning were predominantly psychological in orientation; Rubin (1987) and Wenden (1987) discuss the influence on their work of psychologists such as Bruner (1966) and Carton (1966). In the 1990s the trend has been towards a more social view of language learning in general, reflected in concepts such as *genre, authenticity, interaction*, and this is also true of the literature on learner autonomy: 'Social and co-operative aspects of learning have often been given short shrift in the emphasis on individualisation and independence' (Martyn, 1994: 76).

There was a strong political dimension to early analyses of the role of autonomy (Holec, 1981), and some authors have regretted that this original radicalism has been 'diluted' (Benson, 1996: 30) and 'made bland' (Pennycook, 1997c: 39). However, the advent of critical approaches to language pedagogy (e.g. Pennycook, 1990; Fairclough, 1992) has led to a call to reclaim the original radicalism: 'Learner autonomy can only be the product of a critical practice that questions the legitimacy of existing social relations and the categorisations which support them' (Benson, 1994: 4).

Ultimately, autonomy is both internal and external. We recognise autonomy in psychological attributes (capacity for detachment, critical reflection and strategic choice) as well as in independent action, but at the same time the freedoms implied by autonomy are socially constrained: 'As social beings our independence is always balanced by dependence, our essential condition is one of interdependence; total detachment is a principal determining feature not of autonomy but of autism' (Little, 1990: 7).

Learner training

This concept is based on a positivistic interpretation of research into 'the good language learner' (Naiman, Frohlich and Todesco, 1975; Rubin, 1975), namely, that people can be instructed to become more effective learners of foreign languages. There is no shortage of studies supporting the claim that strategic training can help and that informed strategy training helps most, both in second language learning (e.g. Wenden and Rubin, 1987; Willing, 1988; O'Malley and Chamot, 1990; Wenden, 1991, 1995; White, 1995; Cotterall, 1995; Goh, 1997) and also in the general educational field (Palincsar and Brown, 1984; Palmer and Goetz, 1988). However, there have been more sceptical contributions, notably from Rees-Miller (1993) and Tudor (1996), the latter claiming: 'it would be misleading to assume that . . . strategies can be neatly pedagogised and "taught" to learners in a straightforward manner' (p. 39).

Again, there is a debate about whether *training* is the most appropriate term: some authors prefer *development* or *education* (e.g. Lynch, 1988a; Sheerin, 1989, 1997; Voller and Pickard, 1996; Sinclair, 1996). Yet most critics revert to the term *training*, if reluctantly. For a full discussion of the terminological ins and outs, see Tudor (1996), Benson (1997) and Jordan (1997).

Autonomy in the EAP context

At first sight, relatively few books and articles seem to address the specific pedagogic implications and practical applications of autonomy for EAP teaching/learning, even if we concede that EAP is a minority occupation in TESOL worldwide. Of some 600 titles listed on the major autonomy website maintained by Phil Benson <http://ec.hku.hk/autonomy/bibliog.html>, no more than two dozen include 'EAP', 'university' or 'academic'. Similarly, a substantial recent EAP survey (Jordan, 1997) refers to just 15 publications in sections on 'individualisation and autonomy' and 'awareness raising and learner training', some of which address autonomy from a general perspective, rather than from an EAP-specific point of view.

However, the interest and involvement of EAP practitioners in the autonomy literature is much greater than would appear from scanning the titles of publications. Three recent collections (Gardner and Miller, 1994; Pemberton *et al.*, 1996; Benson and Voller, 1997a) in fact draw heavily on work in institutions where EAP is taught in parallel with the students' on-going degree courses. In addition, some pivotal figures in autonomy, e.g. Edith Esch, David Little and Joan Rubin, work with learners of **other** languages in a university context. So an academic purpose is implicit in the language learning settings of much of the literature.

There may be a commercial motive behind the relative absence of 'EAP' in commercial titles, at least of books. For example, the widely cited collection edited by Brookes and Grundy (1988) comprises papers from the 1987 SELMOUS Conference on 'Individualisation, Autonomy and English for Academic Purposes', but EAP was omitted from the published title *Individualisation and Autonomy in Language Learning*. Similarly, there is no mention of EAP in the title or blurb of Tarone and Yule (1989), which provides a comprehensive rationale for a learner-centred EAP curriculum and sets out its detailed implementation.

Autonomy in the local academic culture

There has been a proliferation of work on 'culture(s)' in language learning and teaching, reflected in both the general literature (e.g. the special issue of *TESOL Quarterly* on 'Language and identity', Vol. 31/3, 1997), in *English for Specific Purposes* (e.g. Flowerdew and Miller, 1996; Cadman, 1997; Paltridge, 1997a), and in EAP collections (e.g. Adams, Heaton and Howarth, 1991; Blue, 1993). A particular strength of EAP-oriented work has been the analysis of cultural learning styles, especially when they are at odds with local expectations in an ESL context. In such work, the status and desirability of autonomy are overarching issues – not a narrow concern with autonomy as a language learner, but the broader autonomy required/expected from a student member of the academic community. Of course, it is worth stressing that misperceptions of local expectations are not confined to non-native or non-local students: doctoral research, for example, is particularly difficult territory for native students, too (Phillips and Pugh, 1994).

Culture has to be seen as one influence among many, and some EAP researchers have stressed the risks of assuming that we know how our students will approach autonomy: 'within-culture differences can be as significant as between-culture differences' (Furneaux, Robinson and Tonkyn, 1988: 99). The level of autonomy varies with circumstances even within the same **individual**, as shown in Houghton, Long and Fanning's (1988) case study of 'Mr Chong'. We have therefore to be wary of our preconceptions about students' attitudes to autonomy.

Negotiating autonomy in EAP

Any move towards autonomy involves the realignment of traditional roles in language learning. Riley has discussed the ways in which the role of the **teacher** has been diversified, to *helper, knower, mentor, adviser* and *consultant* (Riley, 1997), and we might add *facilitator, resource* and *counsellor* (Voller, 1997). Similarly there have been calls for changes to the role of the **learner** and even for the removal of the distinction between teacher and learner: 'the goal of autonomous learning is the negation of the teaching-learning distinction, or the transformation of the learner into a user or producer of language' (Benson, 1996: 33). In EAP the renegotiation of roles has concentrated on ways of involving learners in two activities conventionally considered to be within the teacher's domain: syllabus design, and assessment or evaluation.

Syllabus negotiation might be thought to be particularly suited to EAP courses, given the specific attributes of the learners: '(The students) are frequently quite articulate about their own language problems and are perhaps better aware than their tutors of the learning processes that span numerous activities and sub-skills' (Pugsley, 1988: 60). However, although EAP students may be better able to diagnose their needs than many learners in the wider population, it can be difficult to convert their analysis directly into a negotiated syllabus (particularly with multicultural groups) and even into an agreed methodology: 'while the students' expectations of progress in the language are extremely ambitious, their perceptions of possible options for classroom activity are extremely limited' (Bloor and Bloor, 1988: 65). The teacher still has an important role to play in converting needs analysis outcomes into course content and procedures.

The second realignment of teacher and learner roles in the pursuit of autonomy is in assessment and evaluation. This can be a difficult change to 'sell' to learners, who may be extremely resistant to self- and peer-evaluation, seeing it 'not . . . as an enabling process but as a dereliction of duty' (Wenden, 1995: 79). Nevertheless, there have been a number of attempts to involve EAP learners in assessment: for example self-assessed placement at the start of a pre-sessional course (Ward-Goodbody, 1993); formative course evaluation (Brookes, Grundy and Young-Scholten, 1996); peer evaluation of oral presentations (Lynch, 1988b); self-assessment of progress (Blue, 1988); and course evaluation (Sharp, 1991). A common finding of these and other experiments in autonomy is that what works best is negotiated **shared** responsibility, with teacher and learners making complementary contributions.

Self-access learning

Here I am using *self-access* in the narrow sense of language activity in a self-access centre (SAC). EAP-oriented studies have had a particular impact in this area of autonomy, for example the dedicated collection on self-access of Gardner and Miller (1994), in which most of the contributors write from their experiences of teaching EAP learners. There are also four notable contributions – by Sheerin, Sturtridge, Littlewood and a more critical paper by Littlejohn – in the recent collection edited by Benson and Voller (1997a).

However, the limits on what an SAC can or should offer are a matter of some dispute. Some authors adopt a worm's eye view, concentrating on issues of logistics and ergonomics. Others take a bird's eye view, focusing on the longer-term aim of providing SAC materials and facilities. Littlewood (1997) offers a useful critique of SAC potential, based on his model of language learning as a continuum of (1) pre-communicative work (2) communicative practice (3) structured communication and (4) authentic communication. Any SAC has, he argues, inherent limitations as a site for practice at the 'authentic' end of the scale. Much of the literature of self-access learning is curiously hermetic, concerned with the internal coherence and clarity of the systems, which led Littlejohn (1997) to comment: 'It is as if the notion of self-access work has no significance beyond the walls of the language teaching institution and in other areas of learners' lives' (Littlejohn, 1997: 188–189).

From the psychological perspective, too, self-access learning can appear limited and limiting, which has led some to urge us to expand our horizons, and those of our students, in terms of what SAC materials can offer. To take an obvious example, we should aim to make the materials more open-ended, with commentaries and advice rather than answer keys – a point made a decade ago by Sheerin (1989) and reinforced by Tudor (1996), Little (1997), Aston (1997), Tomlinson (1998) and Gardner and Miller (1999).

Dissatisfaction with the confining features of SAC materials has been expressed in a recasting of the very term *self-access*, to emphasise the individual nature of the language learning enterprise and the need to encourage learners to explore **alternatives** rather than expect **prescriptions**. 'Helping learners in self-access is not just a matter of telling them where they can lay their hands on such-and-such a piece of material; it also necessarily involves some degree of *access to self*' (Riley, 1997: 116).

In Part II of this chapter I discuss work on the PROFILE project, which represents one attempt to help EAP students towards autonomy by building in learner choice and building on learners' experience.

Part 2: PROFILE – a project in EAP learner development

Background

The Institute for Applied Language Studies (IALS) at the University of Edinburgh runs in-session and pre-sessional EAP programmes for students needing English language tuition. Our pre-sessional programme comprises three 3-week courses and a final 4-week course; (for a detailed description and evaluation, see Lynch, 1996). Until 1992 our 'autonomy' activities were limited to one weekly 90-minute SAC session, monitored by the class teacher, and up to 14 hours of open after-class access per week. We gave the students an initial SAC orientation, an annotated list of materials and suggestions for their use. The students completed a self-assessment questionnaire to identify their areas of priority. After this orientation our approach was basically reactive: we encouraged students to ask us for help when they needed it, and we responded with guidance on relevant SAC materials.

In 1992 the pre-sessional programme was assessed for the first time under the BALEAP Accreditation Scheme (for details, see Jordan, 1997) and among the assessors' recommendations was that we should take a more proactive approach to 'learner training', in order to help students continue to learn English after the course, when they would not have SAC opportunities. We therefore decided to incorporate an explicit training component into the summer programme for 1993.

Cycle 1: Introducing 'Learning Strategies'

For summer 1993 we adopted an off-the-shelf solution, *Learning to Learn English* (Ellis and Sinclair, 1989), which offers discussion and reflection tasks in the skill- and knowledge-areas that our students tend to regard as priorities. A particular advantage was its Teacher's Book, including a substantial introduction to teaching 'learner training' classes. We decided to reorder the units to match our students' likely sequence of priorities:

week 1   *Preparation for Language Learning*
     2   *Listening*
     3   *Dealing with grammar*
     4   (new students) *Preparation for Language Learning*
         (continuers) Evaluation of progress in Course 1
     5   *Reading*
     6   *Writing*
     7   (new students) *Preparation for Language Learning*
         (continuers) Evaluation of progress in Course 2
     8   *Dealing with vocabulary*
     9   *Speaking*

We called this part of the programme *Learning Strategies*, to avoid the implications of 'starting from scratch' in the book's title and of the term *training*, which I had expressed objections to some years before (Lynch, 1988a).

The *Learning Strategies* component was evaluated in depth as part of an MSc research project (Stratford, 1993), via (1) observation of three groups' training (two 90-minute sessions per week) over the six weeks of Courses 1 and 2 (2) individual interviews with the three teachers, and (3) student questionnaires. The students' responses to the questionnaires revealed two common criticisms. Firstly, more than half (15 out of 28 students) thought the level of the materials was too low – although that perception was not shared by the teachers. Secondly, there were criticisms that the learners quoted in the book were not EAP students and so would have different needs. Finally, although most students were positive about the ideas underlying *Learning Strategies* (23 of the 28 found the book 'useful' or 'very useful'), they wanted it to be based on materials more relevant to Scotland.

We were alerted to a further weakness by a review of the book (Ho, 1993): that the authors' use of 'What sort of language learner are you?' questionnaires might encourage the assumption that it is possible (and useful) to categorise language learners into pre-existing strategic 'types' – what Dickinson was later to call the 'Zodiac approach' (Dickinson, 1995). Actually, Ho seemed to regard this as a strength and not a weakness: 'From the very first page . . . students are made aware of just what kind of learner they are and which strategies would suit them best' (Ho, 1993: 123). This seemed to us dubious and simplistic.

Cycle 2: Researching and developing our own materials

Following Stratford's study, IALS invested time in research and development of materials that should meet the 1993 students' criticisms by being more challenging linguistically, having greater academic face validity, and being rooted in the local cultural context. The project was the responsibility of my EAP Section colleague Kenneth Anderson and myself.

We kept the overall structure and sequence of *Learning to Learn English*, but added a unit on 'Using Self-Access'. We researched three main sources in preparing for the materials writing. The first was the theoretical and empirical literature: (1) on specific skills (e.g. Kroll, 1990) on writing and Meara (1980) on vocabulary; (2) on strategy training (e.g. Rubin and Thompson, 1982; Wenden and Rubin, 1987); and (3) EAP-specific collections (e.g. Brookes and Grundy, 1988; Adams, Heaton and Howarth, 1991). The second source was relevant methodology books, including Brown and Yule (1983), Anderson and Lynch (1988), Harmer (1987), Kenworthy (1987), McCarthy (1991) and Nunan (1991).

The third source was our past EAP students. Since the 1993 students had recommended writing materials from a specifically local perspective, we asked past students for their insights into informal language learning while studying at Edinburgh. We sent out a letter in early 1994 to approximately 100 graduate students, asking them to describe any techniques for language improvement which they had devised themselves and found useful during their stay in Edinburgh.

Their contribution was invaluable. It is worth bearing mind that very few EAP teachers – ourselves included – have first-hand knowledge of **precisely** what it is like to improve knowledge of an L2 while studying another (non-language) subject in the second-language setting, e.g. studying agriculture in French in France. As it happens, Kenneth Anderson and I both did modern language degrees in Britain

(French and Russian, and German and French, respectively). Although we have also followed L2 courses abroad, we did so as language specialists, unlike our EAP students; and although we have acquired other languages informally through working abroad, we have never had the experience of doing *exactly* what our EAP students do. So we see the involvement of students currently on degrees at the University of Edinburgh as a vital part of the materials development.

Having gathered information from the three sources (research, pedagogy and questionnaire) we faced the problem of how best to convert it into learning materials. We decided that the best way to exploit the textually denser information (especially research data) as classroom material would be to modify it as little as possible. Bearing in mind the criticisms that *Learning to Learn English* had been 'too simple', we wanted to prevent the perception that our own material was linguistically undemanding or insufficiently 'serious' in content. So we deliberately set out to write a text reflecting genre features, such as academic argument and citations, which the students would encounter in their later studies.

The three sources also provided a 'natural' structure for each unit: an introduction to key ideas from applied linguistic research; a description of practical resources that learners might exploit, drawing on the methodological literature and on our own experiences; and, finally, suggestions offered by past students, sharing their first-hand experience at Edinburgh. This tripartite structure also eventually suggested the title for our materials: *PROFILE – Principles, Resources and Options for the Independent Learner of English*, with the acronym emphasising the individual profile of interests and needs that influence a learner's preferences.

The materials were piloted in summer 1994 and were evaluated in a similar way to Stratford's (1993) study, through classroom observation, end-of-course student questionnaires and teacher feedback sheets for each *PROFILE* unit. The students' response was very positive: on only two items (out of 14) was there evidence that we should make adjustments – both related to the time available. Five students (out of 27) thought that there had been too little time on each task, and 11 wanted more time to put into practice the ideas and techniques featured in the materials. The tutors made similar comments on the need to rethink the time management of the sessions.

Cycle 3: Revision and evaluation of PROFILE

The 1994 users' comments suggested that *PROFILE* was appropriate in content and level, but that we should change the balance between in-class reading and active discussion to create more time for class-room practice in the techniques and activities suggested. We decided to make two small changes. First, for summer 1995 we added a cover/contents page for each unit, explaining that there would not be time to do all the tasks, and that the group should choose which ones they wanted to focus on. Secondly, we asked the students to prepare for their *PROFILE* sessions by reading the material as homework.

These changes in fact made little difference to participants' perceptions. Their responses in end-of-course questionnaires indicated that most would still have liked more time on *PROFILE*. The teachers reported being more comfortable about omitting some of the tasks, but this was not a view shared by some of the students, which was on the lines of 'If it's in the materials, the teacher should do it in class'. The teachers said that the time management problems had not been solved by asking the students to do homework preparation; some did not do the homework, which slowed down the class's progress.

Reluctantly – like most materials writers! – we shortened the text and reduced the number of tasks. Over the next two summers (1996 and 1997) we cut *PROFILE* from 155 pages in the original 1994 version to 95 pages in 1997. We now have an average of ten tasks per unit, i.e., five per session, and this seems to have been the key to raising the general level of satisfaction. In questionnaires the majority of students indicate that they think the time allocated to *PROFILE* is adequate, with a few asking for more. Our teaching colleagues also find that it is now a much more manageable component of the EAP programme than the pilot version.

Cycle 4: An independent version of PROFILE

PROFILE was designed for the pre-sessional course, preparing students for informal learning during their period of study at the University of Edinburgh. However, only about a fifth of the University's intake of international students (40 out of 200 in a typical year) attend the IALS summer programme. Some take in-session courses during the academic year, which are offered to students scoring below a 'ceiling' score on a matriculation test of English, but limited resources mean that we have to 'exclude' the higher-scoring students. Over time the number of these excluded students has grown, and we now expect that each year 80 or so will not get a course place and may approach us for advice.

We have now adapted the original classroom *PROFILE* materials into a version that can be used 'independently', i.e., without access to a teacher and class, by the higher-scoring students who cannot find places in our in-session courses. We made four modifications with independent use in mind. First, we altered or removed any rubrics that referred to group discussion, since we assumed that independent learners would be working alone. Second, we removed the unit on Using Self-Access, since it was irrelevant without access to the SAC facilities that pre-sessional students can use. Third, we added a set of Study Notes at the back of the book, slightly modified from the Tutor's Notes used in the summer. Fourthly, we bound the material in book form, rather than as the separate hand-outs used in the classroom. This independent *PROFILE* book went on sale in autumn 1995 and has since been revised (Anderson and Lynch, 1996).

Cycle 5: Evaluating the independent version of PROFILE

In the three years since the independent version became available, we have had very positive informal feedback, in terms of comments from individual users and also in terms of copies sold – roughly 200. We had intended to gather more formal feedback and had inserted a questionnaire into the book for that purpose, but the response rate was practically zero. At the time of writing, we are engaged in a more proactive evaluation by users of the independent *PROFILE*. We have been collecting data in two ways. Firstly, we are now able to use e-mail to follow up the students that buy the book, inviting them to send us comments and queries as they are in the process of using the materials, and to send us feedback when they complete the book. Secondly, one of our in-session speaking skills classes is using discussion tasks from *PROFILE*. The students taking the course receive their own copies of the book to read at home; we ask them to complete and return a short unit questionnaire each week, and also to annotate a photocopy of the Study Notes, showing us which parts of the text or which tasks they find problematic (e.g. inadequate, or hard to follow). In these two ways we hope to gain insights into how the independent user processes *PROFILE* and to make improvements for a third edition.

Conclusion

PROFILE is an attempt to apply key principles in the literature on autonomy in locally relevant ways. The first principle is the imperative need to alert EAP students to the potential for informal language learning beyond the language teaching institution. 'Effective second language development . . . depends ultimately on extensive autonomous interaction with the target language: it cannot be 'taught' in a classroom' (Broady and Kenning, 1996: 10). The independent version of *PROFILE* makes a virtue of the fact that the students using the book are **unable** to get into a language class – much as they might like to – and need to identify and manage learning opportunities in the academic environment around them.

Secondly, *PROFILE* has been written in a conscious attempt to avoid the 'Zodiac approach' to learner *training*. There are no questionnaires leading on to neat answers and cut-and-dried categories. On this issue, we endorse the position of Gremmo and Riley:

> we need to set up types of learning, not types of learners . . . not to transform all learners into 'successful' language learners, with the cognitive and psycho-social features which . . . research has identified, but rather to help learners to come to terms with their strengths and weaknesses, to learn a language efficiently in ways which are compatible with their personalities.
>
> (Gremmo and Riley, 1995: 158)

Thirdly, we did not want to go to the other extreme and 'leave learners to their own devices' (Littlewood, 1997). The Options section of each unit, where we present and discuss the suggestions from past EAP students, could be said to risk leaving the learners to **each other's** devices; however, we have balanced that by including Principles derived from research and Resources based on teaching experience, as well as the first-hand learner insights in Options.

Fourthly, we agree with the view in the literature that any move towards autonomy reduces the divisions between teacher and taught. Our aim has been to make *PROFILE*, in a sense, a forum for contributions from parties who do not normally talk together: language learners, applied linguistic researchers, and language teachers. It is also unusual for current students to 'meet' their predecessors, as they can in the Options section. Tasks are designed to lead the user beyond the page to experimentation in their everyday life use of English – and to do so having 'consulted' the various parties represented in each unit:

> of course, there is no real substitute for practical experience. But neither is there any justification for not learning from other people's mistakes or for trying to reinvent the wheel, so it makes good sense to reflect on previous experience and to try to systematise what has been acquired, so that it can be transmitted and shared in as clear and efficient a way as possible.
>
> (Riley, 1997: 129)

That encapsulates what we have tried to do in *PROFILE*.

Fifth, *PROFILE* is intended to reverse the usual direction of learner education for autonomy. Rather than setting out to transform the (classroom) language *learner* into a language *user* – a widely stated aim of learner training (e.g. Benson, 1996; Little, 1996) – the independent version of *PROFILE* is rooted in **use**, i.e., the student's academic and social discourse, and offers options for harnessing that experience to **learn** language. In this way, it has parallels with the *open-ended self-access* approach, which 'effectively assigns to learners the role of methodological researchers, exploring resources and evaluating their potential for learning' (Aston, 1997: 204).

Finally, we are aware of the likely limitations to the independent version of *PROFILE*, and in particular the current Study Notes. The 'voice' in those notes is very much that of the teacher. Like Tomlinson (1998), we believe that there is greater potential in self-access materials than has been exploited so far. The data we are currently gathering from users of *PROFILE* should enable us to extend the dialogue by bringing in other students' contributions. At the moment the students' 'voice' is restricted to the Options section of each unit, but we would like to incorporate other users' comments and answers into the Study Notes. By so doing, we may contribute to the autonomy of the EAP students and their education as language learners.

Acknowledgements

I would like to acknowledge the key contributions of Sara Stratford, whose original study of *Learning Strategies* led to the decision to design our own EAP-oriented materials, and of my IALS colleague Kenneth Anderson, who has collaborated with me in the design, evaluation and revision of several generations of *PROFILE* (and other) materials.

References

Adams P., B. Heaton, and P. Howarth (Eds.). 1991. *Socio-Cultural Issues in English for Academic Purposes*. Hemel Hempstead: Phoenix ELT.

Adamson, H. D. 1993. *Academic Competence. Theory and Classroom Practice: Preparing ESL Students for Content Courses*. New York: Longman.

Adams-Smith, D. 1984. Planning a university language centre in Oman: Problems and proposals. In *English for Specific Purposes in the Arab World*, J. Swales and H. Mustafa (Eds.). Birmingham: University of Aston Language Studies Unit.

Adler, R. G., and G. Rodman. 1997. *Understanding Human Communication* (6th edition). Orlando, FL: Harcourt Brace.

Ajzen, I. 1991. *Attitudes, Personality, and Behaviour*. Milton Keynes: Open University Press.

Alba, J. W., and L. Hasher. 1983. Is memory schematic? *Psychological Bulletin*, 93: 203–231.

Alderson, J. C. 1984. Reading in a foreign language: A reading problem or a language problem? In *Reading in a Foreign Language*, J. A. Alderson and A. H. Urquhart (Eds.), 1–27. London: Longman.

1988. Testing and its administration in ESP. In *ESP in the Classroom: Practice and Evaluation*, D. Chamberlain, and R. J. Baumgardner (Eds.), 87–97. ELT Document No. 128. Modern English Publications and the British Council.

Alderson, J. C., and A. Beretta. 1992. *Evaluating Second Language Education*. Cambridge: Cambridge University Press.

Alderson, J. C, and A. H. Urquhart. 1985. The effect of students' academic discipline on their performance on ESP reading tests. *Language Testing*, 2 (2): 192–204.

Allen, J. P. B., and H. Widdowson (Eds.). 1974 and later years. *The Focus Series*. Oxford; Oxford University Press.

Allison, D. 1996. Pragmatist discourse and English for academic purposes. *English for Specific Purposes*, 15 (2): 85–103.

Allison, D., and S. Tauroza. 1995. The effect of discourse organisation on lecture comprehension. *English for Specific Purposes*, 14 (2): 157–173.

Allwright, J., and J. Banerjee 1997. Investigating the accuracy of admissions criteria: A case study in a British university. *Language Testing Update*, 22: 36–41.

American Educational Research Association (AERA), American Psychological Association (APA), and National Council on Measurement in Education (NCME). 1985. *Standards for Educational and Psychological Testing*. Washington, DC: American Psychological Association.

Anderson, A., and T. Lynch. 1988. *Listening*. Oxford: Oxford University Press.

Anderson, B. 1983. *Imagined Communities*. London: Verso.

Anderson, J. I. 1980. The lexical difficulties of English medical discourse for Egyptian students. *English for Specific Purposes* (Oregon State University), 37: 4.

Anderson, K., and T. Lynch. 1996. *PROFILE: Principles, Resources and Options for the Independent Learner of English. Self-Study Version*. Institute for Applied Language Studies, University of Edinburgh.

Anderson, R. C., and P. D. Pearson. 1988. A schema-theoretic view of basic processes in reading comprehension. In *Interactive Approaches to Second Language Reading*, P. L. Carrell, J. Devine, and D. E. Eskey (Eds.), 37–55. Cambridge: Cambridge University Press.

Anderson-Hsieh, J., and K. Koelher. 1988. The effect of foreign accent and speaking rate on native speaker comprehension. *Language Learning*, 38: 561–611.

Arden-Close, C. 1993. Language problems in science lectures to non-native speakers. *English for Specific Purposes*, 12 (3): 251–261.

Argyle, M., and R. Ingham. 1972. Gaze, mutual gaze and proximity. *Semiotica*, 6: 32–49.

Arnaudet, M. L., and M. E. Barrett. 1984. *Approaches to Academic Reading and Writing*. Englewood, Cliffs, NJ: Prentice Hall.

1990. *Paragraph Development*. Englewood Cliffs, NJ: Prentice Hall.

Aston, G. 1997. Involving learners in developing learning methods: Exploiting text corpora in self-access. In *Autonomy and Independence in Language Learning*, Benson and Voller (Eds.), 204–214. London: Longman.

Atkinson, D., and V. Ramanathan. 1995. Cultures of writing: An ethnographic comparison of L1 and L2 university writing/language programmes. *TESOL Quarterly*, 29 (3): 539–568.

Attwell, E. 1999. *Machine Translation*. London: British Council.

Axtell, R. E. 1990. *Do's and Taboos Around the World* (2nd edition). New York: Wiley.

Ayers, G. 1993. *A Preliminary Investigation of Abstracts Through a Genre Analysis of the Short Texts Accompanying Articles and Letters in the Scientific Journal Nature*. The University of Birmingham: MA dissertation.

Bachman, L. F. 1986. The Test of English as a Foreign Language as a measure of communicative competence. In *Toward Communicative Competence Testing: Proceedings of the Second TOEFL Invitational*

Conference, C. Stansfield (Ed.), 69–88. Princeton, NJ: Educational Testing Service.

1990. *Fundamental Considerations in Language Testing*. Oxford: Oxford University Press.

Bachman, L. F., F. Davidson, K. Ryan, and I. Choi. 1995. *An Investigation into the Comparability of Two Tests of English as a Foreign Language: The Cambridge-TOEFL Comparability Study*. Cambridge: Cambridge University Press.

Bachman, L. F., B. K. Lynch, and M. Mason. 1995. Investigating variability in tasks and rater judgements in a performance test of foreign language speaking. *Language Testing*, 12: 238–257.

Bakhtin, M. M. 1986. *Speech Genres and Other Late Essays*. Austin: University of Texas Press.

Balcom, P., and Kozar, S. 1994. An ESP speaking course for international graduate students. *TESL Canada Journal*, 12: 58–68.

Baldauf, R. B., and B. H. Jernudd. 1983. Language of publications as a variable in scientific communication. *Australian Review of Applied Linguistics*, 6: 97–108.

Ballard, B., and J. Clanchy. 1984. *Study Abroad: A Manual for Asian Students*. Selangor Darul Ehsan: Longman Malaysia.

1991. *Teaching Students from Overseas*. Melbourne: Longman Cheshire.

Barber, C. L. 1962. Some measurable characteristics of modern scientific prose. In *Contributions to English Syntax and Philology*. Reprinted in J. M. Swales (Ed.), 1988, *Episodes in ESP*. Hemel Hempstead: Prentice Hall International.

Barghiel, V., and L. Muresan. 1995. Training in evaluation in the framework of PROSPER. In *Prodess Colloquium*, 79–91. Manchester: British Council

Barkhuizen, G., and D. Gough. 1996. Language curriculum development in South Africa. *TESOL Quarterly*, 30 (3): 453–472.

Barnes, B. 1982. *T. S. Kuhn and Social Science*. London: MacMillan.

Barron, C. 1992. Cultural syntonicity: Co-operative relationships between the ESP unit and other departments. *Hong Kong Papers in Linguistic and Language Teaching*, 15: 1–14.

Bartholomae, D. 1985. Inventing the university. In *When a Writer Can't Write*, M. Rose (Ed.), 134–165. New York: Guilford.

Bartholomae, D., and A. Petrosky. 1986. *Facts, Artifacts and Counter-facts: A Basic Reading and Writing Course for the College Curriculum*. Pittsburgh: University of Pittsburgh Press.

Bates, L., J. Lane, and E. Lange. 1993. *Writing Clearly: Responding to ESL Compositions*. Boston: Heinle and Heinle.

Bazerman, C. 1988. *Shaping Written Knowledge: The Genre and Activity of the Experimental Article in Science*. Madison: University of Wisconsin.

1994. *Constructing Experience*. Carbondale, IL: Southern Illinois University Press.

Bazerman, C., and J. Paradis (Eds.). 1991. *Textual Dynamics of the Professions*. Madison: University of Wisconsin Press.

Beach, R., and L. Bridwell. 1984. Learning through writing: A rationale for writing across the curriculum. In *The Development of Oral and Written Language in Social Contexts*, A. D. Pellegini and T. D. Yawey (Eds.), 183–198. Norwood, NJ: Ablex.

Beattie, G. 1978a. Sequential temporal patterns of speech and gaze in dialogue. *Semiotica*, 23: 27–52.

1978b. Floor apportionment and gaze in conversational dyads. *British Journal of Social and Clinical Psychology*, 17: 7–15.

Becka, J. V. 1972. The lexical composition of specialised texts and its quantitative aspect. *Prague Studies in Mathematical Linguistics*, 4: 47–64.

Beebe, S. A. 1974. Eye contact: a nonverbal determinant of speaker credibility. *Speech Teacher*, 23: 21–25.

Beglar, D., and A. Hunt. 1999. Revising and validating the 2000 word level and the university word level vocabulary tests. *Language Testing*, 16 (2): 131–162.

Bejarano, Y., T. Levine, E. Olshtain, and J. Steiner. 1997. The skilled use of interaction strategies: Creating a framework for improved small-group communicative interaction in the language classroom. *System* 25, (2): 203–214.

Belanoff, P. 1997. *Portfolios*. Upper Saddle River: Prentice Hall Regents.

Belcher, D. 1994. The apprenticeship approach to advanced academic literacy: Graduate students and their mentors. *English for Specific Purposes*, 13: 23–34.

Belcher, D., and G. Braine (Eds.). 1995. *Academic Writing in a Second Language: Essays on Research and Pedagogy*. Norwood, NJ: Ablex.

Benesch, S. 1988. *Ending Remediation: Linking ESL and Content in Higher Education*. Alexandria, VA: TESOL.

1993. ESL, ideology, and the politics of pragmatism. *TESOL Quarterly*, 27 (4): 705–716.

1996. Needs analysis and curriculum development in EAP: An example of a critical approach. *TESOL Quarterly*, 30 (4): 723–738.

1999. Rights analysis: Studying power relations in an academic setting. *English for Specific Purposes*, 18 (4): 313–327.

Benesch, S., and B. Rorschach. 1989. *Academic Writing Workshop II*. Belmont, CA: Wadsworth.

Benson, M. 1988. The academic listening task: A case study. *TESOL Quarterly*, 23 (3): 421–445.

Benson, M. J. 1991. University ESL reading: A content analysis. *English for Specific Purposes*, 10 (2): 75–88.

Benson, P. 1994. Self-access systems as information systems: Questions of ideology and control. In *Directions in Self-Access Language Learning*, Gardner and Miller (Eds.), 3–12. Hong Kong: Hong Kong University Press.

1996. Concepts of autonomy in language learning. In *Taking Control: Autonomy in Language Learning*, P. Pemberton, E. S. L. Li, W. W. F. Or and H. D. Pierson (Eds.), 27–34. Hong Kong: Hong Kong University Press.

Benson, P. 1997. The philosophy and politics of learner autonomy. In *Autonomy and Independence in Language Learning*, P. Benson, and P. Voller (Eds.), 18–34. London: Longman.

Benson, P., and P. Voller (Eds.). 1997a. *Autonomy and Independence in Language Learning*. London: Longman.

1997b. Introduction. In *Autonomy and Independence in Language Learning*, P. Benson, and P. Voller (Eds.), 1–12. London: Longman.

Beretta, A. 1986. Program-fair language teaching programme evaluation. *TESOL Quarterly*, 20 (3): 144–155.

Beretta, A., and A. Davies. 1985. Evaluation of the Bangalore project. *English Language Teaching Journal*, 39: 121–127.

Berger, V. 1990. The effects of peer and self-feedback. *CATESOL Journal*, 3: 21–35.

Berkenkotter, C., and T. N. Huckin. 1993. Rethinking genre from a socio-cognitive perspective. *Written Communication*, 10: 475–509.

1995. *Genre Knowledge in Disciplinary Communication: Cognition/ Culture/Power*. Hillsdale, NJ: Lawrence Erlbaum.

Berkenkotter, C., T. Huckin, and J. Ackerman. 1991. Social context and socially constructed texts: The initiation of a graduate student into a writing research community. In *Textual Dynamics of the Professions*, C. Bazerman and J. Paradis (Eds.), 191–215. Madison: University of Wisconsin Press.

Bernhardt, E. B. 1990. A content analysis of 'methods texts' for the teaching of second language reading. Paper presented at the National Reading conference, Miami, FL.

1991. A psycholinguistic perspective on second language literacy. In *Reading in Two Languages*, J. H. Hulstijn and J. F. Matter (Eds.), AILA Review, 8: 31–44.

Bhatia, V. K. 1993. *Analyzing Genres: Language Use of Professional Settings*. London: Longman.

Biber, D., S. Conrad, and S. Reppen. 1994. Corpus-based approaches to issues in applied linguistics. *Applied Linguistics*, 15 (2): 169–189.

Biber, D., and E. Finegan. 1994. Intra-textual variation within medical research articles. In *Corpus-based Research into Language*, N. Oostdijk and P. de Haan (Eds.), 201–221. Amsterdam-Atlanta, GA: Rodopi.

Biggs, J. B. 1976. Dimensions of study behaviour: Another look at a.t.i. *British Journal of Educational Psychology*, 46: 68–80.

Bisong, J. 1995. Language choice and cultural imperialism. *ELT Journal*, 49 (2): 122–132.

Bizzell, P. 1982. Cognition, convention and certainty: What we need to know about writing. *PRE/TEXT*, 3: 213–243.

1992. *Academic Discourse and Critical Consciousness*. Pittsburgh: University of Pittsburgh Press.

Blanton, L. L. 1987. Reshaping ESL students' perceptions of writing. *ELT Journal*, 41: 112–118.

Block, J., and L. Chi. 1995. A comparison of the use of citations in Chinese and English academic discourse. In *Academic Writing in a Second Language: Essays on Research and Pedagogy*, D. Belcher and G. Braine (Eds.), 231–274. Norwood, NJ: Ablex.

Bloomfield, L. (1938). Linguistic aspects of science. In *Foundations of the Unity of Science*, O. Neurath, R. Carnap, and C. Morris (Eds.), 215–278. Chicago: The University of Chicago Press.

Bloor, D. 1976. *Knowledge and Social Imagery*. London: Routledge and Kegan Paul.

Bloor, M. 1998. English for specific purposes: The preservation of the species. *English for Specific Purposes*, 17: 47–66.

Bloor, M., and T. Bloor. 1986. Languages for specific purposes: practice and theory. *CLCS Occasional Papers*, 19. Dublin: Trinity College, Centre for Language and Communication Studies.

1988. Syllabus negotiation: The basis for learner autonomy. In *Individualisation and Autonomy in Language Learning*, Brookes and Grundy (Eds.), 62–74. ELT Documents 131. Oxford: Modern English Publications / British Council.

Bloor, M., and M. J. St John. 1988. Project writing: The marriage of process and product. In *Academic Writing: Process and Product*, P. C. Robinson (Ed.), 85–94. ELT Document 129. Modern English Publications and the British Council.

Bloor, T. 1996. Three hypothetical strategies in philosophical writing. In *Academic Writing: Intercultural and Textual Issues*, E. Ventola and A. Mauranen (Eds.), 19–43. Amsterdam: John Benjamins.

Blue, G. 1988. Self-assessment: The limits of learner independence. In *Individualisation and Autonomy in Language Learning*, Brookes and Grundy (Eds.), 100–118. ELT Documents 131. Oxford: Modern English Publications / British Council.

1991. Language learning within academic constraints. In *Socio-Cultural Issues in English for Academic Purposes*, Adams, Heaton, and Howarth (Eds.), 101–117. Hemel Hempstead: Phoenix ELT.

1993. Nothing succeeds like linguistic competence: The role of language in academic success. In *Language, Learning and Success: Studying Through English*, G. Blue (Ed.). Hemel Hempstead: Phoenix ELT.

Borg, S. 1998. Teachers' pedagogical systems and grammar teaching: A qualitative study. *TESOL Quarterly*, 32 (1): 9–38.

Bossers, B. 1991. On thresholds, ceilings and short-circuits: The relation between L1 reading, L2 reading, and L2 knowledge. In *Reading in Two Languages*, J. H. Hulstijn and J. F. Matter (Eds.), AILA Review, 8, 45–60.

Bourdieu, P. 1982. *Ce Que Parler Veut Dire*. Paris: Fayard.

Braine, G. 1980. *The concept of English for science and technology (EST) and a suggested course in EST for BSc. (General) degree students of the University of Kelaniya*. Sri Lanka: Unpublished BA thesis.

1988a. Academic writing task surveys: The need for a fresh approach. *Texas Papers in Foreign Language Education*, 1: 101–118.

1988b. A reader reacts . . . *TESOL Quarterly*, 22: 700–702.

1989. Writing in science and technology: An analysis of assignments from ten undergraduate courses. *English for Specific Purposes*, 8: 3–16.

1995. Writing in the natural sciences and engineering. In *Academic Writing in a Second Language*, D. Belcher and G. Braine (Eds.), 113–134. Norwood, NJ: Ablex.

Bramki, D., and R. C. Williams. 1984. Lexical familiarisation in economics text, and its pedagogic implications in reading comprehension. *Reading in a Foreign Language*, 2 (1): 169–181.

Brannon, L., and C. H. Knoblauch. 1982. On students' rights to their own texts: A model of teacher response. *College Composition and Communication*, 33: 157–166.

Bransford, J. D. 1979. *Human Cognition: Learning, Understanding and Remembering*. Belmont, CA: Wadsworth.

Brewster, J. 1999. Teaching English through content. In *Innovation and Best Practice*, C. Kennedy (Ed.), 83–95. Harlow: Longman.

Bridgeman, B., and S. Carlson. 1983. *Survey of Academic Writing Tasks Required of Graduate and Undergraduate Foreign Students*. TOEFL Research Report No. 15. Princeton, NJ: Educational Testing Service.

Briggs, S. L., and R. Bauman. 1992. Genre, intertextuality and power. *Journal of Linguistic Anthropology*, 2: 131–172.

Briggs, S., V. Clark, C. Madden, R. Beal, S. Hyon, P. M. Aldridge, and J. M. Swales. 1997. *The International Teaching Assistant: An Annotated Critical Bibliography* (2nd edition). Ann Arbor, MI: English Language Institute Test Publications.

Brindley, G. 1989. *Assessing Achievement in the Learner-Centred Curriculum*. Sydney: National Centre for English Language Teaching and Research, Macquarie University.

Brinton, D. M., M. A. Snow, and M. B. Wesche. 1989. *Content-based Second Language Instruction*. New York: Newbury House.

Brinton, D. M. 1993. Content-based instruction and English for specific purposes: Same or different? *TESOL Matters*, August/September: 9.

2000. Out of the mouths of babes: Novice teacher insights into content-based instruction. In *Content-based College ESL Instruction*, L. F. Kasper (Ed.), 48–70. Mahwah, NJ: Lawrence Erlbaum.

Broady E., and M-M. Kenning (Eds.). 1996. *Promoting Learner Autonomy in University Language Teaching*. London: Association for French Language Studies /Centre for Information on Language Teaching and Research.

Brookes A., and P. Grundy (Eds.). 1988. *Individualisation and Autonomy in*

Language Learning. ELT Documents 131. Oxford: Modern English Publications / British Council.

1990. *Writing for Study Purposes*. Cambridge: Cambridge University Press.

Brookes, A., P. Grundy, and M. Young-Scholten. 1996. Tutor and student evaluation of activity design and purpose. In *Evaluation and Course Design in EAP*, Hewings and Dudley-Evans (Eds.), 36–45. Hemel Hempstead: Phoenix ELT.

Brown, G. 1978. Understanding spoken language. *TESOL Quarterly*, 12 (3): 271–283.

Brown, G., and M. Atkins. 1988. *Effective Teaching in Higher Education*. London: Routledge.

Brown, G., and G. Yule. 1983. *Teaching the Spoken Language*. Cambridge: Cambridge University Press.

Brown, J. D. 1993. A comprehensive criterion-referenced language testing project. In *A New Decade of Language Testing Research: Selected Papers from the 1990 Language Testing Research Colloquium*, D. Douglas and C. Chapelle (Eds.), 163–184. Alexandria, Virginia: Teachers of English to Speakers of Other Languages, Inc.

1995. *The Elements of Language Curriculum: A Systematic Approach to Programme Development*. Boston, MA: Heinle and Heinle.

1996. *Testing in Language Programs*. Upper Saddle River: Prentice Hall Regents.

1997. Computers in language testing: Present research and some future directions. *Language Learning and Technology*, 1 (1): 44–59.

Brown, K. 1993. World Englishes in TESOL programmes: An infusion model of curricular innovation. *World Englishes*, 12: 59–73.

Bruffee, K. 1983. Writing and reading as collaborative or social acts. In *The Writer's Mind*, J. N. Hays (Ed.). Urbana: NCTE.

1993. *Collaborative Learning*. Baltimore: The Johns Hopkins University Press.

Bruner, J. S. 1966. *Towards a Theory of Instruction*. Cambridge, MA: Harvard University Press.

1975. Beyond the information given. In *How Students Learn*, N. J. Entwistle and D. Hounsell (Eds.). Lancaster: Institute for Post-Compulsory Education, Lancaster University.

Buck, G. 1990. *The Testing of Second Language Listening Comprehension*. University of Lancaster: PhD dissertation.

Burgess, S. 1997. *Discourse Variation Across Cultures: A Genre-analytic Study of Writing on Linguistics*. University of Reading: Unpublished PhD thesis.

Burstein, J., L. Frase, A. Ginther, and L. Grant. 1996. Technologies for language assessment. In *Annual Review of Applied Linguistics*, 16: 240–260.

Buzan, T. 1995. *Use Your Head*. London: BBC Books.

Bycina, D. 1986. Teaching language through content: English for science and technology at USC. *CATESOL News*, 18 (3): 13.

Byrd, P., and J. M. Reid. 1997. *Grammar in the Composition Classroom. Essays on Teaching ESL for College-bound Students.* Boston: Heinle and Heinle.

Cadman, K. 1997. Thesis writing for international students: A question of identity? *English for Specific Purposes*, 16 (1): 3–14.

Cambridge University. 1990. *Preliminary English Test: Vocabulary list.* Local Examinations Syndicate: International examinations.

Cameron, D. 1995. *Verbal Hygiene.* London: Routledge.

Campion, M. E., and W. B. Elley. 1971. *An Academic Vocabulary List.* Wellington: NZCER.

Canagarajah, A. S. 1996. 'Nondiscursive' requirements in academic publishing, material resources of periphery scholars, and the politics of knowledge production. *Written Communication*, 13 (4): 435–472.

Canale, M., and M. Swain. 1980. Theoretical bases of communicative approaches to second language teaching and testing. *Applied Linguistics*, 1: 1–47.

Candlin, C. N., J. Bruton, and J. M. Leather. 1976. Doctors in casualty: Specialist course design from a database. *International Review of Applied Linguistics*, 14: 245–272.

Carrell, P. L. 1983. Three components of background knowledge in reading comprehension. *Language Learning*, 33: 183–207.

Carrell, P. L., and J. G. Carson. 1997. Extensive and intensive reading in an EAP setting. *English for Specific Purposes*, 16 (1): 47–60.

Carroll, J. B. 1961. Fundamental considerations in testing English language proficiency of foreign students. In *Teaching English as a Second Language* (2nd edition), H. B. Allen and R. N. Campbell (Eds.), 313–321. New York: McGraw-Hill.

1964. Words, meanings, and concepts. *Harvard Educational Review*, 34: 178–202.

Carroll, J. B., P. Davies, and B. Richman. 1971. *The American Heritage Word Frequency Book.* New York: Houghton Mifflin, Boston American Heritage.

Carroll, M. 1994. Journal writing as a learning and research tool in the adult classroom. *TESOL Journal*, 4 (1): 19–22.

Carson, J. G., and I. Leki (Eds.). 1993a. *Reading in the Composition Classroom: Second Language Perspectives.* Boston: Heinle and Heinle.

Carson, J. G., and I. Leki. 1993b. Introduction. In *Reading in the Composition Classroom: Second Language Perspectives*, J. G. Carson, and I. Leki (Eds.), 1–7. Boston: Heinle and Heinle.

Carson, J. G., and G. L. Nelson. 1996. Chinese students' perceptions of ESL peer response group interaction. *Journal of Second Language Writing*, 5: 1–19.

Carson, J. G., J. A. Taylor, and L. Fredella. 1997. The role of content in task-based EAP instruction. In *The Content-based Classroom: Perspectives on Integrating Language and Content*, M. A. Snow, and D. M. Brinton (Eds.), 367–370. White Plains, NY: Addison Wesley Longman.

Carter-Sigglow, J. 1996. Correspondence. *Nature*, 384: 764.

Carton, A. 1966. *The Method of Inference in Foreign Language Study.* New York: Research Foundation of the City of New York.

Carver, D. 1983. Some propositions about ESP. *English for Specific Purposes*, 2: 131–37.

Casanave, C. 1995. Local interactions: Constructing contexts for composing in graduate sociology programme. In *Academic Writing in a Second Language: Essays on Research and Pedagogy*, D. Belcher, and G. Braine (Eds.), 83–110. Norwood, NJ: Ablex.

Celani, M. A. A., J. L. Holmes, R. C. G. Ramos, and M. R. Scott. 1998. *The Brazilian ESP Project: An Evaluation.* Sao Paulo: Editoria de PUC-SP.

Celce-Murcia, M. 1980. Contextual analysis of English: Application to TESL. In *Discourse analysis in Second Language Research*, D. Larsen-Freeman (Ed.), 241–259. Rowley, Mass: Newbury House.

Chamberlain, R. 1981. The SP of the E. In *Team Teaching in ESP*, 97–108. ELT Documents 106. London: The British Council.

Chamot, A. U. 1993. Student responses to learning strategy instruction in the foreign language classroom. *Foreign Language Annals*, 26 (3): 308–321.

Chapelle, C., W. Grabe, and M. Berns. 1997. *Communicative Language Proficiency: Definition and Implications for TOEFL 2000.* Princeton, NJ: Educational Testing Service.

Charge, N., and L. Taylor. 1997. Recent developments in IELTS. *ELT Journal*, 51 (4): 374–380.

Charney, D. 1996. Empiricism is not a four-letter word. *College Communication and Composition*, 47: 567–593.

Chase, G. 1988. Accommodation, resistance and the politics of student writing. *College Composition and Communication*, 39 (1): 13–22.

Chaudron, C. 1983. Simplification of input: topic reinstatements and their effects on L2 learners' recognition and recall. *TESOL Quarterly*, 17 (3): 437–458.

Chaudron, C., L. Loschy, and J. Cook. 1994. Second language listening comprehension and lecture note-taking. In *Academic Listening: Research Perspectives*, J. Flowerdew (Ed.), 75–92. Cambridge: Cambridge University Press.

Chaudron, C., and J. C. Richards. 1986. The effect of discourse markers on the comprehension of lectures. *Applied Linguistics*, 7: 113–127.

Cheung, H. F. 1994. *The Perceived and Actual Effects of Speech Rates on Listening Comprehension.* Department of English, City University of Hong Kong: Unpublished M. A. thesis,.

Chiang, C. S., and P. Dunkel. 1992. The effect of speech modification, prior knowledge, and listening proficiency on EFL listening. *TESOL Quarterly*, 26 (2): 345–374.

Chirnside, A. 1986. Talking for specific purposes. In *ESP for the University*, D. P. L. Harper (Ed.), 141–148. ELT Document 123. Oxford: Pergamon Press and the British Council.

Chiseri-Strater, E. 1991. *Academic Literacies: The Public and Private Discourse of University Students*. Portsmouth, NH: Heinemann/ Boynton-Cook.

Cho, Y. 1998. *Examining the validity of a multiple-choice plagiarism test*. University of Illinois at Urbana-Champaign: Unpublished manuscript.
   (Forthcoming). *The Use of Portfolio Assessment in Large-scale ESL University Placement Testing*. University of Illinois at Urbana-Champaign: Unpublished dissertation.

Christison, M. A., and K J. Krahnke. 1986. Student perceptions of academic language study. *TESOL Quarterly*, 20 (1): 61–81.

Christison, M. A., and F. L. Stoller (Eds.). 1997. *A Handbook for Language Programme Administrators*. Burlingame, CA: Alta Book Centre.

Chu, L., T. Kitchen, and M. L. Chew. 1997. How do we learn best? Preferences and strategies in learning and teaching styles at the National University of Singapore. Paper presented at Singapore Tertiary English Teachers Society / National Tsinghua University Joint Seminar, Hsin Chu, Taiwan, June 1997.

Clapham, C. 1996. *The Development of IELTS: A Study of the Effect of Background Knowledge on Reading Comprehension*. Cambridge: Cambridge University Press.

Clark, R. 1992. Principles and practice of CLA in the classroom. In *Critical Language Awareness*, N. Fairclough (Ed.), 117–140. London: Longman.

Clark, R., and R. Ivanic. 1996. *The Politics of Writing*. London: Routledge.

Clarke, M. A. 1979. Reading in Spanish and English: Evidence from adult ESL students. *Language Learning*, 29 (1): 121–150.

Clegg, J. 1999. Teaching the primary and secondary curriculum through the medium of English. In *Innovation and Best Practice*, C. Kennedy (Ed.), 69–82. Harlow: Longman.

Clerehan, R. 1995. Taking it down: notetaking practices of L1 and L2 students. *English for Specific Purposes* 14 (2): 137–155.

Clerehan, R., and J. Moodie. 1997. A systematic approach to the teaching of writing for supervisors of international students: Perspectives from genre theory. In *Learning and Teaching in Higher Education: Advancing International Perspectives*, R. Murrray-Harvey and H. C. Silins (Eds.). Adelaide: School of Education, Flinders University of South Australia.

Clyne, M. 1987. Cultural differences in the organisation of academic texts. *Journal of Pragmatics*, 11: 211–247.
   1994. *Intercultural Communication at Work*. Cambridge: Cambridge University Press.

Coady, J. 1979. A psycholinguistic model of the ESL reader. In *Reading in a Second Language*, R. Mackay, B. Barkman, and R. R. Jordan (Eds.), 5–12. Rowley, MA: Newbury House.

Cobb, T. 1996. *From Concord to Lexicon: Development and Test of a Corpus-based Lexical Tutor*. Concordia University, Montreal: Unpublished doctoral dissertation. <http://www.er.uqam.ca/nobel/r21270/webthesis/Thesis0.html>

Cobb, T. 1997. Is there any measurable learning from hands-on concordancing? *System,* 25: 301–315.

Cobb, T. (In press). Applied constructivism: A test for the learner-as-scientist. *Educational Technology Research and Development.*

Cohen, A. D. 1987. Student processing of feedback on their compositions. In *Learner Strategies in Language Learning,* A. L. Wenden, and J. Rubin (Eds.), 57–69. Englewood Cliffs, NJ: Prentice-Hall.

1994. *Assessing Language Ability in the Classroom.* Boston: Heinle and Heinle.

1996. Verbal reports as a source of insights into second language learner strategies. *Applied Language Learning,* 7: 5–24.

1998. *Strategies in Learning and Using a Second Language.* London: Longman.

Cohen, A. D., and M. C. Cavalcanti. 1990. Feedback on compositions: Teacher and student verbal reports. In *Second Language Writing: Research Insights for the Classroom,* B. Kroll (Ed.), 155–177. Cambridge: Cambridge University Press.

Cohen, A., H. Glasman, P. R. Rosenbaum-Cohen, J. Ferrara, and J. Fine. 1988. Reading English for specialised purposes: Discourse analysis and the use of student informants. In *Interactive Approaches to Second Language Reading,* P. Carrell, J. Devine, and D. E. Eskey (Eds.), 152–167. Cambridge: Cambridge University Press.

Coleman, H. (Ed.). 1996. *Society and the Language Classroom.* Cambridge: Cambridge University Press.

Collins, H. M. 1992. *Changing Order: Replication and Induction in Scientific Practice.* Chicago: Chicago University Press.

Collins, H., and T. Pinch. 1993. *The Golem: What Everyone Should Know about Science.* Cambridge: Cambridge University Press.

Connor, U. 1987. Argumentative patterns in student essays: Cross cultural differences. In *Writing Across Languages: Analysis of L2 Text,* U. Connor and R. B. Kaplan (Eds.). Reading, MA: Addison-Wesley.

1996. *Contrastive Rhetoric: Cross-cultural Aspects of Second Language Writing.* Cambridge: Cambridge University Press.

1999. 'How you like our fish?' Accommodation in international business communication. In *Business English: Research into Practice,* M. Hewings, and C. Nickerson (Eds.), 116–29.

Connor, U., and K. Asenavage. 1994. Peer response groups in ESL writing classes: How much impact on revision? *Journal of Second Language Writing,* 3: 257–276.

Connor, U., and A. M. Johns (Eds.). 1990. *Coherence in Writing: Research and Pedagogical Perspectives.* Alexandria, VA: TESOL.

Connor, U., and R. Kaplan (Eds.). 1987. *Writing across Cultures: Analysis of L2 Text.* Reading, MA: Addison-Wesley.

Conrad, S. 1996. Investigating academic texts with corpus-based techniques: An example from biology. *Linguistics and Education,* 8: 299–326.

Cook, T., and D. Campbell. 1979. *Quasi-experimentation: Design and Analysis Issues for Field Settings*. Chicago: Rand-McNally.

Cook, V. 1991. *Second Language Learning and Language Teaching*. London: Edward Arnold.

Cooper, J. 1979. *Think and Link*. London: Edward Arnold.

Cooper, M. 1984. Linguistic competence of practised and unpractised non-native speakers of English. In *Reading In a Foreign Language*, J. A. Alderson, and A.H. Urquhart (Eds.), 122–138. London: Longman.

Cooper, R. 1989. *Language Planning and Social Change*. Cambridge: Cambridge University Press.

Corbluth, J. D. 1975. English or special English? *ELT Journal*, 29: 277–286.

Corson, D. J. 1985. *The Lexical Bar*. Oxford: Pergamon Press.

1995. *Using English Words*. Dordrecht: Kluwer Academic Publishers.

1997. The learning and use of academic English words. *Language Learning*, 47 (4): 671–718.

Cortazzi, M. 1990. Cultural and educational expectations in the language classroom. In *Culture and the Language Classroom*, B. Harrison (Ed.). ELT Documents 132.

Cortazzi, M., and L. Jin. 1994. Narrative analysis: Applying linguistics to cultural models of learning. In *Evaluating Language*, D. Graddol, and J. Swann (Eds.), 75–90. Clevedon: Multilingual Matters.

Cotterall, S. 1995. Developing a course strategy for learner autonomy. *ELT Journal*, 49 (3): 219–227.

Cowan, J. R. 1974. Lexical and syntactic research for the design of EFL reading materials. *TESOL Quarterly*, 8 (4): 389–400.

Coxhead, A. 1998. *An Academic Word List*. ELI Occasional Publication No. 18, Victoria University of Wellington, New Zealand.

(Forthcoming). A new academic word list.

Crookes, G., and S. M. Gass (Eds.). 1993a. *Tasks and Language Learning: Integrating Theory and Practice*. Bristol, PA: Multilingual Matters.

Crookes, G., and S. M. Gass (Eds.). 1993b. *Tasks in a Pedagogical Context: Integrating Theory and Practice*. Bristol, PA: Multilingual Matters.

Crystal, D. 1997. *English as a Global Language*. Cambridge: Cambridge University Press.

1999. The future of Englishes. In *Innovation and Best Practice*, C. Kennedy (Ed.), 9–22. Harlow: Longman.

Crystal, D., and D. Davy. 1969. *Investigating English Style*. London: Longman.

Cumming, A. 1985. Responding to the writing of ESL students. *Highway One*, 8: 58–78.

Cummins, J. 1979. Cognitive/academic language proficiency, linguistic interdependence, the optimal age question and some other matters. *Working Papers on Bilingualism*, 18: 197–205.

Dahl, D. A. 1981. The role of experience in speech modifications for second language learners. *Minnesota Papers in Linguistics and Philosophy of Language*, 7: 78–93.

Davidson, F. 1993. Testing English across cultures: Summary and comments. *World Englishes*, 12 (1): 113–125.

1994. The interlanguage metaphor and language assessment. *World Englishes*, 13 (3): 377–386.

1998. Review of Clapham (1996). *Language Testing*, 15 (2): 289–301.

Davies, A. 1991. *The Native Speaker in Applied Linguistics*. Edinburgh: Edinburgh University Press.

Davies, A., and C. Criper. 1988. *ELTS Validation Project Report*. London: The British Council and the University of Cambridge Local Examinations Syndicate.

Davies, F. 1988. Designing a writing syllabus in English for academic purposes: Process and product. In *Academic writing: Process and Product*, P. Robinson (Ed.). ELT Documents 129. London: Modern English Teacher, Macmillan in association with the British Council.

Davis, T. (Ed.). 1997. *Open Doors 1996/7*. New York: Institute of International Education.

Day, R. R., and J. Bamford. 1998. *Extensive Reading in the Second Language Classroom*. Cambridge: Cambridge University Press.

Day, R., and J. Yamanaka. 1998. *Impact Issues*. Singapore: Longman.

DeCarrico, J., and J. R. Nattinger. 1988. Lexical phrases for the comprehension of academic lectures. *English for Specific Purposes*, 7 (2): 91–102.

De Escorcia, B. 1984. Team-teaching for students of economics: A Colombian experience. In *Common Ground: Shared Interests in ESP and Communication Studies*, R. Williams, J. Swales, and J. Kirkman (Eds.), 135–144. ELT Document 117. Oxford: Pergamon Press and the British Council.

DeKeyser, R. 1995. Learning second language grammar rules: An experiment with a miniature linguistic system. *Studies in Second Language Acquisition*, 17: 379–410.

De Lano, L., L. Riley, and G. Crookes. 1994. The meaning of innovation for ESL teachers. *System*, 22 (4): 487–496.

Delpit, Lisa. 1990. Dilemmas of a progressive Black educator. Paper presented at the Conference on College Composition and Communication. Chicago, 22 March.

De Swaan, A. 1998. A political sociology of the world language system (1): The dynamics of language spread. *Language Problems and Language Planning*, 22 (1): 63–75.

DeVito, J. A. 1998. *The Interpersonal Communication Book* (eighth edition). New York: Longman.

Dickinson, L. 1987. *Self-instruction in Language Learning*. Cambridge: Cambridge University Press.

1995. Autonomy and motivation: A literature review. *System*, 23 (2): 165–174.

Dillon, G. 1991. *Contending Rhetorics*. Bloomington: University of Indiana Press.

Dong, Y. R. 1998. Non-native graduate students' thesis/dissertation writing in science: Self-reports by students and their advisors from two US institutions. *English for Specific Purposes*, 17: 369–390.

Dornyei, Z. 1995. On the teachability of communication strategies. *TESOL Quarterly*, 29 (1): 55–85.

Doughty, C., and J. Williams. 1998. Pedagogical choices in focus on form. In *Focus on Form in Classroom Second Language Acquisition*, C. Doughty, and J. Williams (Eds.), 197–262. New York: Cambridge University Press.

Douglas, D., and L. Selinker. 1993. Performance on a general versus field-specific test of speaking proficiency by international teaching assistants. In *A New Decade of Language Testing Research*, C. Chapelle, and D. Douglas (Eds.). Alexandria, VA: TESOL Publications.

Dresher, R. 1934. Training in mathematics vocabulary. *Educational Research Bulletin*, 13 (8): 201204.

Drury, H., and C. Webb. 1991. Teaching academic writing at the tertiary level. *Prospect*, 7 (1): 7–27.

Dubois, B. L. 1987. Something on the order of around forty to forty-four: Imprecise numerical expressions in biomedical slide talks. *Language in Society*, 16: 527–541.

Dudley-Evans, T. 1984a. The team teaching of writing skills. In *Common Ground: Shared Interests in ESP and Communication Studies*, R. Williams, J. M. Swales, and J. Kirkman (Eds.), 127–134. ELT Documents 117. Oxford: Pergamon.

1984b. A preliminary investigation of the writing of dissertation titles. In *The ESP Classroom*, G. James (Ed.), 40–46. Exeter, UK: Exeter Linguistic Studies.

1985. *Writing Laboratory Reports*. Melbourne: Thomas Nelson.

1986. Genre analysis: An investigation of the introduction and discussion sections of MSc dissertations. In *Talking about Text*, M. Coulthard (Ed.). Discourse Analysis Monographs No 13. English Language Research, University of Birmingham.

1991. Socialisation into the academic community: Linguistic and stylistic expectations of a PhD thesis as revealed by supervisor comments. In *Socio-cultural Issues in English for Academic Purposes*, P. Adams, B. Heaton, and P. Howarth (Eds.), 41–51. London: Macmillan.

1993. Variation in communication patterns between discourse communities: The case of highway engineering and plant biology. In *Language, Learning and Success: Studying Through English*, G. Blue (Ed.). London: Modern English Publications in association with The British Council, Macmillan.

1994a. Genre analysis: An approach to text analysis for ESP. In *Advances in Written Text Analysis*, M. Coulthard (Ed.), 219–228. London: Routledge.

1994b. Research in English for Specific Purposes. In *LSP – Problems and Prospects*, R. Khoo (Ed.). Anthology Series 13. Singapore: SEAMEO Regional Language Centre.

1994c. Variations in the discourse patterns favoured by different disciplines and their pedagogical implications. In *Academic Listening: Research Perspectives*, J. Flowerdew (Ed.). Cambridge: Cambridge University Press.

1995. Common core and specific approaches to the teaching of academic writing. In *Academic Writing in a Second Language. Essays on Research and Pedagogy*. D. Belcher, and G. Braine (Eds.), 293–312. Norwood, NJ: Ablex.

Dudley-Evans, T., and W. Henderson. 1990. *The Language of Economics: The Analysis of Economics Discourse*. ELT Documents 134. London: Modern English Publications.

Dudley-Evans, T., and T. F. Johns. 1981. A team teaching approach to lecture comprehension. In *The Teaching of Listening Comprehension*. ELT Documents Special. Oxford: Pergamon in association with the British Council.

Dudley-Evans, T., and M. J. St John. 1998. *Developments in English for Specific Purposes: A Multi-Disciplinary Approach*. Cambridge: Cambridge University Press.

Dudley-Evans, T., and J. Swales. 1980. Study modes and students from the Middle East. In *Study Modes and Academic Development of Overseas Students*, G. M. Greenall and J. E. Price (Eds.). ELT Documents 109.

Duff, P. 1986. Another look at interlanguage talk: Taking task to task. In *Talking to Learn: Conversation in Second Language Acquisition*, R. Day (Ed.), 147–181. Rowley, MA: Newbury House.

Dunkel, P. 1988a. The effect of delivery modification on notetaking and comprehension of L2 lectures. *Journal of Intensive English*, 2 (1): 41–52.

1988b. The content of L1 and L2 students' lecture notes and its relation to test performance. *TESOL Quarterly*, 22 (2): 260–279.

Dunkel, P. A., and J. M. Davis. 1994. The effects of rhetorical signaling cues on the recall of English lecture information by ESL and ENL listeners. In *Academic Listening: Research Perspectives*, J. Flowerdew (Ed.), 55–74. Cambridge: Cambridge University Press.

Dunkel, P., S. Mishra, and D. Berliner. 1989. Effects of note taking, memory and language proficiency on lecture learning for native and nonnative speakers of English. *TESOL Quarterly*, 23 (3): 543–550.

Duran, R., M. Canale, J. Penfield, C. Stansfield, and J. Liskin-Gasparro. 1985. *TOEFL from a Communicative Viewpoint on Language Proficiency: A Working Paper*. Princeton, NJ: Educational Testing Service.

Duszak, A. (Ed.). 1997. *Intellectual Styles and Cross-cultural Communication*. Berlin: Mouton de Gruyter.

Ede, L., and Lunsford, A. 1984. Audience addressed / audience invoked: The role of audience in composition theory and pedagogy. *College Composition and Communication*, 35: 155–171.

Educational Testing Service (ETS). 1998a. *Information Bulletin for TOEFL, TWE and TSE*. Princeton, NJ: Educational Testing Service.

Educational Testing Service (ETS). 1998b. *Information Bulletin for Computer-based Testing.* Princeton, NJ: Educational Testing Service.

Egginton, W. C. 1987. Written academic discourse in Korean: Implications for effective communication. In *Writing across Cultures: Analysis of L2 Text,* U. Connor, and R. Kaplan (Eds.), 153–168. Reading, MA: Addison-Wesley.

Ehrman, M. E., and R. L. Oxford. 1989. Effects of sex differences, career choice, and psychological type on adult language learning strategies. *Modern Language Journal,* 73 (1): 1–13.

1995. Cognition plus: Correlates of language learning success. *Modern Language Journal,* 79 (1): 67–89.

Eisterhold, J. C. 1990. Reading-writing connections: Toward a description for second language learners. In *Second Language Writing: Research Insights for the Classroom,* B. Kroll (Ed.), 88–101. Cambridge: Cambridge University Press.

Elder, C. 1993. Language proficiency as a predictor of performance in teacher education. *Melbourne Papers in Language Testing,* 2 (1): 68–89.

Ellis G., and B. Sinclair. 1989. *Learning to Learn English.* Cambridge: Cambridge University Press.

Emig, J. 1977. Writing as a mode of learning. *College Composition and Communication,* 32: 365–387.

English, S. L. 1986. Kinesics in academic lectures. *ESP Journal,* 4: 161–170.

Entwistle, N. J. (Ed.). 1985. *New Directions in Educational Psychology 1. Learning and Teaching.* London: The Falmer Press.

Entwistle, N. J., and D. Hounsell (Eds.). 1975. *How Students Learn.* Lancaster: Institute for Post-Compulsory Education, Lancaster University.

Entwistle, N. J., and J. D. Wilson. 1977. *Degrees of Excellence: The Academic Achievement Game.* London: Hodder and Stoughton.

Enyedi, A., and P. Medgyes. 1998. ELT in Central and Eastern Europe. *Language Teaching,* January: 1–12.

Eskey, D. 1997. Syllabus design in content-based instruction. In *The Content-based Classroom: Perspectives on Integrating Language and Content,* M. A. Snow, and D. M. Brinton (Eds.), 132–141. White Plains, NY: Longman. (Reprinted from *The CATESOL Journal,* 5 (1): 11–24, 1992.)

Esposito, M., K Marshall, and F. L. Stoller. 1997. Poster sessions by experts. In *New Ways in Content-based Instruction,* D. M. Brinton, and P. Master (Eds.), 115–118. Alexandria, VA: TESOL.

Evensen, L. 1996. The hidden curriculum of technology for academic writing: Toward a research agenda. In *Academic Writing: Intercultural and Textual Issues,* E. Ventola, and A. Mauranen (Eds.), 89–111. Amsterdam: John Benjamins.

Exline, R. V., and C. Eldridge. 1967. Effects of two patterns of a speaker's visual behaviour upon the perception of the authenticity of his verbal message. Paper presented at a meeting of the Eastern Psychological Association, Boston.

Eyraud, K., G. Giles, S. Koenig, and F. L. Stoller. 2000. The word wall approach: Promoting L2 vocabulary learning. *English Teaching Forum*, 38 (3): 2–11.

Fahnestock, J. 1986. Accommodating science: The rhetorical life of scientific facts. *Written Communication*, 3: 275–296.

Faigley, L. 1986. Competing theories of process: A critique and proposal. *College English*, 48: 527–542.

Fairclough, N. 1992. *Critical Language Awareness*. London: Longman.

Farid, A. 1985. *A Vocabulary Workbook*. Englewood Cliffs: Prentice Hall.

Farrell, P. 1990. *Vocabulary in ESP: A lexical analysis of the English of electronics and a study of semi-technical vocabulary*. CLCS Occasional Paper No. 25, Trinity College.

Ferris, D. R. 1995a. Student reactions to teacher response in multiple-draft composition classrooms. *TESOL Quarterly*, 29: 33–53.

1995b. Can advanced ESL students be taught to correct their most serious and frequent errors? *CATESOL Journal*, 8 (1): 41–62.

1995c. Teaching ESL composition students to become independent self-editors. *TESOL Journal*, 4 (4): 18–22.

1997. The influence of teacher commentary on student revision. *TESOL Quarterly*, 31: 315–339.

1998. Students' views of academic aural/oral skills: A comparative needs analysis. *TESOL Quarterly*, 32 (2): 289–318.

1999. The case for grammar correction in L2 writing classes: A response to Truscott (1996). *Journal of Second Language Writing*, 8: 1–10.

Ferris, D., and J. Hedgcock. 1998. *Teaching ESL Composition: Purpose, Process, and Practice*. Mahwah, NJ: Lawrence Erlbaum.

Ferris, D. R., S. Pezone, C. R. Tade, and S. Tinti. 1997. Teacher commentary on student writing: Descriptions and implications. *Journal of Second Language Writing*, 6: 155–182.

Ferris, D., and T. Tagg. 1996a. Academic listening/speaking tasks for students: Problems, suggestions, and implications. *TESOL Quarterly*, 30: 297–320.

1996b. Academic oral communication needs of EAP learners: What subject-matter instructors actually require. *TESOL Quarterly*, 30: 31–58.

Finkel, S. 1995. *Causal Analysis with Panel Data*. Sage University Paper series on Quantitative Applications in the Social Sciences 7–105. Thousand Oaks, CA: Sage.

Flower, L., and John R. Hayes. 1981. A cognitive process theory of writing. *College Composition and Communication*, 32: 365–387.

Flowerdew, J. 1992. Definitions in science lectures. *Applied Linguistics*, 13 (2): 202–221.

1993a. Content-based language instruction in a tertiary setting. *English for Specific Purposes*, 12: 121–138.

1993b. An educational, or process approach to the teaching of professional genres. *ELT Journal*, 47: 305–316.

1993c. Concordancing as a tool in course design. *System*, 21: 231–244.

(Ed.), 1994a. *Academic Listening: Research Perspectives*. Cambridge: Cambridge University Press.

1994b. Specific language for specific purposes: Concordancing for the ESP syllabus. In *LSP – Problems and Prospects*, R. Khoo (Ed.). Anthology Series 13. Singapore: SEAMEO Regional Language Centre.

1994c. Research of relevance to second language lecture comprehension – an overview. In *Academic Listening: Research Perspectives*, J. Flowerdew (Ed.), 7–29. Cambridge: Cambridge University Press.

(In press). Genre in the classroom: A linguistic approach. In *Genres in the Classroom*, A. Johns (Ed.). Mahwah, New Jersey: Erlbaum.

1999. Writing for scholarly publication in English: The case of Hong Kong. *Journal of Second Language Writing*, 8 (2): 123–145.

Flowerdew, J., D. Li, and L. Miller. 1998. Attitudes towards English and Cantonese among Hong Kong Chinese university lecturers. *TESOL Quarterly*, 32: 201–231.

Flowerdew, J., and L. Miller. 1992. Student perceptions, problems and strategies in second language lecture comprehension. *RELC Journal*, 23: 60–80.

1995. On the notion of culture in second language lectures. *TESOL Quarterly*, 29 (2): 345–374.

1996. Lectures in a second language: Notes towards a cultural grammar. *English for Specific Purposes*, 15 (2): 345–373.

1997. The teaching of academic listening comprehension and the question of authenticity. *English for Specific Purposes*, 16 (1): 27–46.

Flowerdew, J., and S. Tauroza. 1995. The effect of discourse markers on second language lecture comprehension. *Studies in Second Language Acquisition*, 17 (4): 435–458.

Fonzari, L. 1999. English in the Estonian multicultural society. *World Englishes*, 18 (1): 39–48.

Frank, M. 1990. *Writing as Thinking: A Guided Process Approach*. Englewood Cliffs, NJ: Prentice Hall.

Fransson, A. 1977. On qualitative differences in learning, IV. Effects of motivation and test anxiety on process and outcome. *British Journal of Educational Psychology*, 47: 244–257.

1984. Cramming or understanding? Effects of intrinsic and extrinsic motivation on approach to learning and test performance. In *Reading in a Foreign Language*, J. C. Alderson, and A. Urquhart (Eds.), 86–121. London: Longman.

Freebody, P., and R. C. Anderson. 1981. Effects of vocabulary difficulty, text cohesion, and schema availability on reading comprehension. Technical Report No. 225. Urbana, IL: University of Illinois Centre for the Study of Reading.

Freedman, A., and P. Medway (Eds.). 1994. *Genre and the New Rhetoric*. London: Taylor and Francis.

Frodesen, J. 1991. Grammar in writing. In *Teaching English as a Second or*

Foreign Language (2nd edition), M. Celce-Murcia (Ed.), 264–276. Boston: Heinle and Heinle.

Frodesen, J. 1995. Negotiating the syllabus: A learner-centred, interactive approach to ESL graduate writing course design. In *Academic Writing in a Second Language*, D. Belcher, and G. Braine (Eds.), 331–350. Norwood, NJ: Ablex.

Fujimura, J. H. 1996. *Crafting Science: A Sociohistory of the Quest for the Genetics of Cancer.* Cambridge, MA: Harvard University Press.

Fulcher, G. 1997. Assessing writing. In *Writing in the English Language Classroom*, G. Fulcher (Ed.), 91–107. Hemel Hempstead: Prentice Hall Europe ELT.

  1999. Assessment in English for academic purposes: Putting content validity in its place. *Applied Linguistics*, 20: 221–236.

Fuller, S. 1997. *Science.* Buckingham: The Open University Press.

Fulwiler, T. 1982. Writing: An act of cognition. In *Teaching Writing in All Disciplines*, C. W. Griffin (Ed.), 15–36. San Francisco: Jossey-Bass.

Furneaux, C., C. Locke, P. Robinson, and A. Tonkyn. 1991. Talking heads and shifting bottoms: The ethnography of seminars. In *Socio-Cultural Issues in English for Academic Purposes. Developments in ELT*, P. Adams, B. Heaton, and P. Howarth (Eds.). Hemel Hempstead: Pheonix ELT.

Furneaux C., P. Robinson, and A. Tonkyn. 1988. Making friends and influencing tutors: Strategies for promoting acculturation in the EAP classroom. In *Individualisation and Autonomy in Language Learning*, Brookes and Grundy (Eds.), 88–99. ELT Documents 131. Oxford: Modern English Publications / British Council.

Gajdusek, L. 1988. Toward wider use of literature in ESL: Why and how. *TESOL Quarterly*, 22: 227–257.

Gardner D., and L. Miller (Eds.). 1994. *Directions in Self-Access Language Learning.* Hong Kong: Hong Kong University Press.

  1999. *Establishing Self-Access: From Theory to Practice.* Cambridge: Cambridge University Press.

Geertz, C. 1975. *The Interpretation of Cultures.* London: Hutchinson.

Genesee, F., and J. Upshur. 1996. *Classroom-based Evaluation in Second Language Education.* Cambridge: Cambridge University Press.

Ghadessy, M. 1979. Frequency counts, word lists, and materials preparation: A new approach. *English Teaching Forum*, 17 (1): 24–27.

Giannoni, D. S. 1998. The genre of journal acknowledgments: Findings of a cross-disciplinary investigation. *Linguistica e Filologia*, 6: 61–83.

Gibbs G. 1985. Teaching study skills. In *New Directions in Educational Psychology 1. Learning and Teaching*, N. J. Entwistle (Ed.). London: The Falmer Press.

Gibbs, W. W. 1995. Lost science in the Third World. *Scientific American*, August, 1995: 76–83.

Giddens, A. (1984). *The Constitution of Society: Outline of the Theory of Structuration.* Cambridge: Polity Press.

Gilbert, G. N., and M. Mulkay. 1984. *Opening Pandora's Box: A Sociological Analysis of Scientists' Discourse.* Cambridge: Cambridge University Press.

Ginther, A., and L. Grant. 1996. A review of the academic needs of native English-speaking college students in the United States. TOEFL Monograph Series, MS-1. Princeton, NJ: Educational Testing Service.

Giroux, Henry A. 1983. *Theory and Resistance in Education: A Pedagogy for the Opposition.* South Hadley: Bergin.

 1992. *Border Crossings: Cultural Workers and the Politics of Education.* New York: Routledge.

Gleitman, L. R., and P. Rozin. 1973. Teaching reading by use of a syllabary. *Reading Research Quarterly,* 8: 447–483.

Godman, A., and M. E. F. Payne. 1981. A taxonomic approach to the lexis of science. In *English for Academic and Technical Purposes: Studies in Honor of Louis Trimble,* 23–39. Newbury House, Rowley, Mass.

Goh, C. 1997. Metacognitive awareness and second language listeners. *ELT Journal,* 51 (4): 361–369.

 1998. Emerging environments of EAP. *RELC Journal,* 29 (1): 20–33.

Goldinger, S. D. 1996. Words and voices: Episodic traces in spoken word identification and recognition memory. *Journal of Experimental Psychology: Leaning, Memory and Cognition,* 22: 1166–1183.

Goldstein, L., C. Campbell, and M. C. Cummings 1997. Smiling through the turbulence: The flight attendant syndrome and writing instructor status in the adjunct model. In *The Content-based Classroom: Perspectives on Integrating Language and Content,* M. A. Snow, and D. M. Brinton (Eds.), 331–339. White Plains, NY: Longman.

Goldstein, L., and S. Conrad. 1990. Student input and the negotiation of meaning in ESL writing conferences. *TESOL Quarterly,* 24: 443–460.

Goleman, D. 1996. *Emotional Intelligence: Why It Can Matter More Than IQ.* London: Bloomsbury Publishers.

Goodman, K S. 1967. Reading: A psycholinguistic guessing game. *Journal of the Reading Specialist,* 6: 126–135.

 1973. Psycholinguistic universals in the reading process. In *Psycholinguistics and Reading,* F. Smith (Ed.), 21–29. New York: Holt, Rinehart and Winston.

Gosden, H. 1992. Discourse functions of marked theme in scientific research articles. *English for Specific Purposes,* 11: 207–224.

Gottman, J. M. 1996. *The Analysis of Change.* Mahwah, NJ: Lawrence Erlbaum.

Grabe, W. 1986. The transition from theory to practice in teaching reading. In *Teaching Second Language Reading for Academic Purposes,* F. Dubin, D. E. Eskey, and W. Grabe (Eds.), 25–48. Reading, MA: Addison-Wesley.

 1988a. English, information access and technology transfer: A rationale for English as an international language. *World Englishes,* 7 (1): 63–72.

 1988b. Reassessing the term 'Interactive'. In *Interactive Approaches to*

Second Language Reading, P. L. Carrell, J. Devine, and D. E. Eskey (Eds.), 56–72. Cambridge: Cambridge University Press.

1991. Current developments in second language reading research. *TESOL Quarterly*, 25: 375–406.

Grabe, W., and R. Kaplan. 1996. *Theory and Practice of Writing. An Applied Linguistic Perspective*. London: Longman.

Graddol, D. 1997. *The Future of English?* London: British Council.

Graham, J. 1987. English language proficiency and prediction of academic success. *TESOL Quarterly*, 21 (3): 505–521.

Green, J. M. 1993. *The Word Wall: Teaching Vocabulary Through Immersion*. Ontario: Pippin Publishing.

Green, J. M., and R. Oxford. 1995. A closer look at learning strategies, L2 proficiency, and gender. *TESOL Quarterly*, 29 (2): 261–297.

Grellet, F. 1981. *Developing Reading Skills*. Cambridge: Cambridge University Press.

Gremmo, M-J., and P. Riley. 1995. Autonomy, self-direction and self access in language teaching and learning: The history of an idea. *System*, 23 (2): 151–164.

Gruba, P., and C. Corbel. 1997. Computer-based testing. In *Encyclopedia of Language and Education*, C. Clapham,and D. Corson (Eds.), 141–149. Dordrecht, the Netherlands: Kluwer Academic Publishers.

Gu, P. Y. 1996. Robin Hood in SLA: What has the learning strategy researcher taught us? *Asian Journal of English Language Teaching*, 6: 1–29.

Gunnarsson, B-L. 1997. Language for specific purposes. In *Encyclopedia of Language and Education, Volume 4: Second Language Education*, G. R. Tucker, and D. Corson (Eds.), 105–117. Amsterdam: Kluwer Academic Publishers.

Gupta, J. K., A. B. L. Srivastava, and K. K. Sharma. 1988. On the optimum predictive potential of change measure. *Journal of Experimental Education* 56: 124–128.

1989. Estimation of true change using additional information provided by an auxiliary variable. *Journal of Experimental Education*, 57: 143–150.

Haas, C. 1994. Learning to read biology: One student's rhetorical development in college. *Written Communication*, 11 (1): 43–84.

Hafernik, J. J., D. Messerschmidt, and S. Vandrick. 1996. What are IEPs really doing about content? *Journal of Intensive English Studies*, 10: 31–47.

Hairston, Maxine. 1982. The winds of change: Thomas Kuhn and the revolution in the teaching of writing. *College Composition and Communication*, 33: 76–88.

1986. On not being a composition slave. In *Training the New Teacher of College Composition*, Charles W. Bridges (Ed.), 117–124. Urbana, IL: NCTE.

Hall, D., and B. Kenny. 1988. An approach to a truly communicative methodology: The AIT pre-sessional course. *English for Specific Purposes*, 7 (1): 19–32.

Hall, S., and D. Crabbe. 1994. *English for Business and Technology Course Design*. Singapore: SEAMEO Regional Language Centre.

Halliday, M. A. K. 1989. *Spoken and Written Language*. Oxford: Oxford University Press.

Halliday, M. A. K., A. McIntosh, and P. Strevens. 1964. *The Linguistic Sciences and Language Teaching*. London: Longman.

Halliday, M. A. K., and R. Hasan. 1976. *Cohesion in English*. London: Longman.

Halliday, M. A. K., and J. R. Martin. 1993. *Writing Science: Literacy and Discursive Power*. Pittsburgh, PA: University of Pittsburgh.

Hamayan, E. 1995. Approaches to alternative assessment. In *Annual Review of Applied Linguistics (1995)*, W. Grabe, (Ed.), 212–226. New York: Cambridge University Press.

Hambleton, R. K., and M. Murphy. 1992. A psychometric perspective on authentic measurement. *Applied Measurement in Education*, 5: 1–16.

Hamilton, J. 1996. *Inspiring Innovations in Language Teaching*. Bristol, PA: Multilingual Matters.

Hamp-Lyons, L. 1990. Second language writing: Assessment issues. In *Second Language Writing: Research Insights for the Classroom*, B. Kroll (Ed.), 69–87. Cambridge: Cambridge University Press.

1991a. Pre-text: Task-related influences on the writer. In *Assessing Second Language Writing in Academic Contexts*, L. Hamp-Lyons (Ed.). Norwood, NJ: Ablex Publishing Corporation.

1991b. Scoring procedures for ESL contexts. In *Assessing Second Language Writing in Academic Contexts*, L. Hamp-Lyons (Ed.), 241–278. Norwood, NJ: Ablex Publishing Corporation.

(Ed.). 1991c. *Assessing Second Language Writing in Academic Contexts*. Norwood, NJ: Ablex.

1996. The challenges of second-language writing assessment. In *Assessment of Writing: Politics, Policies, Practices*, E. M. White, W. D. Lutz, and S. Kamusikiri (Eds.). New York, NY: The Modern Language Association of America.

1998. Ethical test preparation practice: The case of the TOEFL. *TESOL Quarterly*, 32 (3): 329–337.

Hamp-Lyons, L., and W. Condon. 1993. Questioning assumptions about portfolio-based assessment. *College Composition and Communication*, 44: 176–190.

Hamp-Lyons, L., and B. Heasley. 1987. *Study Writing*. Cambridge: Cambridge University Press.

Hansen, C., and C. Jensen. 1994. Evaluating lecturer comprehension. In *Academic Listening: Research Perspectives*, J. Flowerdew (Ed.). Cambridge: Cambridge University Press.

Harklau, L., K. Losey, and M. Siegal (Eds.). 1999. *Language Minority Students, ESL, and College Composition*. Mahwah, NJ: Lawrence Erlbaum.

Harmer J. 1987. *Teaching and Learning Grammar.* London: Longman.

Harris, D. P. 1969. *Testing English as a Second Language.* New York: McGraw-Hill.

Harris, J. 1989. The idea of community in the study of writing. *College Composition and Communication,* 40 (1): 11–22.

Hawkey, R. 1982. An Investigation of Inter-Relationships between Cognitive/Affective and Social Factors and Language Learning. University of London: Unpublished PhD thesis.

Haynes, M. 1993. Patterns and perils of guessing in second language reading. In *Second Language Reading and Vocabulary Learning,* T. Huckin, M. Haynes, and J. Coady (Eds.), 46–62. Norwood, NJ: Ablex.

Hazel, M., and J. Ayres. 1998. Conversational turntaking behaviours of Japanese and Americans in small groups. *JALT Journal,* 20: 91–99.

Hedgcock, J., and N. Lefkowitz. 1994. Feedback on feedback: Assessing learner receptivity to teacher response in L2 composing. *Journal of Second Language Writing,* 3: 141–163.

Henrichsen, L. E. 1989. *Diffusion of Innovations in English Language Teaching: The ELEC Effort in Japan, 1956–1968.* New York: Greenwood Press.

Henry, A., and R. L. Roseberry. 1998. An evaluation of a genre-based approach to the teaching of EAP/ESP writing. *TESOL Quarterly,* 32 (1): 147–156.

Henry, J., and N. Pritchard. 1999. TEFL by distance. In *Innovation and Best Practice,* C. Kennedy (Ed.), 46–58. Harlow: Longman.

Herbert, A. J. 1965. *The Structure of Technical English.* London: Longman.

Herbolich, B. 1979. Box kites. *English for Specific Purposes.* English Language Institute, Oregon State University No. 29. Reprinted in J. M. Swales (Ed.) *Episodes in ESP.* Hemel Hempstead: Prentice Hall International.

Herrington, A. 1985. Writing in academic settings: A study of the contexts for writing in two college chemical engineering courses. *Research in the Teaching of English,* 19: 331–361.

Herrington, A., and C. Moran. 1992. *Writing, Teaching, and Learning in the Disciplines.* New York: Modern Languages Association of America.

Hewings M., and T. Dudley-Evans (Eds.). 1996. *Evaluation and Course Design in EAP.* Hemel Hempstead: Phoenix ELT.

Hewings, M., and C. Nickerson (Eds.). 1999. *Business English: Research into Practice.* Harlow: Longman.

Higgins, J. J. 1966. Hard facts. *ELT Journal,* 21 (1): 55–60.

Higher Education Statistics Agency. 1997. *Higher Education Statistics in the United Kingdom.* London.

Hilke, R., and P. Wadden. 1997. The TOEFL and its imitators: Analysing the TOEFL and evaluating TOEFL-prep tests. *RELC Journal,* 28 (10): 28–53.

Hindmarsh, R. 1980. *Cambridge English Lexicon.* London: Cambridge University Press.

Hinds, J. 1987. Reader versus writer responsibility: A new typology. In *Writing Across Languages: Analysis of L2 text*, U. Connor, and R. Kaplan. (Eds.), 141–152. Reading, MA: Addison Wesley.

Hirsh, D., and P. Nation. 1992. What vocabulary size is needed to read unsimplified texts for pleasure? *Reading in a Foreign Language*, 8: 689–696.

Hirvela, A. 1990. ESP and literature: A reassessment. *English for Specific Purposes*, 9: 237–252.

1997. 'Disciplinary portfolios' and EAP writing instruction. *English for Specific Purposes*, 16 (2): 83–100.

Ho, Y. 1993. Review of 'Learning to Learn English: A Course in Learner Training' (Ellis and Sinclair, 1989). *TESOL Quarterly*, 27 (1): 122–124.

Holec, H. 1981. *Autonomy and Foreign Language Learning*. Oxford: Pergamon.

(Ed.). 1988. *Autonomy and Self-Directed Learning: Present Fields of Application*. Strasbourg: Council of Europe.

Holliday, A. 1992. Tissue rejection and informal orders in ELT projects: Collecting the right information. *Applied Linguistics*, 13 (4): 403–424.

1994. *Appropriate Methodology and Social Context*. Cambridge: Cambridge University Press.

1999. Achieving cultural continuity in curriculum innovation. In *Innovation and Best Practice*, C. Kennedy (Ed.), 23–31. Harlow: Longman.

Holten, C. 1997. Literature: A quintessential content. In *The Content-based Classroom: Perspectives on Integrating Language and Content*, M. A. Snow, and D. M. Brinton (Eds.), 377–387. White Plains, NY: Longman.

Hopkins, A., and T. Dudley-Evans. 1988. A genre-based investigation of the discussion section in articles and dissertations. *English for Specific Purposes*, 7: 113–122.

Hornberger, N. 1994. Literacy and Language Planning. *Language and Education*, 8: 75–86.

Horowitz, D. 1986a. Process not product: Less than meets the eye. *TESOL Quarterly*, 20: 141–144.

1986b. What professors actually require: Academic tasks for the ESL classroom. *TESOL Quarterly*, 20: 445–461.

1990. Fiction and nonfiction in the ESL/EFL classroom: Does the difference make a difference? *English for Specific Purposes*, 9: 161–168.

Horst, M., T. Cobb, and P. Meara. 1998. Beyond A Clockwork Orange: Acquiring second language vocabulary through reading. *Reading in a Foreign Language*, 11 (2): 207–223.

Horzella, M., and G. Sindermann. 1992. Aspects of scientific discourse: Conditional argumentation. *English for Specific Purposes*, 11: 129–139.

Houghton, D., C. Long, and P. Fanning. 1988. Autonomy and individualisation in language learning: the role and responsibilities of the EAP tutor. In *Individualisation and Autonomy in Language Learning*, Brookes and

Grundy (Eds.), 75–87. ELT Documents 131. Oxford: Modern English Publications / British Council.

Howatt, A. P. R. 1984. *A History of English Language Teaching*. Oxford: Oxford University Press.

Huckin, T. N. 1988. Achieving professional communicative relevance in a 'generalised' ESP classroom. In *ESP in the Classroom: Practice and Evaluation*, D. Chamberlain, and R. J. Baumgardner (Eds.), 61–70. ELT Document 128. Modern English Publications and the British Council.

Huddleston, R. N. 1971. *The Sentence in Written English: A Syntactic Study Based on an Analysis of Scientific Texts*. Cambridge: Cambridge University Press.

Hughes, A. 1988. Achievement and proficiency: The missing link? In *Testing English for University Study*, A. Hughes (Ed.), 36–44. London: Modern English Publications and The British Council.

Hutchinson, T., and A. Waters. 1987. *English for Specific Purposes*. Cambridge: Cambridge University Press.

Hwang, K. 1989. *Reading Newspapers for the Improvement of Vocabulary and Reading Skills*. Victoria University of Wellington, New Zealand: Unpublished MA thesis.

Hwang, K., and P. Nation. 1994. *VocabProfile: Vocabulary analysis software*. English Language Institute, Victoria University of Wellington, New Zealand.

Hyland, K. 1997. *Hedging in Scientific Research Articles*. Amsterdam: John Benjamins.

1998. Persuasion and context: The pragmatics of academic discourse. *Journal of Pragmatics*, 30: 437–455.

(In press). Reporting verbs in research articles.

Hyon, S. 1996. Genre in three traditions: Implications for ESL. *TESOL Quarterly*, 30: 693–722.

Irifune, T., N. Nishiyama, K. Kuroda. T. Inoue, M. Isshiki, W. Utsume, K. Funakoshi, S. Urakawa, T. Uchida, T. Katsura, and O. Ohtaka. 1998. The postspinel phase boundary in Mg_2SiO_4 determined by in situ X-ray diffraction. *Science*, 279: 1698–1700.

Isaacs, G. 1994. Lecturing practices and note-taking purposes. *Studies in Higher Education*, 19 (2): 203–216.

Ishiguro, K. 1982/1987. A Family Supper. In *The Penguin Book of Modern British Short Stories*, M. Bradbury (Ed.), 434–442. Harmondsworth, Middlesex: Viking.

Jacobson, W. H. 1987. An assessment of the communication needs of non-native speakers of English in an undergraduate Physics lab. *English for Specific Purposes*, 6: 173–186.

Jacoby, S., D. Leech, and C. Holte. 1995. A genre-based developmental writing course for undergraduate ESL science majors. In *Academic Writing in a Second Language. Essays on Research and Pedagogy*, D. Belcher, and G. Braine (Eds.). Norwood, NJ: Ablex.

Janopoulos, M. 1986. The relationship between pleasure reading and second language writing proficiency. *TESOL Quarterly*, 20: 763–768.

1992. University faculty tolerance of NS and NNS writing errors. *Journal of Second Language Writing*, 1: 109–122.

Janzen, J. 1996. Teaching strategic reading. *TESOL Journal*, 6 (1): 6–9.

Janzen, J., and F. L. Stoller. 1998. Integrating strategic reading in L2 instruction. *Reading in a Foreign Language*, 12 (1): 251–269.

Jenkins, R. 1992. *Pierre Bourdieu*, London: Routledge.

Jensen, C., and C. Hansen. 1995. The effect of prior knowledge on EAP listening test performance. *Language Testing*, 12: 99–119.

Jernudd, B. 1990. Two approaches to language planning. In *Language Use, Language Teaching and the Curriculum*, V. Bickley (Ed.), 48–53. Hong Kong: IELE.

Jernudd, B. H., and R. B. Baldauf, Jnr. 1987. Planning science communication for human resource development. In *Language Education in Human Resource Development*, B. K. Das (Ed.), 144–189. Singapore: SEAMEO Regional Language Centre.

Johns, A. M. 1981. Necessary English: A faculty survey. *TESOL Quarterly*, 15: 51–57.

1988. The discourse communities dilemma: Identifying transferable skills for the academic milieu. *English for Specific Purposes*, 7: 55–59.

1990. L1 composition theories: Implications for developing theories of L2 composition. In *Second Language Writing: Research Insights for the Classroom*, B. Kroll (Ed.), 24–36. Cambridge: Cambridge University Press.

1993. Written argumentation for real audiences: Suggestions for teacher research and classroom practice. *TESOL Quarterly*, 27: 75–90.

1994. Issues in ESP for the 90s. In *LSP – Problems and Prospects*, R. Khoo (Ed.). Anthology Series 13. Singapore: SEAMEO Regional Language Centre.

1995a. Genre and pedagogical purposes. *Journal of Second Language Writing*, 4: 181–190.

1995b. Teaching classroom and authentic genres: Initiating students into academic cultures and discourses. In *Academic Writing in a Second Language*, D. Belcher and G. Braine (Eds.). Norwood, NJ: Ablex.

1997a. *Text, Role and Context*. Cambridge: Cambridge University Press.

1997b. English for specific purposes and content-based instruction: What is the relationship? In *The Content-based Classroom: Perspectives on Integrating Language and Content*, M. A. Snow, and D. M. Brinton (Eds.), 363–366. White Plains, NY: Addison Wesley Longman.

1998. The visual and the verbal: A case study in macroeconomics. *English for Specific Purposes*, 17: 183–197.

2000a. Genre and pedagogy: The introduction. In *Genre and Pedagogy*, A. M. Johns (Ed.). Mahwah, NJ: Lawrence Erlbaum.

(Ed.). 2000b. *Genre and Pedagogy*. Mahwah, NJ: Lawrence Erlbaum.

(Forthcoming). Destabilising and enriching novice students' genre theories.

In *Genres in the Classroom: Theory, Research and Practice*, A. Johns (Ed.). Mahwah, NJ: Lawrence Erlbaum.

Johns, A. M., and T. Dudley-Evans. 1991. English for specific purposes: International in scope, specific in purpose. *TESOL Quarterly*, 25 (2): 297–314.

Johns, C. M., and T. F. Johns. 1977. Seminar discussion strategies. In *English for Academic Purposes*, A. P. Cowie, and J. B. Heaton (Eds.). Reading: BAAL/SELMOUS.

Johns, T. F. (no date). The text and its message: An approach to the teaching of reading strategies for students of Development Administration. Mimeo.

1988. Whence and whither classroom concordancing? In *Computer Applications in Language Learning*, T. Bongaerts, T. van Els, and H. Wekker (Eds.), 9–33. Dordrecht: Foris.

Johns, T. F., and F. Davies. 1983. Text as a vehicle for information: The classroom use of written texts in teaching reading in a foreign language. *Reading in a Foreign Language*, 1: 1–19.

Johns, T. F., and A. Dudley-Evans. 1980. An experiment in team-teaching of overseas post-graduate students of transportation and plant biology. In *Team-Teaching in ESP*, 6–23. ELT Documents 106. London: The British Council.

Johnson, D. M., and D. H. Roen (Eds.). 1989. *Richness in Writing: Empowering ESL Students*. New York: Longman.

Johnson, K 1981. *Communicate in Writing*. London: Longman.

Johnson, R. K., C. K. W. Shek, and E. H. F. Law. 1993. *Using English as the Medium of Instruction (Teaching in Hong Kong No. 6)*. Hong Kong: Longman.

Johnson, S., P. Linton, and R. Madigan. 1994. The role of internal standards in assessment of written discourse. *Discourse Processes*, 18: 231–245.

Jones, K 1982. *Simulations in Language Teaching*. Cambridge: Cambridge University Press.

Jordan, R. R. 1989. English for academic purposes (EAP). *Language Teaching*, 22 (3): 150–164.

1990. *Academic Writing Course*. London: Nelson.

1997. *English for Academic Purposes: A Guide and Resource Book for Teachers*. Cambridge: Cambridge University Press.

Jungheim, N. 1995. Assessing the unsaid: The development of tests of nonverbal ability. In *Language Testing in Japan*, J. Brown, and S. Yamashita (Eds.), 149–163. Tokyo: JALT Publications.

Kachru, B. B. (Ed.). 1982. *The Other Tongue: English Across Cultures*. Urbana, IL: University of Illinois Press.

1985. Standards, codification and sociolinguistic realism: The English language in a global context. In *English in the World: Teaching and Learning the Languages and Literatures*, R. Quirk and H. Widdowson (Eds.), 11–30. Cambridge: Cambridge University Press.

1988. ESP and non-native varieties of English: Towards a shift in paradigm. In *ESP in the Classroom: Practice and Evaluation*, D. Chamberlain and R. J. Baumgardner (Eds.), 9–28. ELT Documents 128. London: Modern English Publications and the British Council.

1991. World Englishes and applied linguistics. In *Languages and Standards: Issues, Attitudes and Case Studies*, M. L. Tickoo (Ed.), 178–205. Singapore: SEAMEO Regional Language Centre.

1995a. World Englishes: Approaches, issues and resources. In *Readings on Second Language Acquisition*, H. D. Brown, and S. Gonzo (Eds.), 229–261. Englewood Cliffs, NJ: Prentice Hall.

1995b. Contrastive rhetoric in World Englishes. *English Today*, 41: 21–31.

Kamler, B., and T. Threadgold. 1997. Which thesis did you read? In *Policy and Practice of Tertiary Literacy*, Z. Golebiowski (Ed.). Proceedings of the First National Conference on Tertiary Literacy: Research and Practice. Volume 1. Melbourne: Victoria University of Technology.

Kaplan, R. B. 1966. Cultural thought patterns in intercultural education. *Language Learning*, 16: 1–20.

1987. Cultural thought patterns revisited. In *Writing Across Languages: Analysis of L2 Text*, U. Connor, and R. B. Kaplan (Eds.). Reading, MA: Addison Wesley.

1989. Language planning v planning language. In *Language Learning and Community*, C. Candlin, and T. McNamara (Eds.). 193–203. Sydney: NCELTR.

Kaplan, R. B., and P. A. Shaw. 1983. *Exploring Academic Discourse. A Textbook for Advanced Level ESL Reading and Writing Students*. Rowley, Mass: Newbury House.

Kasper, L. F. 1995a. Theory and practice in content-based ESL reading instruction. *English for Specific Purposes*, 14: 223–230.

1995b. Discipline-oriented ESL reading instruction. *Teaching English in the Two-Year College* 22: 45–53.

1995/96. Using discipline-based texts to boost college ESL reading instruction. *Journal of Adolescent and Adult Literacy*, 39: 298–306.

1997. The impact of content-based instructional programmes on the academic progress of ESL students. *English for Specific Purposes*, 16: 309–320.

Kendon, A. 1967. Some functions of gaze-direction in social interaction. *Acta Psychologica*, 26: 22–63.

Kendon, A., and M. Cook. 1969. The consistency of gaze patterns in social interaction. *British Journal of Psychology*, 60: 481–494.

Kennedy, C. (Ed.). 1984. *Language Planning and Language Education*. London: Allen and Unwin.

1985. Language planning – state of the art. In *Language Teaching Surveys*, V. Kinsella (Ed.), 19–45. Cambridge: Cambridge University Press.

1986. Language planning, channel management, and ESP. In *Language in Education in Africa*, 69–100. Centre for African Studies. Edinburgh: University of Edinburgh Press.

1987a. The future of ELT. *System*, 14 (3): 307–314.

1987b. Innovating for a change: Teacher development and innovation. *ELT Journal*, 41 (3): 163–170.

1988. Costs, benefits, and motivation in ESP. *ESPMENA*, 30: 15–24.

(Ed.). 1989. *Language Planning and Language Teaching*. Hemel Hempstead: Prentice Hall.

1996. Teachers as agents of change. In *Quality Management and the Management of Change*, J. O'Dwyer (Ed.), 12–19. Ankara, Turkey: University of Bilkent and Whitstable: IATEFL.

1997. Training trainers as change agents. In *Learning to Train*, I. McGrath (Ed.), 127–139. Hemel Hempstead: Prentice Hall.

1999. Fit or split – innovation and best practice. In *Innovation and Best Practice*, C. Kennedy (Ed.), 1–8. Harlow: Longman.

Kennedy, C., and J. Kennedy. 1996. Teacher attitudes and change implementation. *System*, 24 (3): 351–360.

Kennedy, G. 1992. Preferred ways of putting things with implications for language teaching. In *Directions in Corpus Linguistics*, J. Svartvik (Ed.). Berlin: Mouton de Gruyter.

Kenworthy J. 1987. *Teaching English Pronunciation*. London: Longman.

Kern, R. G. 1989. Second language reading strategy instruction: Its effects on comprehension and word inference ability. *Modern Language Journal*, 73 (2): 135–149.

King, P. 1994. Visual and verbal messages in the engineering lecture: Note-taking by post-graduate L2 students. In *Academic Listening: Research Perspectives*, J. Flowerdew (Ed.), 219–238. Cambridge: Cambridge University Press.

Knapp, M. L., and J. A. Hall. 1997. *Nonverbal Communication in Human Interaction* (4th edition). Orlando, FL: Harcourt Brace.

Knorr-Cetina, K. D. 1981. *The Manufacture of Knowledge*. Oxford: Pergamon Press.

Koda, K. 1988. Cognitive processes in second-language reading: Transfer of L1 reading skills and strategies. *Second Language Research*, 4: 133–156.

Koh, M. Y. 1985. The role of prior knowledge in reading comprehension. *Reading in a Foreign Language*, 3: 375–380.

Kramsch, C. J. 1993. *Context and Culture in Language Teaching*. Oxford: Oxford University Press.

Krashen, S. D. 1989. We acquire vocabulary and spelling by reading: Additional evidence for the input hypothesis. *Modern Language Journal*, 73: 440–464.

1993. *The Power of Reading: Insights from the Research*. Englewood, CO: Libraries Unlimited.

Kress, G. 1990. Critical discourse analysis. *Annual Review of Applied Linguistics*, 11: 84–99.

Kroll, B. (Ed.). 1990. *Second Language Writing: Research Insights for the Classroom*. Cambridge: Cambridge University Press.

1998. Assessing writing abilities. In *Annual Review of Applied Linguistics*, W. Grabe (Ed.), 18: 219–240.

Kroll, B., and J. Reid 1994. Guidelines for developing writing prompts: Clarifications, caveats and cautions. *Journal of Second Language Writing*, 3: 231–255.

Ku, P. Y. N. 1997. Predictors of strategy choice by EFL students in Taiwan. Paper presented at RELC Seminar, Singapore, April 1997.

Kucera, H. 1982. The mathematics of language. In *The American Heritage Dictionary* (2nd College edition). Boston: Houghton Mifflin.

Kunz, L. 1972. *26 Steps. A Course in Controlled Composition for Intermediate and Advanced ESL Students*. New York: Language Innovations.

Kuo, C-H. 1993. Problematic issues in EST materials development. *English for Specific Purposes*, 12: 171–181.

Kusel, P. 1992. Rhetorical approaches to the study and composition of academic essays. *System*, 20 (4): 457–469.

Kusuyama, Y. 1998. *Grammar Instruction in Content-based EAP: From 'Fluency vs. Accuracy' to 'Fluency and Accuracy'*. University of California, Los Angeles: Unpublished manuscript.

Kwan-Terry, A. 1988. *Interactive Writing*. London: Prentice Hall.

LaBerge, D., and S. J. Samuels. 1974. Toward a theory of automatic information processing in reading. *Cognitive Psychology*, 6: 293–323.

Latour, B., and S. Woolgar. 1979. *Laboratory Life: The Social Construction of Scientific Facts*. Beverly Hills, CA: Sage Publications.

1986. *Laboratory Life: The Social Construction of Scientific Facts*. Beverly Hills, CA: Sage Publications; (2nd Edition), Princeton: Princeton University Press.

Laufer, B. 1992. How much lexis is necessary for reading comprehension? In *Vocabulary and Applied Linguistics*, P. J. Arnaud and H. Béjoint (Eds.), 126–132. London: Macmillan.

Laufer, B., and P. Nation. 1995. Vocabulary size and use: Lexical richness in L2 written production. *Applied Linguistics*, 16 (3): 307–322.

1999. A vocabulary size test of controlled productive ability. *Language Testing*, 16 (1): 33–51.

Laufer, B., and D. D. Sim. 1985. Taking the easy way out: Non-use and misuse of clues in EFL reading. *English Teaching Forum*, April: 7–10.

Lay, N. D. S. 1995. Response journals in the ESL classroom: Windows to the world. *Teaching English in the Two-Year College*, 22: 38–44.

Leeds, B. (Ed.). 1996. *Writing in a Second Language: Insights from First and Second Language Teaching and Research*. New York: Longman.

Leki, I. 1989. *Academic Writing: Techniques and Tasks*. New York: St Martin's Press.

1990a. Coaching from the margins: Issues in written response. In *Second Language Writing: Research Insights for the Classroom*, B. Kroll (Ed.), 57–68. Cambridge: Cambridge University Press.

1990b. Potential problems with peer responding in ESL writing classes. *CATESOL Journal*, 3: 5–19.

1991a. Twenty-five years of contrastive rhetoric: Text analysis and writing pedagogies. *TESOL Quarterly*, 25 (1): 123–143.

1991b. The preferences of ESL students for error correction in college-level writing classes. *Foreign Language Annals*, 24: 203–218.

1992. *Understanding ESL Writers*. Portsmouth, NH: Heinemann.

1995a. *Academic Writing: Exploring Processes and Strategies* (2nd Edition). New York: St Martin's Press.

1995b. Coping strategies of ESL students in writing tasks across the curriculum. *TESOL Quarterly* 29 (4): 235–260.

Leki, I., and J. Carson. 1994. Students' perceptions of EAP writing instruction and writing needs across the disciplines. *TESOL Quarterly* 28 (1): 81–101.

1997. 'Completely different worlds': EAP and the writing experiences of ESL students in university courses. *TESOL Quarterly*, 31 (1): 39–69.

Light, R. L., X. Ming, and J. Mossop. 1987. English proficiency and academic performance of international students. *TESOL Quarterly*, 21 (2): 251–261.

Lipp, E., and J. P. Wheeler. 1991. Sustaining the interest of academically oriented ESL students. *TESOL Quarterly*, 25: 185–189.

Little, D. 1990. Autonomy in language learning: Some theoretical and practical considerations. In *Autonomy in Language Learning*, I. Gathercole (Ed.), 7–15. London: Centre for Information on Language Teaching and Research.

1996. Freedom to learn and compulsion to interact: Promoting learner autonomy through the use of information systems and information technologies. In *Taking Control: Autonomy in Language Learning*, R. Pemberton, E. S. L. Li, W. W. F. Or and H. D. Pierson (Eds.), 203–218. Hong Kong: Hong Kong University Press.

1997. Responding authentically to authentic texts: A problem for self-access learning? In *Autonomy and Independence in Language Learning*, Benson and Voller (Eds.), 225–236. London: Longman.

Littlejohn, A. 1997. Self-access work and curriculum ideologies. In *Autonomy and Independence in Language Learning*, P. Benson and P. Voller (Eds.), 181–191. London: Longman.

Littlewood W. 1997. Self-access: Why do we want it and what can it do? In *Autonomy and Independence in Language Learning*, P. Benson and P. Voller (Eds.), 79–91. London: Longman.

Liu, H. 1997. *Constructing and Validating Parallel Forms of Performance-based Writing Prompts in an Academic Setting*. University of Illinois at Urbana-Champaign: Unpublished doctoral dissertation.

Ljung, M. 1991. Swedish TEFL meets reality. In *English Computer Corpora*, S. Johansson, and A-B. Stenstrom (Eds.). Berlin: Mouton de Gruyter.

LoCastro, V. 1994. Learning strategies and learning environments. *TESOL Quarterly*, 28 (2): 409–414.

Lockhart, C., and P. Ng. 1995. Analyzing talk in peer response groups: Stances, functions, and content. *Language Learning*, 45: 605–655.

Loehlin, J. C. 1987. *Latent Variable Models*. Mahwah NJ: Lawrence Erlbaum.

Long, D. R. 1990. What you don't know can't help you. *Studies in Second Language Acquisition*, 12: 65–80.

Long, M. H. (In press). *Task-Based Language Teaching*. Oxford: Blackwell.

Long, M. H., and G. Crookes. 1992. Three approaches to task-based syllabus design. *TESOL Quarterly*, 26: 55–98.

Long, M. H., and P. Porter. 1985. Group work, interlanguage talk and second language acquisition. *TESOL Quarterly*, 19: 207–227.

Long, M. H., and P. Robinson. 1998. Focus on form: Theory, research, practice. In *Focus on Form in Classroom Second Language Acquisition*, C. Doughty, and J. Williams (Eds.), 15–41. New York: Cambridge University Press.

Love, A. 1991. Process and product in geology: An investigation of some discourse features of two introductory textbooks. *English for Specific Purposes*, 10 (2): 89–109.

Lowenberg, P. 1993. Issues of validity in tests of English as a world language: Whose standards? *World Englishes*, 12 (1): 95–106.

Lumley, T. (In progress). The process of assessment of writing performance: The rater's perspective.

Lund, R. L. 1991. A comparison of second language listening and reading comprehension. *Modern Language Journal*, 75: 196–204.

Lunsford, A. 1978. What we know – and don't know – about remedial writing. *College Composition and Communication*, 29: 47–52.

Lynch, B. K. 1996. *Language Programme Evaluation*. New York: Cambridge University Press.

Lynch, B. K., and F. Davidson. 1994. Criterion-referenced language test development: Linking curricula, teachers, and tests. *TESOL Quarterly*, 28: 727–743.

Lynch, T. 1988a. The teacher and self-directed learning: Sharing or shirking responsibility? Paper presented at the CELTA Conference on Self-Directed Learning, Cambridge, March 1988.

    1988b. Peer evaluation in practice. In *Individualisation and Autonomy in Language Learning*, A. Brookes, and P. Grundy (Eds.), 119–125. ELT Documents 131. Oxford: Modern English Publications/British Council.

    1994. Training lecturers for international audiences. In *Academic Listening: Research Perspectives*, J. Flowerdew (Ed.), 269–289. Cambridge: Cambridge University Press.

    1996. Influences on course revision: An EAP case study. In *Evaluation and Course Design in EAP*, Hewings and Dudley-Evans (Eds.), 26–35. Hemel Hempstead: Phoenix ELT.

Lynch, T., and K. Anderson. 1991. Do you mind if I come in here? – A comparison of EAP seminar/discussion materials and the characteristics of real academic interaction. In *Socio-Cultural Issues in English for Academic Purposes. Developments in ELT*, P. Adams, B. Heaton, and P. Howarth (Eds.). Hemel Hempstead: Phoenix ELT.

Lynn, R. W. 1973. Preparing word lists: A suggested method. *RELC Journal*, 4 (1): 25–32.

McArthur, T. 1998. *The English Languages*. Cambridge: Cambridge University Press.

McCarthy, L. P. 1987. A stranger in strange lands: A college student writing across the curriculum. *Research in the Teaching of English*, 21 (3): 233–265.

McCarthy, M. 1991. *Discourse Analysis for Language Teachers*. Cambridge: Cambridge University Press.

McCarthy, M., and R. Carter. 1994. *Language as Discourse: Perspectives for Language Teaching*. London: Longman.

McClelland, J., D. E. Rumelhart, and G. E. Hinton. 1986. The appeal of parallel distributed processing. In *Parallel Distributed Processing: Explorations in the Microstructure of Cognition*, D. E. Rumelhart, J. McClelland, and the PDP Research Group (Eds.), Vol. 1, 3–44. Cambridge, MA: MIT Press.

McDaniel, E. R. 1997. Nonverbal communication: A reflection of cultural themes. In *Intercultural Communication: A Reader* (8th edition), L. Samover, and R. Porter (Eds.), 256–265. Belmont, CA: Wadsworth.

Mach, T., and F. L. Stoller. 1997. Synthesising content on a continuum. In *New Ways in Content-based Instruction*, D. M. Brinton, and P. Master (Eds.), 61–63. Alexandria, VA: TESOL.

Mach, T., F. L. Stoller, and C. Tardy. 1997. A gambit-driven debate. In *New Ways in Content-based Instruction*, D. M. Brinton, and P. Master (Eds.), 64–68. Alexandria, VA: TESOL.

Mackay, R. 1993. Embarrassment and hygiene in the classroom. *English Language Teaching Journal*, 47 (1): 32–39.

McKenna, E. 1987. Preparing students to enter discourse communities in the US. *English for Specific Purposes*, 6: 187–202.

Mackey, M. 1997. Good-enough reading: Momentum and accuracy in the reading of complex fiction. *Research in the Teaching of English*, 31: 428–458.

McKnight, A. 1994. The business of listening at university (or: Do international students learn by 'not' listening to lectures?). *Eric Document*. ED 374 663.

McNamara, T. F. 1996. *Measuring Second Language Performance*. London: Longman.

Maggio, M., and C. Gay. 1986. Intercultural communication as an integral part of an ESL program: The University of Southern California experience. In *Teaching Across Cultures in the University ESL Program*, P. Byrd (Ed.), 93–98. Washington, DC: NAFSA.

Mangelsdorf, K. 1989. Parallels between speaking and writing in second language acquisition. In *Richness in Writing: Empowering ESL Students*, D. Johnson, and D. Roen (Eds.), 134–145. New York: Longman.

——— 1992. Peer reviews in the ESL composition classroom: What do the students think? *English Language Teaching Journal*, 46: 274–284.

Mangelsdorf, K., and A. L. Schlumberger. 1992. ESL student response stances in a peer-review task. *Journal of Second Language Writing*, 1: 235–254.

Markee, N. 1986. The relevance of socio-political factors to communicative course design. *English for Specific Purposes*, 5 (1): 3–16.

——— 1997. *Managing Curricular Innovation*. Cambridge: Cambridge University Press.

Markham, P. L., and M. Latham. 1987. The influence of religion-specific background knowledge on the listening comprehension of adult second language students. *Language Learning*, 37: 157–170.

Markus, G. B. 1979. *Analyzing Panel Data*. Sage University Paper series on Quantitative Applications in the Social Sciences 07–018. Thousand Oaks, CA: Sage.

Marshall, S., and M. Gilmour. 1993. Lexical knowledge and reading comprehension in Papua New Guinea. *English for Specific Purposes*, 13: 69–81.

Martin, A. V. 1976. Teaching academic vocabulary to foreign graduate students. *TESOL Quarterly*, 10 (1): 91–97.

Martin, J. R. 1985. Process and text: Two aspects of human semiosis. In *Systemic Approaches on Discourse, Vol. 1*, J. D. Benson, and W. S. Greaves (Eds.), 248–274. Norwood, NJ: Ablex.

——— 1993. Genre and literacy: Modelling context in educational linguistics. *Annual Review of Applied Linguistics*, 13: 141–172.

Martin, J. R., and R. Veel (Eds.). 1998. *Reading Science: Critical and Functional Perspectives on Discourses of Science*. London: Routledge.

Marton, F. 1975. What does it take to learn? In *How Students Learn*, N. J. Entwistle, and D. Hounsell (Eds.). Lancaster: Institute for Post-Compulsory Education, Lancaster University.

Martyn, E. 1994. Self-access logs: Promoting self-directed learning. In *Directions in Self-Access Language Learning*, D. Gardner, and L. Miller (Eds.), 65–77. Hong Kong: Hong Kong University Press.

Mason, A. 1994. By dint of: Student and lecturer perceptions of lecture comprehension strategies in first-term graduate study. In *Academic Listening: Research Perspectives*, J. Flowerdew (Ed.), 199–218. NY: Cambridge University Press.

Master, P. A. 1987. Generic *the* in *Scientific American*. *English for Specific Purposes*, 6: 165–186.

——— 2000. Grammar in content-based instruction. In *Content-based College ESL Instruction*, L. F. Kasper (Ed.), 93–106. Mahwah, NJ: Lawrence Erlbaum.

Matsuda, P. (In preparation). *ESL Writing in 20th Century US Higher Education: The Formation of an Interdisciplinary Field*. The University of Purdue.

Mauranen, A. 1993a. *Cultural Differences in Academic Rhetoric*. Frankfurt: Peter Lang.

——— 1993b. Contrastive ESP rhetoric: Metatext in Finnish-English economics texts. *English for Specific Purposes*, 12 (1): 3–22.

May, R. M. 1997. The scientific wealth of nations. *Science*, 275: 793–796.
1998. The scientific investments of nations. *Science* 281: 49–51.
Meara, P. 1980. Vocabulary acquisition: A neglected aspect of language learning. *Language Teaching and Linguistics Abstracts*, 13 (4): 221–246.
1993. Tintin and the world service: A look at lexical environments. *IATEFL: Annual Conference Report*: 32–37.
Medgyes, P., and R. Kaplan. 1992. Discourse in a foreign language: The example of Hungarian scholars. *IJSL*, 98: 69–102.
Mehrabian, A., and M. Williams. 1969. Nonverbal concomitants of perceived and intended persuasiveness. *Journal of Personality and Social Psychology*, 13: 37–58.
Mellinkoff, D. 1963. *The Language of the Law*. Boston: Little, Brown and Company.
Meloni, C., and S. Thompson. 1980. Oral reports in the intermediate ESL classroom. *TESOL Quarterly*, 14: 503–514.
Melton, C. D. 1990. Bridging the cultural gap: A study of Chinese students' learning style preferences. *RELC Journal*, 21 (1): 29–54.
Mendelsohn, D. J. 1998. Teaching listening. *Annual review of Applied Linguistics*, 18: 81–101.
Mendolsohn, D., and J. Rubin (Eds.). 1995. *A Guide for the Teaching of Academic Listening*. San Diego, CA: Dominie Press.
Mendonca, C. O., and K. E. Johnson. 1994. Peer review negotiations: Revision activities in ESL writing instruction. *TESOL Quarterly*, 28: 745–769.
Mervis, J., and D. Normile. 1998. Agencies embrace peer review to strengthen research base. *Science*, 279: 1471–1473.
Meyer, P. G. 1990. Non-technical vocabulary in technical language. Paper delivered at AILA congress in Thessalonika.
Mezynski, K. 1983. Issues concerning the acquisition of knowledge: Effects of vocabulary training on reading comprehension. *Review of Educational Research*, 53: 253–279.
Miller, C. R. 1984. Genre as social action. *Quarterly Journal of Speech*, 70: 151–167.
Milton, J., and P. Meara. 1995. How periods abroad affect vocabulary growth in a foreign language. *ITL Review of Applied Linguistics*, 107/108: 17–34.
Minsky, M. 1977. Frame system theory. In *Thinking: Readings in Cognitive Science,* P. N. Johnson-Laird, and P. C. Wason (Eds.), 335–376. Cambridge: Cambridge University Press.
Mittan, R. 1989. The peer review process: Harnessing students' communicative power. In *Richness in Writing: Empowering ESL Students*, D. M. Johnson, and D. H. Roen (Eds.), 207–219. New York: Longman.
Mohan, B. A. 1986. *Language and Content*. Reading, MA: Addison Wesley.

Mohan, B. A., and Winnie Au-Yeung Lo. 1985. Academic writing and Chinese students: Transfer and developmental factors. *TESOL Quarterly*, 19: 515–534.

Mohr, L. B. 1992. *Impact Analysis for Programme Evaluation*. Newbury Park, CA: Sage.

Montgomery, S. L. 1996. *The Scientific Voice*. New York: The Guilford Press.

Moody, K. 1974. *Frames for Written English*. Oxford: Oxford University Press.

Moore, H. 1996. Language policies as virtual reality. *TESOL Quarterly*, 30 (3): 473–498.

Motta-Roth, D., and G. Hendges. 1997. The abstract as means of access to the international scientific community. Paper presented at XIV ENPULI, Belo Horizonte, Brazil, July 1997.

Mueller, G. A. 1980. Visual contextual cues and listening comprehension: An experiment. *Modern Language Journal*, 64: 335–340.

Mullins, P. 1992. *Successful English Language Learning Strategies of Students Enrolled in the Faculty of Arts, Chulalongkorn University, Bangkok, Thailand*. United States International University, San Diego, CA. Unpublished doctoral dissertation.

Munby, J. 1978. *Communicative Syllabus Design*. Cambridge: Cambridge University Press.

Murison, E., and C. Webb. 1991. *Writing a Research Paper*. Sydney: Learning Assistance Centre, University of Sydney.

Murphey, T. 1992. The discourse of pop songs. *TESOL Quarterly*, 26 (4): 770–774.

Murphy, J. M. 1996. Integrating listening and reading instruction in EAP programmes. *English for Specific Purposes*, 15 (2): 105–120.

Mustafa, Z. 1995. The effect of genre awareness on linguistic transfer. *English for Specific Purposes*, 14: 247–256.

Myers, G. 1989. The pragmatics of politeness in scientific articles. *Applied Linguistics*, 10: 1–35.

   1990. *Writing Biology: Texts in the Construction of Scientific Knowledge*. Madison, WI: University of Wisconsin Press.

   1991. Lexical cohesion and specialised knowledge in science and popular science tests. *Discourse Processes*, 14: 1–25.

Nagy, W. 1997. On the role of context in first- and second-language vocabulary learning. In *Vocabulary: Description, Acquisition, Pedagogy*, N. Schmitt, and M. McCarthy (Eds.), 64–83. New York: Cambridge University Press.

Nagy, W. E., P. A. Herman, and R. C. Anderson. 1985. Learning words from context. *Reading Research Quarterly*, 20: 233–253.

Naiman, N., M. Frohlich, and A. Todesco. 1975. The good language learner. *TESL Talk*, 5 (1): 58–75.

Nation, I. S. P. 1990. *Teaching and Learning Vocabulary*. Boston: Heinle and Heinle.

1993. Using dictionaries to estimate vocabulary size: Essential, but rarely followed, procedures. *Language Testing*, 10 (1): 27–40.

1999. *Learning Vocabulary in Another Language*. English Language Institute, Victoria University of Wellington.

Nation, P. 1982. Beginning to learn foreign vocabulary: A review of the research. *RELC Journal*, 13 (1): 14–36.

1997. Vocabulary size, text coverage & word lists. In *Vocabulary: Description, Acquisition, Pedagogy*, N. Schmitt, and M. McCarthy (Eds.), 6–19. New York: Cambridge University Press.

Nayar, P. B. 1997. ESL/EFL dichotomy today. *TESOL Quarterly*, 31 (1): 9–38.

Nelson, G. L., and J. G. Carson. 1998. ESL students' perceptions of effectiveness in peer response groups. *Journal of Second Language Writing*, 7: 113–132.

Nelson, G. L., and J. M. Murphy. 1993. Peer response groups: Do L2 writers use peer comments in revising their drafts? *TESOL Quarterly*, 27: 135–142.

Neustupny, J. 1985. Problems in Australian-Japanese contact situations. In *Cross-cultural Encounters*, J. Pride (Ed.), 44–64. Melbourne: River Seine Publications.

Ng, W. 1996. Natural languages not a top priority for engineering students. *CUHK Newsletter*, 88: 2.

Nicholls, A. 1983. *Managing Educational Innovation*. London: Allen and Unwin.

Nickerson, C. 1998. Corporate culture and the use of written English within British subsidiaries in the Netherlands. *English for Specific Purposes*, 17 (3): 281–294.

Norris, J., J. D. Brown, T. Hudson, and J. Yoshioka. 1998. *Designing Second Language Performance Assessments*. Second Language Teaching and Curriculum Centre Technical Report No. 18: University of Hawaii Press.

Norton, B. 1998. Language, identity, and the ownership of English. *TESOL Quarterly*, 31: 409–429.

Numrich, C. 1995. *Consider the Issues: Advanced Listening and Critical Thinking Skills* (2nd edition). White Plains, NY: Longman.

Nunan D. 1988a. *The Learner-Centred Curriculum*. Cambridge: Cambridge University Press.

1988b. *Syllabus Design*. Oxford: Oxford University Press.

1991. *Language Teaching Methodology*. Hemel Hempstead: Prentice Hall.

1996. Learner strategy training in the classroom: An action research study. *TESOL Journal*, Autumn: 35–41.

Nuttall, C. 1996. *Teaching Reading Skills in a Foreign Language*. Oxford: Heinemann ELT.

Nwogu, K. N. 1997. The medical research paper: Structure and functions. *English for Specific Purposes*, 16 (2): 119–138.

O'Dwyer, J. 1995. (Ed.). *Quality Management and the Management of Change*. Ankara, Turkey: University of Bilkent and Whitstable: IATEFL.

O'Dwyer, J., J. Anderson, and G. Gilroy. 1995. Quality improvement through focused evaluation. In *Quality Management and the Management of Change*, J. O'Dwyer (Ed.), 117–126. Ankara, Turkey: University of Bilkent and Whitstable: IATEFL.

Office of International Student Affairs. 1998. Report on International Student Enrollments for 1998–1998, prepared for the 14 October 1998 Graduate Programme Directors Workshop. University of Illinois at Urbana-Champaign.

Okara, Gabriel. 1990. Towards an evolution of the African language for African literature. *Kunapipi*, 12 (2): 11–18.

Oldenburg, H. 1992. *Angewandte Fachtextlinguistik*. Tubingen: Narr.

Olsen, L. A., and T. N. Huckin. 1990. Point-driven understanding in engineering lecture comprehension. *English for Specific Purposes*, 9: 33–47.

O'Malley, J. M. 1987. The effects of training in the use of learning strategies on learning English as a second language. In *Learner Strategies in Language Learning*, A. Wenden, and J. Rubin (Eds.), 133–143. Englewood Cliffs, NJ: Prentice Hall.

O'Malley, J. M., and A. Chamot. 1990. *Learning Strategies in Second Language Acquisition*. Cambridge: Cambridge University Press.

O'Malley, J. M., A. U. Chamot, and L. Küpper. 1989. Listening comprehension strategies in second language acquisition. *Applied Linguistics*, 10 (4): 418–437.

Orwell, G. 1936/1968. Shooting an elephant. In *The Collected Essays, Journalism and Letters of George Orwell, Vol. 1*, S. Orwell, and I. Angus (Eds.), 235–242. New York: Harcourt, Brace & World.

Oshima, A., and A. Hogue. 1992. *Writing Academic English* (2nd edition). Reading, MA: Addison Wesley.

    1998. *Introduction to Academic Writing*. Reading, MA: Addison Wesley.

Oster, J. 1985. The ESL composition course and the idea of a university. *College English*, 47: 66–76.

Ostler, S. E. 1980. A survey of academic needs for advanced ESL. *TESOL Quarterly*, 14: 489–502.

Oxford English Software. 1993. *MicroConcord Corpus Collections*. Oxford: Oxford University Press.

Oxford, R. L. 1990. *Language Learning Strategies*. Boston: Heinle and Heinle.

Oxford, R. L., and J. A. Burry-Stock. 1995. Assessing the use of language learning strategies worldwide with the ESL/EFL version of the Strategy Inventory for Language Learning (SILL). *System*, 23 (1): 1–23.

Oxford, R. L., and D. Crookall. 1989. Research on language learning strategies: Methods, findings, and instructional issues. *Modern Language Journal*, 73 (4): 404–419.

Oxford, R. L., D. Crookall, A. Cohen, R. Lavine, M. Nyikos, and W. Sutter. 1990. Strategy training for language learners: Six situational case studies and a training model. *Foreign Language Annals*, 22 (3): 197–216.

Oxford, R. L., and M. Nyikos. 1989. Variables affecting choice of language learning strategies by university students. *Modern Language Journal*, 73 (3): 291–300.

Pakir, A. 1999. Connecting with English in the context of internationalisation. *TESOL Quarterly*, 33: 103–114.

Palincsar, A., and A. Brown. 1984. Reciprocal teaching of comprehension-fostering and comprehension-monitoring activities. *Cognition and Instruction*, 1: 117–175.

Palmer, D., and E. Goetz. 1988. Selection and use of study strategies: The role of the studier's beliefs about self and strategies. In *Learning and Study Strategies: Issues in Assessment, Instruction and Evaluation*, C. Weinstein, E. Goetz, and P. Alexander (Eds.). New York: Academic Press.

Paltridge, B. 1995a. Analysing genre: A relational perspective. *System*, 23: 503–511.

1995b. An integrated approach to language programme development. *English Teaching Forum*, 33: 41–44.

1997a. Thesis and dissertation writing: Preparing ESL students for research. *English for Specific Purposes*, 16: 61–70.

1997b. Genre, discourse and academic listening. In *New Ways in Teaching Adults*, M. Lewis (Ed.). Alexandra, VA: TESOL.

1999. Reading across the curriculum: A genre-based perspective. In *New Ways in Teaching English at the Secondary Level*, D. Short (Ed.). Alexandra, VA: TESOL.

2000. Genre, text type and the EAP classroom. In *Genre and Pedagogy*, A. M. Johns (Ed.). Mahwah, NJ: Lawrence Erlbaum.

Park, D. B. 1982. The meanings of audience. *College English*, 44: 247–257.

1986. Analysing audiences. *College Composition and Communication*, 37: 478–488.

Parry, K. 1996. Culture, literacy, and L2 reading. *TESOL Quarterly*, 30: 665–692.

Parthasarathy, R. 1976. *Rough Passage*. Delhi: Open University Press.

Pascale, R. 1990. *Managing on the Edge*. London: Penguin.

Patthey-Chavez, G. G., and D. R. Ferris. 1997. Writing conferences and the weaving of multi-voiced texts in college composition. *Research in the Teaching of English*, 31: 51–90.

Peirce, B. N. 1989. Towards a pedagogy of possibility in teaching of English internationally. *TESOL Quarterly*, 23: 401–420.

1992. Demystifying the TOEFL reading test. *TESOL Quarterly*, 26 (4): 665–692.

Pemberton, R., E. Li, W. Or, and H. Pierson (Eds.). 1996. *Taking Control:*

Autonomy in Language Learning. Hong Kong: Hong Kong University Press.

Pennington, M. 1998. The folly of language planning. *English Today*, 54 (14/2): 25–32.

Pennycook, A. 1989. The concept of 'method', interested knowledge, and the politics of language teaching. *TESOL Quarterly*, 23: 589–618.

1990. Towards a critical applied linguistics for the 1990s. *Issues in Applied Linguistics*, 1 (1): 8–28.

1994a. *The Cultural Politics of English as an International Language.* London: Addison Wesley Longman.

1994b. Vulgar pragmatism, critical pragmatism, and EAP. *English for Specific Purposes*, 16 (4): 253–269.

1996a. Borrowing others' words: Text, ownership, memory and plagiarism. *TESOL Quarterly*, 30 (2): 201–230.

1996b. TESOL and critical literacies: Modern, post or neo? *TESOL Quarterly*, 30 (1): 163–171.

1997a. Critical applied linguistics and education. In *Encyclopedia of Language and Education*, Vol. 1, *Language Policy and Political Issues in Education*, R. Wodak, and D. Corson (Eds.). Dordrecht: Kluwer Academic Publishers.

1997b. Vulgar pragmatism, critical pragmatism, and EAP. *English for Specific Purposes*, 15: 85–103.

1997c. Cultural alternatives and autonomy. In *Autonomy and Independence in Language Learning*, P. Benson and P. Voller (Eds.), 35–53. London: Longman.

1998. *English and the Discourses of Colonialism.* London: Routledge.

Perry, W. G. Jr. 1975. Intellectual and ethical development in the college years. In *How Students Learn*, N. J. Entwistle, and D. Hounsell (Eds.). Lancaster: Institute for Post-Compulsory Education, Lancaster University.

1977. Studying and the student. *Higher Education Bulletin*, 5: 120–124.

Phillips, E., and D. Pugh. 1994. *How to Get a PhD*. Milton Keynes: Open University Press.

Phillips, M. K. 1981. Toward a theory of LSP methodology. In *Language for Specific Purposes: Programme Design and Evaluation.* Rowley, MA: Newbury House.

Phillips, M. K., and C. C. Shettlesworth. 1978. How to ARM your students: A consideration of two approaches to providing materials for ESP. In *English for Specific Purposes*, ELT Documents 101, 23–35. London: British Council.

Phillipson, R. 1992. *Linguistic Imperialism.* Oxford: Oxford University Press.

Phillipson, R., and T. Skutnabb-Kangas. 1996. English only worldwide or language ecology? TESOL Quarterly 30 (3): 429–452.

Pica, T. 1994. Questions from the language classroom: Research perspectives. *TESOL Quarterly*, 28 (1): 49–79.

Pica, T., R. Kanagy, and J. Falodun. 1993. Choosing and using communication tasks for second language research and instruction. In *Task-based Learning in a Second Language*, S. M. Gass, and G. Crookes (Eds.), 9–34. Clevedon, Avon: Multilingual Matters.

Pickering, A. 1992. From science as knowledge to science as practice. In *Science as Practice and Culture*, A. Pickering (Ed.), 1–26. Chicago: Chicago University Press.

Pinker, S. 1989. *Learnability and Cognition: The Acquisition of Argument Structure*. Cambridge, MA: MIT Press.

Popham, W. J. 1978. *Criterion-referenced Measurement*. Englewood Cliffs, NJ: Prentice Hall.

Powers, D. E. 1986. Academic demands related to listening skills. *Language Testing*, 3 (1): 1–38.

Praninskas, J. 1972. *American University Word List*. Longman, London.

Pratt, M. L. 1991. Arts of the contact zone. *Profession*, 91. 33–40.

Price, J. E. 1977. Study skills – with special reference to seminar strategies and one aspect of academic writing. In *English for Specific Purposes*, S. Holden (Ed.). London: MEP.

Prior, P. 1991. Contextualising writing and response in a graduate seminar. *Written Communication*, 8 (3): 267–310.

1995. Redefining the task: An ethnographic examination of writing and response in graduate seminars. In *Academic Writing in a Second Language: Essays on Research and Pedagogy*, D. Belcher, and G. Braine (Eds.), 47–81. Norwood, NJ: Ablex.

1998. *Writing/Disciplinarity: A Sociohistorical Account of Activity in the Academy*. Mahwah, NJ: Lawrence Erlbaum.

Pugsley, J. 1988. Autonomy and individualisation in language learning: Institutional implications. In *Individualisation and Autonomy in Language Learning*, Brookes and Grundy (Eds.), 54–61. ELT Documents 131. Oxford: Modern English Publications / British Council.

Purves, A. C. (Ed.). 1988. *Writing across Languages and Cultures: Issues in Contrastive Rhetoric*. Newbury Park, CA: Sage.

1992. Reflections on research and assessment in written composition. *Research in the Teaching of English*, 26 (1): 108–122.

Pyo, K. H. (Forthcoming). *Construct Validation of EAP Testing Using an Integrated Approach*. University of Illinois at Urbana-Champaign: Unpublished doctoral dissertation.

Quirk, R. 1991a. Language varieties and standard language. In *Languages and Standards: Issues, Attitudes and Case Studies*, M. L. Tickoo (Ed.), 165–177. Singapore: SEAMEO Regional Language Centre.

1991b. The question of standard in the international use of English. In *Languages and Standards: Issues, Attitudes and Case Studies*, M. L. Tickoo (Ed.), 153–164. Singapore: SEAMEO Regional Language Centre.

Radecki, P., and J. Swales. 1988. ESL student reaction to written comments on their written work. *System*, 16: 355–365.

Raimes, A. 1985. What unskilled ESL students do as they write: A classroom study of composing. *TESOL Quarterly*, 19: 229–258.

1987. Language proficiency, writing ability, and composing strategies: A study of ESL college student writers. *Language Learning*, 37: 439–468.

1991. Out of the woods: Emerging traditions in the teaching of writing. *TESOL Quarterly*, 25: 407–430.

Ramanathan, V., and R. B. Kaplan. 1996. Audience and voice in current L1 composition texts: Some implications for ESL student writers. *Journal of Second Language Writing*, 5: 21–34.

Ramani, E., T. Chacko, S. J. Singh, and E. H. Glendinning. 1988. An ethnographic approach to syllabus design: A case study of the Indian Institute of Science, Bangalore. *English for Specific Purposes*, 7: 81–90.

Ramanujan, A. K. 1990. Is there an Indian way of thinking? An informal essay. In *India through Hindu Categories*, M. McKim (Ed.), 41–58. New Delhi: Sage.

Rampton, M. B. H. 1990. Displacing the 'native speaker': Expertise, affiliation, and inheritance. *ELT Journal*, 44 (2): 97–101.

Raphan, D. 1996. A multimedia approach to academic listening. *TESOL Journal*, 6 (2): 24–28.

Reading and Thinking in English, 1979, 1980. Oxford: Oxford University Press (no authors acknowledged).

Redman, S., and R. Ellis. 1991. *A Way With Words: Vocabulary Development Activities for Learners of English, Vols. 1–4*. Cambridge: Cambridge University Press.

Rees-Miller, J. 1993. A critical appraisal of learner training: Theoretical bases and teaching implications. *TESOL Quarterly*, 27 (4): 679–689.

Reid, J. 1984a. The radical outliner and the radical brainstormer: A perspective on composing processes. *TESOL Quarterly*, 18: 529–533.

1984b. Comments on Vivian Zamel's 'The composing process of advanced ESL students: Six case studies'. *TESOL Quarterly*, 18: 149–159.

1987. The learning style preferences of ESL students. *TESOL Quarterly*, 21 (1): 87–111.

1988. *The Process of Composition*. Englewood Cliffs, NJ: Prentice Hall.

1989. English as a second language composition in higher education: The expectations of the academic audience. In *Richness in Writing: Empowering ESL Students*, D. M. Johnson and D. H. Roen (Eds.), 220–234. New York: Longman.

1993. *Teaching ESL Writing*. Englewood Cliffs, NJ: Prentice Hall.

1994. Responding to ESL students' texts: The myths of appropriation. *TESOL Quarterly*, 28: 273–292.

Reid, J., and B. Kroll. 1995. Designing and assessing effective classroom writing assignments for NES and ESL students. *Journal of Second Language Writing*, 4: 17–41.

Reid, J. M., and M. Lindstrom. 1985. *The Process of Paragraph Writing*. Englewood Cliffs, NJ: Prentice Hall.

Reppen, R. 1995. A genre-based approach to content writing instruction. *TESOL Journal*, 4: 32–35.

Ricento, T., and N. Hornberger. 1996. Unpeeling the onion: Language planning and policy and the ELT professional. *TESOL Quarterly*, 30 (3): 410–428.

Richards, J. C. 1983. Listening comprehension: Approach, design, procedure. *TESOL Quarterly*, 17 (2): 219–240.

Richards, J. C., and C. Lockhart. 1994. *Reflective Teaching in Second Language Classrooms*. Cambridge: Cambridge University Press.

Riley, P. 1997. The guru and the conjurer: Aspects of counselling for self-access. In *Autonomy and Independence in Language Learning*, P. Benson and P. Voller (Eds.), 114–131. London: Longman.

Robinson, P. J. 1989. A rich view of lexical competence. *ELT Journal*, 43 (4): 274–282.

1991. *ESP Today: A Practitioners' Guide*. New York: Prentice Hall.

Robinson, P. 1995. Attention, memory and the 'noticing' hypothesis. *Language Learning*, 45: 283–331.

1997. Generalizability and automaticity of second language learning under implicit, incidental, enhanced and instructed conditions. *Studies in Second Language Acquisition*, 19: 223–248.

1998a. State of the art: SLA theory and second language syllabus design. *The Language Teacher*, 22 (4): 7–14.

1998b. Task complexity, cognitive resources and second language syllabus design. In *Cognition and Second Language Instruction*, P. Robinson (Ed.). New York: Cambridge University Press.

Robinson, P., and S. Ross. 1996. The development of task-based assessment in English for Academic Purposes programmes. *Applied Linguistics*, 17: 455–476.

Rodriguez, R. 1981. *Hunger of Memory: The Education of Richard Rodriguez*. Boston: Godine.

Rogers, E. M. 1995. *Diffusion of Innovations* (4th edition). New York: Free Press.

Rose, M. 1989. *Lives on the Boundary*. New York: Penguin.

Ross, S. 1998. *Measuring Gain in Language Programs: Theory and Research*. Sydney: National Centre for English Language Teaching and Research, Macquarie University.

Rost, M. 1990. *Listening in Language Learning*. London: Longman.

1994. On-line summaries as representations of lecture understanding. In *Academic Listening: Research Perspectives*, J. Flowerdew (Ed.), 93–127. Cambridge: Cambridge University Press.

1997. Strategies in L2 listening. Plenary paper presented at Research Meets Practice: Listening Skills (Conference organised by IATEFL Research Group, Cambridge, UK, 28 February–2 March 1997).

Rounds, P. 1987. Characterising successful classroom discourse for NNS teaching assistant training. *TESOL Quarterly*, 21: 643–671.

Rubin, J. 1975. What the 'good language learner' can teach us. *TESOL Quarterly*, 9 (1): 41–45.

1987. Learner strategies: Theoretical assumptions, research history and typology. In *Learner Strategies in Language Learning*, A. Wenden, and J. Rubin (Eds.), 15–29. Englewood Cliffs, NJ: Prentice Hall.

Rubin, J., and I. Thompson. 1982. *How to Be a Successful Language Learner*. Boston: Heinle and Heinle.

Rudwick, M. J. S. 1985. *The Great Devonian controversy*. Chicago: The University of Chicago Press.

Ruhe, V. 1996. Graphics and listening comprehension. *TESL Canada Journal*, 14 (1): 45–60.

Rumelhart, D. E. 1977. Towards an interactive model of reading. In *Attention and Performance VI*, S. Dornic (Ed.). Hillsdale, NJ: Erlbaum.

St John, M. J. 1987. Writing processes of Spanish scientists publishing in English. *English for Specific Purposes*, 6: 113–120.

Salager-Meyer, F. 1994. Hedges and textual communicative function in medical English written discourse. *English for Specific Purposes*, 13: 163–197.

Samuels, S. J. 1977. Introduction to theoretical models of reading. In *Reading Problems*, W. Otto (Ed.). Boston, MA: Addison Wesley.

Santos, T. 1988. Professors' reactions to the academic writing of nonnative speaking students. *TESOL Quarterly*, 22: 69–90.

1992. Ideology in composition: L1 and ESL. *Journal of Second Language Writing*, 1 (1): 1–15.

Saragi, T., I. S. P. Nation, and G. F. Meister. 1978. Vocabulary learning and reading. *System*, 6: 72–78.

Sato, C. 1982. Ethnic styles in classroom discourse. In *On TESOL '81*, M. Hines, and W. Rutherford (Eds.), 11–24. Washington, DC: TESOL.

Savignon, S. J. 1972. *Communicative Competence: An Experiment in Foreign-language Teaching*. Philadelphia, PA: The Centre for Curriculum Development.

1983. *Communicative Competence: Theory and Classroom Practice*. Reading, MA: Addison Wesley.

Saville-Troike, M. 1984. What really matters in second language learning for academic achievement? *TESOL Quarterly*, 18: 199–219.

Sawyer, M. 1989. Language learning by the case method. In *Language Teaching and Learning Styles Within and Across Cultures*, V. Bickley (Ed.), 138–143. Hong Kong: Institute of Language in Education, Education Department.

Schank, R. C., and R. Abelson. 1977. Scripts, plans and knowledge. In *Thinking: Readings in Cognitive Science*, P. N. Johnson-Laird, and P. C. Wason (Eds.), 421–432. Cambridge: Cambridge University Press.

Schenck, M. J. 1988. *Read, Write, Revise. A Guide to Academic Writing*. New York: St Martin's Press.

Schmidt, R. 1990. The role of consciousness in second language learning. *Applied Linguistics*, 11: 129–158.

Scollon, R. 1996. Plagiarism and ideology: Identity in intercultural discourse. *Language in Society*, 24: 1–28.

1997. Contrastive rhetoric, contrastive poetics, or perhaps something else? *TESOL Quarterly*, 31: 352–363.

Scott, H., and J. Scott. 1984. ESP & Rubic's cube: Three dimensions in course design & materials writing. In *English for Specific Purposes in the Arab World*, J. Swales, and H. Mustafa (Eds.). Birmingham: University of Aston Language Studies Unit.

Segalowitz, N., C. Poulsen, and M. Komoda. 1991. Lower level components of reading skill in higher level bilinguals: Implications for reading instruction. In *Reading in Two Languages*, AILA Review 8, J. H. Hulstijn, and J. F. Matter (Eds.), 15–30.

Sellen, D. 1982. *Skills in Action*. London: Hulton Educational.

Shalom, C. 1993. Established and evolving spoken research process genres: Plenary lecture and poster session discussions academic conferences. *English for Specific Purposes*, 12 (1): 37–50.

Sharp, A. 1991. Staff/student participation in course evaluation: A procedure for improving course design. *ELT Journal*, 44 (1): 132–137.

Shaw, P. 1991. Science research students' composing processes. *English for Specific Purposes*, 10: 189–206.

Sheerin, S. 1989. *Self-Access*. Oxford: Oxford University Press.

1997. An exploration of the relationship between self-access and independent learning. In *Autonomy and Independence in Language Learning*, P. Benson, and P. Voller (Eds.), 54–65. London: Longman.

Shih, M. 1986. Content-based approaches to teaching academic writing. *TESOL Quarterly*, 20: 617–648.

1992. Beyond comprehension exercises in the ESL academic reading class. *TESOL Quarterly*, 26 (2): 289–318.

Shoham, M., A. S. Peretz, and R. Vorhaus. 1987. Reading comprehension tests: General or subject specific? *System*, 15: 81–88.

Shohamy, E. 1995. Performance assessment in language testing. In *Annual Review of Applied Linguistics (1995)*, 15, W. Grabe (Ed.), 188–211. New York: Cambridge University Press.

1998. Applying a multiplism approach. In *Testing and Evaluation in Second Language Education*, E. S. L. Li, and G. James (Eds.), 99–114. Hong Kong: Language Centre, The Hong Kong University of Science and Technology.

Silva, T. 1988. Comments on Vivian Zamel's 'recent research on writing pedagogy': A reader reacts . . . *TESOL Quarterly*, 22: 517–520.

1990. Second language composition instruction: Developments, issues, and directions in ESL. In *Second Language Writing: Research Insights for the Classroom*, B. Kroll. (Ed.), 11–23. Cambridge: Cambridge University Press.

1993. Toward an understanding of the distinct nature of L2 writing:

The ESL research and its implications. *TESOL Quarterly*, 28: 657–677.

1997. On the ethical treatment of ESL writers. *TESOL Quarterly*, 31: 359–363.

1998. The author responds . . . *TESOL Quarterly*, 32: 342–351.

Silva, T., I. Leki, and J. Carson. 1997. Broadening the perspective of mainstream composition studies: Some thoughts from the disciplinary margins. *Written Communication*, 14: 398–428.

Simner, M. 1997. *Position Statement on the Use of the Test of English as a Foreign Language as a University Admission Requirement*. Ottawa: Canadian Psychological Association.

Sinclair, B. 1996. Materials design for the promotion of autonomy: How explicit is 'explicit'? In *Taking Control: Autonomy in Language Learning*, R. Pemberton, E. S. L. Li, W. W. F. Or, and H. D. Pierson (Eds.), 149–165. Hong Kong: Hong Kong University Press.

Sionis, C. 1995. Communicative strategies in the writing of scientific research articles by non-native speakers. *English for Specific Purposes*, 14: 99–113.

Skehan, P. 1989. *Individual Differences in Second-Language Learning*. London: Edward Arnold.

1998. *A Cognitive Approach to Language Learning*. Oxford: Oxford University Press.

Smagorinsky, P. 1989. The reliability and validity of protocol analysis. *Written Communication*, 6: 463–479.

Smith, H. 1999. Managing ELT Projects. In *Innovation and Best Practice*, C. Kennedy (Ed.), 40–45. Harlow: Longman.

Smith, S. 1997. The genre of the end comment: Conventions in teacher responses to student writing. *College Composition and Communication*, 48: 249–268.

Snow, M. A. (Ed.). 1992. *Project LEAP: Learning-English-for-Academic-Purposes*. Training Manual – Year One. Los Angeles: California State University, Los Angeles.

1993a. Discipline-based foreign language teaching: Implications from ESL/EFL. In *Language and Content: Discipline- and Content-based Approaches to Language Study*, M. Krueger, and F. Ryan (Eds.), 37–56. Lexington, MA: D.C. Heath.

(Ed.), 1993b. *Project LEAP: Learning-English-for-Academic-Purposes*. Training Manual – Year Two. Los Angeles: California State University, Los Angeles.

(Ed.). 1994. *Project LEAP: Learning-English-for-Academic-Purposes*. Training Manual – Year Three. Los Angeles: California State University, Los Angeles.

Snow, M. A., and D. M. Brinton. 1997. *The Content-based Classroom: Perspectives on Integrating Language and Content*. White Plains, NY: Longman.

Snow, M. A., and L. D. Kamhi-Stein. (Eds.). 1996. *Teaching Academic*

Literacy Skills: Strategies for Content Faculty. Los Angeles: California State University, Los Angeles.

Snow, M. A., M. Met, and F. Genesee. 1989. A conceptual framework for the integration of language and content in second/foreign language instruction. *TESOL Quarterly*, 23 (2): 201–217.

Soars, J., and L. Soars. 1991. *Headway* (Vols. 1, 2 & (3). London: Oxford University Press.

Sommers, N. 1982. Responding to student writing. *College Composition and Communication*, 33: 148–156.

Spack, R. 1985. Literature, reading, writing, and ESL: Bridging the gap. *TESOL Quarterly*, 19: 703–725.

Spack, R. 1988. Initiating students into the academic discourse community: How far should we go? *TESOL Quarterly*, 22: 29–51.

1990. *Guidelines*. New York: St Martin's Press.

1994. *Blair Resources for Teaching Writing: English as a Second Language*. Englewood Cliffs, NJ: Prentice Hall.

Spanos, G. 1987. On the integration of language and content instruction. *Annual Review of Applied Linguistics*, 10: 227–240.

Spencer, D. 1967. *Guided Composition Exercises*. London: Longman.

Spiro, R. J. 1980. Constructive processes in prose comprehension and recall. In *Theoretical Issues in Reading Comprehension*, R. J. Spiro, B. C. Bruce, and W. F. Brewer (Eds.). Hillsdale, NJ: Erlbaum.

Spolsky, B. 1978. Introduction. In *Advances in Language Testing 2: Approaches to Language Testing*. Washington, DC: Centre for Applied Linguistics.

1990. The prehistory of TOEFL. *Language Testing*, 7: 98–118.

1993. Testing across cultures: An historical perspective. *World Englishes*, 12: 87–93.

1995. *Measured Words*. Oxford: Oxford University Press.

Stanovich, K. E. 1980. Toward an interactive-compensatory model of individual differences in the development of reading fluency. *Reading Research Quarterly*, 16: 32–71.

Stevens, V. 1991a. Classroom concordancing: Vocabulary materials derived from relevant authentic text. *English for Specific Purposes*, 10 (1): 35–46.

1991b. Concordance-based vocabulary exercises: A viable alternative to gap-fillers. In *Classroom Concordancing: English Language Research Journal*, 4, T. Johns, and P. King (Eds.), 47–63. University of Birmingham: Centre for English Language Studies.

Stevens, V., and S. Millmore. 1987. *Text Tanglers*. Stonybrook, NY: Research Design Associates. Computer programme.

Steward, S. 1999. *An Investigation of Writing Features which have Predictive Evidence of Validity for EPT Placement Levels*. Division of English as an International Language, University of Illinois at Urbana-Champaign: Unpublished Master's thesis.

Stoller, F. L. 1995. *Managing Intensive English Programme Innovations*.

NAFSA Working Paper No. 56. Washington, DC: NAFSA (Association of International Educators).

1997. The catalyst for change and innovation. In *A Handbook for Language Programme Administrators*, M. A. Christison, and F. L. Stoller (Eds.), 33–48. Burlingame, CA: Alta Book Centre.

1999. Time for change: A hybrid curriculum for EAP programmes. *TESOL Journal*, 8 (1): 9–13.

Stoller, F. L., and W. Grabe. 1997. A six T's approach to content-based instruction. In *The Content-based Classroom: Perspectives on Integrating Language and Content*, M. A. Snow, and D. M. Brinton (Eds.), 78–94. White Plains, NY: Addison Wesley Longman.

Stratford, S. 1993. *An Analysis of the Role of the Teacher in Learner Training and the Implications for Teacher Preparation*. University of Edinburgh. MSc dissertation.

Straub, R. 1997. Students' reactions to teacher comments: An exploratory study. *Research in the Teaching of English*, 31: 91–119.

Strevens, P. 1973. Technical, technological, and scientific English. *ELT Journal*, 27 (3): 223–234.

1977. *New Orientations in the Teaching of English*. Oxford: Oxford University Press.

1988a. ESP after twenty years: A re-appraisal. In *ESP: State of the Art*, M. Tickoo (Ed.), 1–13. Singapore: SEAMEO Regional Language Centre.

1988b. The learner and teacher of ESP. In *ESP in the Classroom: Practice and Evaluation*, D. Chamberlain and R. J. Baumgardner (Eds.), 39–44. ELT Document 128. Modern English Publications/British Council.

Sturtridge, G. 1997. Teaching and learning in self-access centres: Changing roles. In *Autonomy and Independence in Language Learning*, Benson and Voller (Eds.), 66–78. London: Longman.

Sutarsyah, C., P. Nation, and G. Kennedy. 1994. How useful is EAP vocabulary for ESP? A corpus based study. *RELC Journal*, 25 (2): 34–50.

Svalberg, A. 1998. Nativisation in Brunei English. *World Englishes*, 17 (3): 325–344.

Swain, M. 1995. Three functions of output in second language learning. In *Principle and Practice in Applied Linguistics: Studies in Honour of H. G. Widdowson*, G. Cook and B. Seidlhoffer (Eds.), 125–144. Oxford: Oxford University Press.

Swales, J. 1981. *Aspects of Article Introductions*. Birmingham: Aston University, Language Studies Unit.

1984a. Research into the structure of introductions to journal articles and its application to the teaching of academic writing. In *Common ground: Shared Interests in ESP and Communication Studies*, R. Williams, J. Swales, and J. Kirkman (Eds.), 77–86. Oxford: Pergamon.

1984b. A review of ESP in the Arab world 1977–1983: Trends, developments, and retrenchments. In *English for Specific Purposes in the Arab World*, J. Swales, and H. Mustafa (Eds.), 9–21. Birmingham: University of Aston Language Studies Unit.

1985. *Episodes in ESP*. Oxford: Pergamon Press.

1986. A genre based approach to language across the curriculum. Paper presented at the RELC Seminar, Singapore, April 1986.

1987. Utilising the literatures in teaching the research paper. *TESOL Quarterly*, 21 (1): 41–68.

(Ed.). 1988a. *Episodes in ESP*. Hemel Hempstead: Prentice Hall.

1988b. Discourse communities, genres and English as an international language. *World Englishes*, 7: 211–220.

1990. *Genre analysis: English in Academic and Research Settings*. Cambridge: Cambridge University Press.

1996. Occluded genres in the academy: The case of the submission letter. In *Academic Writing: Intercultural and Textual Issues*, E. Ventola, and A. Mauranen (Eds.), 45–58. Amsterdam: John Benjamins.

1997. English as Tyrannosaurus rex. *World Englishes*, 16 (3): 373–382.

1998. *Other Floors, Other Voices: A Textography of a Small University Building*. Mahwah, NJ: Lawrence Erlbaum.

Swales, J. M., U. K Ahmad, Y-Y. Chang, D. Chavez, D. F. Dressen, and R. Seymour. 1998. Consider this: The role of imperatives in scholarly writing. *Applied Linguistics*, 19 (1): 97–121.

Swales, J. M., and C. B. Feak. 1994. *Academic Writing for Graduate Students*. Ann Arbor, MI: University of Michigan Press.

Swales, J. M., and H. Najjar. 1987. The writing of research article introductions. *Written Communication*, 4: 175–192.

Swinbanks, D., and R. Nathan with R. Triendl. 1997. Western research assessment meets Asian cultures. *Nature*, 389: 113–117.

System, 23 (2). 1995. Special Issue on Learner Autonomy.

Tadros, A. A. 1985. *Prediction in Text*. Birmingham: University of Birmingham, English Language Research.

Tan, S. H. 1990. The role of prior knowledge and language proficiency as predictors of reading comprehension among undergraduates. In *Individualising the Assessment of Language Abilities*, J. H. A. L. de Jong and D. K Stevenson (Eds.), 214–224. Clevedon, PA: Multilingual Matters.

Tannacito, D. J. 1995. *A Guide to Writing in English as a Second or Foreign Language: An Annotated Bibliography of Research and Pedagogy*. Alexandria, VA: TESOL.

Tarone, E. S., S. Dwyer, S. Gillette, and V. Icke. 1981. On the use of the passive in two astrophysics journal papers. *English for Specific Purposes*, 1: 123–140.

Tarone, E., and G. Yule. 1989. *Focus on the Language Learner*. Oxford: Oxford University Press.

Tauroza, S. 1994. The Hong Kong corpus of computer science and information systems lectures. In *The Practice of LSP: Perspectives, Programmes and Projects*, R. Khoo (Ed.), 68–84. Singapore: SEAMEO Regional Language Centre.

1998. Ensuring quality in quantitative studies of L2 lecture comprehension: A review of research on how L2 listeners unpackage the text of lectures. In *Text in Education and Society*, D. Allison, L. Wee, B. Zhiming and S. A. Abraham (Eds.), 126–137. Singapore: Singapore University Press and World Scientific Publishing.

Tauroza, S., and D. Allison. 1994. Expectation-driven understanding in information systems lecture comprehension. In *Academic Listening: Research Perspectives,* J. Flowerdew (Ed.), 35–54. Cambridge: Cambridge University Press.

Taylor, C., D. Eignor, M. Schedl, and F. DeVincenzi. 1995. TOEFL 2000: A project overview and status report. Paper presented at Language Testing Research Colloquium, Baltimore, MD, March.

Taylor, G., and T. Chen. 1991. Linguistic, cultural and subcultural issues in contrastive discourse analysis: Anglo-American and Chinese scientific texts. *Applied Linguistics*, 12 (3): 319–336.

TESOL Quarterly, 31 (3). 1997. Special Issue on Language and Identity.

Thompson, D. K. 1993. Arguing for experimental 'facts' in science: A study of research article results sections in biochemistry. *Written Communication*, 10: 106–128.

Thompson, S. 1994. Frameworks and contexts: a genre-based approach to analysing lecture introductions. *English for Specific Purposes*, 13 (2).

Threadgold, T. 1989. Talking about genre: Ideologies and incompatible discourses. *Cultural Studies*, 3: 101–127.

Thurston, J., and C. N. Candlin. 1997. *Exploring Academic English. A Workbook for Student Essay Writing.* Sydney: National Centre for English Language Teaching and Research, Macquarie University.

1998. Concordancing and the teaching of the vocabulary of academic English. *English for Specific Purposes*, 17 (3): 267–280.

Tickoo, M. L. 1994. Approaches to ESP: Arguing a paradigm shift. In *LSP: Problems and Prospects*, R. Khoo (Ed.), 30–48. Singapore: SEAMEO Regional Language Centre.

Tollefson, J. 1989. The role of language planning in second language acquisition. In *Language Planning and Language Teaching*, C. Kennedy (Ed.), 22–31. Hemel Hempstead: Prentice Hall.

1991. *Planning Language, Planning Inequality.* Harlow: Longman.

(Ed.). 1995. *Power and Inequality in Language Education.* Cambridge: Cambridge University Press.

Tomlinson, B. 1998. Access-self materials. In *Materials Development on Language Teaching*, B. Tomlinson (Ed.), 320–336. Cambridge: Cambridge University Press.

Tracy, K. 1997. *The Colloquium.* Norwood, NJ: Ablex.

Tricamo, J., and A. Snow. 1995. *Improving University Instruction for Language Minority Students: Strategies from Project LEAP* [Videotape]. (Available from Project LEAP, Learning Resource Centre, California State University, Los Angeles.)

Trimble, L. 1985. *English for Science and Technology: A Discourse Approach.* Cambridge: Cambridge University Press.

Tripathi, P. 1998. Redefining Kachru's outer circle of English. *English Today* 56: 55–58.

Truscott, J. 1996. The case against grammar correction in L2 writing classes. *Language Learning,* 46: 327–369.

Tsou, C-L. 1998. Science and scientists in China. *Science,* 280: 528–529.

Tudor, I. 1996. *Learner-Centredness as Language Education.* Cambridge: Cambridge University Press.

Tudor, I., and R. Tuffs. 1991. Formal and content schemata in L2 viewing comprehension. *RELC Journal,* 22 (2): 79–97.

University of Cambridge Local Examinations Syndicate (UCLES)/The British Council/IDP Education Australia. 1998. *IELTS Annual Review,* 1997/98.

Ur, P. 1996. *A Course in Language Teaching. Practice and Theory.* Cambridge: Cambridge University Press.

Valentine, J. F. Jr., and L. M. Repath-Martos. 1997. How relevant is relevance? In *The Content-based Classroom: Perspectives on Integrating Language and Content,* M. A. Snow, and D. M. Brinton (Eds.), 233–247. White Plains, NY: Longman.

Valero-Garces, C. 1996. Contrastive ESP rhetoric: Metatext in Spanish-English economics texts. *English for Specific Purposes,* 15 (4): 279–294.

Vande Kopple, W. 1985. Some exploratory discourse on metadiscourse. *College Communication and Composition,* 36: 82–93.

Van der Walt, C. 1999. Business English and international comprehensibility. In *Business English: Research into Practice,* M. Hewings and C. Nickerson (Eds.), 44–52. Harlow: Longman.

Vandrick, S. 1997. Diaspora literature: A mirror for ESL students. *College ESL,* 7: 53–69.

Vann, R. J., and R. G. Abraham. 1990. Strategies of unsuccessful language learners. *TESOL Quarterly,* 24 (2): 177–198.

Vann, R., F. Lorenz, and D. Meyer. 1991. Error gravity: Faculty response to errors in written discourse of nonnative speakers of English. In *Assessing Second Language Writing in Academic Contexts,* L. Hamp-Lyons (Ed.), 181–195. Norwood, NJ: Ablex.

Vann, R., F. Lorenz, and D. Meyer. 1984. Error gravity: A study of faculty opinion of ESL errors. *TESOL Quarterly,* 18: 427–440.

Vaughan, C. 1991. Holistic assessment: What goes on in the rater's mind? In *Assessing Second Language Writing in Academic Contexts,* L. Hamp-Lyons (Ed.). Norwood, NJ: Ablex.

Veel, R., and C. Coffin. 1996. Learning to think like an historian: The language of secondary school history. In *Literacy in Society,* R. Hasan, and G. Williams (Eds.). London: Longman.

Ventola, E. 1996. Packing and unpacking information in academic text. In *Academic Writing: Intercultural and Textual Issues*, E. Ventola and A. Mauranen (Eds.), 153–194. Amsterdam: John Benjamins.

Ventola, E., and A. Mauranen, A. (Eds.). 1996. *Academic Writing: Intercultural and Textual Issues*. Amsterdam: John Benjamins.

Villamil, O. S., and M. C. M. deGuerrero. 1996. Peer revision in the L2 classroom: Social-cognitive activities, mediating strategies, and aspects of social behaviour. *Journal of Second Language Writing*, 5: 51–75.

Visser, A. 1989. Learning core meanings. *Guidelines*, 11 (2): 10–17.

Vogely, A. 1995. Perceived strategy use during performance on three authentic listening comprehension tasks. *Modern Language Journal*, 79: 41–56.

Voller, P. 1997. Does the teacher have a role in autonomous language learning? In *Autonomy and Independence in Language Learning*, P. Benson, and P. Voller (Eds.), 98–113. London: Longman.

Voller, P., and V. Pickard. 1996. Conversation exchange: A way towards autonomous language learning. In *Taking Control: Autonomy in Language Learning*, R. Pemberton, E. S. L. Li, W. W. F. Or and H. D. Pierson (Eds.), 115–132. Hong Kong: Hong Kong University Press.

Vukadinovic, N. 1998. When chemistry is bonded with English: A case study of team-teaching. Mimeo.

Walters, K. 1998. New Year Happy – some sociolinguistic observations on the way to the 'anglicisation' of Tunisia. Paper presented at TSAS 4th International Annual Conference 'English in North Africa'. Carthage, April 1998.

Walvoord, B., and L. P. McCarthy. 1990. *Thinking and Writing in College: A Naturalistic Study of Students in Four Disciplines*. Urbana, IL: NCTE.

Wang, Z. G., L. Delva, M. Gaboli, R. Rivi, M. Giorgi, D. Cordon-Cardo, F. Grosveld, and P. P. Pandolfi. 1998. Role of PML in cell growth and the retinoic acid pathway. *Science*, 279: 1547–1551.

Wang, and Wu. 1990. *Composition (Chinese)*.

Ward-Goodbody, M. 1993. Letting the students choose: A placement procedure for a pre-sessional course. In *Language, Learning and Success: Studying through English*, G. Blue (Ed.). Hemel Hempstead: Phoenix ELT.

Waters, A. 1996. A review of research into needs of English for academic purposes of relevance to the North American higher education context. TOEFL Monograph Series, MS-6. Princeton, NJ: Educational Testing Service.

1997. Theory and practice in LSP course design. In *Applied Languages: Theory and Practice in ESP*, J. Piqué, and D. Viera (Eds.). Valencia, Spain: Universitat de Valencia.

Waters, M., and A. Waters. 1992. Study skills and study competence: Getting the priorities right. *English Language Teaching Journal*, 46 (3): 264–273.

1995. *Study Tasks in English*. Student's Book, Teacher's Book and Cassettes. Cambridge: Cambridge University Press.

Wa Thiong'o, Ngugi. 1986. *Decolonising the Mind: The Politics of Language in African Literature*. London: Currey, Heinemann.

1990. Return of the native tongue. *Times Literary Supplement*, September 14–20, 972, 985.

Webb, C. 1991. *Writing an Essay in the Humanities and Social Sciences*. Sydney: Learning Assistance Centre, University of Sydney.

Weeks, W. H., P. B. Pedersen, and R. W. Brislin. 1982. *A Manual of Structured Experiences for Cross-cultural Learning*. Washington, DC: SIETAR.

Weigle, S. C., and L. Jensen. 1997. Issues in assessment for content-based instruction. In *The Content-based Classroom: Perspectives on Integrating Language and Content*, M. A. Snow, and D. M. Brinton (Eds.), 201–212. White Plains, NY: Longman.

Weir, C. J. 1990. *Communicative Language Testing*. Hemel Hempstead: Prentice Hall.

1993. *Understanding and Developing Language Tests*. Hemel Hempstead: Prentice Hall.

1997. The testing of reading in a second language. In *Encyclopedia of Language and Education*, C. Clapham, and D. Corson (Eds.), 39–49. Dordrecht, the Netherlands: Kluwer Academic Publishers.

Weir, C. J., and A. H. Urquhart. 1998. *Reading in a Second Language: Process, Product and Practice*. London: Longman.

Weissberg, B. 1993. The graduate seminar: Another research-process genre. *English for Specific Purposes*, 12 (1): 23–35.

Weissberg, R., and S. Buker. 1990. *Writing up Research. Experimental Report Writing for Students of English*. Englewood Cliffs, NJ.: Prentice Hall.

Wenden, A. L. 1986. Incorporating learner training in the classroom. *System*, 14 (3): 315–325.

1987. Incorporating learner training in the classroom. In *Learner Strategies in Language Learning*, A. Wenden, and J. Rubin (Eds.), 159–168. Englewood Cliffs, NJ: Prentice Hall.

1991. *Learner Strategies for Learner Autonomy*. Englewood Cliffs, NJ: Prentice Hall.

1995. Learner training in context: A knowledge-based approach. *System*, 23 (2): 183–194.

Wenden, A., and J. Rubin (Eds.). 1987. *Learner Strategies in Language Learning*. Englewood Cliffs, NJ: Prentice Hall.

Wesche, M. B. 1993. Discipline-based approaches to language study: Research issues and outcomes. In *Language and Content: Discipline- and Content-based Approaches to Language Study*, M. Krueger, and F. Ryan (Eds.), 57–82. Lexington, MA: D. C. Heath.

West, M. 1953. *A General Service List of English Words*. London: Longman, Green and Co.

458   *References*

West, R. 1994. Needs analysis in language teaching. *Language Teaching*, 27: 1–19.

White, C. 1995. Autonomy and strategy use in distance foreign language learning: Research findings. *System*, 23 (2): 207–221.

White, L., and F. Genesee. 1996. How native is near-native? The issue of ultimate attainment in adult second language acquisition. *Second Language Research*, 12 (3): 233–265.

White, R. 1988. *The ELT Curriculum*. Oxford: Blackwell.

White, R., and D. McGovern. 1994. *Writing*. Hemel Hempstead: Phoenix ELT.

Widdowson, H. G. 1979. *Explorations in Applied Linguistics*. Oxford; Oxford University Press.

    1983. *Learning Purpose and Language Use*. Oxford: Oxford University Press.

    1997. EIL/ESL/EFL: Global issues and local interests. *World Englishes*, 16 (1): 135–146.

Wiley, T. 1996. Language planning and policy. In *Sociolinguistics and Language Teaching*, S. McKay and N. Hornberger (Eds.), 103–148. Cambridge: Cambridge University Press.

Wilkins, D. 1976. *Notional Syllabuses*. Oxford: Oxford University Press.

Williams, J. 1992. Planning, discourse marking, and the comprehensibility of international teaching assistants. *TESOL Quarterly*, 21: 643–671.

Williams, R. 1976. *Keywords: A Vocabulary of Culture and Society*. New York: Oxford University Press.

    1985. Teaching vocabulary recognition strategies in ESP reading. *English for Specific Purposes Journal*, 4 (2): 121–131.

Willing, K. 1988. *Learning Styles in Adult Migrant Education*. Adelaide: National Curriculum Resource Centre.

Willis, J. 1996. *A Framework for Task-based Instruction*. London: Longman.

Wong, R., E. H. Glendinning, and H. Mantell. 1987. *Becoming a Writer*. New York: Longman.

Wood, A. S. 1982. An examination of the rhetorical structures of authentic chemistry texts. *Applied Linguistics*, 3 (2): 121–143.

    1997. Scientific English: A World English based on an international discourse community. Paper presented at the Fourth International Conference on World Englishes, Singapore 19–21 December 1997.

Woods, D. 1996. *Teacher Cognition in Language Teaching: Beliefs, Decision-Making and Classroom Practice*. Cambridge: Cambridge University Press.

Woolgar, S. 1993. *Science: The Very Idea*. London: Routledge.

The World Almanac and Book of Facts. 1998. New York: Newspaper Enterprise Association.

Worthington, D., and P. Nation. 1996. Using texts to sequence the introduction of new vocabulary in an EAP course. *RELC Journal*, 27 (2): 1–11.

Wu, R. 1998. 3.2 million students take MET today. *China Youth Daily*, 7th June.

Xue, Guoyi, and I. S. P. Nation. 1984. A university word list. *Language Learning and Communication*, 3 (2): 215–229.

Yakhontova, T. 1995. Bahktin at home and abroad. *Journal of Advanced Composition*, 17: 83–94.

Yang, Huizhong. 1986. A new technique for identifying scientific/technical terms and describing science texts. *Literary and Linguistic Computing*, 1 (2): 93–103.

Yorio, C. A. 1986. Consumerism in second language learning and teaching. *Canadian Modern Language Review*, 42 (3): 668–187.

Young, L. 1994. University lectures – macro-structure and micro-features. In *Academic Listening: Research Perspectives*, J. Flowerdew (Ed.), 159–179. Cambridge: Cambridge University Press.

Yule, G. 1997. *Referential communication tasks*. Mahwah, NJ: Lawrence Erlbaum.

Yunick, S. 1997. Genres, registers and sociolinguistics. *World Englishes*, 16: 321–336.

Zamel, V. 1982. Writing: The process of discovering meaning. *TESOL Quarterly*, 16: 195–209.

1983. The composing process of advanced ESL students: Six case studies. *TESOL Quarterly*, 17: 165–187.

1985. Responding to student writing. *TESOL Quarterly*, 19: 79–102.

1987. Recent research on writing pedagogy. *TESOL Quarterly*, 21: 697–715.

1993. Questioning academic discourse. *College ESL*, 3 (1): 28–39.

Zamel, V., and R. Spack (Eds.). 1998. *Negotiating Academic Literacies: Teaching and Learning Across Languages and Cultures*. Mahwah, NJ: Lawrence Erlbaum.

Zhang, S. 1995. Re-examining the affective advantage of peer feedback in the ESL writing class. *Journal of Second Language Writing*, 4: 209–222.

Zimmerman, M. 1988. *Texas Indexer/browser, V. 0.27*. Silver Spring, Maryland.

Zughoul, M., and R. Hussain. 1985. English for higher education in the Arab world. *English for Specific Purposes*, 4: 133–152.

Index

References to *figures* and *tables* are indicated by italics. References to authors are listed under the first author.